MW00991925

READING THUCYDIDES

READING THUCYDIDES

James V. Morrison

The Ohio State University Press
Columbus

Library of Congress Cataloging-in-Publication data
Morrison, James V., 1956–
  Reading Thucydides / James V. Morrison.
    p. cm.
  Includes bibliographical references and index.
  ISBN-13: 978-0-8142-1035-2 (cloth : alk. paper)
  ISBN-10: 0-8142-1035-X (cloth : alk. paper)
  ISBN-13: 978-0-8142-9112-2 (cd-rom)
  ISBN-10: 0-8142-9112-0 (cd-rom)
  1. Thucydides. History of the Peloponnesian War. 2. Greece—History—
Peloponnesian War, 431–404 B.C.—Historiography. I. Title.
  DF229.T6M67 2006
  938'.05072—dc22
                                    2006008845

Cover design by DesignSmith.
Type set in Goudy.
Printed by Thomson-Shore, Inc.

9 8 7 6 5 4 3 2 1

To the memory of John B. McDiarmid,
who taught me so much about Ancient Greece

Contents

LIST OF ABBREVIATIONS

JOURNAL TITLES

AHB   *Ancient History Bulletin*
AJP   *American Journal of Philology*
BICS   *Bulletin of the Institute of Classical Studies of the University of London*
BMCR   *Bryn Mawr Classical Review*
CA   *Classical Antiquity*
CJ   *Classical Journal*
CP   *Classical Philology*
CQ   *Classical Quarterly*
CRAI   *Comptes rendus de L'Académie des Inscriptions et Belles-Lettres*
CW   *Classical World*
GRBS   *Greek, Roman and Byzantine Studies*
HSCP   *Harvard Studies in Classical Philology*
ICS   *Illinois Classical Studies*
JHS   *Journal of Hellenic Studies*
JRS   *Journal of Roman Studies*
LCM   *Liverpool Classical Monthly*
PCPS   *Proceedings of the Cambridge Philological Society*
QUCC   *Quaderni Urbinati di Cultura Classica*
REA   *Revue des Études Anciennes*
REG   *Revue des Études Grecques*
RM   *Rheinisches Museum*
RPh   *Revue de Philologie*
TAPA   *Transactions and Proceedings of the American Philological Association*
WS   *Wiener Studien*
YCS   *Yale Classical Studies*

OTHER ABBREVIATIONS

Ath. Pol. *Athenaion Politeia* (Constitutions of the Athenians)
ATL   *Athenian Tribute List*
HCT   *A Historical Commentary on Thucydides*
HG   *Historia Graeca*

ACKNOWLEDGMENTS

This project began at a 1989 NEH Summer Institute led by Elaine Fantham on "The Greek Enlightenment." It was here that I was first introduced to the ideas of Eric Havelock that have influenced this book. I am grateful to Elaine and the other scholars from that institute; I also wish to thank the NEH for its funding of such valuable interactions among scholars and teachers. I am also indebted to the participants of the 2000, 2002, and 2004 Orality conferences for their ideas and probing questions.

Many people have improved the quality and clarity of my ideas about Thucydides over the past two decades. I would especially like to mention those who read and commented on my papers, articles, and chapters: Paula Debnar, Stewart Flory, Michael Flower, Irene de Jong, Ludwig Koenen, Peter Krentz, Don Lateiner, and Ruth Scodel. It has been my good fortune to have benefited from the advice of such warm and knowledgeable friends and colleagues.

The material in several chapters has appeared in earlier form as articles. I should like to acknowledge the kind permission to reuse such material from the Johns Hopkins University Press for material in chapters 5 and 6: "Historical Lessons in the Melian Episode," *TAPA* 130 (2000): 119–48 and "A Key Topos in Thucydides: The Comparison of Cities and Individuals," *AJP* 155.4 (1994): 525–41; from the University of California Press for material in chapters 2 and 3: "Preface to Thucydides: Rereading the Corcyrean Conflict (1.24–55)," *Classical Antiquity* 18 (1999): 94–131; and from Brill Publishing for material in chapters 9 and 10: "Memory, Time, and Writing: Oral and Literary Aspects of Thucydides' *History*," ed. C. Mackie, *Oral Performance and its Contexts* (2004): 95–116.

Many friends and relatives have supported me over the past sixteen years in the making of this book. I especially appreciate the tolerance of my wife, Ruth, who endured the anarchy of notes, files, and books that proliferated throughout our house—perhaps the written word does have its drawbacks. I would also like to thank Eugene O'Connor who initially expressed an interest in this book and has always been supportive.

My first contact with Thucydides in Greek was at the University of Washington in a class taught by Merle Langdon. After Pericles' Funeral Oration we focused on book four and the topography of Sphacteria. There have been many rereadings since, but I am grateful to Merle for his spirited introduction to an often difficult author. It was also in Seattle that I studied with John B. McDiarmid, who was my first mentor in the mysteries of the Pre-Socratic philosophers, Aeschylus, Pindar, and Aristotle. He was a wonderful teacher who is sorely missed. It is to his memory that I dedicate this book.

PART ONE
INTRODUCTION

1

IN DIALOGUE WITH THUCYDIDES

Often when reading Thucydides, I ask myself: what does Thucydides himself think? Does he endorse this argument? Should I compare these two situations? Why has he withheld his own judgment? The premise of this book is that these reactions are the result of deliberate strategies on the part of Thucydides. Of course, at times Thucydides is at the reader's side, explaining, judging, tying together passages, events, and arguments (1.1.1, 1.23.6, 1.55.2, 2.65, 3.82–83). But the reader also encounters a reticent and less intrusive side of Thucydides as this authoritative presence recedes.

The goal of this book is to examine Thucydides' techniques of presentation and the effects of those techniques on the reader's experience. Indeed, it will be valuable to approach the *History* in part from the perspective of the reader's experience, for the *History* is an *interactive* work in which Thucydides invites the reader to juxtapose one argument with another, compare speech and narrative, and test maxim against a particular episode. There is what we might call a *dialogic* quality to his presentation that is found not only in the pairs of speeches which respond to one another; the narrative itself raises questions and encourages the reader to pursue multiple lines of possible action and consequence. The *History* lives as an interactive text by putting the reader in a position to confront arguments, make connections, and—vicariously—decide the best course of action. There are four main features to this book's analysis: Thucydides' method of presenting speech and narrative, the reader's experience, Thucydides' view of history, and Thucydides' position in the context of oral and written culture. In this introductory chapter, I would like to present these areas of inquiry before turning in the second chapter to a more in-depth examination of Thucydides' narrative techniques and the reader's tasks.

The first feature in the *History* to be explored is Thucydides' presentation of speech and narrative. This general approach has been labeled "narratology" (with its attendant "narrator," "narratee," "analepsis," "prolepsis," etc.), but regardless of the terminology, the focus is upon *the method of presentation of the history*. There is nothing revolutionary about observing the effect of the narrator conveying certain information or of a figure such as Pericles interpreting past events or anticipating the future. This approach basically examines how the author presents events and speeches to the readers of the text. Such analysis means paying attention to who perceives or interprets an event—who "focalizes" it. The narrator may recount what happens, a character may describe something, but sometimes *within the narrative*, events are presented from the perspective *not* of the narrator, but from the perspective of one of the characters. When the narrator presents events through a character's perceptions, thoughts, emotions, or words, this is referred to as "embedded focalization." Narrative analysis also studies many other features, such as the ordering of events, the juxtaposition of speech and narrative, and flashbacks and foreshadowings that link earlier and later events to the situation being described.

The second feature I explore is the effect of Thucydides' presentation on the reader. That is, we may approach the *History* on the one side in terms of the narrator's decisions to present, withhold, and comment, and from the opposite perspective we may explore the reactions and experiences of the reader. Thucydides often encourages his reader to adopt the position of figures within the work and to view matters from several perspectives. To the extent that readers are able to view past events in this manner, the overall effect is a feeling of open-endedness in terms of possible responses, and alternative argument and action.

The reader then encounters an interactive, participatory type of literature in which Thucydides expects his reader to play an active, intellectual role. White comments:

> The text is like the world itself . . . Thucydides' purpose . . . [is not] to present a narrative of events and to explain them . . . [but] by reduplicating them in clarified and intensified form will force upon the reader the difficulties Thucydides himself faces . . . the experience of this text is like an experience of the world.[1]

Thucydides appeals to the reader's involvement by bringing written literature as close as possible to the live, extemporaneous, face-to-face debate of Greek politics. The audience is engaged in a unique way that we might term "dialogic" rather than "dogmatic."

At several points in this book, I have found it profitable to compare Thucydides and Plato: this is the first occasion. What Thucydides has accomplished is analogous to Plato with respect to the function of the work itself. The works of Plato, in particular, the early, "aporetic" Platonic dialogues, are left in an important sense without resolution. If Euthyphro's definitions of piety are inadequate, for example, the reader is implicitly invited to join in and continue that search. The *History* and the Platonic dialogues share this special quality of eliciting the reader's engagement.

Thucydides presents an implicit model for thinking about one of the reader's most important tasks. At pivotal points in the *History* Thucydides emphasizes the activity by statesmen and historians of juxtaposing, comparing, and extrapolating—captured by the Greek term *eikazein* (1.9–10, 1.138, 4.36). Thucydides also claims that in the future, events comparable to those from the past may take place (1.22.4). Passages such as these offer a model for the engaged reader: just as statesmen, historians, and citizens must draw connections between past events and the present or between argument and possible courses of action, Thucydides encourages his reader's engagement in extrapolation and conjecture (*eikazein*) with respect to both past and future: readers must project themselves into the past and view what is past to them as part of an indeterminate future.[2] At some level, the reader knows that everything described in the *History* has already taken place. Nevertheless, we may distinguish between the retrospective reader who understands where various events are leading and the engaged reader who experiences an atmosphere of contingency.

A possible motivation for the ultimate form of Thucydides' project—especially his means of presentation—was that he was striving to produce an alternative way to address his fellow Athenians, for participation in civic affairs was no longer available to him.[3] When Thucydides was sent into exile in 424 BCE, he could no longer point out the proper course of action or warn of mistaken policy in the assembly. Exile cut him off from these opportunities for civic engagement. Yet even in exile Thucydides strove to engage his fellow citizens and his fellow Greeks, but now it was no longer in a living, face-to-face conversation; rather it was in a written medium, aimed at both a more immediate audience (Athenians and other Greeks ca. 400 BCE) and a more distant audience—as suits "a possession forever."[4] I will explore the events of Thucydides' life and their possible effects on his work more fully in chapters 9 and 10.

The third feature is Thucydides' view of the past which grows out of this atmosphere of open-ended contingency. I will argue that because the reader is encouraged to adopt the position of figures within the *History* and view what has already happened as part of an indeterminate future, we come to appreciate the radical nature of Thucydides' non-teleological history. Thucydides repeatedly indicates—both implicitly and explicitly—how events might have taken another direction: there is nothing inevitable about the course of history. A consequence of Thucydides' sort of presentation is that readers may also view the past from this perspective.

Alternative scenarios proliferate in Thucydides' work. The *History* is continually raising possibilities, revealing alternatives, and considering hypothetical situations in order to emphasize the contingent nature of the events of the Peloponnesian War. Thucydides' presentation reveals that events are not governed by divine guidance; history has no ultimate goal (we might contrast both Homer and Herodotus).[5] This, of course, does not mean that certain things are not likely to take place, but the *open-endedness* of Thucydides has not, in my view, been sufficiently recognized.

Flory notes that explicit counterfactual hypotheses occur with comparably high frequency only in the work of Homer and Thucydides, and thinks these hypotheses mark Thucydides' "style of speculation as a significant peculiarity of the *History*." Flory concludes that Thucydides:

> shows us that, in fact, the sequence of events is not inevitable, for the outcome of a battle often hinges upon tiny and unpredictable accidents. When Thucydides looks back on the war that Athens lost, he sees that defeat might have been only the result of a concatenation of trivial mishaps beyond human control.[6]

At times authorial comment and foreshadowing indicate the ultimate direction of events—or indeed the outcome of the war itself—yet along the way Thucydides constantly emphasizes choices and decisions which may have led to other outcomes. While Flory analyzes explicit hypotheses expressed in the historian's own voice, Thucydides utilizes diverse means for suggesting alternative scenarios in both speech and narrative. We have much to learn about Thucydides' view of history by applying Flory's insights more broadly.[7]

Up to now I have been speaking about the *reader's* experience and the *reader's* engagement, but the matter is not so simple. The fourth and final feature for examination is Thucydides' special role in the transition from a predominantly oral culture in fifth-century Athens to a more literate culture. The issue here is in part that of *reception*: how Thucydides' work would have been made accessible to other Greeks. Thucydides' *History* may be regarded as a pivotal work that seeks to recreate the earlier world of spoken argument, yet it does so as a text that may be read and reread.

While the *History* may be explored in terms of narrative analysis, this method needs to be adapted to a work that, in part, may have been *heard* rather than *read*. Ultimately I will argue that Thucydides' intended audience includes both readers and auditors.

In order to locate Thucydides' position on the oral-written continuum in terms of sources, composition, and reception, I would like to provide a brief sketch of orality and literacy in ancient Greece. There are three significant stages for our survey: primary orality (pre-750 BCE), various stages of proto-literacy (750–400 BCE), and the period of alphabetic dependency (400 BCE and after). The first period, often called the "Dark Ages" of Greece, was a 450-year period (1200–750 BCE) when no system of writing existed. Greeks still spoke about the past, but they did so in part by means of an oral poetic tradition handed down from one generation of singers to the next. This was a tradition in which the composition, performance, and reception of heroic stories was undertaken without the aid of any system of writing. This does not mean that the tales told were unsophisticated, yet these stories are lost to us because they were never written down—the technology of writing simply did not exist.[8]

In Archaic Greece (beginning in the eighth century BCE), the Greek alphabet was invented (based on the Phoenician syllabary). This writing system has continued in use till today (including the Romans' adaptation of it that pretty much constitutes our familiar 26-letter alphabet). Although from the mid-700s BCE the alphabet existed in the ancient Greek world (extending in the east to coastal Asia Minor and in the west to Italy and Sicily), scholars have distinguished between different stages of literacy. For example, even though the alphabet existed in Homer's own lifetime (during the 700s), the *Iliad* and the *Odyssey* are very much products of that oral tradition from the Dark Ages (whether Homer himself was literate or not remains a controversial question).[9]

This second stage might be characterized as a mixed period distinguished by various degrees of proto-literacy that lasted until about 400 BCE.[10] The alphabetic system was employed for dedicatory, proprietary, legal, and funerary inscriptions as well as for the recording of epic, lyric, and dramatic verse. In the fifth century the Athenians' large maritime empire required extensive use of documents, including correspondence, record-keeping, and court business (among Athenians and also between Athenians and their subject city-states).[11] Yet even though a new technology—the alphabetic writing system—existed throughout this period (750–400 BCE), the culture remained a predominantly oral culture. That is, the mindset of poets, politicians, and thinkers remained to a large degree an oral mindset for 350 years or more. While the songs of Homer, Sappho, and Pindar were recorded—written down by someone on papyrus—the primary access to these works by the vast majority of the population was by the *ear* (they heard them) rather than by the *eye*. This was also true of the tragedies of Aeschylus, Sophocles, and Euripides that were performed at the festival of Dionysus as well as the speeches of the Athenian statesman Pericles, heard live and out loud in the Athenian assembly.

The third stage, beginning right around the year 400 BCE, has been called the era of alphabetic dependency or alphabetic literacy. For the first time poets and thinkers composed works that were intended to be *read* by their audiences (readers) rather than *heard*. We see this new sensibility also reflected in the court system in which written documents of a witness' testimony supplanted the spoken words of that witness; also lawsuits had to accord with written law. Robb concludes: "By the early fourth century, writing and documents manifestly are becoming a presumption of the daily functioning of the courts and of legal procedures."[12]

Robb also argues that in Aristotle's Lyceum in the mid-fourth century "educational activity . . . indisputably centered around its characteristic texts."[13] By this time the transition to a book-reading public (however elite) was complete. There is much else to be said, but I trust that this admittedly sketchy and simplified survey provides a context for the innovations of Thucydides.

A pivotal work analyzing the transition from the second stage of proto-literacy to the third stage of alphabetic literacy is *Preface to Plato* (1963) by Eric Havelock whose interest lies in the classical period (fifth and fourth centuries BCE). Havelock argues that it was not until Plato in the fourth century that someone recognized the potential—and the problems—of writing for a reading public. Although forty years ago this was an extremely controversial idea, it has now become largely accepted that during this second period from roughly 750–400 BCE there was a long, gradual shift from an audience that learned by hearing, memorizing, and reciting spoken discourse to a perhaps relatively select audience that would read and reread written texts.

Plato grew up in a fifth-century oral culture, but he augurs a new era by his reflections on written literature. Allow me to briefly describe the situation Plato faced. Someone would ask a question: Is Pericles wise? The answer given might well be based on a recollection of earlier literature, often a passage from Homer (what Havelock calls "the Homeric encyclopedia"). In Plato's *Republic* (from the second quarter of the fourth century), the figure of Socrates is still complaining that "Homer educated Hellas

. . . and people live their entire lives according to this poet" (*Rep.* 606e). Havelock argues that the "cultural situation described by Plato is one in which oral communication still dominates all the important relationships and valid transactions of life."[14] According to Havelock, part of Plato's response to this situation was a new type of discourse (dialectic), but he also developed his philosophy of the "forms" (*ideai*). The true reality—the forms—was unchanging, immaterial, and knowable, unlike the words of the poets that could be twisted to suit a particular context. Plato's "ideas" were fixed and absolute—like writing—and provided a new way for thinking about the world. Robb describes Plato's role:

> To appreciate Plato in the context of his time requires our seeing him as both the great heir of a still dominantly oral culture—in place by habit or preference, not technological necessity—and simultaneously its destroyer. . . . [Plato] finally destroyed the cultural situation in which for most people, high and low, important knowledge was transmitted across generations orally, in performances.[15]

But was Plato the first to recognize the drawbacks of a primarily oral culture? Was he the first to anticipate the potential of writing? I would like to go back one generation to that of Thucydides. The dates of the composition of Thucydides' *History* are certain: 431–ca. 400 BCE (1.1, 5.26). In view of this fact, the intellectual climate of Thucydides' lifetime may help us to position the *History* in its cultural context. Thucydides (465?–ca. 400 BCE) was also raised in fifth-century Athens which consisted primarily of an oral culture. In the law courts and political assemblies, at the dramatic festivals, even encountering Socrates in the agora, intellectual exchange took place orally in a live, face-to-face, and often spontaneous manner. The Sophists dazzled the public by presenting display pieces; they also offered instruction for how to be successful in public speaking contests. This was very much a "performance culture." Yet in the fourth century, we find the beginnings of a reading culture, in which literature and ideas were composed in writing for a reading "audience." Thucydides sits on the cusp of that transition from a predominantly oral culture to the beginnings of a new self-awareness for literature that was meant to be read.

One of the fascinating aspects of Thucydides' *History* is that it is a written text, yet it still recreates the dynamism of oral exchange.[16] The quality of "engagement" found in Thucydides' work mentioned above derives in part from the *innovative* nature of this work. That is, this work still retains the habits and practices of the oral culture Thucydides grew up in

yet he, like Plato, also had a sensitivity and self-awareness of written literature's potential. Thucydides was, I believe, engaged in a project—analogous to what Plato did for philosophy—by challenging the ways in which
Greeks thought about the past. And like Plato's creation of a "literary"
Socrates, Thucydides has recreated the political arena in Greece with
respect to fifth-century oral debate and to military strategy and battle.[17]
Both Thucydides and Plato, the first two great authors of Attic prose, were
responding to the same conditions of restricted literacy in essentially the
same period. Thucydides obviously intended his written work to address a
contemporary audience in some manner and he seems to have anticipated, at least in part, an audience of listeners.

By exploring the *History* from this perspective, I hope to bring
Thucydides into the debate surrounding the long transition from orality to
literacy in Ancient Greece. Thucydides deserves greater attention for his
self-conscious reflections on the issues of oral and written sources, presentation, and reception. Preceding Plato by a generation, he grandly pro-
nounces that his work will be a "possession for all time" (1.22.4). This
suggests an awareness of the capacity of a written work to transcend the
moment in ways that ephemeral speech and performance cannot.[18] The
result is that my method of exploring Thucydides' presentation of speech
and narrative is basically a narratological approach but we must understand the unique features of its compositional structure in terms of the culture of the historian's own time and place. The reception of Thucydides'
work—by both readers and auditors—will be addressed in the final two
chapters.

These are the four features I will explore: the presentation of speech and
narrative, the reader's experiences, Thucydides' view of history, and
Thucydides as a transitional figure between oral and literary culture. I am
not advancing a single overarching thesis. One thing I have learned is that
it is a mistake to try to reduce Thucydides' complex work to a single argument. In fact, Thucydides himself apparently delights in setting up a thesis and then later undermining that argument by showing its weaknesses
and inconsistencies. Whatever success I have had in grappling with
Thucydides has come when I have focused on particular problems or specific events: this is the path I will follow in this book.

Many scholars have influenced my interpretation of Thucydides. I have
already mentioned Havelock, Flory, and Robb. Regarding Thucydides' narrative, works by Connor, Hornblower, de Jong, Rood, and Stahl have also been
especially valuable.[19] Provocative work on Plato's dialogues by Blondell and
Hershbell offers many insights relevant to the interactive, "dialogic" nature

of Thucydides' work.[20] Concerning contingent history—and against seeing the past as inevitable—Flory is joined by Bernstein, Ferguson, Gould, Stahl, and Varnadoe.[21] Regarding oral culture and literacy in antiquity, I should mention the scholarship of Edmunds, Harris, Ong, and Thomas.[22]

In addition to such scholarly works, a major influence upon my analysis has been my own personal experience, in reading, probing, and teaching Thucydides. As teachers know, the words of Thucydides' (and Plato's) texts—both in substance and style—are ideal prompts for discussion that can lead to conflicting interpretations of what Thucydides is up to. This is no accident; rather, Thucydides has adopted a means of presenting the war so that the reader plays a role in testing, analyzing, and extrapolating.

The organization of this book is as follows. Chapter 2 presents a fuller discussion of how Thucydides' techniques force readers to become active participants in assessing and anticipating events. These basic techniques—multiple perspective, authorial reticence, and episodic structure—engage both the "retrospective" reader and the "engaged" reader, who is encouraged to relive the past as though the outcome were still in doubt.

In "Part Two. Participatory, Punctuated, and Retrospective History: Corcyra, Plataea, and Melos," chapters 3, 4, and 5 will examine how Thucydides' presentation of particular city-states encourages different sorts of participation on the reader's part. Chapter 3 analyzes "participatory history," in which Thucydides encourages the reader to consider events in the Corcyrean conflict from the perspective of the participants involved; indeed, we come to appreciate how Thucydides presents actions and argument in such a way that the reader may re-experience them and become engaged with questions, such as the "inevitability" of the war. In chapter 4, the city of Plataea offers an excellent example of "punctuated presentation," as Thucydides links speech and narrative across separate episodes. Especially important are the ways in which early action leads to later consequences and the manner in which speakers reinterpret past events. Chapter 5 argues that the true significance of Athens' conflict with Melos may be best understood in terms of "retrospective" engagement, for the reader is led back to earlier juxtapositions of speech and event which offer "lessons" pertinent to this particular conflict. Each city—Corcyra, Plataea, and Melos—offers a different sort of challenge to the reader. Certainly Part Two is not comprehensive: I have selected what I believe to be representative examples of Thucydides' presentation of cities' arguments, actions, and the consequences of those actions.[23]

In "Part Three. Argument and Reverberation: Comparison, Maxim, and Metaphor," chapters 6, 7, and 8 explore how rhetorical language presents a different sort of challenge to the reader. Chapter 6 explores the comparison between cities and individuals that raises questions about the behavior, character, and interaction of cities. In chapter 7, we find that maxims often bridge the gap between domestic politics and international conflict. Chapter 8 focuses on Thucydides' use of metaphorical phrases, such as "Athens, the tyrant-city," which suggest comparisons for the reader's investigation. Thucydides' work as a whole—even though indisputably unfinished—achieves a kind of unity due to these recurrent comparisons, maxims, and metaphors.

In "Part Four. Biography and Reception," chapter 9 considers Thucydides' explicit claims and probable motivations for his work, while reflecting upon the events in his own life. Chapter 10 explores the reception of his work, for both readers and auditors—ancient and modern—are addressed by the *History*. In chapters 3 through 8, I refer to Thucydides' "reader" and the sort of engagement available to a reading audience. Since this may differ from how Thucydides envisioned the reception for his work, these final chapters examine the ways in which Thucydides, while privileging his own work as written—and therefore superior to oral discourse—invites the engagement of both readers and auditors.

My intended audience includes scholars and specialists in ancient history, philosophy, politics, and literature, yet I hope that my discussion will also interest those studying the transition from orality to literacy in the ancient world. I have attempted to shed new light on many important passages and themes in Thucydides so that undergraduate and graduate students in history and classics may find particular chapters useful to their study and research. With these readers in mind, all passages are presented either in English (with key Greek phrases inserted) or in Greek with an English translation following.

While exploring Thucydides' presentation and his techniques, I hope to offer a greater appreciation of his innovations. Thucydides reveals his own awareness of doing something novel. Indeed, he presents a new way of viewing the past, seeks to present accurately speeches and events, claims everlasting value for his work, and suggests the advantages of written over oral communication. Thucydides recognized that it is possible to transcend one's own immediate circumstances—the here and now—but it is impossible to do so if you go to the agora, the Pnyx, or the Theater of Dionysus. To transcend the moment with words, you must use words that will live beyond your own lifetime. Thucydides' phrase, "a possession forever" (κτῆμά τε ἐς αἰεί–1.22.4), suggests a broad conception of his "target" audience, not limited to the immediate postwar Greek world. He includes us, too, as modern readers.[24]

2

THE READER'S TASK

The goal of this chapter is to examine in greater depth how Thucydides'
unusual sort of presentation forces readers (and auditors) to become
active participants. Thucydides achieves this effect by using several inter-
related techniques, in particular, multiple perspective, authorial reticence,
and episodic structure. The major effects are a balanced presentation and
the absence of rhetorical and military closure that induce the reader to take
on an active role. Before turning to techniques and effects, I will speak
briefly about focalization and the reader, who is encouraged to engage in
extrapolation and conjecture (*eikazein*) with respect to both the past and
future. Subsequent chapters will present detailed analyses of specific conflicts and arguments. My larger goal in this book is to understand
Thucydides' authorial strategies and to recover the experience of reading
the *History*, though I reiterate that in the final two chapters I will consider the reception by both readers *and* auditors.

In the introductory chapter I mentioned the value of the concept of
"focalization." In general terms, focalization means that Thucydides
chooses to present actions or experiences from a particular point of view.
Primary focalization refers to the presentation of events through the perspective of the narrator. Yet frequently Thucydides introduces secondary
(or embedded) focalization when events are seen through the eyes of those
involved.[1] Thucydides may explicitly signal such secondary focalization by
indicating an intellectual or emotional experience of an individual or
group within the *History*: "they noticed," "wanting . . . ," "fearing . . . ,"
etc. To be sure, at times Thucydides merely describes what someone does
or what happens and there is no heightened sense that we are meant to
view that event from the point of view of someone involved. Such passages
often convey a more objective and distant feel. Quite frequently, however, Thucydides chooses to invite us to view the action from the point of
view of a particular figure or group; indeed, his success in engaging his
reader in large part derives from such embedded focalization.[2]

It may be useful to distinguish such "intellectual" or "psychological" focalization of perception and emotion from what we might call "rhetorical" focalization. When Thucydides presents speeches (or speeches reported in the third person), he is also offering us the perspective of those involved—that is, it is a type of secondary focalization. Yet a speech is a more public way of presenting someone's perspective and contrasts significantly with the more private and internal perceptions and emotions mentioned above. When speeches present a point of view, there is an objectivity to the words spoken—whether the report is direct or indirect—while with psychological focalization, Thucydides allows us to "get into the character's head" with more private intellectual and emotional focalization.[3]

In addition to discussing focalization, I should consider the reader's task. For the purposes of analysis in chapters 3–8, I will limit my discussion to the hypothetical reader constructed from Thucydides' text. This reader, implied by the History, reads the narrative and speeches as Thucydides has structured them. While it is possible to distinguish a first-time reader from a re-reader or a modern reader from an ancient one, I would like to employ the idea of a double perspective for this implied reader.[4] On one side, it is possible for the reader to enjoy a leisurely, distant view by looking at events in retrospect: this first perspective is that of the "distant" or "retrospective" reader, who knows the course of the war in outline, with the Athenian defeat in 404 providing the terminus towards which events are headed. There is, however, a second viewpoint: the engaged perspective. We find Thucydides employing techniques that produce a vivid, participatory experience for the "engaged" reader.[5] From this perspective, the reader must respond actively in contemplating past possibilities and potential future events.

I acknowledge that retrospective readers may still be "engaged" in some sense and that readers with a more "immediate" perspective may still analyze the situation. And at some level, every reader is simultaneously aware of both aspects. Nevertheless, the distinction between the distant and engaged reader may prove useful, provided we remain cognizant of how the reader is led to switch back and forth between these two perspectives.[6] At times, Thucydides encourages a more distant or passive mode by overtly connecting one sequence, episode, or event with another, but much more commonly finding those connections and juxtaposing relevant passages remains the task of the reader.[7] This forces the reader to participate actively in creating the meaning of the History. For example, when Cleon says that the Athenian empire is a tyranny, the reader should hear the near-echo of Pericles (3.37.2; cf. 2.63.2). Because of the interruption (3 years and some 50 pages)—and Thucydides' failure in book 3 *explicitly* to highlight this echo—when this "significant reminiscence" occurs, it is the reader's task to connect the two sections, compare the contexts, and judge whether the same idea is being expressed and how such a metaphor might apply to the new situation.[8] In the Corcyrean conflict (1.24–55) explored in chapter 3, the reader may juxtapose ideas and themes from this episode with (a) earlier sections of the *History* (the Preface, Archaeology and Methodology–1.1–23); (b) later sections of book 1 and the war books (2–8); and (c) the circumstances of the reader's own experience and world.[9]

As I have mentioned above, in chapters 3–8 when I refer to Thucydides and the reader (or auditor), strictly speaking I mean the narrator and the implied or hypothetical reader. I limit my initial analysis to contemplating the implied reader's experience in order to lay the basis for our appreciation of Thucydides' *History*. I am not overly fond of jargon ("narratee" still makes me wince), and my feeling is that theoretical distinctions are valuable only as a means to an end. Yet positing an implied reader with a double perspective and employing the concept of focalization will bring us closer to our goal. The important point is that when Thucydides and readers (or auditors) are mentioned in chapters 3–8, these entities are reconstructions based on the text. Having said this, I am extremely interested in the historian's life and times and in actual readers, both ancient and modern. I will turn to the historian's biography and the experience of actual flesh and blood readers in chapters 9 and 10. But until then I believe analyzing the experience of the hypothetical reader implied by the text will be a productive way to approach the diverse challenges of Thucydides' *History*.[10] Without being too loose in terminology, I will do my best to write in a reasonable and accessible way.

To return to the double lens of the reader: when Thucydides demands an engaged, participatory attitude on the part of the reader, in a sense, he is asking the reader to suspend previous knowledge of subsequent events. The effect is that readers at some level are able to project themselves into the past situation as constructed by Thucydides. Thucydides can be especially effective in recreating past events, offering the reader an opportunity to "relive" that particular situation. Connor describes this aspect of Thucydides' text as "experiential" or "participatory," and characterizes him as "a writer who keeps drawing his readers into the narrative of events until they feel they are themselves present, actually experiencing them."[11] Of course, such an experience is vicarious; nevertheless, this is a deliberate effect of Thucydides' techniques.

The best model for both engaged and distant readers may be found in Thucydides' description of what historians and politicians are able to do. Concerning the engaged reader, Thucydides praises statesmen who have the capacity to see likenesses, extrapolate from present evidence and circumstances, and attempt to foresee the probable course of events. He uses the word *eikazein* and related words: "to compare" and "to make conjectures on the basis of comparisons."[12] For example, the statesman Themistocles successfully looks to the future, anticipating the importance of walls for Athenian autonomy (1.90–91), the potential for the Piraeus as a port (1.93.3), and the link between sea power and Athenian dominance (1.93.3–4). Summing up his ability, Thucydides calls Themistocles "the finest at forecasting" (ἄριστος εἰκαστής–1.138.3).[13] To the extent that engaged readers project themselves into the situations Thucydides presents, they too can extrapolate from past contexts and anticipate later events.[14]

Alternatively, in contemplating our task as retrospective readers, we should note that in some situations the reader's labor is not unlike that of the historian. In the Archaeology, Thucydides reasons that accounts of the Greeks journeying to Troy might serve as a basis for approximating the scope of previous expeditions. "We must make reasonable conjectures [εἰκάζειν δὲ χρή] from this expedition about other expeditions before that time" (1.9.4).[15] In this instance the historian uses Homeric evidence to establish a view of the capabilities of military ventures in early Greece. Surely in the year 431 Thucydides himself engaged in the process of conjecture (*eikazein*) toward the future. At the start of the war, he "expected (*elpisas*) the war would be great and more noteworthy to record (*axiologotaton*) than previous wars" (1.1.1). In a sense, Thucydides has challenged his reader to take on the labor which he, as historian, has taken up in attempting to discover what actually happened. Thucydides' address to the reader in 1.22 (with its many purposes) follows his discussion of the historian's labor to find the truth in spite of bias and inaccuracy. Others, such as poets and political orators, do not rigorously examine accounts of the past. For his part, Thucydides has found that participants in recent events do not say the same thing due to favoritism or (lapses of) memory (εὐνοίας ἢ μνήμης–1.22.3). An awareness of inconsistent accounts, untested variants, and the labor necessary to uncover the truth offers a picture of what the historian must contend with. By the same token, the *History* we encounter—with its multiple perspective and other challenges—forces the reader to negotiate some of the same problems which the historian has had to confront.

The reader's reward will be a type of wisdom. Yet if my work is judged useful (*ophelima*) by as many as wish to look clearly at both past events and those in the future which, in accordance with human nature, will be similar and will resemble past events, that will suffice. (1.22.4)

Thucydides suggests that his retrospective reader may gain a clear understanding of the past, and that this understanding offers something useful: he postulates the idea of repetition of the same sorts of events in the future. But the apprehension of such similar situations requires a facility for judgment and comparison (*eikazein*)—the same intellectual and imaginative capacity Thucydides has implied is necessary for historians. The relevance for us is that Thucydides has set up a dynamic situation and challenged his readers to engage in the activities of extrapolation, conjecture, and prediction—both from the engaged perspective (that of the participants) and from the distant perspective (that of the historian).[16]

I now turn to the techniques found in the *History* which offer this special type of experience for the reader. A number of features are essential for constructing what I broadly call the recreation of the political arena of fifth-century Greece. First, we find that Thucydides employs *multiple perspective* in both speech and narrative. In the Corcyrean conflict (1.24–55), for example, both Corcyra and Corinth present arguments; as the internal audience, the Athenians offer a third perspective. The reader is implicitly asked to view that conflict from these three points of view and needs to be critical of what is said in speeches, evaluating whatever claims are made. We find speech and narrative structured in such a way as to encourage us to adopt diverse points of view: actively from Corcyrean and Corinthian perspectives and deliberatively from the position of Athens.

In thinking about the experience of reading this text, I have found useful Yunis' notion of "instructional rhetoric," which, Yunis argues, renders the governing body "capable of autonomous, conscientious decision-making."[17] This political exchange suggests a model for reading the text of Thucydides. A politician may instruct his citizens concerning the best policy; so, according to Yunis, Thucydides "instructs his readers about Athenian policy through Pericles' speeches."[18] The reader's critical evaluation of the speeches will lead to a more knowledgeable position from which to think about politics, conflict, and war. By actively analyzing the speeches, the reader may be in a better position (like Themistocles or Pericles) to judge what can or should be done in a particular situation. Evidently Thucydides has decided that to achieve such an appreciation, the reader must be exposed to more than one viewpoint.[19]

We also find *multiple perspective* in Thucydides' presentation of action in the narrative. He frequently switches points of view, allowing the reader to see how the battle of Sybota (1.44–55), for example, was experienced by several of the participants through the use of secondary or embedded focalization. I would suggest that the equivalent of the viewpoints offered in paired speeches (rhetorical focalization) is the multiple perspective on action found in the narrative (intellectual or emotional focalization). One of the ways in which Thucydides makes his history "useful" (*ophelima*–1.22.4) for his reader is by refraining from offering a single, authoritative account of events.[20] Thus in both speech and narrative the reader is invited to see events from the point of view of the participants: speakers, audience, soldiers, politicians, and others.

Simply offering multiple perspectives by itself does not guarantee the reader's active involvement; such engagement is also promoted by *authorial reticence*. It has been noted that Thucydides frequently refrains from commenting upon or judging speech and narrative—he is very sparing in intruding his opinions.[21] He generally does not actively promote one group over another. He tells us "The Plataeans spoke . . . ," "The Thebans spoke . . . ," "The Athenians made the following decisions. . . ." Yet he neither openly condemns either set of speakers for inconsistent or fallacious arguments, nor does he explicitly endorse, say, the voting of the Athenians. As a result, the feature of multiple perspective coupled with authorial reticence activates the evaluative capacities of his audience; the reader must step in to assess the validity of claims and to judge the diplomatic and military strategies employed. In fact, Thucydides' audience would be familiar with such authorial reticence, for it is also found in Homer. As Aristotle says in the *Poetics*:

> Among Homer's many other laudable attributes is his grasp—unique among epic poets—of his status as a poet. For the poet himself should speak as little as possible, since when he does so he is not engaging in mimesis . . . Homer, after a short preamble, at once "brings onto stage" a man, woman, or some other figure. (*Poetics* ch. 24, 1460a5–11)[22]

Although at times Thucydides goes a long way toward distancing himself from poets (e.g., 1.21; cf. 2.41.4), both Homer and Thucydides exemplify the principle articulated by Aristotle regarding restraint in explicit authorial commentary.

One effect of Thucydides' use of multiple perspective and authorial reticence is what might be called a *balanced presentation*. Because Thucydides offers differing perspectives, the reader gets the impression of an equitable presentation. This does not mean that Thucydides is totally disinterested; he does not "objectively" present only the events themselves. There is, of course, a careful process of selection and placement that creates a variety of intellectual and emotional experiences for the reader. In many conflicts, however, we are told both sides' motivations before argument and action; each side is given equal opportunity to put forward an argument; battles are viewed from the perspectives of the various sides involved. Thucydides' section on methodology anticipates such an equitable approach. Flory has argued that when Thucydides characterizes his history as lacking what is often translated as "the romantic element" or "the storytelling element" (τὸ μυθῶδες–1.22.4), we should understand the expression in a political sense. In this context, τὸ μυθῶδες means patriotic stories, "stories which exaggerate and celebrate the glories of war."[23] If this interpretation is right, Thucydides is warning us early on that he will be avoiding chauvinism; he will offer no biased or exaggerated stories of Athenian patriotism—or of any other city-state. By using multiple perspective and reining in his own opinions, Thucydides strives to achieve an evenhanded presentation.

Another effect of Thucydides' type of presentation is a *lack of closure* in rhetorical and military conflict. In speech, the arguments do not generally achieve a satisfying conclusion. While some decision is reached (to make an alliance, to declare war, etc.), the issues brought up are not dealt with definitively. One such issue is the relevance of morality to foreign policy. The Athenians consistently argue against cities acting justly toward one another and de Ste. Croix endorses this view as revealing Thucydides' own beliefs.[24] This viewpoint, however, is only a part of a dialogue. The historian allows opposing viewpoints to be expressed, but seldom passes judgment in his own voice. From a sophistic point of view, it is possible to argue persuasively both sides of the argument, and it may well be true that a fixed, authoritative perspective—a single view—would oversimplify such complex situations.[25] This is in the nature of dialogue, at least in Thucydides' use of it. My point is that because such issues are not resolved wholly one way or the other, because Thucydides refrains from commenting on the validity of these arguments, the reader is forced to consider both arguments, to inspect the consequences of following one course of action rather than the other, and ultimately is left with a deeper understanding of the complexities of the political situation and the rhetoric which attempts to describe it. If there is to be any resolution, it is the reader who must provide it.[26]

We find a similar situation regarding the narrative, although here we must assess this lack of closure from both a local and a more distant perspective. From a local perspective—in the context of each narrative episode—when Thucydides offers no commentary, it is the reader who must assign significance to the various events presented. Of course, Thucydides implies that certain facts are significant by including those facts and not others, but seldom will he remark "this is important," or "the significance of the following is . . . ."[27] Lack of closure may here be better recast as "lack of guidance" on Thucydides' part. Again the reader must actively evaluate. From a more distant perspective—when an episode is set in the broader context of the entire *History*—we find a different type of *absence of closure*, one that requires a different sort of involvement for the reader. Thucydides generally does not make explicit connections between one episode and a later one— even one deserving comparison because of cause and effect, the same participants, or similar (or significantly reversed) contexts. In chapter 4, I will examine how the four separate episodes involving Plataea present many challenges to the reader, in part due to Thucydides' lack of guidance concerning the significant connections between these episodes. The Corcyrean conflict is unusual in that Thucydides explicitly links this dispute to the outbreak of the war, that is, Thucydides tells us how this section relates to the war which book 2 presents (1.23.6, 1.55.2; cf. 1.146). Still in 1.24–55 the speeches and narrative are typical in that Thucydides does not draw explicit connections between a particular argument or strategy in this episode and other parts of the *History*, even though such features reverberate in a variety of ways throughout this work.[28]

Another way to describe the *History* is to characterize it as "episodic" or "punctuated," deriving from the entrances and exits of the major participants, central issues, and striking metaphors in various conflicts. By "episodic" I do not mean the sort of thing Aristotle discusses in the *Poetics* where he criticizes the lack of unity in many works (see *Poetics* ch. 17, 1455b13; cf. ch. 8, 1451a16–35). The extraordinary thing about Thucydides' *History*—in spite of the fact that it is clearly unfinished and does not bring us down to the end of the war in 404—is that its design is immensely rich because of the way it engages the reader by building links from early sections to later ones: echoes and reminiscences are integral to the ethos of the work, regardless of the abrupt end in the year 411. Given the often pejorative sense of "episodic" (and "annalistic" does not do much better), perhaps a better label is "punctuated history": Thucydides presents one episode after another, each as a discrete point or unit (*punctum*), yet each is related to other events and ideas in a multitude of ways.[29]

With regard to figures and city-states, the larger movement of Thucydides' *History* follows what we might call "presentation, interruption, and resumption"—that is, punctuated history. After key figures or cities appear and play their roles on center-stage (*presentation*), Thucydides then shifts his attention to a new context without telling us, for example, the aftermath in Corcyra (*interruption*). The chronological framework that follows winter and summer, year by year, inevitably makes the reading experience fragmentary or "punctuated" in this sense. Only in reaching the events of the year 431 or 427 do we learn what happened in Corcyra after 433 (*resumption*).

The effects of this strict chronology—an organizational decision on Thucydides' part—are tremendous. Each figure, each city, each idea—once introduced—is not kept continually before our eyes. Due to the fact that so many of these figures, cities, and themes inevitably return at some later point in the *History*, each episode retains a "to-be-continued" feel. It is incumbent upon the reader to keep track of the details and circumstances. The issues raised in the speeches, and the strategies and maneuvers described in the narrative will reappear with relevance outside the original context. Although in a local sense rhetorical and military conflicts receive some sort of provisional pause, the figures and ideas return later in the work in other situations: the reader must be in a position to juxtapose those later sequences with the earlier episodes. Now that we have considered Thucydides' techniques—multiple perspective, authorial reticence, and episodic structure (or punctuated presentation)—and the common effects of balanced presentation and avoidance of closure, let us examine specific conflicts involving Corcyra, Plataea, and Melos.

Part Two
Participatory, Punctuated, and Retrospective History: Corcyra, Plataea, and Melos

3

THE CORCYREAN CONFLICT (1.24–55)

Let us now examine the Corcyrean conflict. The analysis of chapters 3–5 concerns multiple perspective and authorial reticence—and the effects of these techniques—with a focus on particular city-states. Thucydides' account of the Corcyrean conflict (1.24–55) serves in many ways as a programmatic introduction to the complexities of rhetoric and action found in the *History*.[1] With the reader viewing the situation from the perspective of the speakers and audience during the speeches at Athens and from that of the combatants during the battle of Sybota, Thucydides uses this first extended episode to present the world of political discourse, deliberation, and battle. The Corcyrean conflict may be viewed as programmatic for a number of reasons: it is the first episode with a pair of speeches; Thucydides ties this episode directly to the outbreak of the war; certain questions, such as morality's relevance to foreign policy, are introduced here for the first time; and, most importantly, it is here that Thucydides establishes what the reader's role is to be throughout the *History*.

I should begin by acknowledging a special debt to two articles: Connor's "Narrative Discourse in Thucydides" (1985) and Arnold's "The Persuasive Style of Debates in Direct Speech in Thucydides" (1992).[2] Connor attempts to answer the question: Why do we believe Thucydides' account? What makes the *History* so persuasive and compelling? His answer points to three aspects: first, the Archaeology offers a demonstration of his historical method; second, Thucydides successfully "replicates the intractability of historical experience" by his use of multiple perspectives in narrating events; and third, Thucydides creates an "experiential" or "participatory" type of narrative. Whereas Connor examines the narrative, Arnold focuses on speeches and seeks to demonstrate that "Thucydides creates for his readers an experience analogous to that which would have been experienced by an audience listening to political oratory."[3] By building on these insights, I hope to show how speech and narrative constitute two integral parts of Thucydides' recreation of the political arena of fifth-century Greece. For all the significance of Thucydides' Archaeology and Statement of Method (1.2–23), the "participatory" dimension of the *History* begins with the Corcyrean conflict. It is only with the introduction of speeches that the reader must address the ways in which speech and narrative confirm and undermine each other, as the historian's voice now alternates and competes with that of his characters in speech.[4]

For purposes of analysis, it will be valuable to divide Thucydides' account of the Corcyrean conflict into three sections: (1) Background and Conflict (1.24–31.3); (2) Speeches and Assemblies (1.31.4–44); and (3) Further Conflict: the Battle of Sybota (1.45–55). In the first section, Thucydides guides us by providing background information as well as several explanations for certain decisions and events. The first section does not demand "participation" from the reader in the same way as the subsequent two sections: the narrative is simply less intense, lacking dramatic detail about the perceptions and emotions of the participants. Thucydides' second section offers full-fledged "participatory" history of one type, employing multiple perspective in the paired arguments of the debate. With the battle of Sybota, a rapid succession of focalized experiences—the emotional and perspectival reactions of the participants—contrasts sharply with the opening section.

BACKGROUND AND CONFLICT (1.24–31.3)

In this opening section I begin by noting the sort of facts and events included. My particular interest is in Thucydides' selectivity regarding which events receive explanation and how detailed that explanation is.[5] The three Greek cities of Epidamnus, Corcyra, and Corinth provide the focus.[6] Thucydides begins with Epidamnus: its location, the circumstances of its colonization, its subsequent growth, and the ongoing civil war. Thucydides tells us that Corcyra established the city although a Corinthian, Phalius, served as founder (*oikistes*) with Corinthians among the settlers (1.24.2). When civil war arises in Epidamnus, the people (*demos*) expel the oligarchs and, finding themselves under pressure, send to Corcyra for help. This diplomatic cry is ignored (1.24.4–7). The Epidamnians' second move is to consult the Delphic oracle, which endorses the idea of sending to Corinth. Corinth's promise of aid (and the arrival in Corcyra of the oligarchical exiles) triggers the Corinthian conflict with Corcyra (1.25–26.2; cf. 1.26.3).

In the opening two and a half paragraphs (1.24–26.2) Thucydides presents geographical information, as well as historical background which both reaches back several hundred years and covers up-to-date political conflict. The relationships between the cities—especially "mother-city" (*metropolis*) and colony—are sketched out.[7] The divine element plays a role in two instances: the Epidamnian ambassadors are suppliants to Corcyra in the temple of Hera (1.24.7); and the oracle of Apollo advises the Epidamnians to set up the Corinthians as "leaders" (*hegemonas*–1.25.1). The restrictions are clear as well: in part this simply means a lack of detail. We find no dates other than the very vague "before the present war" (πρὸ τοῦδε τοῦ πολέμου–1.24.5).[8] For the first five chapters (1.24–28), no individuals other than Phalius are mentioned. We may contrast the absence of named individuals here with Thucydides' discussion of Agamemnon, Minos, and the tyrants in the Archaeology. One effect early on in this conflict is that the communities appear to discuss, act, and fight as collectives: "the Corinthians say . . ." "the Corcyreans perceived . . . ." This apparent unity within cities is of course belied by the fact that Epidamnus, for example, is split between popular and oligarchical factions. This tension between the ideal of a united polis and factionalism operates repeatedly in the *History* for the cities of Plataea, Mytilene, Corcyra, Thebes, Samos, and Athens.[9]

While the focus is very much on information and action rather than argument or justification, the following items do receive explanation. (a) Thucydides tells us that an ancient custom specified that a Corinthian— that is, someone from the *metropolis* of Corcyra—serve as founder of Epidamnus for the Corcyreans (κατὰ δὴ τὸν παλαιὸν νόμον–1.24.2). (b) Civil war in Epidamnus was caused, "it is said," by the barbarian war on the mainland (1.24.4).[10] (c) The Epidamnians originally send to Corcyra because it was their *metropolis* (ὡς μητρόπολιν οὖσαν–1.24.6). (d) When the Epidamnians "realize" (*gnontes*–1.25.1) that no help is forthcoming, they send to the oracle. As Lang points out, Thucydides has adopted the Herodotean practice of concisely indicating motivation by a participle.[11] (e) We are not told why the Corcyraeans reject the Epidamnian supplication, but an extensive account is given explaining the Corinthians' decision to help Epidamnus. It was just (κατὰ . . . τὸ δίκαιον), the Corinthians believed, for them to intervene because Epidamnus was as much their colony as it was the Corcyraeans' (1.25.3).[12] A second factor was Corinthian hatred of Corcyra due to Corcyra's lack of respect for Corinth (1.25.3–4). Such were the "causes for complaint" (*enklemata*–1.26.1) which motivated the Corinthian intervention in

Epidamnus.[13] Overall we see that the items which receive explanation are predominantly political, having to do with *metropolis* and colony, civil war, diplomatic entreaty, and Corinth's decision to help another city.[14]

To pick up the narrative thread: Corcyra sends ships and makes an overture to Epidamnus; this is rejected and a siege ensues (1.26.3–27). As the Corinthians learn of the siege, we find that the number of Greek cities involved greatly increases: Megara, Pales on Cephallonia, Epidaurus, Hermione, Troezen, Leucas, Ambracia, Thebes, and Elis all play a role (1.27.2).[15] The Corcyreans object that the problems in Epidamnus have nothing to do with Corinth; still they are willing to go to arbitration. Corcyra and Corinth could mutually choose Peloponnesian cities to act as arbitrators and the colony would go to whichever side the arbitrators decided; or, the Corcyreans suggest, the matter could be referred to Delphi. The Corinthians, however, want Corcyra to lift the siege *before* they go to arbitration, but the Corcyreans insist that the Corinthian expedition must withdraw before they lift the siege (1.28). These efforts at negotiation fail.[16] The battle of Leucimme follows (435 BCE), with Corcyra claiming victory and setting up a trophy; on the same day the city of Epidamnus negotiates a surrender to Corcyra (1.29–30). Out of anger, the Corinthians begin a shipbuilding enterprise.[17] The Corcyreans hear of this and decide to approach the Athenians in order to gain allies. The Corinthians in turn also send ambassadors to dissuade the Athenians from joining with Corcyra and its navy (1.31).

In his book *Athens and Corcyra*, Wilson remarks that "it is a great pity that Thucydides tells us practically nothing about the sea-fight [of Leucimme]."[18] It is true that there is a quantitative leap in terms of vivid detail from this battle to Thucydides' recreation of the battle of Sybota in the third section. Still in paragraphs 1.26.3–31.3 we note some specificity with regard to geography, the names of generals, and the numbers of ships and men. This account allows us to some extent to visualize the strength of forces, the terrain, and the actual individuals involved, yet all diplomatic exchange continues to be told briefly in the third person (e.g., 1.28, 1.29.5; cf. 1.24.6).[19] That is, Thucydides chooses not to include speeches in the early phases of the conflict; he waits until Athens is approached after the first battle. Yet even without the inclusion of speeches, this opening episode offers us a paradigm: failed negotiation leads to war. In miniature, the proposals and counterproposals made by Corcyra and Corinth immediately before the fight anticipate the failure in the rest of book 1 to find a negotiated settlement (by arbitration or otherwise) between the Athenians and the Spartan alliance. As

Thucydides has structured the narrative leading up to war, Pericles' final words of book 1 are a plea for arbitration (1.144–145); book 2 begins the war narrative.

We also observe that in this first section there is virtually no mention of Athens and Sparta. Thucydides' decision to begin with Epidamnus nicely demonstrates the connection between a remote and apparently irrelevant city and the larger alliances of Athens and Sparta.[20] A second sort of rationale—not preempting the first—follows Flory's interpretation of τὸ μυθῶδες discussed in chapter 2 (1.22.4). If Thucydides is claiming that he will not tell exaggerated patriotic stories, his choice to start somewhere other than Athens or Sparta may indicate his decision to avoid opening the "causes of war" section with a situation which would inevitably trigger some sort of emotional response.[21] Beginning the narrative with a major conflict featuring either Athens or Sparta would be likely to provoke fifth-century animosities. In the second section the Athenians listen, in the third they become involved, but Thucydides begins far from the centers of power.

Thucydides expects the reader to know a few basic facts: where the Ionian Gulf and Apollonia are (1.24.1, 1.26.2), what god resides in Delphi (1.26.1–2; cf. 1.26.4). On the whole, however, Thucydides appears to be offering mostly general background information necessary to welcome even a relatively unknowledgable reader into the story.[22] In the second and third sections, the demands increase as the level of encouragement for the reader's involvement rises. In this first section, however, we do not find vivid "experiential" history. Thucydides has prepared us for the looming conflict with the following in place: the main "actors" are cities; the details concern political and military matters; the fullest explanation concerns the Corinthian decision to become involved; and one model with later relevance shows unsuccessful negotiations leading to war.

Speeches and Assemblies (1.31.4–44)

In the second section, Thucydides presents two speeches addressed to the Athenians: the Corcyreans argue for an alliance with Athens (1.32–36); the Corinthians argue against such an alliance (1.37–43). It is here that Thucydides begins his fully vivid recreation of one aspect of the political arena: the world of political discourse (in the third section Thucydides offers an "experiential" account of battle). The key ingredients of this recreation are multiple perspective and authorial reticence. Thucydides keeps the presentation evenhanded by offering two perspectives: the reader is able to appreciate the situation in 433 from both the Corcyrean and Corinthian points of view.[23]

This recreation is made to feel rather open-ended because Thucydides is sparing in making authorial comments. For example, in introducing the speakers, Thucydides briefly indicates the motivation of each side, but makes no comment between the two speeches other than to note the change of speakers (1.31.2–31.4; 1.37.4). We find no authorial judgement as to the validity of the claims made until Thucydides comments on Athenian motivation and reasoning.[24] Still the structure encourages the reader not only to appreciate the complexities of the situation but also to examine critically the two arguments from the perspective of 433 BCE. That is, there is a sense in which the reader is put into the position of the Athenians. Like them, readers are not called on to articulate an argument of their own, but must listen, assess, and—by extension—make a decision. While at one level Thucydides' readers know war will come, by offering speeches with little comment he provokes the engaged reader to judge the merits of both speeches and ponder the consequences of Athenian action as though looking ahead from the year 433. While we are not actually hearing these two speeches in 433, Thucydides has structured the narrative in such a way as to encourage us to adopt these diverse points of view—both actively from Corcyrean and Corinthian perspectives and from the reactive and deliberative stance of Athens.

Because Thucydides offers multiple perspectives (with paired speeches and in his account of the battle of Sybota), the reader is able to appreciate the various points of view of the key cities. But more is asked of the reader. Once put in those positions, the reader needs to be active, engaging in the process of "extrapolation" (*eikazein*). Based on the present situation, what is likely to happen? From the perspective of 433 (as recreated by Thucydides), what is the probable course of events? The engaged reader must contemplate Athens' best move. Thucydides drives home the importance of the reader's role by not anticipating in speech or narrative the actual decision of Athens. The reader's engagement is provoked not only by multiple perspective and lack of authorial comment; in this case, the outcome comes as a surprise in terms of the preceding text. After the speeches, the Athenian assembly at first accepts the Corinthians' argument and votes to reject an alliance (*symmachia*) with Corcyra; a second meeting on the next day, however, determines that a defensive alliance (*epimachia*) with Corcyra would be the best course of action (1.44.1). Neither Corcyra nor Corinth mentioned the possibility of a defensive alliance.

In thinking of this entire episode as a kind of test for the engaged read-er, we find two viewpoints put forth; authorial comment comes only at the end. The issue between Corcyra and Corinth concerns whether—given the problem of Epidamnus and previous treaty obligations—Athens should make an alliance with Corcyra. The two arguments are vigorously put for-ward, aiming to persuade or dissuade the Athenians.[25] However persuasive and cogent each argument is, the Athenians apparently must choose one alternative over another: either ally with Corcyra or not.[26] The reader comes to learn, however, that speeches from cities who potentially have much to gain may skew a third city's options into an "either/or" situation; in fact, more flexibility is possible.[27] The Athenians adopt an option *not* expressed by Corinth or Corcyra. The reader has been in no way prepared in the speeches for a defensive alliance, and thus is alerted to the possibil-ity of imaginative (and more moderate) diplomacy. One lesson is that it may be necessary for the reader to go beyond what is said in the speeches to reach a decision best advancing one's own interests. This is an example of how the reader is encouraged to be engaged by anticipating a variety of choices. The active reader should be asking whether there are choices other than the alternatives Corcyra and Corinth present. A passive read-er—like unimaginative citizens in the Athenian assembly—will be left with a more limited and less advantageous set of options.[28]

So much for a quick overview of the speeches from the reader's point of view. This first set of speeches also introduces the reader to a broad spec-trum of issues, some of which have not yet been articulated in the *History*. There are four broad areas: the first three touch on justice, advantage, and relations between cities (treaties, etc.); the fourth concerns interpreting the past and anticipating the future. Each topic is significant in a different way. For example, the topic of justice is one that has not been anticipated in any way until this point of the *History*. The reader has not been pre-pared to think of foreign policy in moral terms until the speeches begin. The fourth category of looking to the past and future may well bear upon the reader's experience of reading history. That is, interpretation of the past and anticipation of the future may be seen as relevant to Athens in think-ing about a potential alliance with Corcyra—Athens must ruminate on the past and try to foresee the future—yet these skills of interpretation and anticipation are necessary for the engaged reader of Thucydides' *History*. I will comment briefly on the first three topics, and then explore at greater length this fourth issue.[29]

Both sides insist that considerations of justice should lead the Athenians to follow their recommendation. The Corcyreans begin each of their first three paragraphs with the idea of justice (including the first word spoken in the *History*): "It is 'just' [*dikaion*], since we have done no previous service to you and have no treaty in effect, to make especially clear . . . what advantage will come to Athens" (1.32.1; cf. 1.33.1, 1.34.1). The Corcyreans' more persuasive appeal may be their offer of a large navy (an appeal to Athenian self-interest), yet they begin by trying to show themselves as victims of injustice.[30] The Corinthians find it necessary to begin their speech by responding to these accusations of injustice made by the Corcyreans. The Corinthians feel no less strongly that justice resides on their side, for it is the Corcyreans who have "acted from evil motives [*kakourgia*], not for good [*arete*]; Corcyra wanted no allies because her actions were wrong [*adikemata*] and she was ashamed to call in others to witness her deeds" (1.37.2). If the Athenians refrain from the proposed alliance, according to the Corinthians, they would avoid joining the Corcyreans in committing injustice (ἵνα μὴ ξυναδικῶσιν); better to let them alone be guilty of injustice (ὅπως κατὰ μόνας ἀδικῶσι–1.37.4).[31]

I would emphasize that from the reader's perspective, these speeches are significant in raising the issue of justice at all. The reader has had no preparation for moral issues in the first 31 chapters of book one, and for the first time the reader needs to think about the relationship between justice and foreign policy.[32] White offers an intelligent reading of the importance of justice—or at least justification—in foreign policy.

> [Although] it is not particularly important to Athens that what she does actually be right . . . it is important that she be able to claim it is right. . . . While the talk about expediency is meant to persuade the Athenians directly to a particular course of action . . . the talk about justice . . . is meant to demonstrate what can be said in the future for and against the justice of the recommended courses of action. . . . The arguments are in this sense less about justice than about justifiability.[33]

This reading may be cynical, calling into question whether morality has any true relevance to foreign policy, but it fits Thucydides' comments at 1.44. When he tells us which factors actually influenced the second Athenian decision, they were matters of self-interest: naval strength and trade routes (1.44.2–3). As part of the reader's introduction to the rhetorical world of international negotiations, we find that even if moral considerations are not essential for motivation, such appeals are important for providing a set of justifications for Athenian action.[34]

The second area of appeal is self-interest. Both sides argue that Athens would benefit from either forming or refraining from the proposed alliance. Such appeals are more compelling in the Corcyreans' speech. The first sentence of the Corcyreans couples justice with advantage, for they wish to show "what advantages [ksumphora] will come to Athens" (1.32.1). The specific gains are two: first of all, Corcyra's navy will make Athens stronger (1.35.5). When war comes (and they insist it will) Athens will be the stronger side with two of three major navies (1.33.2, 1.36.1–3).[35] A second specific advantage is the "most profitable" (ksymphorotaton) location of Corcyra, for it is on the way to Italy and Sicily (1.36.2). Corinth's best response concerning Athenian self-interest appears to be a redefinition of advantage recommending caution:

"τό τε γὰρ ξυμφέρον ἐν ᾧ ἄν τις ἐλάχιστα ἁμαρτάνῃ μάλιστα ἕπεται."

"Advantage goes to him who makes the fewest mistakes." (1.42.2)

The mistake here apparently is to think that war will come when it instead lies uncertainly in the future (the likelihood of war is discussed below).[36]

A third set of issues concerns relations between cities, such as foundation ties, treaties, alliances, and the notions of "friendship" and "enmity" between cities.[37] Concerning relations between colony and "mother-city," Corinth makes two particularly weak claims: first, they call Epidamnus "their colony" ('Επίδαμνον ἡμετέραν οὖσαν–1.38.5) when it is at best more of a joint colony (1.24.2). Second, they make the false analogy between (1) the Samian revolt of 440 and Athens' right to punish its own allies (ksymmachous–1.43.1) and (2) their standing in 433 with regard to Corcyra. Although Corcyra is not an ally, the Corinthians claim the same right to deal with the Corcyreans as the Athenians have to deal with cities within the empire.[38] Of greatest urgency regarding the interpretation of treaties is whether an Athenian alliance with Corcyra would violate the treaty between Athens and Sparta from 446. Is Corcyra eligible to join either side? The Corcyreans argue:

"λύσετε δὲ οὐδὲ τὰς Λακεδαιμονίων σπονδὰς δεχόμενοι ἡμᾶς μηδετέρων ὄντας ξυμμάχους."

"In receiving us into an alliance you will not be breaking the treaty since we are allies to neither side." (1.35.1)

Corinth responds that the spirit of the 446 treaty precludes cities not originally involved (τῶν ἀγράφων πόλεων) from joining an alliance simply for the freedom to wrong others (1.40.2–40.3).[39]

We also find the language of friendship and enmity characterizing relations between cities.[40] These speeches introduce concepts relevant not only to how cities relate to one another but also to how they may rhetorically envisage such relationships which involves hierarchy, obligation, and maintaining treaties (also not anticipated earlier).[41] These three issues—justice, advantage, and international relations—confront the reader in this first experience of diplomatic discourse. Thucydides' presentation of views from two opposing sides offers the reader an appreciation both of the past isolation and current goals of Corcyra, and of Corinth's insistence on the spirit if not the letter of the treaty still in effect. The reader's engagement also flows from a need to weigh the validity and force of opposing claims in order to arrive at some sort of assessment as to which argument is stronger on which particular points. The reader as addressee (that is, in the position of the Athenians) is better able to view these arguments with a specific question in mind—what should Athens do? That is, Thucydides has contextualized these problems: while the distant reader may consider these issues in terms of their abstract or general validity, the engaged reader must apply these ideas to a specific case.

Of particular interest in these speeches is the fourth area of dispute: consideration of the past and the future. These remarks are not only relevant to the immediate situation, but may apply more generally toward the act of reading, specifically interpreting and learning from the past and anticipating the future. The arguments in these speeches do not straightforwardly reflect Thucydides' own ideas; rather, views about the importance of the past and the possibility of anticipating the future are advanced in dynamic fashion for the reader.[42] These speeches help the reader explore different ways of interpreting the past and of conjecturing (eikazein) about what the future may hold.

Both the Corcyreans and the Corinthians raise the idea of teaching and learning. At the first and most obvious level this refers to the Athenians understanding the issues. The Corcyreans wish to "teach" (anadidaksai–1.32.1) the Athenians the advantages of an alliance with Corcyra.[43] The Corinthians, too, find it necessary that the Athenians "learn" (μαθεῖν χρή—1.40.1) why it is not just for them to join the Corcyreans in an alliance.[44] This is a case where the reader needs to think about how learning from the past may be relevant to this conflict. In these speeches we find echoes of terminology and criteria invoked in Thucydides' remarks in the

Archaeology and Method, such as the importance of clarity and the role of evidence. The Corcyreans assert that the Corinthians' injustice is clear (ὡς δὲ ἠδίκουν σαφές ἐστιν–1.34.2–34.3); we recall Thucydides' remarks that his audience should consist of those wishing clearly to understand the past (τὸ σαφὲς σκοπεῖν–1.22.4).[45] The Corcyreans also introduce Corinth's treatment of Corcyra as "evidence" (*tekmerion*) of how the Corinthians would behave toward the Athenians (1.34.3). Such terms are familiar to readers of the early sections of the *History* which are presented in Thucydides' own voice.[46] In this self-referential way, these echoes call upon the reader to examine the clarity of argument in these two speeches and to assess the type of evidence the Corcyreans and Corinthians introduce—set against the standards explicitly proposed by the historian. Are the arguments sufficiently clear with adequate evidence to support making or abstaining from a treaty with Corcyra?

Each speech presents a different view of the past; neither is disinterested; both are polemical and self-serving. In recalling the past help (*euergesia*) they have given the Athenians, the Corinthians cite past events as a basis for present decisions and anticipations of the future.[47] When the Samians revolted, Corinth supported Athens and refused to assist the revolting city (1.40.5). Even earlier—before the Persian War—the Corinthians aided the Athenians with twenty ships against Aegina (1.41.2). That is, the Corinthians would have the Athenians base their decision regarding Corcyra on past service (selectively adduced) received from Corinth. In part, this is an example of traditional Greek morality— after you receive help from your friends, you should return the favor[48]; in part, the point concerns the relevance of history for the Corinthians, who see the past as critical in determining present action. Given their past isolation, the Corcyreans are more interested in the future, but they too feel they must explain their past, most prominently those actions which in retrospect are seen to be mistakes. "What once appeared to be wisdom [ἡ δοκοῦσα ἡμῶν πρότερον σωφροσύνη] now appears as lack of foresight and a source of weakness [νῦν ἀβουλία καὶ ἀσθενία φαινομένη]" (1.32.4).[49] Their previous policy of non-alliance and isolation has come to be seen as "an error of thought" (δόξης . . . ἁμαρτία—1.32.5). The Corinthians argue from their own past actions for Athenian quiescence, but the problem is they do not have much to offer Athens now. The Corcyreans have no past favor to cite as precedent, but lay greater emphasis on the future with the promise of a navy.

In a sense, these conflicting views of the past stand as two models for the value of history. The Corinthians use their past actions to set precedents, to establish a relationship, and in this case to seek recompense for previous favors. This view of the past implies a continuity and a structure that help guide subsequent actions. Upsetting this view is the problem of unpredictability and error. Situations change; people make mistakes. What appeared to be a good idea at one time (Corcyrean neutrality, for example) looks less desirable in a new light. After citing their previous errors, the Corcyreans go on to say that if the Athenians think war will not come, the Athenians are making a mistake (γνώμης ἁμαρτάνει–1.33.3). The Corcyreans prefer their vision of a future in which Athens joins them and they would then repay the Athenians for helping them: the Corcyreans' "historical" precedent lies with future actions on both sides.[50]

Both speeches cannot simply be read as offering instructions to the reader: the speeches are not authorial statements and, in addition, we find inconsistency related to past and future. The Corcyreans' argument may be seen as emphasizing human inability to anticipate the future: they have made mistakes in the past and characterize the Athenians' potential rejection of their offer as such a mistake. Yet paradoxically it is the Corcyreans who maintain a definite vision of the future: war will come; the Athenians will benefit from their navy. If the Athenians do not join them, they predict, the Athenians will look back on this in retrospect as an error in judgment. They even argue that if war comes, their proposed alliance will bring no danger or expense (ἄνευ κινδύνων καὶ δαπάνης διδοῦσα ἑαυτήν–1.33.2).[51] Based on the previous mistakes of their past behavior, however, the Corcyreans do not have much to recommend themselves as reliable prognosticators. The Corinthians on the other hand look confidently to the past as a guide to action. Yet they now insist that:

"τὸ μέλλον τοῦ πολέμου . . . ἐν ἀφανεῖ ἔτι κεῖται."

"The coming of war still lies in uncertainty." (1.42.2)

The Corinthians are also trying to have it both ways. They argue that an Athenian alliance with Corcyra would bring about war instead of peace (1.40.2), yet this will presumably happen in what they label the "uncertain" future. Such contradictions complicate the reader's assessment of each speech's recommendations. The reader becomes wary of basing decisions on the advice either of someone who has made mistakes in the past but is now certain of what will come, or of someone who argues the future is uncertain but that a particular action will bring war.[52]

Lying behind all this talk of past and future, of precedent and mistake, is the issue of whether war will come. Is the future course of events inevitable? Thucydides structures his narrative and speeches in such a way that his reader certainly knows that war will come. The markers are obvious. The subject of his history—the greatest war that has ever taken place—is announced by Thucydides at the opening of the *History* (1.1); immediately before the Corcyrean conflict he catalogues the suffering and upheaval caused by this war: exile, civil war, famine, disease (1.23). He even goes so far as to cite the conflict over Epidamnus as one of the two immediate causes of the war (1.23.6; cf. 1.55.2). The reader knows in advance that war will come. In tracing the steps leading up to war in his book *ANAΓKH in Thucydides*, Ostwald cites de Romilly: "the narrative is so compelling that the reader cannot envision the events happening in any other way."[53] We must conclude that one aspect of this early reading experience is a clear realization on the retrospective reader's part that war will come.

But there is another side—that of the engaged reader. In spite of Thucydides' references to the impending war, one question we as readers confront in sections 1.33–43 is the issue of whether war was inevitable. For the first time in the *History* Thucydides is not simply telling us what happened or why; instead in the speeches he has introduced arguments from two cities as part of his recreation of the political discourse of that time. The perspectives of those two sides advance as the authorial presence recedes. There is a sense in which, by "reliving" these speeches of 433, the engaged reader is able to consider anew the question of what may be about to happen. If war were inevitable, the Athenians would want the Corcyrean navy. But would an Athenian alliance with Corcyra help precipitate a war which is not imminent?[54] From the perspective of 433, what should the Athenians have done? Thucydides' prior announcements about Athenian growth and Spartan fear notwithstanding, he has reconstructed the scenario in such a way that we need to rethink that very question. For thirty-one chapters Thucydides has determined our view of events in an authoritative, almost omniscient manner; that guidance now ends. As Arnold says, "even in the narrative the knowledge that the reader has of the outcome of the war at times ironically strains against the apparent line of the author's argument."[55] This is the first of many instances where contemplating the experience of the speakers (Corcyreans and Corinthians) and the internal audience (the Athenians) instructs us as readers—in fact, it shows us *how* to be engaged readers. By adopting the viewpoints of the participants, we are in a position to regain the atmosphere of a contingent future.[56]

Thucydides' vivid recreation of the political arena offers us a sense that what is actually past to us (the war) still lies ahead in an indefinite future. I would argue that this is one of the defining features of Thucydides' *History*. In sections such as this, Thucydides induces the reader to project himself or herself into the past and view the situation from that time frame.[57] At one level, the reader knows war will come; at another, the reader is asked whether it had to happen as it did. Our engagement with Thucydides' work goes beyond seeking to understand the past. This section—something like an experiment run for the reader under controlled conditions—offers us training in the process of extrapolation and conjecture (*eikazein*). In this case, extrapolation consists of seeing the possibilities that had existed—not only what actually happened but what might have happened but did not.[58] Of course, in some sense we see (or foresee) the end result, yet the reader is being asked *to some degree* to suspend previously acquired knowledge in order to contemplate the options available to Athens in 433.

In his book *On the Origins of War and the Preservation of Peace*, Kagan notes that the later vote of the Spartans to go to war was not decided by a large majority (1.87). "We may deduce that not everyone thought the war was inevitable . . . not everyone thought it was necessary."[59] He goes on to explore alternatives which might have been pursued and remarks that "at each step [in the events leading to war] it is clear that the decisions were not preordained . . . any assertion that war was inevitable after the Thirty Years' Peace of 446–45 does not arise from the evidence but must be imposed *a priori*."[60] It is possible to read Thucydides, that is, and not agree with his conclusion that Athenian growth and Spartan fear "forced the war" (ἀναγκάσαι ἐς τὸ πολεμεῖν–1.23.6). The idea that war could have been avoided runs counter to this announcement of Thucydides, yet the narrative is sufficiently open-ended to suggest viable alternatives in 433 that at least might have postponed irreparable discord. In fact, Athens' decision to form only a defensive alliance with Corcyra may be seen as a moderate response, aimed at diffusing potential escalation of this conflict.[61]

The Corcyreans' and Corinthians' remarks on past and future do not represent Thucydides' own opinions. These ideas are part of his reconstruction of diplomatic dialogue which bears on how to view past and future. Arguments in the speeches may fit with the narrative elsewhere, at times even reinforcing authorial comments. When the Corcyreans assert that war will come because of Spartan fear (1.33.3), this clearly echoes Thucydides' own statements (1.23.6); nevertheless, Thucydides uses the two views of the future advanced by Corcyra and Corinth to deepen our understanding of the complex situation in 433. What in hindsight appears to have been unavoidable exists in an uneasy tension with the vividly contingent atmosphere of this "participatory" recreation. To the extent we put ourselves in the position of the Athenians in 433, we must look ahead from that perspective and ask not only was war inevitable but what actions might have resolved these international disputes. This is always an issue when reading history. Did what happened have to happen? Were there other options?[62] Thucydides himself offers no authoritative statement but leaves the issue open. Although we know the war took place, these speeches call into question the inevitability of that war. Part of Thucydides' project is to represent the past as present so that the reader may anticipate later historical events—past to the reader but subsequent to 433—as lying in an uncertain future. The reader—like the statesman or member of the Athenian assembly—must extrapolate (*eikazein*).

FURTHER CONFLICT: THE BATTLE OF SYBOTA (1.45–55)

In this third section we look at narrative focusing on a single battle, in a sense the narrative equivalent of the speeches just examined. Thucydides uses multiple focalization or points of view to represent how the Corcyreans, Corinthians, and Athenians experienced the battle. There is an even-handedness to the extent that these cities are all given serious attention; the effect for the reader is a vivid recreation of events. As we saw, the speeches were open-ended in that Thucydides did not pass judgment regarding the claims made in the speeches: the reader must become involved and weigh the disputed issues. The narrative in section 1.45–55 is open-ended in another sense. Thucydides does not assign significance to each event as it takes place, preferring to present these events in a way which allows the reader to seek what is most important. As seen from a distant perspective, the task of juxtaposition (a facet of *eikazein*) obliges the reader to make connections between this episode and other sections of the *History*, although in this opening conflict Thucydides explicitly reminds the reader of how this sequence fits into the larger course of events (1.55.2).

Following the Athenians' second assembly, ten ships are sent with a difficult set of instructions. They are not to break the treaty by attacking Corinth but are to help the Corcyrean fleet if it is attacked. We are given greater detail (names of generals, numbers of ships, and geography),

although dating is still vague ("not much later" [οὐ πολὺ ὕστερον]–1.45.1).
The fleet led by Corinth numbers 150 ships—90 of them are
Corinthian; the Corcyrean fleet of 110 ships is now supported by the 10
from Athens (1.47). This battle is much more fully described than that
of Leucimme.[63]

There are thirteen embedded (or secondary) focalizations in paragraphs
1.48–53, that is, passages in which events are presented from the perspective of a figure or group involved. Thucydides switches from one perspective to another showing what each side experienced. First the battle array
is described. The Athenians are on the far right flank supporting the three
squadrons of the Corcyreans. Opposing them are the Megarians and
Ambracians on the right wing, and (facing the Athenians) the
Corinthians on their left wing (1.48).[64] The first focalization is a paired
focalization: "When they [the Corinthians and the Corcyreans] saw each
other, they lined up opposite to one another" (ὡς δὲ κατεῖδον
ἀλλήλους–1.48.3). Section 1.49 describes the general character of the
battle which was "very similar to a land battle" (πεζομαχία δὲ τὸ πλέον
προσφερὴς οὖσα–1.49.2).[65] The second embedded focalization begins
broadly ("confusion and disorder reigned everywhere"–1.49.4), but
resolves into another double outlook or paired focalization. The
Athenians imposed fear on the Corinthians, as the Athenian generals
themselves feared the prohibition from fighting ordered by Athens (φόβῳ
μὲν παρεῖχον . . . δεδιότες–1.49.4).[66] Thucydides has already offered the
reader the perspectives of the Corcyreans, Corinthians, and Athenians
during the speeches. Now with the unfolding of battle, Thucydides puts the
reader into the position of the various combatants by indicating perceptions and emotions.

Third, the Athenians find that attempting to defend Corcyra is a deli-
cate business. In the chaotic fighting, the Athenians try to frighten anyone approaching the Corcyreans; as difficulties facing the Corcyreans
grow, the Athenians support them more aggressively (1.49.4–7). Soon the
Athenians, "seeing the Corcyreans pressed" (ὁρῶντες τοὺς Κερκυ-
ραίους πιεζομένους–1.49.7) are drawn in, and fight openly against the
Corinthians.[67]

Thucydides switches perspective more rapidly now. A fourth view:
the Corcyreans panic, thinking they will not make it to land
(deisantes–1.50.4). We return, in a fifth view, to the Corinthians, who
attempt to follow up their initial success, but an additional twenty ships
from Athens appear dissuading further action. Thucydides emphasizes the
suddenness of the appearance of the twenty Athenian ships from the per-

spective of the Corinthians, who take fright, thinking there may be more ships. This leads to a withdrawal (ἐξαπίνης . . . κατιδόντες . . . δείσαν-τες–1.50.5–51.1). In a sixth view, the Corcyreans are surprised at the Corinthian retreat until they see the ships arriving (ἐθαύμαζον . . . πρὶν . . . ἰδόντες–1.51.2). They, too, are struck with fear, thinking the additional ships are the enemy; soon they come to recognize them as Athenian and seek harboring for the night as battle comes to an end (ἐφοβήθησαν . . . ἔγνωσαν–1.51.5).

Thucydides has introduced six embedded focalizations (for the three central participants) with swift changes in 1.48–51.[68] While Thucydides' recreation of the arena of political discourse requires the reader to examine paired arguments, his recreation of this sea-battle builds on both objective factors—the number of ships, geography, strategy, and tactics—and on the deliberative and emotional experience of the combatants who plan, watch, act, and are struck with fear and surprise. While certainly selective, Thucydides' recreation is designed to make the reader's experience closer to that of the participants. This is brought home most powerfully by Thucydides' decision to *deprive* the reader of foreknowledge that a second Athenian contingent of twenty ships is on its way. Neither the Corinthians nor the Corcyreans knew of this and experience surprise— shared by the first-time reader—and fear. In a way this is the narrative equivalent of the third option adopted by Athens regarding the Corcyrean alliance. In that case there had been no advance notice in the speeches of Athens' decision to make a defensive alliance. Both the Athenian decision there (1.44) and the sudden arrival of a second Athenian contingent in this section introduce the ingredient of the unexpected; there is no way for the first-time reader to anticipate such outcomes based on the *History* alone. Again we may see this as "training" for the reader. During speeches the reader should always be asking whether there are options other than the ones presented. For the narrative, the reader recognizes that the course of battle cannot be accurately predicted, for the participants are often not fully cognizant of the resources each side may draw on. Given the apparently exhaustive description at 1.47–1.48, the arrival of twenty first-class ships hits the reader even harder. Thucydides' deliberate suppression of this later Athenian decision to send reinforcements implies the need for a flexible type of anticipation on the reader's part.[69]

On the following day we again find changing perspectives. (7) The Athenians and Corcyreans, wanting to know if there will be further battle (βουλόμενοι εἰδέναι εἰ ναυμαχήσουσιν–1.52.1), sail into the harbor where the Corinthian fleet has retreated for the night. Then we turn to

(8) the Corinthian perspective: they fear that the Athenians think the treaty has been broken and will prevent them from sailing away (*dediotes*–1.52.2–3). A dialogue ensues. (9) In addressing the Athenians (a rhetorical focalization) and ignoring the Corcyreans, the Corinthian envoys argue that the Athenians have committed an injustice (*adikia*) and have broken the treaty. Here Thucydides gives a brief speech in a few sentences (1.53.2). (10) The Corcyreans (presented in the third person) shout out, calling for the death of the envoys.[70] (11) The Athenians respond to Corinth, insisting that they did not begin the battle: "We are not beginning a war, O Peloponnesians, nor are we breaking the treaty. We came to help our allies, the Corcyreans" (1.53.4). It is noteworthy that the first words of the Athenians in the *History* are a response to charges that they have committed injustice and have broken a treaty. This provides an initial template for the first book, further expanded with the Corinthian charges at the first gathering of the Peloponnesian allies (1.69 ff.).[71] The Corinthians then journey home and the Corcyreans retrieve corpses.[72] Here, too, the perspective of all three cities are presented, two in direct speech and one reported in the third person.

Thucydides' use of multiple perspective to present battle is analogous to the two speeches in the debate: just as both Corinthians and Corcyreans are able to voice their arguments, so in the narrative the battle experience is presented from several sides. Such use of multiple viewpoint is underlined by the fact that two trophies were set up: each side had the opinion that it had won the battle of Sybota and indeed Thucydides expresses for each side a rationale for claiming victory with two final embedded focalizations. (12) The Corinthians feel they were victorious in the sea-battle in capturing over a thousand prisoners and sinking approximately seventy ships (1.54.2). (13) While sinking only thirty ships, the Corcyreans forced the Corinthian retreat (1.54.2).[73] Again we note the equitable balance of Thucydides' presentation.[74] Still the battle is not decisively won by either side—if both could claim victory, it does not resolve much of anything. Nevertheless, it leads to a great war. The closing paragraph reemphasizes the point Thucydides began with: this was the first cause (*aitia*) of the war for the Corinthians against the Athenians, as the seabattle with the Corcyreans took place while a treaty was in effect (ἐν σπονδαῖς–1.55.2; cf. 1.68.4).

Considered in the context of the *History* as a whole, the Corcyrean conflict exemplifies the episodic or punctuated nature of Thucydides' work. Corcyra, Corinth, and Athens play major roles in this episode—both in debate and in the battles which take place off the coast of northwestern Greece—yet in section 1.56 Thucydides breaks off without saying what happens later in Corcyra and shifts his attention to Potidaea. As Wilson remarks, "The importance of the Corcyrean navy to Athens is not in any way followed up."[75] As time passes, Corinth, Corcyra, Athens, Sicily, Italy, and the importance of navies will all return to our attention. Most importantly, the issues raised in the speeches—justice, advantage, and abiding by treaties—will reappear with application to other situations. Thucydides has introduced points of controversy which—although in a local sense receive a sort of provisional resolution—recur later in the work. The reader must be in a position to recall and juxtapose the arguments of those other episodes with this early sequence. This is the task to be explored in chapter 4 with a focus on Plataea.

In this chapter I have tried to show that, for all the significance of Thucydides' Archaeology and Statement of Method (1.2–23), the "participatory" dimension of the History begins with the Corcyrean conflict. While Thucydides explicitly links this opening episode with the coming of war in 431, he becomes more reticent with such comments as the History unfolds and the reader's task becomes proportionately more demanding.

4

PUNCTUATED HISTORY:
THE CASE OF PLATAEA

The previous chapter examined Thucydides' introduction of participatory history to the reader. We now turn to punctuated history, which derives from Thucydides' chronological framework. While we could track various cities through the *History*, such as Corcyra, Athens, or Syracuse, in this chapter we will examine the presentation of Plataea: how Thucydides explores this city, interrupts and shifts his focus, and then later returns. What happens to Plataea does not significantly affect the outcome of the war, yet Thucydides begins book 2—after his proclamation of the war's inauguration—with the Theban invasion of Plataea.[1] This chapter analyzes the role of this minor city that takes on paradigmatic importance for understanding punctuated history with respect to the following: the way in which past actions lead to later consequences; the rhetoric which describes and reinterprets previous action; the manner in which Plataea—in terms of its situation and choices—is implicitly compared with Mytilene, Corcyra, Melos, and Athens; and finally the ability to compare and extrapolate (*eikazein*), especially from the perspective of the Plataeans who must look ahead to an uncertain future.[2] Once more Thucydides highlights the open-ended future by demonstrating how decisions and chance events lead to outcomes that were not inevitable.

There are four extended passages focusing on Plataea: the Thebans enter the city at the start of the war (431 BCE—2.2–6); Sparta offers to allow Plataea to remain neutral, and then puts the city under siege (429 BCE–2.71–78); 212 Plataeans escape (428 BCE—3.20–24); and after the city surrenders, the Plataeans and Thebans debate the Plataeans' fate before Spartan "judges" (427 BCE—3.52–68). Badian calls this a "tragedy in a prelude and three acts."[3] To be sure, the whole sequence culminates in the execution of the inhabitants and the destruction of the city. Thucydides establishes links between early episodes and later ones in a variety of ways, most obviously by using the city of Plataea as a connect-

44

ing thread. These passages in turn present a new task for the reader who is challenged to follow the city in different stages of its historical development, gauge early words and actions with those found later in the *History*, and tie early action and rhetoric with later consequences. After examining each section in its own context, I will turn to Thucydides' overall presentation of Plataea in the *History*, seeking to retrieve those aspects of the reader's task that are most important for understanding Plataea's role.

My analysis of these four episodes explores tensions between: (1) goal and outcome; (2) knowledge and ignorance; and (3) choices and forced decisions. The issue of comparison and extrapolation is also prominent, both implicitly and explicitly. The first tension is created by the articulation of goals at the beginning of each episode set against the actual outcomes. Often, of course, there is a disjunction between the various participants' intentions and the ultimate result of a particular sequence of events. Figures in Thucydides' *History* are invariably disappointed: the Thebans fail to gain control of Plataea in 431; the Spartans fail to burn the city in 429. Indeed, the successes of the Plataeans in the first three sections—regaining control of their city, the avoidance of conflagration for Plataea, and the nighttime escape—depend upon desperate action, luck, and the aid of the elements. It seems more than coincidence that in the first three sections, fortuitous "interventions"—rain, wind, and a new moon—play such an important role in assisting the Plataeans. While another Greek might attribute such narrow escapes to the gods, Thucydides may only be suggesting that factors such as the weather are unpredictable and at times favor the more vulnerable side. These first three positive outcomes contrast sharply with the execution in 427 (3.68), which comes to be viewed as almost inevitable—even by the Plataeans themselves.[4]

In addition to goals and outcomes, a second tension concerns knowledge and ignorance of events each set of participants has. Thucydides often highlights these viewpoints by the use of embedded (or secondary) focalization. Perhaps the dominant experience of figures in both sections 1 and 3 is that of misperception or lack of knowledge, when events do not proceed as planned or anticipated. Certainly in the first episode the Plataeans (other than the pro-Theban Plataeans) were totally unaware of Theban plans to enter the city. As Thucydides notes, there was no guard set (φυλακῆς οὐ προκαθεστηκυίας–2.2.3); some Plataeans were outside the city walls, for they did not expect trouble in times of peace (οἷα ἀπροσδοκήτου κακοῦ ἐν εἰρήνῃ γενομένου–2.5.4). Once the Thebans are inside, the Plataeans at first mistakenly think there were more

Thebans than there actually were. The Thebans *wrongly* think that it would be easy to persuade the Plataeans to capitulate and attempt to come to an agreement with the populace. Later the advantage gained from superior knowledge and unanticipated aggression shifts from the Theban plotters to the Plataean resistance; in this case, the Plataean plan works successfully (2.3–4). In the third section, the Plataean escape is also grounded in surprise, misdirection, and confusing the besieging army.

Degrees of knowledge range along the spectrum from total ignorance (of the Plataeans on the eve of the Theban invasion) to conspiratorial action. This theme of misperception and lack of knowledge, however, operates not only for Thebes, Plataea, and Athens, but also at the level of the reader's own experience.[5] In general, the reader learns various facts of which the participants are unaware, as Thucydides exploits the possibilities of dramatic irony. But Thucydides not only effectively uses focalization to show how—at different times—participants experienced the events and encourages the reader to adopt the position of the participants[6]; at times, the reader's perspective is manipulated. For example, at 2.5.5–6, Thucydides suggests that the Plataean herald reports what was actually agreed upon when, in fact, he has only presented *the Thebans' version* of the "negotiation" between the second contingent of the Thebans and the Plataeans who have just regained control of their city.

Based on goals and varying levels of knowledge, particular decisions are made. For example, unexpected invasions and escapes occur in episodes 1 and 3. In the second section, negotiations appear pretty flexible; in the fourth section, the options dwindle to death or deception (and death). Whenever choices are made, they grow out of limited information—a narrow perspective—but also out of the human incapacity accurately to foretell later events. The reader must ask: Were such errors inevitable? To what extent were these events and their consequences unpredictable? Were there viable alternatives to those taken? Plataea resists Archidamus' overtures in episode 2, based on an Athenian promise of rescue, which is not fulfilled. Should the Plataeans in 429 have counted on such a promise? Was the Athenian promise even made in good faith? More generally we need to examine later consequences of Theban and Plataean action. Once the Thebans entered Plataea, could anything have prevented war? And how should we describe the entry of these 300 Thebans—as forced entry or as a response to an invitation? When Plataea becomes Thucydides' focus in two sections of book 3, as retrospective readers, we need to recall the decisions and actions made at the start of the war. Goals and outcomes are dependent in large part on the participants' perspectives and their sense of viable choices. We should not view these various tensions—goal and outcome, knowledge and ignorance, choices and forced decisions—as discrete and unrelated. Nevertheless, these categories will be useful for purposes of analysis.

The issue of comparison and extrapolation (*eikazein*) is relatively open-ended. Of the three levels of analysis—local (the passage itself), distant (comparing one section with another), and extratextual (comparing an episode in Thucydides' *History* with events outside the history), comparison of the four Plataean episodes constitutes a type of distant analysis. Part of the reader's task is to make connections between these four passages and other sections of the *History* based on thematic connections (such as the option of neutrality, linking Plataea to Corcyra and Melos) and with cities in comparable situations (Plataea's affinities with Athens and Mytilene). The retrospective reader is asked to recollect earlier sections when engaged with the later narrative. We discover a movement from actions presented in pure narrative to speeches in sections 2 and 4; a shift from various choices offered early on to the Plataeans to severely restricted options; and the role of chance and the elements unexpectedly aiding the Plataeans ultimately reduced to total despair.

Plataea and the Beginning of the Peloponnesian War (2.2–6)

Let us turn to the first episode. The lack of speeches in this opening section means that Thucydides will present a particular sort of drama for the reader's experience. Rather than grappling with the complexities of argument and counterargument, the reader becomes more of a spectator to a drama, holding a position of knowledge superior to that of the participants involved. Thucydides has recreated the events by combining objective facts with the deliberations and emotional experience of the participants. Thucydides begins the first section (2.2–6) from the perspective of the pro-Theban Plataeans and the Thebans who enter the city; then we are shown the shock and subsequent resistance of the Plataeans; Thucydides later shifts outside the walls to the perspective of the Theban contingent that knows little of what is going on within Plataea; the Athenians give advice on the basis of only limited information; finally the herald is sent to deliver a message, only to learn on arrival that his advice arrives too late. Yet throughout this first section, Thucydides provides such vivid detail that the reader is able also to take an engaged perspective.

Thucydides is very restrictive as to what he includes in his narrative, yet he does supply information about the motivation of various participants.[7] The Thebans themselves, anticipating (*proidontes*) war, wanted to control Plataea since it was always hostile (*diaphoron*) to them, even in peace (2.2.3). Once the invading force has apparently gained control, the Plataeans surrender, in part because the Thebans took no violent measures toward anyone (οὐδὲν ἐνεωτέριζον–2.3.1). Yet the majority of Plataeans (τῷ γὰρ πλήθει) did not wish to revolt from Athens (2.3.2). While the preliminary step of entering the city is successfully achieved, the pro-Theban Plataeans and the Thebans fail to maintain control of Plataea; only after the year 427 (the fourth episode) do the Thebans finally take full control of Plataea.

Thucydides employs eleven embedded or secondary focalizations in section 2.2–6 describing the first event triggering the war in 431 BCE. The first focalization occurs in connection with the invitation for the Thebans to enter the city. Thucydides indicates the pro-Theban Plataean faction's three goals: personal power, the death of their enemies, and bringing Plataea into the Theban sphere of influence (2.2.2). Second, there is a change of plan when the Thebans ignore the advice of the pro-Theban faction and call an assembly. They think it would be easy to come to an agreement with the Plataeans (νομίζοντες . . . ῥᾳδίως–2.2.3–4). The Thebans' goal has not changed, but there is an alteration in the means pursued to achieve that outcome.[8] Thucydides reports the herald's announcement:

γνώμην δ' ἐποιοῦντο κηρύγμασί τε χρήσασθαι ἐπιτηδείοις καὶ ἐς ξύμβασιν μᾶλλον καὶ φιλίαν τὴν πόλιν ἀγαγεῖν καὶ ἀνεῖπεν ὁ κῆρυξ, εἴ τις βούλεται κατὰ τὰ πάτρια τῶν πάντων Βοιωτῶν ξυμμαχεῖν, τίθεσθαι παρ' αὐτοὺς τὰ ὅπλα.

[The Thebans] issued a proclamation in reasonable terms, aimed at leading the city into a friendly arrangement; and their herald proclaimed that anyone wishing to be an ally in accordance with the ancestral practice of all Boeotians should ground his arms with them. (2.2.4; cf. 2.3.4)

A question arises concerning perspective of this second focalization: is it the Thebans who find the terms "reasonable" (*epitedeiois*) or is this Thucydides' authorial comment?

Third, Thucydides lets us experience the shock the Plataeans feel (ᾔσθοντο . . . ἐξαπιναίως–2.3.1).[9] The sudden entrance of the Thebans causes fear (*katadeisantes*) and confusion, as the Plataeans believe (*nomisantes*) that there are more Thebans within the city than in fact there are (2.3.1). Continuing the narrative from the Plataeans' perspective, Thucydides tells us that they then noticed (*katenoesan*) there were not so many Thebans and they began to orchestrate a night attack by cutting through walls and setting up barricades (2.3.2–3). (4) The Thebans recognize the trap (οἱ δ' ὡς ἔγνωσαν ἐξηπατημένοι) and attempt to repel the attack, but then out of fear (*ephobethesan*) they flee through the city (2.4.1–2). Thucydides provides considerable detail in recreating this nocturnal chase.

ἔπειτα πολλῷ θορύβῳ αὐτῶν τε προσβαλόντων καὶ τῶν γυναικῶν καὶ τῶν οἰκετῶν ἅμα ἀπὸ τῶν οἰκιῶν κραυγῇ τε καὶ ὀλολυγῇ χρωμένων λίθοις τε καὶ κεράμῳ βαλλόντων, καὶ ὑετοῦ ἅμα διὰ νυκτὸς πολλοῦ ἐπιγενομένου, ἐφοβήθησαν καὶ τραπόμενοι ἔφευγον διὰ τῆς πόλεως, ἄπειροι μὲν ὄντες οἱ πλείους ἐν σκότῳ καὶ πηλῷ τῶν διόδων ᾗ χρὴ σωθῆναι καὶ γὰρ τελευτῶντος τοῦ μηνὸς τὰ γιγνόμενα ἦν.

Then there was a tremendous uproar from the men who were attacking them, and shouting and yelling from the women and slaves on the roofs, who hurled down stones and tiles; at the same time it had been raining hard all night. Finally in a panic [the Thebans] turned and fled through the city, most of them clueless as to which way to go in the darkness and mud in order to escape (for it was also a moonless night at the end of the month). (2.4.2)

With vivid mention of shouting, rain, tiles hurled down from roofs, and the darkness of the night, Thucydides recreates the Thebans' desperate circumstances. He contrasts the bewildered Thebans (who are "clueless"–*apeiroi*) with the experienced Plataeans who know their ways around in their own city (ἐμπείρους δὲ ἔχοντες–2.4.2).[10]

Subsequent events are then recounted. An unnamed Plataean shuts the gate by which the Thebans entered (2.4.3). Various groups of Thebans jump to their death or die in scattered groups. Some escape with the help of an axe given by an anonymous Plataean woman, but this leads to (5) a quick Plataean point of view: not many Thebans escaped, "for [the Plataeans'] perception was quick [αἴσθησις γὰρ ταχεῖα ἐπεγένετο]" (2.4.4). Most of the Thebans retreat to a large building. The Plataeans see them within (*horontes*) and deliberate whether to burn the building with those inside or follow another course of action (2.4.6). The Thebans surrender and Thucydides shifts to the scene outside the city walls.

We might note at this point the unforced decisions by the Thebans (to invade, to invite the Plataean populace into an alliance, and to surrender rather than fight to the death) and by the Plataeans (to resist and to ponder the means of slaughtering the Thebans). Thucydides presents each of these actions as autonomous and in response to desire and circumstance. With respect to chance events that might have turned out otherwise, we are about to learn that the Thebans only "just" manage to cross the Asopos River (*molis*–2.5.3). If the river had been a bit more flooded, they never would have made it to Plataea at all.

(6) After viewing events from the perspective of the Thebans and Plataeans within the city, events are now focalized by a second contingent of Thebans approaching Plataea. The Theban troops receive news of what has happened, learning (*eisthonto*) that some Thebans have died and others have been taken prisoner (2.5.1–4). They consider seizing the Plataeans still in the countryside outside the city walls (2.5.4). (7) Suspecting (*hypotopesantes*) such a seizure, the Plataeans within are fearful (*deisantes*). At 2.5.5 we see things from the Plataeans' perspective.

οἱ δὲ Πλαταιῆς ἔτι διαβουλευομένων αὐτῶν ὑποτοπήσαντες τοιοῦτόν τι ἔσεσθαι καὶ δείσαντες περὶ τοῖς ἔξω.

While [the Thebans] were still discussing it, the Plataeans suspected that this [the Theban plan to seize Plataeans outside] was what they might do and feared for the safety of those outside the walls. (2.5.5)

The next thing we read is that the Plataeans send out a herald, who says that what the Thebans did in peace was sacrilegious (οὔτε . . . ὅσια–2.5.5) and that they should not harm the Plataeans outside the city.[11]

κήρυκα ἐξέπεμψαν παρὰ τοὺς Θηβαίους, λέγοντες ὅτι οὔτε τὰ πεποιημένα ὅσια δράσειαν ἐν σπονδαῖς σφῶν πειράσαντες καταλαβεῖν τὴν πόλιν, τά τε ἔξω ἔλεγον αὐτοῖς μὴ ἀδικεῖν· εἰ δὲ μή, καὶ αὐτοὶ ἔφασαν αὐτῶν τοὺς ἄνδρας ἀποκτενεῖν οὓς ἔχουσι ζῶντας· ἀναχωρησάντων δὲ πάλιν ἐκ τῆς γῆς ἀποδώσειν αὐτοῖς τοὺς ἄνδρας.

They sent a herald to the Thebans, saying that this attempt to seize their city in time of peace was contrary to divine sanction; they told them not to harm those who were outside. If they did, the Plataeans said that they would kill the Thebans whom they held as prisoners. If, on the other hand, the Thebans would withdraw from their land, the Plataeans would give the prisoners back to them. (2.5.5)

The previous section indicated a shift in focalization: the Plataeans suspected that the Thebans had plans to seize the Plataeans outside the walls (the first half of 2.5.5). Because there is no explicit indication that the focalization has changed, the next section—the second half of 2.5.5—appears either to be objectively told (with Thucydides as sole focalizer) *or* to be a continuation of events as seen from the Plataean perspective (the seventh focalization). The reader is given the impression that this section is an objective description of the herald's speech. (Note the similarities to the herald's speech given in the third person at 2.4.4 quoted above.)

But Thucydides has misled his reader. The account of what the herald tells the Thebans is *the Theban account*, given presumably after the fact. That is, this is very much a secondary focalization, as Thucydides presents what was said from the Theban point of view. Thucydides now reveals this:

Θηβαῖοι μὲν ταῦτα λέγουσι καὶ ἐπομόσαι φασὶν αὐτούς· Πλαταιῆς δ᾽ οὐχ ὁμολογοῦσι.

The Thebans say this and swear to it, but the Plataeans do not agree. (2.5.6)

Subsequently we learn the Plataean account. They maintain they did not promise to give back the prisoners; they swore no oath, but said they would negotiate after the Plataeans were released.

What Thucydides has done is to introduce an eighth focalization from the Theban point of view—their version of what the herald said (2.5.5)—without alerting the reader to this shift in perspective. Then a ninth viewpoint gives the Plataean account (2.5.6). Nevertheless, the reader has been led to believe that the account of the herald is objective (or presented from the Plataean point of view). This striking instance of manipulation on Thucydides' part has the effect of unsettling the reader's experience.[12] According to the conventions of Thucydides' presentation, he generally lets the reader know when a shift in perspective has taken place. Yet here Thucydides manipulates these conventions and disrupts the illusion of confidence the reader may feel at this critical point (2.5.5–6). Much like the ambushed Plataeans—or, later, like the Thebans within the city, who are themselves the target of a surprise attack—the reader is misled as to what was actually happening, or whose perspective is being presented. In fact, Thucydides never indicates which account—the Theban or the Plataean—is accurate.[13]

From 2.5.7–6, we find more factual description, as Thucydides presents the subsequent sequence of events. The Thebans outside the city leave; the Plataeans bring their property and people into the city, and then kill the 180 Theban prisoners. They send a message to Athens and the Athenians immediately arrest all Boeotians in Athens. This is not a question of perspective: these events are presented more objectively. (10) At this point, we shift to the perspective of Athens, learning of the Athenians' advice (*keleuontes*–2.6.2) that the Plataeans should do nothing until they consult Athens. Thucydides emphasizes the Athenians' lack of knowledge, telling us that they knew nothing of the prisoners having been put to death (οὐ γὰρ ἠγγέλθη αὐτοῖς ὅτι τεθνηκότες εἶεν . . . καὶ τῶν ὕστερον οὐδὲν ᾔδεσαν. οὕτω δὲ οὐκ εἰδότες οἱ ᾿Αθηναῖοι ἐπέστελ-λον–2.6.3). (11) The final view is that of the anonymous Athenian herald who arrives in Plataea to discover that the Theban prisoners had been put to death (*eure*–2.6.3). The Athenians then send supplies and men to Plataea and Thucydides shifts from this episode to the preparation for war.[14]

Part of extrapolation and comparison concerns connecting this episode (2.2–6) to the rest of the *History*. In this broader context we should first note that Thucydides uses this episode to mark the beginning of the Peloponnesian War, the greatest war ever to affect the Greek world. Thucydides raises the anticipation of war for the reader in book 1; this now receives fulfillment, although the prominent roles Thebes and Plataea play have not previously been anticipated.[15] In contrast to the various causes of the war presented in book one, the Plataean episode is the first engagement, the trigger that sets the war in motion. In paragraph 2.2 Thucydides offers various means of dating this beginning, yet the temporal setting is wholly subordinate to the act of the 300 armed Thebans entering the city of Plataea. Thucydides notes that with the Theban invasion, the treaty has now clearly been broken (λελυμένων λαμπρῶς τῶν σπονδῶν–2.7.1; cf. 2.10.1). Later the first Peloponnesian invasion of Attica will be defined as taking place on the eightieth day after the

Plataean episode (2.19.1). This opening incident of the war is significant not only because it marks the start of the war, but also because in retrospect this action bears on later control of Plataea and the overall responsibility for the war itself.[16]

This first section is also important due to what has immediately preceded it: not only the dating (2.2.1), but also the close of book one which includes Pericles' offer of arbitration and the lack of a Spartan response (1.143–146), and the articulation of Pericles' war strategy which expresses the idea that the Athenians should think of themselves as islanders (nesiotai–1.143.5). This idea of "Athens as an island" has crucial consequences for their ally Plataea. The Athenians are powerful at sea, but they do not aid landlocked Plataea later in the war (the Athenians do send troops and supplies in 431–2.6.4). Although Thucydides may be implicitly contrasting the landlocked Plataeans with Athenian "islanders," in some ways the experiences of Plataea and Athens are quite similar. Following the Peloponnesian invasion of Attica, Athens is repeatedly put under attack—a crisis Plataea will undergo in the years 429–427. Both are in a defensive position behind walls, as citizens and property are brought within and their land is ravaged (2.5.7, 2.14, 2.21–22; cf. 2.71.1). The difference is that the Plataeans, as they later put it, are "mainlanders" (epeirotai–3.54.4). I will return to the significance of this juxtaposition after examining episodes 2 and 3.

PLATAEA AND THE OFFER OF NEUTRALITY (2.71–78)

We now move to the second section in the History where Plataea plays a major role, specifically their negotiations with the Spartan King Archidamus and the resulting siege of Plataea. There is virtually no mention of Plataea between the spring of 431 (2.6) and the spring of 429 (2.71). For 64 chapters all we have heard of Plataea is that it was one of Athens' allies (in the catalog at 2.9.4) and that part of the Boeotian forces went to Plataea, rather than Athens (2.12.5). That is, until we encounter Plataea in 2.71, there has been little intervening comment concerning what happened there after the Athenian herald arrived to find out that the 180 Theban prisoners had been put to death and that Athens subsequently sent men and supplies (2.6.4).[17]

For the purposes of analysis, this episode may be divided into two parts. In the first part we have five short speeches: two by the Plataeans, three by Archidamus (the earlier Plataean episode contained only narrative).

The second half of this section is pure narrative with seven focalizations as Thucydides describes the efforts of the allied Peloponnesian and Boeotian forces to take the city. Topics of particular interest in this passage include: the expectations of participants, the range of choices offered to the Plataeans, the viability of those choices, and Archidamus' critical role as a negotiator. It is significant that the effect of the siege is to cut off Plataea from the rest of the Greek world; we also find an implied comparison between Plataea and Athens.

The choices as envisioned by participants are limited by expectations, including the expectation at the beginning of this section that the Peloponnesian force will invade Attica once again rather than Plataea. The Greeks (and perhaps the first-time reader) may expect that in the summer of 429, the Peloponnesians would once again invade Attica. Thucydides begins with the usual pattern:

τοῦ δ' ἐπιγιγνομένου θέρους οἱ Πελοποννήσιοι καὶ οἱ ξύμμαχοι ἐς μὲν τὴν Ἀττικὴν οὐκ ἐσέβαλον, ἐστράτευσαν δὲ ἐπὶ Πλάταιαν.

In the coming summer, the Peloponnesians and their allies into Attica *did not invade, but marched against Plataea.* (2.71.1)

It is not until the negative (*ouk*) that Thucydides makes clear that this year the Peloponnesian forces would *not* invade Attica, but instead would march against Plataea. I will return below to the idea of Plataea as a "surrogate" Athens.

The goal of the Peloponnesians and Boeotians is to remove Plataea as an Athenian ally. Archidamus suggests that neutrality is all they wish. In the fifth speech, he says, "We have not come for empire (*arche*) nor will we now act unjustly (*adikos*) to this land" (2.74.2). The Plataeans suspect that the Theban goal is the enslavement of Plataea (ἐπὶ δουλείᾳ τῇ ἡμετέρᾳ–2.71.3). The Plataeans hope to survive and ideally maintain their autonomy.

Yet the contingent future contains several options for the Plataeans. Indeed, Archidamus shows considerable flexibility in suggesting various options as he attempts to avoid forcing Plataea into an either/or situation. Most importantly, Archidamus has thought up novel ways of getting around the apparent alternatives that Plataea must either fight with or against the Spartans. The Spartan king argues that if the Plataeans do not wish to join Sparta and its allies to help liberate Greece, they could become a neutral state.

"ἡσυχίαν ἄγετε νεμόμενοι τὰ ὑμέτερα αὐτῶν, καὶ ἔστε μηδὲ μεθ᾽ ἑτέρων, δέχεσθε δὲ ἀμφοτέρους φίλους, ἐπὶ πολέμῳ δὲ μηδετέρους."

"Remain at peace and join with neither side, but receive both as friends and wage war against neither." (2.72.1)

Such an arrangement would be acceptable to Sparta. Archidamus should be recognized as an innovator for his flexibility: he is willing to offer the Plataeans more than one choice.[18]

In the third speech (given in direct discourse), Archidamus tries another improvised solution. The Plataeans could turn the city of Plataea—all their households and property—over to Sparta, mark the boundaries and count the trees, and leave the territory during the war. Then, when the war ends, the Plataeans might come back and everything would be returned to them. For a second time, Archidamus shows his skills as a negotiator by avoiding the appearance of forcing the Plataeans into accepting or rejecting a narrow range of demands. Here he offers the option of putting the city into "receivership" until the war comes to a close. Archidamus emphasizes his efforts to come up with a reasonable solution (προκαλεσάμενοι γὰρ πολλὰ καὶ εἰκότα–2.74.2). The apparent abundance of options voiced here contrasts sharply with the narrow path Plataea must follow in book 3 when they surrender their city to the Spartans.

According to the Plataeans, the threatening action of Sparta is unjust and unworthy of the Spartans and their ancestors. The Plataeans advance the idea that justice and precedent based on duty to one's ancestors lead to the same position: Plataea must be allowed to determine its own foreign policy. In particular, the Plataeans use the past to argue for "comparable" behavior from the Spartans in the current situation. Plataea's idea of just action is related to past Panhellenic enterprises, freedom, and the gods. They recall Pausanias' liberation of Greece when Xerxes was repulsed. In joining together in common danger, the Greeks sacrificed in Plataea's agora to Zeus, the god of Freedom (*Zeus Eleutherios*). Pausanias called upon his allies to allow Plataea to live independently (αὐτονόμους οἰκεῖν) and to refrain from unjust action leading to slavery (στρατεῦσαί τε μηδένα ποτὲ ἀδίκως ἐπ᾽ αὐτοὺς μηδ᾽ ἐπὶ δουλείᾳ–2.71.2). The Plataeans argue that the past deeds of Pausanias should be seen as setting the standard against which later Spartans should act.[19]

"οὐ δίκαια ποιεῖτε οὐδ᾽ ἄξια οὔτε ὑμῶν οὔτε πατέρων ὧν ἐστέ, ἐς
γῆν τὴν Πλαταιῶν στρατεύοντες."

"It is not just nor is it worthy of you or your fathers to invade the land of
the Plataeans." (2.71.2)

The Spartans' fathers (*patres*) guaranteed Plataean independence and sovereignty, yet the Spartans are now acting in contrary fashion. Justice, the
oaths of Spartan ancestors, and sacrifices to the gods all urge the Spartans
to reconsider their actions against Plataea. The Plataean peroration appeals
to the gods as witnesses and to the oaths sworn by both Spartan and
Plataean: the Spartans should continue to honor Pausanias' original decision (καθάπερ Παυσανίας ἐδικαίωσεν–2.71.4). The Plataeans imagina-
tively reconstruct the past to argue for their own autonomy.

Archidamus in turn argues that the Spartans' actions are consistent
with the tradition of their ancestors. The current war itself is being fought
for the sake of freedom.

"παρασκευή τε τοσήδε καὶ πόλεμος γεγένηται αὐτῶν ἕνεκα καὶ τῶν
ἄλλων ἐλευθερώσεως."

"This army has been raised and the war itself has broken out in order to
free them [that is, the Greeks who fought for freedom against Xerxes] and
others like them." (2.72.1)

What the Plataeans have *said* is fine; the problem, according to
Archidamus, lies in the fact that their *actions* do not match those sentiments
(ἢν ποιῆτε ὁμοῖα τοῖς λόγοις–2.72.1). That is, setting word against
action, Archidamus finds the Plataeans' words noble, but their actions fail
to match that nobility. Archidamus answers almost every appeal of the
Plataeans with a counterargument. Regarding the claims to justice, he
asserts that just acts should match just words. As a representative of freedom and autonomy, Pausanias guides united Greek action now no less than
previously (καθάπερ γὰρ Παυσανίας ὑμῖν παρέδωκεν–2.72.1). In his
last speech, returning once more to the idea of justice Archidamus calls
upon the gods and heroes of the land.

"οὔτε νῦν, ἤν τι ποιῶμεν, ἀδικήσομεν· προκαλεσάμενοι γὰρ πολλὰ
καὶ εἰκότα οὐ τυγχάνομεν. ξυγγνώμονες δὲ ἔστε τῆς μὲν ἀδικίας
κολάζεσθαι τοῖς ὑπάρχουσι προτέροις, τῆς δὲ τιμωρίας τυγχάνειν

τοῖς ἐπιφέρουσι νομίμως."

"Nor will we be acting wrongly now [adikesomen], if we do anything; for although we have offered many reasonable proposals, we have failed. Grant that those who were the first to do injustice be punished for it and that those lawfully [nomimos] seeking retribution obtain it." (2.74.2)

At this point the Spartans make preparations for war.

Three strategic issues are linked to this scenario: Why has Sparta invaded Plataea? Were the options voiced by Archidamus and the Athenian promise for aid given sincerely? And—whatever the answer to the second question—what was the likelihood of Athenian aid?

First, why did Sparta invade Plataean territory instead of Attica in 429? One view, expressed by Connor, is that Archidamus and the Spartans had "in effect, been defeated." After failing to force a land battle with Athens, they move on to Boeotia. Yet Connor views both enterprises as challenges to the Periclean strategy, by tempting the Athenians to engage in a land battle.[20] Perhaps Archidamus is showing his inventiveness as a military strategist by trying to provoke a land war in a new way. Kagan points to three factors for the march on Plataea: Theban pressure, the thoroughness of the destruction in Attica from the previous year, and danger of infection from the plague. While all these motivations may play a role, the way in which Thucydides orders his opening ("into Attica, they did *not* invade . . .") suggests that Plataea has become in a sense a surrogate target in place of Athens.[21]

The second issue concerns the sincerity of what both Archidamus and Athens tell the Plataeans. Kagan says that both offers are "a charade." The Spartan "offer had been made impossible by the unprovoked attack," yet later he qualifies this assertion: in 429 the Plataeans "could have yielded on reasonable terms had not Athens held her [Plataea] to the alliance and promised help."[22] After consulting with Athens, the Plataeans reject the various offers of Archidamus (alliance, neutrality, receivership), having obtained a promise that Athens would help the Plataeans (2.73.3). Kagan believes that the Athenian promise "must reflect the momentary ascendancy of the war party . . . the promise was honestly intended, but it could not be kept." Badian is quite skeptical: the Athenians' guarantee was a "formal promise of aid which they well knew they would not be able to give."[23]

Regardless of the sincerity of Archidamus' or the Athenians' promises, a third related issue concerns the likelihood of Athenian aid to Plataea.

The Plataeans invoke their past relationship with Athens: "our [Plataean] fathers swore oaths never to do violence (μηδὲν νεωτερίζειν) to the alliance with Athens" (2.73.3). What should the Plataeans have reckoned as their best decision? The Plataeans are forced to extrapolate from past and present circumstances in order to anticipate the likelihood of several future possiblities. Rusten argues that "given Pericles' strategy of abandoning the Attic countryside . . . the town [of Plataea] was doomed." Kagan calls the strategy which required Athenian assistance for land-locked Plataea "untenable."[24] From the first-time reader's perspective, there is no clear answer; rather, we are left up in the air. The question of Plataea's best choice is not definitively answered. The engaged reader is put into the Plataean position of weighing these alternatives, ignorant of what lies ahead.

The Plataeans apparently expected to get help from the Athenians. Although Thucydides does not report the exchange between the Plataeans and the Athenians in Athens, the Athenians appear to have reassuringly emphasized the past, vowing similar aid in the future. Promises are made, but the specifics are never addressed: how will the Athenians come to help the land-locked Plataea? There is a brief, sobering note in the middle of the second Mytilenian section that Salaethus offers to lead the Peloponnesians away from Plataea, but he is put to death by the Athenians (3.36.1). No explicit comment by Thucydides links this decision to Athens' previous guarantee of aid.

In the second half of this section, Thucydides presents the Peloponnesian attempt to take Plataea. Seven focalizations are used to describe the activities of attack and defensive maneuver in pure narrative.[25] We view these undertakings very much from the perspective of the participants. The plans, the emotions, and—significantly—the expectations of what is likely to happen are focalized by the Spartans and their allies on one side and by the Plataeans on the other.

(1) The Spartans and their allies go to work, by bringing wood from Cithaeron, "expecting (elpizontes) to take the city very quickly" (2.75.1). They work continuously day and night.[26] (2) The Plataeans then see (horontes) what is happening and put up their own wall, attempting to make it equally high. They also consider demolishing part of their wall near the Peloponnesian mound (2.75.4–6).

(3) The Peloponnesians perceive (aisthomenoi–2.76.1) the activity of the Plataeans and begin measuring and filling up gaps with clay. (4) We then switch to the Plataean perspective and their digging of a mine inside their city out to a spot under the Peloponnesian mound as they remove

material from under the mound. (5) Thucydides comments that the Peloponnesians knew nothing of this (καὶ ἐλάνθανον ἐπὶ πολὺ τοὺς ἔξω–2.76.2). (6) Still the Plataeans fear (*dediotes*–2.76.3) that with their relatively low numbers they will not hold out against the more numerous Peloponnesians and their allies. That is, the Plataeans' expectation appears to confirm the Spartans' anticipation that Plataea will soon be taken (2.75.1). The Plataeans then come up with a plan (προσεπεξηῦρον τόδε). They stop building "the large structure opposite their ramp" and from the tall wall build an inner wall in a crescent shape to offer protection, with the intention that if the big wall were taken, this inner structure would hold out (2.76.3).[27]

(7) Out of fear (τοὺς Πλαταιᾶς ἐφόβησεν–2.76.4), the Peloponnesians construct new "devices" (*mechanas*), by setting up beams and a chain. The Peloponnesians find that their contrivances have no effect, and believe (*nomisantes*) that they will not take the city with their current plans (2.77.1). Before preparing for a siege (*periteichisin*), however, they attempt to burn the city by throwing flaming material into the city. That is, their goal remains to take Plataea—if possible—without the expense of a siege (εἴ πως σφίσιν ἄνευ δαπάνης καὶ πολιορκίας προσαχθείη–2.77.2). The wind causes a big flame as they expected (ὅπερ καὶ ἤλπιζον οἱ ἐναντίοι)—note that this is from the perspective of "the enemy." The phrase "so great a flame" (καὶ ἐγένετο φλὸξ τοσαύτη ὅσαν–2.77.4) raises the reader's expectations of Peloponnesian success. Thucydides goes out of his way with a hypothetical comment to emphasize how close danger came.

πνεῦμά τε εἰ ἐπεγένετο αὐτῇ ἐπίφορον, ὅπερ καὶ ἤλπιζον οἱ ἐναντίοι, οὐκ ἂν διέφυγον.

If a wind had come up and carried the fire around it, as the enemy expected, [the Plataeans] would not have escaped. (2.77.5)

But rain comes, "it is said," and puts out the fire (2.77.6). We appreciate how fortuitous circumstances may lead to significant outcomes: here, the lucky appearance of rain saves a city.[28]

Thucydides himself does not in any way anticipate the failure of the Peloponnesians' efforts. We are made to experience this frenetic activity as ongoing; Thucydides encourages us to project ourselves back into the events as they unfold.[29]

Thucydides then shifts to Plataean concerns: women, children, and elders are sent to Athens (2.78.3; cf. 2.6.4). Four hundred Plataeans remain besieged with 80 Athenians, 10 women, and 100 on kitchen duty (*sitopoioi*). Thucydides emphasizes that these are the only ones within the city, in part rounding off the section with provisional closure, in part preparing for events in 428–427.

τοσοῦτοι ἦσαν οἱ ξύμπαντες ὅτε ἐς τὴν πολιορκίαν καθίσταντο, καὶ ἄλλος οὐδεὶς ἦν ἐν τείχει οὔτε δοῦλος οὔτ' ἐλεύθερος...τοιαύτη μὲν ἡ Πλαταιῶν πολιορκία κατεσκευάσθη.

Such was the total when they set up the siege, and no one else was within the walls, neither slave nor free . . . . This was the sort of siege set up against the Plataeans. (2.78.4)

At 2.79 Thucydides shifts to separate business in the northern Aegean. That is, we leave Plataea in this state until the next year (early in book 3).[30] It is significant that by the end of this section, the Peloponnesian siege effectively shuts Plataea off from the rest of the Greek world. Unlike Athens, with its navy, maritime trade, and exchange of information by sea, Plataea is cut off both from what happens and from *what is said*—in particular, political and diplomatic discourse, such as that found in the Mytilenian debate.

We may make connections between section 2.71–78 and other passages in different ways. First, we find a wide range of topics introduced in the five speeches. Similar to the Corcyrean and Corinthian speeches discussed in chapter 3, here we also encounter the issues of justice, relations between cities—and the possibility of neutrality—and interpreting the past and anticipating the future. In addition, we find the topics of freedom, slavery and independence, and appeals to the gods and local heroes. Archidamus' flexibility may remind the reader of the Athenians' action in 433, when they came up with an option (a defensive alliance) not envisioned in either the Corcyreans' or the Corinthians' speeches. Whether Archidamus' offers were made in good faith, the impression Thucydides gives is that the Plataeans could have chosen from among an array of options: they were free to decide.

Second, the situation of Plataea may be compared and contrasted with that of Athens. The Peloponnesians prepared to ravage the land (ἔμελλε δῃώσειν τὴν γῆν–2.71.1, 2.73.1), much as they did in Attica (2.12.5). Note especially the Athenian advice reported by the Plataean heralds:

"ἀλλ' ἀνέχεσθαι καὶ γῆν τεμνομένην, εἰ δεῖ, ὁρῶντας καὶ ἄλλο πάσχοντας ὅτι ἂν ξυνβαίνῃ."

"Endure your land being ravished also, if it is necessary, watching and suf-fering whatever else happens." (2.74.1)

That is, what happens to Plataea evokes what has been happening to the Athenians on the Attic peninsula (cf. 2.19–21). The crucial difference, of course, is that landlocked Plataea is utterly cut off after the siege begins, while Athens has access to the outside world with its navy.[31]

In looking to the future the Plataeans expect Athenian help to arrive. The reader, too, must exercise his or her judgment to determine the like-lihood of such a rescue. In the fourth speech, addressing the Plataean cit-izens, their ambassadors point to justice and the relationship established between Athens and Plataea—this is an appeal to history. The Athenians have never previously abandoned them when in trouble.

"'Αθηναῖοί φασιν ἐν οὐδενὶ ὑμᾶς προέσθαι ἀδικουμένους οὔτε νῦν περιόψεσθαι, βοηθήσειν δὲ κατὰ δύναμιν."

"The Athenians say that they have never ignored us in trouble before and they will not now overlook us, but will come to our aid with force." (2.73.3)

The Plataeans receive assurances about the future: the Athenians will help them "with force" (κατὰ δύναμιν). There is a promise of full Athenian support against the siege, yet there is no attempt later to prevent or to relieve the siege. Only the miraculous rain saves the city from being burned.[32]

THE PLATAEAN ESCAPE (3.20–24)

We now turn to book three where Plataea figures in two episodes: the escape from Plataea, and the debate before Spartan "judges" which leads to the remaining Plataeans' execution. These third and fourth sections offer a study in contrasts: action and words, success and failure, surprise and pre-dictability. The precarious situation of the Plataeans in 428–427 is clearly a

result of the Plataean decision to reject Archidamus' offers and the unful-
filled Athenian promise of aid (both made in 429–2.73.3). Then Plataean
desperation—and no sign of help—lead to bold successful action.[33] This is
also the third of the Plataean episodes in which chance and the elements aid
the Plataeans. For once, a successful outcome matches their goal of escape.

In some ways the third episode is a mirror image of the first episode at
the opening of the war: in the first episode, there was an unexpected
nighttime attack by the Thebans; here, there is a surprise event at night,
but instead of an invasion there is an escape, balancing the entrance of the
Thebans in 431. Although besieged, the Plataeans now have the advantage of surprise and superior knowledge. These third and fourth sections
are also intertwined with the Mytilenian revolt and the Mytilenian debate
at Athens (3.2–19, 3.25–50). The significance of this implied comparison
will be addressed below, but let us first examine sections 3 and 4.

Two choices apparently face the Plataeans: wait for help or act boldly.
Yet the Plataeans despair of gaining aid from the Athenians.

ἀπὸ τῶν Ἀθηνῶν οὐδεμία ἐλπὶς ἦν τιμωρίας οὐδὲ ἄλλη σωτηρία
ἐφαίνετο.

There was no expectation of rescue from Athens, nor did any other means
of survival appear. (3.20.1)

The Plataeans decide to risk an escape (3.20.1). Planning is critical to success, but we also find assistance from the elements. The ice, wind, and
magnitude of the storm on the evening of their venture are all essential to
the escape (3.23.5).[34]

Regarding knowledge and perspective, the escape is presented mostly
from the Plataean point of view. The Plataeans are in a superior epistemological position: they calculate the height of the surrounding walls by
observation; they know (*eidotes*) that the battlements would be deserted on
a cold, wet night (3.22.3; cf. 3.21.4); in the midst of the escape, when the
besieging army brings torches, the Plataeans could see the 300 enemy
troops better than they themselves could be seen, which puts them in a
better position to launch arrows and javelins (ἑώρων μᾶλλον . . . αὐτοὶ
δὲ ἐν τῷ ἀφανεῖ ὄντες ἧσσον διὰ τὰς λαμπάδας καθεωρῶν-
το–3.23.24)[35]; on their way to Thebes, they see (ἑώρων) the
Peloponnesians on the road to Cithaeron toward Athens, but are not seen
themselves (3.24.1). This contrasts, of course, with the ignorance of the
Peloponnesian and Boeotian besiegers: misperception frustrates the

besieging army and aids the brave escapees. Describing the construction of the two projections (*periboloi*), Thucydides indicates the besiegers' goals of keeping the Plataeans trapped and of preventing the arrival of outside help, in case Athens sends any (3.21.1).[36] The Peloponnesian and Boeotian focalizations generally reflect mistaken belief and confusion.

Time and again Thucydides indicates the superior knowledge of the Plataeans in contrast to the Peloponnesians and Thebans outside. The Peloponnesians and Thebans know nothing of the plan to escape. Note Thucydides' use of dramatic irony.

ἔπειτα προσέμειξαν [οἱ Πλαταιῆς] τῷ τείχει τῶν πολεμίων **λάθο-ντες τοὺς φύλακας**, ἀνὰ τὸ σκοτεινὸν μὲν **οὐ προϊδόντων αὐτῶν, ψόφῳ δὲ τῷ ἐκ τοῦ προσιέναι αὐτοὺς** ἀντιπαταγοῦντεος τοῦ ἀνέμου **οὐ κατακουσάντων**.

Then [the Plataeans] reached the wall of the enemy *without the guards noticing*, for *they did not see them* in the darkness and *they did not hear any noise of them coming* due to the wind blowing the other way. (3.22.1)

In addition to not hearing or seeing the Plataeans, the outside army did not know what the situation was.

[τὸ στράτοπεδον] οὐ γὰρ ᾔδει ὅτι ἦν τὸ δεινὸν σκοτεινῆς νυκτὸς καὶ χειμῶνος ὄντος.

[The army] did not know what the danger was in the dark night with the storm in progress. (3.22.5)

To add to the enemies' confusion, the Plataeans remaining behind manipulate the expectations and countermeasures of the besieging army. They set up a diversion on the opposite side of the city from the escape, "so that the Peloponnesians and Boeotians would least have an idea of the Plataean plan . . . [and would be] *at a loss in figuring out what was happening*" (ἀλλ᾽ ἐν ἀπόρῳ ἦσαν εἰκάσαι τὸ γιγνόμενον–3.22.5). In anticipating the use of Theban fire signals to send for help, the Plataeans within set up so many signals that the Theban message is unclear from a distance and no help is sent (3.22.7–8). Finally, when the Plataean escapees head toward Thebes rather than to Athens, they succeed in anticipating the Thebans' belief (*nomizontes*) that the Plataeans would not advance into enemy territory (3.24.1).

The overall plan goes extremely well.[37] Still, we must note the difference between the escaping Plataeans and those Plataeans left behind, who
remain cut off from the outside world and know nothing about anyone's
escape or survival (τῶν μὲν γεγενημένων εἰδότες οὐδέν–3.24.3). In fact,
the Plataeans who turned back before scaling the towers give the false
report that no one survived. Only at daybreak when asking to bury the
Plataean corpses, do the Plataeans learn the truth (μάθοντες δὲ τὸ
ἀληθές–3.24.3).[38] The reader is in a superior position: while linked especially to the escaping Plataeans, the reader appreciates the confusion of
both the Boeotians and Plataeans who remain behind.

Another aspect of this episode concerns comparison and extrapolation,
best captured by the Greek term *eikazein*, a combination of comparison,
improvization, and extrapolation. Here this skill is treated thematically:
this episode presents us with an exercise in *eikazein* at several levels. First,
a successful escape for the Plataeans depends upon successful guessing and
approximation. In order to construct ladders of the appropriate height, the
Plataeans must approximate the height of the outside walls by counting the
number of bricks at a distance.[39]

> τὴν μὲν οὖν ξυμμέτρησιν τῶν κλιμάκων οὕτως ἔλαβον, ἐκ τοῦ
> πάχους τῆς πλίνθου **εἰκάσαι** τὸ μέτρον.

> They took the measurement of the ladders in this manner, and *approxi-*
> *mated* the distance from the thickness of a brick. (3.20.4)

This contrasts with the Peloponnesians and their allies, who must attempt
to guess what has happened (ἄλλο τι νομίσαντες τὸ γιγνόμενον εἶναι
ἢ τὸ ὂν **εἰκάσαι** τὸ γιγνόμενον–3.22.5–6). Their mistaken beliefs aid the
Plataeans in escaping. As I have suggested in previous chapters, the ability of statesmen and historians (and, by extension, readers) to improvise and
conjecture is essential both for understanding the past and for anticipating the future. In this section, Thucydides calls our attention to ways in
which it is possible to succeed or to fail in the difficult art of extrapolation
(*eikazein*). This skill means survival for the escaping Plataeans (their ladders are high enough to reach the towers); the besiegers' failure to figure
out what might be happening allows the escapees to continue on to safety.

At a different level, the reader is being implicitly asked to compare and
contrast the Plataean escape described here with other parts of the *History*.
First, we may compare this situation to that of the first two Plataean

episodes. During the invasion of 431, rain played a role in increasing the difficulties for the Thebans chased through town (2.4.2); then rain put out the blaze set by the Peloponnesians (2.77.6). Just as the Thebans waited for a moonless night in the first section, so here the Plataeans await a dark and stormy night for their escape (3.22.1). To be sure, Thucydides makes no connection between rain and divine aid, but we may easily compare such lucky events favoring Plataea in the first, second, and third sections—all in sharp contrast to the fourth episode where not only do the Athenians bring no aid, but no other "miraculous" rescue saves the Plataeans who are put to death by the Spartans.[40]

The Plataean Debate (3.52–68)

The fourth episode in which Plataea plays a major role is presented after the Mytilenian crisis has been "resolved" with the execution of a thousand leaders of the Mytilenian revolt. As Thucydides has structured the narrative, the Plataeans then surrender their city to Spartan "judges" (*dicastai*— 3.52.2, 3.52.3, 3.53.1).[41] Upon request, the Plataeans are allowed to address the Spartans at length, the Thebans reply, and the Spartan then execute the Plataeans.

This fourth section consists of two speeches with a narrative frame, contrasting with the third section. While the third section offers *successful Plataean action*, the fourth presents the *unsuccessful words of the Plataeans*. In contrast to various options earlier, the Plataeans are now wholly reduced to begging for their lives. The outcome is predictable— even as viewed by the Plataeans in their speech—in the sense that the only choices left apparently are those expressed in the two arguments. Neither the Spartan "dicasts" nor anyone else improvises by articulating even a third possibility.[42] Also in contrast to the three earlier sections, there is no unexpected rescue by the elements or the Athenians to save the Plataeans.

The goal of the Plataeans—faced with a choice of starvation or surrender (3.52.1)—is survival, perhaps living in exile or as prisoners until a truce.[43] In response, the Thebans speak out of fear that the Spartans may give in (3.60); clearly they seek control of Plataea and vengeance for the death of the Theban prisoners at the start of the war (3.66.3; cf. 2.6). The Spartans' motivations are more apparent to the reader than to either the Plataeans or the Thebans. At first they ask a brief question of the Plataeans ("Have you done any good for the Spartans and their allies in the present war"–3.52.4), but decide to allow a longer speech. At the end of the episode, their goals boil down to courting Theban favor for the future in an effort to win the war, rather than paying any gratitude to Plataea for past actions (3.68.4).[44]

Ultimately the Thebans are successful: the Plataeans are not saved, more than 200 Plataeans and 25 Athenians are put to death, and the women are enslaved. Hornblower comments on this tragic precision (*akribeia*): "how little use that long-standing alliance [with the Athenians] was to the Plataians."[45] The Spartans gain the help of the Thebans, for they are "useful" (*ophelimous*–3.68.4; cf. 3.56.4, 3.58.1). Megarian refugees and pro-Spartan Plataeans then settle the city for a year; later the city is razed, and the land is leased out to Thebans. Of course, if Thucydides were strictly annalistic (as he sets out in his program), he would wait until his account of the year 426 to mention the razing of Plataea (3.68.3).[46]

Regarding knowledge and focalization, the bulk of this section consists of rhetorical focalization in the two speeches, yet the frame outside the speeches deserves mention. Most striking is Plataean ignorance about Spartan motivations, the Spartans' idea of justice, and political discourse current at this time. The Plataeans in the besieged city do not know what the reader has learned: that the Spartan goal is to have Plataea surrender, rather than taking it by force, so that when they eventually make a treaty with Athens, Plataea would not have to be restored to the Athenian sphere of influence (μὴ ἀνάδοτος–3.52.2).[47] While Thucydides makes Sparta's motivations available to the reader, the fact that these motivations are not apparent to the Plataeans surely heightens the pathos. In the coda, Thucydides does reveal the Spartan motivation: they believed that by Pausanias' treaty, they could have expected neutrality from the Plataeans. This looks back to episode 2 (3.68.1; cf. 2.72.1). This explicit retrospective link connects the present consequences to those earlier decisions: before the siege an offer of neutrality was made but was rejected by the Plataeans; now the Spartans feel they are released from any treaty obligations (*ekspondoi*).[48]

The Plataeans certainly seem to have misunderstood the Spartans' initial offer. Before giving themselves over to the Spartans, the Plataeans assume that no one will be "unjustly" condemned (παρὰ δίκην–3.52.2–3); they expect "fairness" (τὸ ἴσον) from the dicasts, yet this turns out to be a mistake (*hemartekamen*–3.53.1).[49]

A more intricate pattern—at a larger scale of presentation but also based on contiguous episodes—is the "interweaving" of two or more episodes, with Thucydides' presentation of the Mytilenian revolt and the events concerning Plataea in book 3. First, Thucydides presents an episode of speech and narrative concerning Mytilene (3.2–19); there fol-lows a narrative account of the escape of 212 Plataeans (3.20–24); then Mytilene's surrender leads to the Athenian debate (3.25–50); finally, Plataea's surrender brings on the debate before the Spartan "judges" (3.52–68). In his presentation, Thucydides links and contrasts the cities of Mytilene and Plataea in a number of ways. Both cities are put under siege and later surrender. In one case, an Athenian ally, Mytilene, revolts: as an island, no help reaches it from Sparta (a land power). In the other case, an Athenian ally is loyal but landlocked, so that no help arrives from Athens (a sea power).[50] Thucydides might have presented these conflicts in several ways—the Corcyrean conflict (1.24–55) occurred over several years, but was presented without interruption. Alternation of the two cities in book 3 (with a reminder of Plataea at 3.36.1) reveals a conscious pattern designed to contrast the situations in an overt manner for the reader.[51]

One effect of this pattern is to highlight the fact that the Plataeans have been cut off from the world of the Peloponnesian War, not only in a literal sense, but also rhetorically. They have not been "privy," as the read-er has been, to the Mytilenian debate which has just been presented to the reader. Diodotus proclaims morality to be irrelevant to foreign policy (3.44.4), yet the Plataeans are unaware of such a principle. A similar situ-ation occurs later in the History, when the Athenian garrison at Oenoe is tricked into turning over their position to the Thebans, "for they knew nothing on account of being besieged [καὶ οὐκ εἰδότες οὐδὲν διὰ τὸ πολιορκεῖσθαι]" (8.98.3). As Thucydides sets up the contrast, we note the sharp divergence between the Plataeans' appeals to "conventional" moral ideas and Diodotus' more "realistic" ideas about expediency to the exclusion of justice.[52] The Plataean and Theban speeches look to the past and employ the language of the lawcourt, yet this contrasts not only with the Spartan decision (based on the Thebans' usefulness to them) but also with Diodotus' rejection of Cleon's claim that justice and advantage may be combined when determining foreign policy.

Let us turn to the two speeches. According to the Plataeans, the three most important issues are their past actions and an expected reciprocity; traditional conceptions of justice, law, and Panhellenic religion; and ram-ifications for the future.

The first issue the Plataeans raise is the significance of the past. In con-nection with past service, the Plataeans point to two incidents. They have helped Greece both when fighting the Persians and when they aided the Spartans during the Helot revolt after an earthquake at Ithome (3.54.5).

The Plataeans keep returning to their service during the Persian war: they proved to be "brave" (*agathoi*–3.54.3); the Persians posed a danger to all the Greeks (3.54.4; cf. 3.56.4); the Plataeans served the cause of Greece (3.59.4). The Plataeans invoke the name of Pausanias: they fought with Pausanias and had a friendship with him (3.54.4, 3.58.5; cf. 2.71.4). They recall their joint service with the ancestors of those Spartans who inscribed the names of the Plataeans on the tripod on Delphi (3.57.2; cf. 3.59.1); the tombs of Spartan ancestors are buried on Plataean soil (3.58.4; cf. 3.59.2). In summary, the Plataeans characterize themselves as "benefactors of Greece [ἡμῶν τῶν εὐεργετῶν τῆς Ἑλλάδος]" (3.57.1; cf. 3.58.3, 3.59.1).[53] In appealing to their past service, the Plataeans evidently see these actions as relevant to the current situation: their past bravery against Xerxes merits special consideration in the present war. In part, this suggestion is based on what we might call traditional morality. Because the Plataeans have previously helped Greece in general and the Spartans in particular—because they have performed service as benefactors (*euergetai*)—the Spartans are obliged to repay such service by sparing their lives now. It is *just* to help friends in their hour of need and to balance the current miscalculation now (ἡμῶν τῆς νῦν ἁμαρτίας) against their previous action (3.56.5).[54]

In addition to recalling the past, the Plataeans also bring up a broader moral appeal by invoking justice, law, and religion. The Plataeans characterize themselves as acting justly. They wish to put forth their "just differences" towards the Thebans, the Spartans, and the other Greeks (δίκαια . . . διάφορα–3.54.1; cf. 3.56.5).[55] Also the Spartans have not suffered injustice (or harm) from the Plataeans (οὐκ ἀδικεῖσθαι ὑμᾶς–3.54.2; cf. 3.55.2, 3.59.1).[56] In fact, if the Spartans are friends (*philoi*), it is the Spartans who have wrongly marched against the Plataeans (*hamartanein*–3.54.2). The Thebans, however, are accused of injustice for seizing the city of Plataea during peacetime in the midst of a sacred festival (3.56.1). Connected with the question of justice is that of responsibility: here the Plataeans attribute their decision to make their alliance with Athens to the Spartans: "you are responsible [ἡμεῖς δὲ αἴτιοι]" (3.55.1).[57]

Beyond appealing to the conventional morality of "friendship," the Plataeans invoke laws that bind all people and are honored by the Greeks. The Plataean action against the Theban prisoners who had invaded in 431 is justified in terms of self-defense, a universal law established for all.

"ἐτιμωρησάμεθα κατὰ τὸν πᾶσι νόμον καθεστῶτα."

"We avenged ourselves according to the law [nomos] established for all."
(3.56.2)[58]

In the current situation, the Spartans should respect the Plataeans as suppliants. The "law" of the Greeks forbids the killing of suppliants.

"ὅτι ἑκόντας τε ἐλάβετε καὶ χεῖρας προϊσχομένους (ὁ δὲ νόμος τοῖς
Ἕλλησι μὴ κτείνειν τούτους)."

"You took us who were willing and holding out our hands [as suppliants]
(and the law for the Greeks is not to kill such people)." (3.58.3)[59]

At the end of their speech, the Plataeans shift from supplication to invoking the gods.

"ἡμεῖς τε, ὡς πρέπον ἡμῖν καὶ ὡς ἡ χρεία προάγει, αἰτούμεθα ὑμᾶς,
θεοὺς τοὺς ὁμοβωμίους καὶ κοινοὺς τῶν Ἑλλήνων ἐπιβοώμενοι,
πεῖσαι τάδε."

"And we, as is appropriate and as the need impels us, beseech you to be
persuaded of this, as we invoke the gods whose altars we share and are common to [all] Greeks." (3.59.2)[60]

The ideas of justice, law, the gods, and helping friends (who have done you
a good turn) are wholly missing from Spartan thinking—at least concerning the question they ask both before and after the speeches and according to the motivations attributed to the Spartans by Thucydides. This
array of moral concepts is also excluded by Diodotus as irrelevant to foreign policy. But again, the Plataeans are unaware of this.[61]

Relevant to these moral, legal, and religious ideas are the issues of freedom and slavery in geopolitical terms. Freeing Greece, the Plataeans
argue, should *not* be accomplished by the destruction of Plataea ("Don't
enslave what was freed"–3.58.5). The final words of the Plataeans are:
"Don't free the rest of Greece, but destroy us" (3.59.4).

In addition to dwelling on the past in terms of conventional morality
and of what they define as legal and religious norms, the Plataeans also look
to the future.[62] They have little to promise Sparta in a material sense;
instead they ponder the sort of reputation the Spartans will acquire. This
depends upon the actions they take.

"προσκέψασθέ τε ὅτι νῦν μὲν παράδειγμα τοῖς πολλοῖς τῶν
Ἑλλήνων ἀνδραγαθίας νομίζεσθε· εἰ δὲ περὶ ἡμῶν γνώσεσθε μὴ τὰ
εἰκότα (οὐ γὰρ ἀφανῆ κρινεῖτε τὴν δίκην τήνδε, ἐπαινούμενοι δὲ περὶ
οὐδ' ἡμῶν μεμπτῶν), ὁρᾶτε ὅπως μὴ οὐκ ἀποδέξωνται ἀνδρῶν
ἀγαθῶν πέρι αὐτοὺς ἀμείνους ὄντας ἀπρεπές τι ἐπιγνῶναι, οὐδὲ
πρὸς ἱεροῖς τοῖς κοινοῖς σκῦλα ἀπὸ ἡμῶν τῶν εὐεργετῶν τῆς
Ἑλλάδος ἀνατεθῆναι. δεινὸν δὲ δόξει εἶναι Πλάταιαν Λακεδαι-
μονίους πορθῆσαι, καὶ τοὺς μὲν πατέρας ἀναγράψαι ἐς τὸν
τρίποδα τὸν ἐν Δελφοῖς δι' ἀρετὴν τὴν πόλιν, ὑμᾶς δὲ καὶ ἐκ παντὸς
τοῦ Ἑλληνικοῦ πανοικεσίᾳ διὰ Θηβαίους ἐξαλεῖψαι."

"And reflect that now you are regarded by most Greeks as an example of
upright qualities; but if you reach a decision about us that is not right (for
you will not be judging this case in obscurity, as men of renown judging us
who are not contemptible), beware of their abhorrence that an unseemly
decision about good men was upheld by you, their betters, and that spoils
from us, benefactors of Greece, would have been dedicated in the common
shrines. And it will seem monstrous for the Spartans to destroy Plataea,
that your fathers recorded the city on the tripod at Delphi for its bravery
while you will erase it in its entirety from Greek civilization for the sake
of the Thebans." (3.57.1–2)[63]

The consequence of Sparta's condemnation, the Plataeans claim, is that
other Greeks will certainly take notice with public opinion condemning
the actions of Sparta.[64]

    With its emphasis on how past action is relevant to present circum-
stances, there is a retrospective quality to the Plataeans' speech. Yet in
reinterpreting the past *and* anticipating the future, the Plataean endeavor
to show how past, present, and future interconnect.[65] This results from
comparison and extrapolation (*eikazein*) within their speech. Because earlier sections of Thucydides' *History*—such as the Theban invasion at the
opening of book 2—are presented once again in a new light (first narra-
tively, now rhetorically), the reader is also asked to make connections
between past actions, present circumstances, and the current reinterpreta-
tion of those past actions.

    In speaking about the past, the Plataeans are attempting to offer a new
perspective on earlier events. At 3.56, for example, there is a long series of
"then" and "now," where earlier situations contrast with the present
dilemma.[66] The overall effect is to propel the reader to also contrast ongoing events with previous situations.

"καίτοι εἰ **νῦν** ὑμῖν ὠφέλιμοι δοκοῦσιν εἶναι, πολὺ καὶ ἡμεῖς καὶ οἱ ἄλλοι Ἕλληνες μᾶλλον **τότε** ὅτε ἐν μείζονι κινδύνῳ ἦτε. **νῦν** μὲν γὰρ ἑτέροις ὑμεῖς ἐπέρχεσθε δεινοί, **ἐν ἐκείνῳ** δὲ τῷ καιρῷ, ὅτε πᾶσι δουλείαν ἐπέφερεν ὁ βάρβαρος, οἵδε μετ' αὐτοῦ ἦσαν. καὶ δίκαιον ἡμῶν τῆς **νῦν** ἁμαρτίας, εἰ ἄρα ἡμάρτηταί τι, ἀντιθεῖναι τὴν **τότε** προθυμίαν· καὶ μείζω τε πρὸς ἐλάσσω εὑρήσετε καὶ **ἐν καιροῖς** οἷς σπάνιον ἦν τῶν Ἑλλήνων τινὰ ἀρετὴν τῇ Ξέρξου δυνάμει ἀντιτάξασθαι, ἐπηνοῦντό τε μᾶλλον οἱ μὴ τὰ ξύμφορα πρὸς τὴν ἔφοδον αὐτοῖς ἀσφαλείᾳ πράσσοντες, ἐθέλοντες δὲ τολμᾶν μετὰ κινδύνων τὰ βέλτιστα."

"Though if the Thebans seem useful to you *now, in the past* at a time when you were in greater danger, we and the other Hellenes were much more useful. *Now* you are in a position to take the offensive and to make others fear you; but *in those days*, when the foreign invader threatened us all with slavery, Thebes was on his side. It is just, therefore, for us to set any errors *now*—if we have committed any—against our valor *then*. You will find that our merits greatly outweigh our faults, and that they were shown *at a time when* it was rare to find courage among the Greeks opposed to the might of Xerxes, and when all the greater praise was given to those who, instead of meeting the invasion by acting in the interest of their own safety, were willing to dare the noblest actions in the midst of danger." (3.56.4–5)

According to the Plataeans, similar actions—both past and present— should be gauged by the same standard. What the Plataeans accomplished in the past on behalf of the Greeks—for the sake of freedom—is now used to "enslave" the Greeks.

"ὧν ἡμεῖς γενόμενοι καὶ τιμηθέντες ἐς τὰ πρῶτα νῦν **ἐπὶ τοῖς αὐτοῖς** δέδιμεν μὴ διαφθαρῶμεν, Ἀθηναίους ἑλόμενοι δικαίως μᾶλλον ἢ ὑμᾶς κερδαλέως. καίτοι χρὴ ταὐτὰ περὶ τῶν αὐτῶν ὁμοίως **φαίνεσθαι γιγνώσκοντας**, καὶ τὸ ξυμφέρον μὴ ἄλλο τι νομίσαι ἢ τῶν ξυμμάχων τοῖς ἀγαθοῖς ὅταν αἰεὶ βέβαιον τὴν χάριν τῆς ἀρετῆς ἔχωσι καὶ τὸ παραυτίκα που ὑμῖν ὠφέλιμον καθιστῆται."

"We, who were among these [who dared in the midst of danger] and held in the highest honor, now fear that we will be destroyed *by the same conduct by choosing the Athenians justly rather than yourselves for gain. And yet*

consistency ought to be prominent when you make comparable decisions about
comparable situations, and you ought to believe that there is no expediency except when what is perhaps to your immediate advantage is also established by continuing to keep firm your gratitude for the courage of those
who were good allies." (3.56.6–7)

If in the past the Plataeans chose rightly in fighting Xerxes, then for
choosing rightly now and not deserting the Athenians—without regard for
advantage—they should not be penalized. A brave ally should be able to
count on gratitude.[67] The Plataeans' speech advances the idea that even
though the current situation may differ from a time when Greeks opposed
Persians, the Plataeans have acted in a similar way. Consistent action in
two situations implies comparison and, according to the Plataeans, a reductive prescription: the same rule should apply in all situations.

We now turn to the speech of the Thebans who respond to this by
emphasizing shifting circumstance. Yet before addressing the issues of past
conduct—in historical and moral terms—the Thebans begin by challenging the need for the Plataeans to speak beyond answering the Spartans'
original brief question (3.61.1; cf. 3.52.4–5).[68] Because the Plataeans have
spoken at length and brought accusations against the Thebans and
defended themselves (κατηγορία . . . ἀπολογία), the Thebans must
offer a refutation (*elengkos*–3.61.1). Two points should be made here. First,
the Thebans raise the question not only of what is allowable in discourse,
but whether debate is even needed to decide the fate of the Plataeans.[69]
This anticipates the more severe limits on discourse imposed by the
Athenians upon the Melians (5.89).[70] Second, the Thebans—like the
Plataeans—make extensive use of legalistic language (*kategoria, apologia,
adikia, hekon/akon*, etc.). That is, both the Thebans and the Plataeans
make rhetorical appeals to law and justice; the Spartans' ultimate decision,
however, is based on the usefulness of Theban cavalry and troops
(3.68.4).[71]

In addressing the past, the Plataeans focused on only two incidents—
the Persian war and their help during the Helot uprising—yet the
Thebans range more broadly. In chronological order, the Thebans mention: (1) the founding of Plataea; (2) the Persian War; (3) the battle of
Coronea; (4) the Theban "entrance" into Plataea in 431; and (5) Theban
action in the Peloponnesian War.[72] That is, the Thebans consider more
incidents from the past in their argument, evidently feeling that the
Plataeans have been excessively selective. The Thebans' interpretation of
the past contrasts sharply with that of the Plataeans.

(1) The Thebans begin with the founding of the city of Plataea, which was established by Thebans. Despite this, when in danger the Plataeans turned to Athens and caused harm to Thebes. The Thebans emphasize the Plataean transgression of their ancestral customs (παραβαίνοντες τὰ πάτρια –3.61.2). Their first charge is that the Plataeans violated their local (i.e., Boeotian) affinities.

(2) In turning to Plataean and Theban action during the Persian War, the Thebans do not dispute that the Plataeans fought against the Persians, but they are more interested in the motivation behind these actions. The Plataeans have just asserted that "we alone of the Boeotians" (μόνοι Βοιωτῶν) resisted the Persians (3.54.3), but the Thebans throw the Plataeans' phrase "we alone" (monoi) back at them.[73] According to the Thebans, the Plataeans chose not to "collaborate with the Persians" or "medize," because the Athenians did not. That is, the Plataeans modeled their behavior on that of the Athenians.[74] While the Plataeans have argued that they are acting justly as they did during the Persian war, the Thebans turn this supposed consistency against the Plataeans. They agree that the Plataeans are behaving in the same way, but then give that behavior a new name: the Plataeans always "atticize" or "collaborate with Athens" (attikismon–3.64.5).[75] Plataean motivation is suspect.

Part of the reader's task is to see how well each speech answers or anticipates the charges of the other speech. The Plataeans' "uniqueness" (monoi) is only one of many examples. The Thebans also respond to the Plataeans' claims regarding their role as benefactors of Sparta, taking responsibility for behavior, the proper treatment of suppliants (the Plataeans now, the Theban prisoners in 431), and the question of which city should function as an example (Sparta or Plataea–3.57.1, 3.67.6).[76] Note that the Thebans do follow the spirit of the Plataeans' speech to this extent: the charges made against Thebes are answered as though this were a courtroom. After all, "judges" (dicastai) are listening to these arguments, waiting to pronounce judgment.

Concerning the issue of independent action, one must be autonomous to be considered guilty. In their defense, the Thebans maintain that during the Persian War their city was not in control of itself (autokrator); rather a faction of oligarchs (dunasteia) dominated the city, which is "closest to tyranny" (3.62.3).[77] The city was wrong but not guilty (οὐδ᾽ ἄξιον αὐτῇ ὀνειδίσαι ὧν μὴ μετὰ νόμων ἥμαρτεν–3.62.4).

Plataean aid during the helot revolt is apparently ignored by the Thebans.[78] (3) Once the Thebans are governed by law, their behavior becomes more defensible. Their defeat of Athens at Coronea is seen as advancing the cause of freedom:

"εἰ μαχόμενοι ἐν Κορωνείᾳ καὶ νικήσαντες αὐτοὺς ἠλευθερώσαμεν
τὴν Βοιωτίαν καὶ τοὺς ἄλλους νῦν προθύμως ξυνελευθεροῦμεν."

"If we fought and defeated the Athenians at Coronea and freed Boeotia,
we now are also eagerly freeing others with you." (3.62.5)

(4) The question of the Theban invasion of Plataea is delayed. (5) During
the current war the Thebans have also joined in the liberation of Greece
(*ksuneleutheroumen*–3.62.5). The Thebans are on board now, fighting for
freedom (3.63.1). So much for the Theban *apologia* in response to Plataea's
charges against them.[79]

By framing the issues as they do, the Thebans get around the question
of reciprocity and obligation for past good deeds. They ignore Plataea's
past help to Sparta; Thebes' alliance with Persia is "spun" in terms of lacking independence of action, for they claim they were not in control of
their own city. The Thebans now, however, are helping Sparta and deserve
its favor. They also lead Sparta to focus on the future advantages of maintaining the alliance with Thebes.

The Plataeans have accused the Thebans of injustice and appealed to
law and religion. In their interpretation of the past, the Thebans examine
what justice and injustice are, what factors are relevant, and who is truly
guilty by focusing on injustice and independent action. There are four
parts to the Theban counterargment.

First, the question of willing versus unwilling: the Thebans unwillingly
acted with the Persians, but the Plataeans "willingly and not under compulsion" (ἑκόντες καὶ οὐ βιαζόμενοι) joined the Athenians against the
rest of Greece (3.63.2). The Plataeans have not been acting in self-
defense; they are now guilty. The Thebans, however, were not responsible
(*aitioi*) for past injustice (*adikia*).[80]

Second, they indirectly address Plataea's service to Sparta and Greece.
The Thebans argue that if it is shameful (*aischron*) to betray benefactors,
it is still more shameful and more unjust (αἴσχιον καὶ ἀδικώτερον) for
Plataea to betray all Greece.[81] If what the Thebans have done is bad,
Plataean conduct has been even worse, for they have now joined Athens
as accomplices to injustice (τοῖς ἀδικοῦσιν ἄλλους ξυνεργοὶ
κατέστητε–3.63.3–4).

Third, while the issue of willing versus unwilling carries a legalistic
tone, a separate issue is that of ideology.[82] Past actions are not as important
as the agenda underlying these actions. The Plataeans are guilty of following the Athenian political program, captured by the term *attikismon*,

perhaps coined here for the first time as a parallel with *medismon*. If the Thebans "medized," that is, "collaborated with Persia" during the earlier war, the Plataeans are doing something just as bad now: they are "atticizing" or "collaborating with the Athenians."[83] The motivation for Plataean action during the Persian war is the same as the motivation for their actions now: they would follow the Athenians anywhere. Rather than the Plataeans being pardoned for their past action, they must stand or fall with Athens. The Plataeans left their earlier alliance and joined in the enslaving of Greece with Athens (*ksugkatedoulousthe*); they have done this willingly—no one forced them (cf. 3.64.3).

Fourth, Plataea had the option of remaining neutral before the city was put under siege, but rejected the offer. This, the Thebans argue, reveals the true nature of the Plataeans (3.64.4). The past (good) deeds of the Plataeans were not in line with their actual character (οὐ προσήκοντα); the Plataeans may have presented an appearance of virtue (*andragathian*), the Thebans argue, but Plataean action (doing "evil"—*kakon*—to Greeks) makes them justly hated by the Greeks.

Returning to their own defense, the Thebans respond to the charge that they entered Plataea in 431 while there was a truce in effect (ἐν σπονδαῖς) during a sacred period (*hieromenia*). The Thebans quibble on the meaning of "injustice" (*adikia*).

> "We would have committed injustice, if we had arrived and fought and laid waste your land; but did we commit injustice if your men willingly invited us? . . . They were citizens, they opened the gates as friends, they were restoring our kinship [*suggeneian*]." (3.65.2–3)

The different views of past action here—action narrated by Thucydides in the first Plataean episode—raise a number of difficult issues, one of which is who speaks for a community: a faction, the leaders, or a majority of citizens?[84] If *some* Plataeans did invite the Thebans into Plataea, is this truly an "invasion"?

If crimes took place, the Thebans argue, all of them—three in number—were committed by the Plataeans. The Plataeans broke the agreement (*ksumbasis*) they made with the Thebans in the agora (2.2.4–3.1); they put the Theban prisoners of war to death; and they violated their oath not to kill the prisoners. It was the Thebans who were killed "illegally," stretching out their hands as suppliants, while, as the Thebans later say, the Plataeans are now not truly suppliants.[85]

"ἔννομα γὰρ πείσονται καὶ οὐχὶ ἐκ μάχης χεῖρας προισχόμενοι,
ὥσπερ φασίν, ἀλλ᾽ ἀπὸ ξυμβάσεως ἐς δίκην σφᾶς αὐτοὺς παρα-
δόντες."

"For they will suffer by the laws and are not holding out their hands [as
suppliants] coming from battle, as they claim, but they surrendered themselves for judgment by agreement." (3.67.5)

The Thebans accuse the Plataeans of deserving punishment for their
crimes (3.66.3). The Thebans assert that their demand for vengeance is
"more holy" than the plea of the Plataeans (ὁσιώτερον τιτιμω-
ρημένοι–3.67). Whatever the Plataeans were like in the past, they are
worse now and thus are deserving of double the penalty (διπλασίας
ζημίας–3.67.2).[86] The Thebans insist that emotion is irrelevant to decision-making: in this case, the Plataeans should not be aided by feelings
such as compassion or pity (olophurmo, oikto–3.67.2).[87] Pity is appropriate
in cases of undeserved suffering; bringing punishment to those who
deserve it, such as the Plataeans, should bring rejoicing (epichartoi–3.67.4).
While the Plataeans may point to the graves of their Plataean ancestors,
this consideration is outweighed by the young Thebans who died in 431
and the Theban ancestors who brought Coronea over to the Spartan side
(3.67.3).

And what of the future? The Plataeans had asked the Spartans to consider what would happen to the Spartans' reputation if the Plataeans were
put to death. The Spartans' task, according to the Thebans, is to defend
the law which was broken by Plataea, give "deserved favor" (χάριν
δίκαιαν) to Thebes, and make an example of the Plataeans to all Greeks
(paradeigma–3.67.6).[88] Punishing the Plataeans will demonstrate that it is
by *deeds* which men should be judged, rather than by *words*. In fact—
returning to an idea raised at the beginning of their speech—for good
deeds, a short report is sufficient; for mistakes, words merely serve as a
"cloak" (prokalummata–3.67.6; cf. 3.61.1).[89]

There is a nagging question for the reader: since the Spartans base their
decision on advantage (3.68.4), why has Thucydides included speeches at
all? Does this not render moot much that both the Plataeans and Thebans
argue for? As Hornblower notes, for all the forensic language, this is not a
trial. In chapter 3.68, "the Spartans simply repeat their original question
as if the speeches had never been delivered at all."[90] Macleod sees one purpose to the speeches: "The history, like the tragedy, illustrates the
inevitable fraudulence of moral argument in war and politics."[91] In his

Rhetoric, Aristotle argues that while forensic rhetoric seeks just outcomes, deliberative debate seeks advantage. Though Thucydides precedes Aristotle, he raises questions about such boundaries: the rhetoric of both speeches belongs to the forensic courtroom, yet the outcome is determined by expediency.[92]

Conclusion

Thucydides has used the city of Plataea as an obvious marker to define four stages in this sequence of action and argument. At this point we should explore the various ideas, motifs, and situations connected to Plataea's role in the *History*. We may begin by comparing and contrasting material from the fourth Plataean episode with earlier Plataean episodes. The sequence moves from all narrative in the first section to a full set of speeches in the fourth. In the first three episodes focusing on Plataea, unpredictable weather or luck arrived in time to save Plataea; in the fourth, neither allies nor "supernatural" aid arrive at all. As the Plataeans see it, the Spartans are their only hope (ἡ μόνη ἐλπίς–3.57.4).[93] The Plataeans ask the Spartans to be their saviors (*soteras*–3.59.4). Such pleas are rejected.

With regard to the first incident, we are given new information in this fourth episode from the Plataeans. We learn that the invasion in 431 took place at the sacred time of month (3.56.2). More significantly, when the Plataeans appeal to the law of all Greeks not to kill suppliants (3.58.3; cf. 3.56, 3.59.2), we should recall their actions against the Theban prisoners executed at 2.5.7. Were the Thebans suppliants? If so, have the Plataeans themselves violated the very principle they cite here? Are the Plataeans truly suppliants in 427? If so, does the earlier Plataean action permit the Spartans to deal harshly with them now? The Thebans surrendered to the Plataeans after invading their city. The Plateans have surrendered themselves to the "judgment" of the Spartans. Thucydides sets up the situation so that the reader recalls the earlier incident, seen now in the light of two competing interpretations.

With regard to the second episode, the Thebans recall the Plataeans' opportunity to "opt out" of the war—they could have remained neutral (3.64.3; cf. 2.74). Thucydides himself says that the Spartans believe the Plataean rejection of this offer frees them from earlier obligations toward Plataea (3.68.1). When in book 3 the Plataeans anticipate the probable success of convincing the Spartans to spare their lives, they appeal to Pausanias (3.58.5) and invoke the Spartans' ancestors' graves (3.59.2). Yet the Plataeans (and the reader) should recall that an earlier Plataean attempt to evoke Pausanias and the battle of Plataea did not succeed (2.74.2). At that time, Archidamus had a ready answer to the Plataeans' appeals. How is the situation in 427 different? Is a similar argument likely to have different results now?[94]

In the third episode, the Plataeans executed their escape successfully; here their words are unsuccessful. That is, in action they were almost wholly successful with only a single casualty (3.24.3); their appeals to the Spartans now are totally unsuccessful: more than two hundred Plataeans are executed. The Plataeans have made choices in the past: to kill the Thebans prisoners (2.4.6, 2.6.1); to reject Archidamus' offers (2.72–74); to escape (3.20–24); and finally to hand over their city to the Spartan judges (3.52). They must now abide by the consequences of these actions.

The fourth episode also has links to other speech and action in the *History*, most prominently the Mytilenian debate and narrative. As Connor notes: the "first part of the third book develops a parallelism between the events on Lesbos and the continuing siege of Plataea"; he then enumerates an extensive list of parallels which promotes this comparison.[95] In book 3, Thucydides has structured the narrative in such a way that we are asked to compare the Plataeans' plight with that of the Mytilenians. There is also rhetorical responsion. The labeling of the Spartans as "judges" (*dicastai*) recalls the point disputed by Cleon and Diodotus concerning whether justice is the goal of the Athenian assembly, and to what extent the members of the assembly should think of themselves as being in a courtroom.[96] After the relevance of justice to foreign policy has been explicitly debated in the Athenian assembly—which, in a close vote, endorses Diodotus' recommendation—it is striking to find both the Plataeans and Thebans appealing to justice in their speeches. For example, the Plataeans ask whether the Spartans would actually choose their own immediate "advantage" (*chresimon*) and ignore their obligation to Plataea for past actions.[97]

"εἰ γὰρ τῷ αὐτίκα χρησίμῳ ὑμῶν τε καὶ ἐκείνων πολεμίῳ τὸ δίκαιον λήψεσθε, τοῦ μὲν ὀρθοῦ φανεῖσθε οὐκ ἀληθεῖς κριταὶ ὄντες, τὸ δὲ ξυμφέρον μᾶλλον θεραπεύοντες."

"If you are going to take as your standards of justice your own immediate advantage and their hostility toward us, you will clearly not be true judges of right, but rather servants of advantage." (3.56.3)

The Spartans will be seen not to be "true judges" (οὐκ ἀληθεῖς κριταὶ ὄντες); rather they will have chosen advantage (τὸ ξύμφερον) over the right thing (τοῦ ὀρθοῦ).

Noting that both speeches in the Plataean debate are "filled with the language of justice and piety," Connor says the effect is that the speeches emphasize:

> the discrepancy between the real world and an ideal world in which such appeals would be effective . . . [we are left with the] ineffectiveness of promises, of oaths, of obligations to friends and benefactors, indeed of anything except triumphant, dominant self-interest or advantage.[98]

Macleod remarks that the Spartans "still make a show of their reputed virtue by allowing a kind of trial, whose apparent purpose is to establish guilt or innocence (52.2, 53.4). But this trial is a travesty of legal forms."[99] The Plataean argument insists that if they are executed, the Spartans are not true judges, yet the immediately preceding debate over Mytilene has called into question the validity of morality for foreign policy. This may be seen as a clear example of how "dated" the Plataeans are. The effect of a two-year siege has cut them off from what passes for effective argument.

On the questions of alliance and neutrality, past action and future advantage, we find thematic connections between the Plataean and Corcyrean debates. The reader may well recall the first debate in the *History* where these issues were originally voiced (1.33–43). The Corinthians argued that their past service to the Athenians should induce the Athenians to reject the proposed alliance with Corcyra, who could point to no such past service. The Corcyreans could only promise future advantages (somewhat like the Thebans in this case, from the Spartan perspective). The Athenians then acted in terms of self-interest (1.44); now during wartime the Spartans act in the same way.[100]

Along these lines, there is an obvious point to make. Thucydides uses paired speeches for the Corcyrean and the Plataean debates to recreate for his readers (and auditors) the experience of *hearing* competing arguments that would have been familiar to a late fifth-century Athenian audience. That is, the arguments are modeled on oral discourse found in the Athenian assembly and courtrooms. With its emphasis on guilt, responsibility, and punishment (or acquittal), the Plataean debate in particular evokes forensic speech. A significant distinction is that rather than individuals speaking, Thucydides presents the cities of Plataea and Thebes as unified communities functioning as defendants and prosecutors—as in the Corcyrean debate.[101]

Other connections are implicitly suggested. We have already compared and contrasted this episode with the situation of the Mytilenians in book 3. The Mytilenian revolt is triggered by a Spartan promise to receive Lesbos as an ally, yet the Spartans fail to provide aid (3.25–35). Despite their impressive strength on the sea (3.18–19), the Athenians cannot reach Plataea. Thucydides has once again drawn the contrast of the Peloponnesian strength on land with that of the Athenians at sea.[102]

In the next chapter I will look at Melos and return to the question of neutrality—for both Melos and Plataea. I would close now with one other juxtaposition already mentioned: namely, Plataea's situation in comparison with that of Athens. Both have their territory invaded and are put under attack; the Peloponnesian forces move "not to Attica but to Plataea" (2.71). The points of comparison with Athens include siege and defensive strategy. When, however, the Plataeans refer to themselves as "mainlanders" (*epeirotai*–3.54.4), we note a stark contrast: in Pericles' war strategy the Athenians are asked to think of themselves as "islanders" (*nesiotai*–1.143.5). There are enough similarities between the two situations to see a connection, but the contrasts—Athenian access to the sea, a powerful navy, etc.—distinguish Plataea and also serve to highlight their mistake in trusting Athenian promises of help in all circumstances.[103]

Thucydides' presentation of Plataea offers us an example of punctuated history. When each episode breaks off and Thucydides fails to connect an early passage to a later one, the reader's task is to make those connections. The flip side, that is, of the historian's structuring of the narrative with presentation, interruption, and resumption, is the task of juxtaposition on the reader's part. As we read and reread, we come to appreciate the interconnectedness of this work: the arguments and events which are presented early in the work are later echoed, adapted, and transformed. The reader needs actively to create such links. An aspect of conjecture and extrapolation—a part of *eikazein*, etymologically—is to find the "similarity" or "likeness" (*eikon*) episode A shares with episodes B, C, or D. The reader may develop a facility for juxtaposition and application in other contexts by keeping track of the various figures, cities, conflicts, and arguments which arise—in this case, we have focused on Plataea.[104] Because Thucydides' modern audience consists of readers, such juxtapositions are physically and intellectually feasible: a reader may return to compare an earlier section (available on papyrus roll, codex, or CD) from a more distant, retrospective perspective. To the extent that Thucydides' original audience may have included readers and auditors, juxtaposition and comparison may have been most effectively accomplished by a group. I will discuss such a scenario in chapters 9 and 10.

5

HISTORICAL LESSONS IN THE
MELIAN EPISODE

This chapter on the Melian episode (5.84–116) focuses on the experience of the reader, yet this is a case where we ought to distinguish between multiple experiences of the text. On the one hand, the first-time reader may assume an engaged perspective, viewing the conflict from the perspective of the figures involved. Indeed, dialogue is a particularly useful form for securing such an engagement. Yet this episode may also be viewed productively from the more distant stance of the retrospective reader. While I will not ignore the experience of the engaged reader, I will be emphasizing the significance of the retrospective vantage point.

Thucydides calls attention to the Melian episode by its unique form: it presents the only extended dialogue in the *History*. This chapter argues that in addition to this unusual feature, a second aspect—both unusual and insufficiently noted—is that both sides' arguments offer the type of instruction which is parallel to that offered by Thucydides to his reader.[1] These connections are implicit and are best appreciated by the re-reader (or second-time auditor). Indeed, by considering the experience the reader has gained from the earlier books of the *History*, we are able to uncover and appreciate the lessons of history relevant to this confrontation. The Athenians attempt to teach the Melians what the reader has already learned in the *History*: that in spite of the conventional appeals found in diplomatic discourse, cities base their decisions on expediency. For their part, in seeking to persuade Athens to allow them to remain neutral, the Melians must be able to refer to both past action and future possibility. Although the Athenians say such discussion is out-of-bounds, here, too, the reader appreciates the importance of what the Melians try to do, for a second lesson of the *History* is that statesmen—and citizens—must consider the past and speculate about the future. By setting what the Athenians and the Melians say and do in the broader context of

Thucydides' *History* and applying the lessons of the first five books (some of which has been analyzed in chapters 3 and 4), the reader is in an excellent position to evaluate argument and action.[2] Thucydides' employment of a novel format helps to drive home the lessons that the reader is expected to have learned from considering the *History* as a whole. In essence, the Athenian-Melian exchange has become a kind of test case for the reader, asking how much the reader has learned by the end of five books.

Much of scholarly opinion concerning this conflict insists that the reader must make a choice. The Melians may be seen as victims, as de Romilly argues:

> The choice is obvious, as far as sympathy is concerned. The Melians are presented as having a very vivid sense of their independence ([5.]100); they act justly (104) and courageously (113): all these features are compliments for Thucydides when he can apply them to Athens. Similarly, he takes care to secure the reader's sympathy for the Melians by frequently recalling the cruel situation in which they are placed, and the fact that they have right on their side.[3]

Alternatively, the Athenians—if amoral—may be thought of as merciful in their quest to avoid bloodshed. Bosworth goes so far as to label this approach of the Athenians "humanitarian." Rather than simply overpowering the small city, he contends, Athens gives the Melians the opportunity to save themselves:

> Harsh as [the Athenians'] language undoubtedly is . . . it has a humanitarian end, to convince the Melian oligarchs of the need to capitulate and save themselves and the commons the horrors of a siege. If they acted sensibly, there would be no bloodshed, or even damage to property.[4]

This problem of interpretation arises from the authorial reticence of Thucydides, who withholds judgment and commentary. Thucydides omits any explicit judgment about the prudence or morality of Melos or Athens. Never in his own voice does Thucydides call the Athenians evil or clever, nor does he ever label the Melians foolish or brave.[5] This reticence, of course, is almost universal throughout the *History*: as Westlake notes, Thucydides seldom renders an explicit judgment of individuals, groups, or their decisions.[6]

In the end, each side fails to persuade the other; neither Athens nor

Melos wins the argument. One effect of the dialogue form and the lack of rhetorical resolution is that a balance is created between the claims of the Melians and the Athenians. I find myself endorsing Wasserman's assessment from almost sixty years ago:

> Thucydides uses the form of the dialogue to make his readers listen to the arguments from both sides. Both his Athenians and his Melians so convincingly advance their points that either side has been taken mistakenly as his mouthpiece, while in reality both parties are intended to be seen together to give the complete picture.[7]

The failure of either side to convince the other reflects both strengths and weaknesses in each side's arguments. Only a retrospective reading of the dialogue will allow us, as readers, accurately to assess both arguments and the reasons for the Melians' and Athenians' failure to persuade one another.[8]

GOALS

Let us begin by juxtaposing the goals of each side with possible consequences. Early on, the Melians express their apprehension regarding *war*, if they are in the right and do not give in to Athens, or *slavery*, if the Athenians are persuasive (5.86). Much of the discourse thereafter consists of the Melians arguing to maintain their neutral status, or to evoke images of a successful resistance with help from Sparta or the gods. There are three apparent avenues for Melos: to give in and "join" Athens (that is, become subject allies), to remain neutral, or to resist. Clearly the third option of resistance is more open-ended and dangerous: it is an all-or-nothing decision, leading to success or destruction.[9] The first two possible outcomes—acquiescence or neutrality—can result only from negotiation.

On the Athenian side, there appear to be the same three options from the opposite perspective: persuade the Melians, allow them to remain neutral, or attack. (Neutrality is dismissed, but theoretically the Melians could prove persuasive.) But before considering these choices from the Athenian point of view, we should emphasize the significant option of discourse itself. The military situation has put the Athenians in a position to attack immediately, but they choose to discuss the situation with the Melians first. If they begin an assault and Melos resists, the city could be destroyed with its value to Athens diminished. We may conclude that the

Athenians initiate the dialogue with a single goal in mind: to gain control of an intact city and rule Melos "without toil" (*aponos*–5.91.2).[10] In light of this, we should recognize that while the Athenians have the option of attacking and putting the city under siege, the very fact that they are talking at all implies that they would prefer to persuade the Melians.

Rules for Discourse

Each side fails to convince the other: the Melians do not acquiesce; the Athenians reject neutrality.[11] Why? As we turn to a detailed analysis of the arguments in the dialogue, we note the importance of rules regarding how to proceed. The failure of each side derives partly from a rejection of exploring all possibilities in discussion. Let us examine the various restrictions placed on context and discussion, concerning audience, format, and subject. First, as the dialogue is not spoken before a majority of citizens, the spokesmen—that is, the interlocutors—for the Melians are just a few of their citizens who hold office (5.84.3).[12] According to the Athenians, this advances the Melians' interests in at least two ways:

"ὅπως δὴ μὴ ξυνεχεῖ ῥήσει οἱ πολλοὶ ἐπαγωγὰ καὶ ἀνέλεγκτα ἐσάπαξ ἀκούσαντες ἡμῶν ἀπατηθῶσιν."

"So that a majority of citizens may not hear a continuous speech—at the same time attractive and immune from cross examination—and be deceived." (5.85)

The audience is restricted—the majority (*hoi polloi*) are not addressed. Without the majority of the Melians, who may favor accommodation with Athens, the small set of Melians involved concentrates its energies on the goal of neutrality.[13] A second and related restriction is that—in contrast to all previous speeches[14]—the Athenians propose a point-by-point discussion, allowing for immediate response. This is justified in part by reference to the deceptive power of set speeches (5.85).[15] From the reader's perspective, not only is the format of dialogue striking, but we must also reckon with what the Athenians say about long speeches, namely, that they are deceptive because they are "attractive and immune from cross examination" (ἐπαγωγὰ καὶ ἀνέλεγκτα–5.89). This must cause some uneasiness for the reader, who is now forced to revisit the previous speeches within the *History* in an entirely new light.[16] To what extent have the speeches

from the first five books been deceptive? When have they been manipulative? In what sense are they unanswerable or irrefutable? Thucydides has
highlighted the choice of format for this discussion by raising the question
as to whether the dialogue form is actually a better way to arrive at the
truth.[17] By criticizing set speeches, Thucydides is able to privilege dialogue
over extended speech at this point of the *History*. This may also be seen as
advice to employ dialogue when the audience discusses the *History* (yes,
more of this in chapters 9 and 10—I realize that by now expectations for
these chapters must be quite high).

Besides concerns of audience and format, the third stipulation established by the Athenians imposes severe restrictions upon what is "allowed"
to be explored. The encounter between Athens and Melos, as Thucydides
has structured it, is not a military contest; rather it is rhetorical. A dialogue
would appear to grant both sides equal standing, but the fact that Athens
has insisted that the discussion follow a prescribed route reduces the
advantages Melos may gain from a point-by-point discussion.[18] The range
of subjects is not open-ended, as the Athenians continually try to eliminate certain topics from discussion. Nonetheless, the dialogue format
tremendously helps the Melians, who are able to make repeated efforts to
redefine and restructure the discourse in order to allow for a broader range
of exchange. If the Athenians had laid out the ground rules in a first set
speech, there could have been no Melian response. The dialogue form not
only permits Melos to challenge Athenian assertions, but it also allows
them to call into question and resist the rules of discussion as laid down by
the Athenians. Purely from the Melian point of view, the first two stipulations (small audience and dialogue form) are sufficiently advantageous to
allow them to neutralize the third restriction regarding admissible topics.[19]

ADVANTAGE, NOT JUSTICE: THE ATHENIANS' LESSON

Let us survey how Athens restricts the range of allowable issues. Early
in the dialogue when the Melians say that if they are in the right
(περιγενομένοις μὲν τῷ δικαίῳ–5.86) war will come, the Athenians
immediately insist that the discussion is only about the survival (*soteria*) of
the city of Melos.[20]

"Εἰ μὲν τοίνυν ὑπονοίας τῶν μελλόντων λογιούμενοι ἢ ἄλλο τι
ξυνήκετε ἢ ἐκ τῶν παρόντων καὶ ὧν ὁρᾶτε περὶ σωτηρίας
βουλεύσοντες τῇ πόλει, παυοίμεθ' ἄν· εἰ δ' ἐπὶ τοῦτο, λέγοιμεν ἄν."

"If you have met to weigh your suspicions about the future or for any other reason except to deliberate concerning the safety for your city on the basis of the present circumstances as you see them, we would stop; but if that [the safety for your city] is the reason, we would speak." (5.87)

In part, the Athenians object to "suspicions about the future" (discussed below), but it also appears that the Melians' mention of justice (5.86) leads the Athenians to threaten to cut off dialogue entirely: the Melians must limit discussion to the issue of survival. The Athenians themselves rephrase this restriction in a number of ways: only the issues of survival,[21] safety,[22] reasonable expectation,[23] and the disparity between strong and weak are relevant.[24] That is, the Athenians attempt to collapse a large number of potential topics for discussion into one basic idea: the continued existence of Melos.[25]

The Athenians consider off-limits any mention of justice, fine deeds, freedom, shame, and the past or future. Regarding justice, the Athenians openly say:

"῾Ημεῖς τοίνυν οὔτε αὐτοὶ μετ᾽ ὀνομάτων καλῶν, ὡς ἢ **δικαίως** τὸν Μῆδον καταλύσαντες ἄρχομεν ἢ **ἀδικούμενοι** νῦν ἐπεξερχόμεθα, λόγων μῆκος ἄπιστον παρέξομεν, οὔθ᾽ ὑμᾶς ἀξιοῦμεν ἢ ὅτι Λακεδαιμονίων ἄποικοι ὄντες οὐ ξυνεστρατεύσατε ἢ ὡς **ἡμᾶς οὐδὲν ἠδικήκατε** λέγοντας οἴεσθαι πείσειν."

"Then we on our side will use no fine phrases to furnish a lengthy, unconvincing speech ourselves about *having a right* to rule because we defeated the Persians, or attacking now *because we were wronged*. We do not expect you to think you will persuade us by saying that you are colonists of Sparta and have not joined them in war, or *that you have never done us any harm*." (5.89)

Any mention of justice (δικαίως, ἀδικούμενοι, οὐδὲν ἠδικήκατε) is rejected. The idea that justice is irrelevant to foreign policy recurs prominently in the *History*—this is explored more fully in the Mytilenian debate.[26] Here Athens argues that justice must yield to self-interest (5.90, 5.104); the only law (*nomos*) is the law of ruling where one is strong (οὗ ἂν κρατῇ ἄρχειν–5.105).[27] There are other issues which the Athenians declare out of bounds. When the Melians insist that they are "still free" (ἔτι ἐλευθέροις) and it would be "cowardly and base" (πολλὴ κακότης καὶ δειλία–5.100) if they submitted to Athens, the Athenians respond

that the issue is not goodness or shame (ἀνδραγαθίας . . . αἰσχύνην
–5.101), but rather survival (*soteria*–5.101). In fact, to be defeated—and
yet survive—is "not unseemly" (οὐκ ἀπρεπές–5.111.4).[28]

Remarkable throughout is the utterly frank way in which the
Athenians address the Melians.[29] Yet a lesson lies here, for the reader—
with the advantage of having read the *History*—recognizes the disparity
between speech and action. Previously in the *History* when one city has
attempted to persuade another in diplomatic discourse, the usual practice
is to invoke justice, honor, and the glorious deeds of the past, in addition
to the advantages to be gained.[30] The audiences of such speeches at the
very least hear that a particular course of action has both strategic *and*
moral implications. We have seen this in the Corcyrean and Corinthian
speeches in book 1 and the Plataean debate in book 3 (chapters 3 and 4).
And yet, as Thucydides demonstrates, cities make decisions on the basis
of advantage. For example, the Athenians bring the Corcyreans into a
defensive alliance due to their navy and the important route to the west
(1.44.2–3). Although the rhetoric in the Plataean debate is laden with
moral language, Sparta executes the Plataeans because the Thebans were
"useful" (*ophelimous*–3.68.4).[31] By pointedly indicating after speeches
what the actual motives were, Thucydides highlights the "disconnect"
between the rhetoric of justice found in debates and the decisions themselves which are based on expediency. What is so unusual about the
Melian dialogue is that the Athenians have called into question a whole
set of basic appeals normally used in diplomatic discourse. Andrewes
comments:

> Thucydides distorts his political picture by leaving out arguments which
> may have seemed superficial to him but played a practical part in per-
> suading fifth-century assemblies to their decisions. The still starker exclu-
> sion of ὀνόματα καλά ["fine phrases"] from the Dialogue is a still more
> violent distortion. The danger of stripping away the pretences, attractive
> as the attempt may be to a critical historian, is that with them you strip
> away the actual incentives which decide the ordinary man's vote.[32]

Yet this is precisely what the Athenians have done. They have stripped
away the elevated appeals to country, honor, and justice. How are we to
explain this attempt to narrow the discussion?

We have just referred to the way in which Thucydides frequently jux-
taposes diplomatic discourse in speech (which includes moral language)
with the actual bases for decisions as recounted in the narrative (which are

offered exclusively in terms of expediency). Given this backdrop, we may view what the Athenians are doing here—arguing that the discussion must be restricted to advantage and survival—as a kind of instruction for the Melians which is analogous to what Thucydides teaches the reader of his *History*. Of course, such lessons are introduced in a particular context and may not be applied simplistically to all other situations. Here, however, it is evident the Athenians are attempting to teach the Melians what the reader has already learned: that decisions are based on considerations of advantage, not elevated sentiments or a rosy picture of the past. If the Melians are hoping to affect the outcome of the current conflict, they need to limit their discussion to factors that will *actually* influence the Athenians. The rest is superfluous.[33] On this reading, even the third restriction on permissible topics may be seen as having Melian interests at heart. In the end the Athenians fail to teach the Melians this lesson. Such a lesson, however, must be taken seriously, because by this point of the *History* the reader has already witnessed how decisions are made. What Athens says to the Melians should strike the reader as accurate. When the Melians fail to limit their argument to the topics of safety and advantage, this ultimately dooms their attempt to persuade the Athenians to allow them to remain neutral.

Before turning to the Melians' arguments, we should note the distance created between the reader and the Melians. In one sense, the reader may be fully engaged, actively trying to assess and supplement the arguments of both sides, but in another sense there is a marked gap between what the reader knows and what the Melians insist on doing. To the extent that by reading Thucydides' *History* the reader has "experienced" the war, the reader is now better versed in the ways of the world than the Melians, whose survival depends upon a sounder appreciation of *Realpolitik*. In this case, the Melians appear to be unaware of the gulf between diplomatic discourse and actual decision-making. Thucydides' *History* not only makes this distinction clear, but uses Melos to illustrate the danger of failing to distinguish between moral appeals and prudent decisions. The effect is one of strong dramatic irony and pathos.[34]

Redefining Advantage: The Melians' Argument

Let us now turn to the Melians' arguments as they try to dissuade Athens from attacking. Clearly the Melians have a difficult task. They are outmatched in terms of military power; all they have are words and arguments, yet even here they face restrictions.[35] In a variety of ways, however, the Melians redefine or simply disregard Athenian limitations on possible discourse. We might think the Melians would do better to speak directly, as the Athenians do, and to limit their remarks to matters of expediency. To this extent, they have failed to learn the lesson of the Athenians—and of Thucydides' *History*. In one area, however, the Melians offer valuable advice, namely, in their discussion of past and future, a lesson which the Athenians fail to appreciate.

The Melians begin by trying to redefine the concept of justice (which the Athenians will not allow) in terms of advantage (which the Athenians prize).[36]

"Ἦι μὲν δὴ νομίζομέν γε, χρήσιμον ἀνάγκη γάρ, ἐπειδὴ ὑμεῖς οὕτω παρὰ τὸ δίκαιον τὸ ξυμφέρον λέγειν ὑπέθεσθε μὴ καταλύειν ὑμᾶς τὸ κοινὸν ἀγαθόν, ἀλλὰ τῷ αἰεὶ ἐν κινδύνῳ γιγνομένῳ εἶναι τὰ εἰκότα καὶ δίκαια,[37] καί τι καὶ ἐντὸς τοῦ ἀκριβοῦς πείσαντά τινα ὠφεληθῆναι."

"Then we at least believe it an advantage [χρήσιμον]—necessarily, since you require us to speak of expediency [τὸ ξυμφέρον] apart from justice [τὸ δίκαιον]—that you should not destroy a universal good [τὸ κοινὸν ἀγαθόν]—but that at all times there should be such a thing as fairness and justice [τὰ εἰκότα καὶ δίκαια] for those in danger and that it should be permissible to find help by an argument that falls short of precision." (5.90)

This is not so much collapsing justice and advantage, as it is pointing out the advantages of justice.[38] Even the Athenians, the Melians suggest, might find themselves in a situation where the concept of justice is valuable. Part of the Athenians' response is a lack of concern for the empire's demise—they willingly take on this risk—but the Athenians' other point is that the Melians are speculating about the future. The Athenians wish to speak only about the present, in terms of advantage to their empire and the survival of Melos (5.91). The Melians then ask how it could be advantageous (*chresimon*) for them to accept slavery (*douleusai*–5.92). The Athenians respond that "we would assess as profit" (κερδαίνοιμεν ἄν) not being destroyed (5.93).

The Melians attempt to equate justice with advantage and slavery with disadvantage. The Athenians reject these equations, countering that survival is an advantage and not being annihilated is profit.[39] At this point the Athenian restriction holds: the only accepted coin is advantage. The question for Melos is whether survival is enough of an advantage to relinquish autonomy—perhaps an advantage in itself—yet their continued efforts at debate indicate that mere survival is not enough of an advantage for them to sacrifice their independence.

But restricting discussion to advantage is not irrelevant to the Athenians. Where does their advantage lie? The Melians, who raise this issue, argue that if safety (*asphaleia*) is the highest goal of the Athenians, the Athenians may be less "safe" (that is, in a less advantageous position) by attacking Melos, for this would encourage other neutral powers to turn away from Athens, thus helping Athens' enemies (5.98). The Athenians respond that—as for now—neutral mainlanders are not as threatening as Melos.

> "We do not consider dangerous states on the mainland [*epeirotai*] due to their liberty, for their precautions against us will be a long time in coming [πολλὴν τὴν διαμέλλησιν]. We do consider dangerous islanders like yourselves, who are outside the empire [νησιώτας. . . ἀνάρκτους], and subjects who have already [ἤδη] become exasperated by our empire's constraints. These are the people who are most likely to act in a reckless manner [τῷ ἀλογίστῳ] and to bring both themselves and us into foreseeable danger." (5.99)

We have already learned that the Melians are not like other islanders, because they are not willing to follow Athens (οὐκ ἤθελον ὑπακούειν ὥσπερ οἱ ἄλλοι νησιῶται–5.84.2). Athens finds the Melians threatening, as "islanders . . . outside the the empire" (νησίωτας. . . ἀνάρκτους–5.99), and, as a naval power (*naukratoron*–5.97, 5.109), cannot allow Melos to remain neutral. To this extent, it is the island status of Melos that concerns Athens. Neutral islands make Athens appear weak, thus encouraging reckless attacks (5.97, 5.99). Yet although the Athenians distinguish between immediate threat and what may occur at some point in the future, they imply that if neutrals on the mainland pose no immediate threat, they may be disregarded. Only the here and now is important.

The Melians have attempted to redefine justice and safety by considering the advantages of morality and neutrality; they hypothesize a potential "turning of tables" by sketching out the future consequences of Athenian action. Given the Athenian response, the Melians then begin to resist the Athenians' rhetorical restrictions. While such resistance is ultimately unsuccessful in persuading Athens, the Melians' arguments at 5.100ff. amount to a nullification of the original stipulations on permissible discourse. The Melians revert to appealing to moral concepts, such as shame (5.100), freedom (5.112), and justice.[40] For example, "Nevertheless we trust in chance from god not to be defeated, as righteous men who stand in opposition to unjust ones [ὅσιοι πρὸς οὐ δικαίους]" (5.104). By resisting the Athenians' "rules," the Melians are able to raise a broader range of issues than the Athenians are willing to address. This does not affect the short-term outcome: the Spartans do not help; Athens is victorious with its siege; Melos is destroyed. Although the Athenians win militarily, however, their prohibitions fail to constrain the Melians' words. As "masters of the sea" the Athenians are successful; as "masters of discourse" they cannot control the Melians.[41] In countering and nullifying Athenian restrictions, the Melians raise an important issue: the long-term consequences of Athenian policy.[42] Let us now turn to the significance of pondering history and the future.

Past and Future: A Lesson of Thucydides' *History*

The Melians' goal in the dialogue is to persuade the Athenians to allow their neutral status. Yet it appears that if the Melians are to be successful, they have to deal with past events and future possibilities—with what Thucydides' *History* itself addresses. We recall that early in the dialogue the Athenians threaten to stop the discussion if the Melians speculate about the future (5.87). In her discussion of the Thebans' speech in book 3, Arnold remarks that "while the Spartans in effect deny the relevance of the past, in the Melian dialogue the Athenians reject the relevance of the future."[43] In fact, the dialogue is more complex: we find that both Athens and Melos discuss not only the present but also the past and future, albeit in extremely restricted ways.

The Athenians apparently assert the irrelevance of the past. They will not be introducing recollections of their victory over the Persians and their right to empire; in turn, however, they do not wish to hear about the Melians' innocence (5.89). Past actions, the Athenians maintain in this passage, are not applicable to the current confrontation.[44] Elsewhere, however, the Athenians themselves do look to the past. At the end of the dialogue, they remind the Melians that they have never previously given up a siege out of fear of other powers (5.111.1). The Athenians' characterization of the cautious behavior of the Spartans (5.105.3–4, 5.107, 5.109) is evidently based on the past—certainly the reader has noted incidents prior to 416 which support this (for example, the Spartans fail to assist the Mytilenians in their attempted revolt—3.25–33). That is, they selectively recount the past in order to persuade Melos. The Athenians' apparent rejection of discussing past and future is stated broadly; they do not want events concerning justice or innocence brought up. The past, however, is relevant for the Athenians when it concerns power and action. The Melians themselves disregard this prohibition concerning the past, basing their final rejection of Athens on history, specifically their seven hundred years of freedom (5.112).

Both Athens and Melos present extremely restricted visions of the past. This narrowness results from each side's refusal to acknowledge issues the other side introduces. Melos has no response to the Athenians' characterization of past Spartan action—which the reader knows to a large extent to be accurate. By failing to acknowledge the significance of previous caution and tentativeness on the part of the Spartans, the Melians put themselves in a poor position to determine the chances of their receiving future aid. On the other side, by refusing to allow shame, justice, or freedom into the discussion, the Athenians ignore an essential component of how the Melians define themselves in terms of their own history.

We also find each side making fine distinctions regarding the future. The Melians equate action with hope and inaction with despair.

"καὶ ἡμῖν τὸ μὲν εἶξαι εὐθὺς ἀνέλπιστον, μετὰ δὲ τοῦ δρωμένου ἔτι καὶ στῆναι ἐλπὶς ὀρθῶς."

"And for us to yield immediately is to give up hope, but with action there is still the hope of success." (5.102)

The Melians look ahead to a variety of possibilities. Aid may come from Sparta in the future (5.104, 5.106, 5.108, 5.110, 5.112.2); the Athenian empire may fall (5.90, 5.98, 5.110); the gods may intervene (5.104, 5.112.2).[45] In support of the likelihood of successful military resistance are chance, hope, and the idea that the Spartans will take on the risk.[46] The Spartans may even, the Melians speculate, attack Athenian land (5.110).

At first the Athenians say they are dismissive of thinking about the future. Hope is expensive (ἐλπίς . . . δάπανος γὰρ φύσει) and belongs to the "invisible future" (ἐπὶ τὰς ἀφανεῖς) in a category containing prophecies and oracles (5.103).[47] In part, this is a rhetorical move on the Athenians' part. By cutting off objections the Melians might raise, they set the rules of the debate in such a way that their victory is guaranteed. The

Athenians characterize the Melians' speculation as "senselessness" (τὸ ἄφρον–5.105) and denigrate their claim to foresee the future more clear-ly than what is actually in front of them.

"τὰ μὲν μέλλοντα τῶν ὁρωμένων σαφέστατα κρίνετε, τὰ δὲ ἀφανῆ τῷ βούλεσθαι ὡς γιγνόμενα ἤδη θεᾶσθε."

"You consider the future as clearer than what is before your eyes, and in using wishful thinking you already look on the unforeseeable as taking place." (5.113)

Throughout the dialogue the Melians attempt to get the Athenians to think about the possible consequences of their action (neutrals allying themselves with Sparta, Sparta coming to help, divine intervention, the fall of the empire)—not as certainties, but as plausible contingencies which should influence Athenian decision-making.[48] The Melians ignore Athenian limits on discussion, but the Athenians reject contemplation of these future scenarios.[49]

Two points should be made. First, the Athenians themselves fail to observe their own restriction on future speculation. In fact, the Athenians find their own vision of the future worth contemplating. The Athenians assume that if the Melians resist, the city will be destroyed (πρὸ τοῦ τὰ δεινότατα παθεῖν–5.93)[50]; the Melians may hope for Spartan aid but the Spartans will never arrive (5.105, 5.107).[51] While shutting out the alter-native scenarios of the Melians, the Athenians advance an optimistic set of possibilities promoting their own interest. Just as the Athenians have failed to "teach" Melos the importance—even the necessity—of arguing in terms of advantage, so the Melians have failed to "teach" Athens the value of recollecting the past and contemplating future contingencies.[52]

A comparison between the Melian Dialogue and a Socratic dialogue offers an instructive parallel. Any dialogue—as a means of communication, exploration, and persuasion—has the potential to raise questions which may bring the interlocutor to realize his or her own misconceptions. Yet the only side to ask questions is that of Melos. In part, this reflects the reluctance of the Athenians to take on the role of learner; they evidently think their only purpose is to teach.[53] Subsequently, they fail to pay ade-quate attention to issues the Melians raise.

The second and more important point has to do with the value of history and the possibility of conjecturing usefully about the future. Macleod criti-cizes the selective vision of Athens, commenting that the Athenians' "refusal to look into the future is far removed from the foresight (πρόνοια) which characterizes the Thucydidean statesman." Contemplating what may transpire is what "Diodotus conceives to be the object of political deliberation."[54] In both speech and narrative of the *History*, probing attention is given to the importance of the past and the ability to plan for the future—we have seen this especially in the case of Plataea and its trust in future Athenian aid.[55] From the reader's perspective—at this point in the *History*—saying that the past is irrelevant goes against the entire spirit of Thucydides' work: history is useful, similar sorts of things may happen in the future, study of the past may lead to learning (see especially 1.22.4).[56] Just like Thucydides' readers, politicians, generals, citizens—and here, the Athenians and the Melians—must contemplate the future and consider whether the consequences of a particular action may lead to any advantage.

It is one thing to argue that a particular consequence is unlikely and give reasons for such a conclusion. At least Archidamus (1.80–85) and Pericles (1.140–44) give a rationale for their strategies and try to account for the strengths and weaknesses of the opposing side. But to make such a blanket dismissal of the future as irrelevant, as Athens does here, is clearly condemned by what Thucydides himself has already emphasized in his work. The reader has learned to consider both the short- and long-term effects of decisions and actions. For example, the Plataeans' actions—execution of the Theban prisoners in 431 (2.5.7) and their rejection of the Spartan offer of neutrality in 429 (2.72–74)—are used against them in 427, leading to their execution (3.66–67, 3.68.1). In the Melian episode, however, the Athenians are interested only in the short term. More generally then, from the first five books of Thucydides' *History*, the reader is able to appreciate lessons concerning not only moral language and practical decision-making, but also the significance of the past and the necessity of anticipating the future. Thus the reader is sensitive to the Melians' "pig-headedness"[57] in insisting on moral sentiments, as well as Athens' misguided neglect of past and future. By contrasting how Athens and Melos argue and behave with what is taught in the preceding sections of the *History*, the retrospective reader recognizes the inflexibility of Melos and the recklessness of Athens.[58] Let us turn now to other significant connections the Melian episode has with the *History*.

Parallels and Contrasts with Melos

Beyond the general lessons of Thucydides' *History*, scholars have seen a great many connections between the Melian episode and other specific situations, arguments, and themes from the *History*. While Thucydides never explicitly tells us the significance of the Melian episode, the retrospective reader is encouraged to engage in juxtaposition and comparison concerning the context and motifs introduced in the Melian episode. In addition to the relevance of Mytilene and Plataea,[59] many have viewed the significance of Melos in connection with the subsequent narrative, in particular, regarding the Sicilian expedition in books 6–7, the defection of allies (8.2ff.), and the end of the war in 404 (see Xen. *HG* 2.2.3).

Immediately after Athens takes Melos, Thucydides turns his attention to the Sicilian expedition at 6.1. Like Melos, Sicily is an island, although much larger and more powerful.[60] The Athenians are successful with Melos, whereas they meet with unprecedented disaster in Sicily.[61] Cartwright comments on the sequence of Melos followed by Sicily: "a minor victory is followed by a major defeat, both arising from the same cause, a paradoxical aspect of Athenian power revealed by the dialogue: in some ways it limits, rather than enlarges, Athenian freedom of action."[62] Connor notes: "the reader knows that another island, Sicily, will soon overcome an Athenian attack . . . [Athens, like Melos, is] forced to rely on hope, chance, and speculation about the gods" (esp. 7.77.4).[63]

Once again in the case of Sicily, we might say that the Athenians recklessly dismiss a serious consideration of future possibilities. Scholars who make these connections are fully engaged in a process of comparison, juxtaposition, and extrapolation (captured by the Greek word *eikazein*).[64] The retrospective reader is encouraged actively to participate in these very exercises, for Thucydides' use of self-reference within his *History* stimulates such juxtapositions. I would like to focus upon one particular issue crucial to the Melian episode: neutrality.

Thucydides himself calls attention to the neutral status of Melos at 5.84.2:[65]

ἀλλὰ τὸ μὲν πρῶτον οὐδετέρων ὄντες ἡσύχαζον, ἔπειτα ὡς αὐτοὺς ἠνάγκαζον οἱ Ἀθηναῖοι δηοῦντες τὴν γῆν, ἐς πόλεμον φανερὸν κατέστησαν.

But at first [the Melians] remained neutral toward both sides, but then when the Athenians pressured them by ravaging their land, they became engaged in open war. (5.84.2)[66]

This passage and earlier mentions of Melos in the *History* raise several questions. First, was Melos neutral or hostile to Athens in 416? When war began in 431, Thucydides indicated that Thera and Melos were the only Cycladic islands not allied with Athens (2.9.4). In 426, Nicias took sixty ships and two thousand hoplites to Melos. Thucydides observed that the Melians did not wish to submit to Athens; after ravaging their land, the Athenians sailed away (3.91.1–2).[67] In 431, Melos was neutral; five years later, it resisted an Athenian attack of short duration. Before the confrontation in 416, Melos appears to have had little involvement in the war. Yet when Thucydides says that the Melians "were forced to come to open war" (ἐς πόλεμον φανερὸν κατέστησεν–5.84.2), to what occasion is he referring? Apparently not to 416, for the Athenians have not yet begun hostilities; they send ambassadors before attacking (5.82.3).[68] Does the open hostility refer to the raid of 426?[69] If so, is Melos still hostile in 416–ten years later? How then can it claim neutrality? Could Melos possibly have resumed neutrality—perhaps in 421 with the peace of Nicias? But if so, why does Thucydides omit any indication of this?[70]

The salient point, I think, is that in the incident from 416—as presented by Thucydides—the Athenians do not adduce earlier conflicts they have had with Melos. Presumably they could have used the resistance of the Melians in 426 as an excuse for their aggression, but they choose not to do so. In part, this removes the dialogue somewhat from its historical context, and gives it a more universal meaning.[71] But from the reader's perspective, knowledge of that previous conflict heightens an awareness of Athens' utter disregard of past action, as Thucydides shows the forces—and blindness—which drive Athens on. Thucydides apparently has presented this conflict in such a way as to show that even if Melos were completely and unambiguously neutral, Athens would still act to incorporate the island.[72] By this point Athens no longer needs recourse to past hostility to explain its own aggressiveness—the will to power is its own driving force and no longer needs further justification.[73]

This is borne out by the Melians' argument as well. In rejecting submission and yet desiring to avoid war, the Melians say they hope that Athens will allow them to remain neutral. They even offer a definition of neutrality:

"ὥστε ἡσυχίαν ἄγοντας ἡμᾶς φίλους μὲν εἶναι ἀντὶ πολεμίων, ξυμμάχους δὲ μηδετέρων, οὐκ ἂν δέξαισθε;"

"Would you not accept us keeping the peace, friends instead of enemies, and allies of neither side?" (5.94)

The Melians raise the specter—if Athens besieges them—of other neutrals joining Sparta, thus strengthening Athens' enemies (5.98). That is, the Melians try to fit their goal of neutrality into the Athenian set of values, which is apparently limited to power, safety, and advantage.[74] The final words of the Melians—after invoking freedom, chance, and hope of Spartan aid—are an invitation to Athens:

"προκαλούμεθα δὲ ὑμᾶς φίλοι μὲν εἶναι, πολέμιοι δὲ μηδετέροις, καὶ ἐκ τῆς γῆς ἡμῶν ἀναχωρῆσαι σπονδὰς ποιησαμένους αἵτινες δοκοῦσιν ἐπιτήδειοι εἶναι ἀμφοτέροις."

"We invite you to be our friends, and to be enemies to neither side, and that you make a treaty which seems appropriate to both sides and then leave our land." (5.112.3)

But the Athenians have already stated their objection to neutrality. Friendship, they say, is associated with weakness (ἡ φιλία μὲν ἀσθενίας) and brings harm rather than hatred (5.95).[75] Power alone has become its own justification.

In terms of Thucydides' *History*, the option of neutrality was first considered by the Corcyreans when they sought an Athenian alliance.[76] They concluded in retrospect that such a policy was a mistake (1.32) and successfully pursued an alliance with Athens. The Corcyrean episode prior to the war forces us to consider seriously when neutrality could be a viable option. If an island at the northwest edge of the Greek world can argue that a policy of isolation is foolish, what chance does Melos—without a navy and located in the Aegean (Athens' sphere of domination)—have for disengagement? Archidamus later offered the option of neutrality to the Plataeans, which would have removed Plataea from the Athenian alliance (2.72). Yet neutrality was again rejected, as Plataea insisted on maintaining its relationship with Athens.[77] Athens now insists that Melos not remain neutral, for Athens controls the sea and Melos is an island. The issue is not whether neutrality is an option. The question is whether neutrality is a viable option for this weak island at this time.

The situation in the Melian episode is similar to these previous situations in some respects, significantly reversed in others. Like Corcyra, Melos has had, or at least claims, a policy of neutrality; unlike Corcyra, however, Melos wishes to maintain such a status. Corcyra was independent and had a navy; Melos is virtually without defense. Corcyra came to consider neutrality a mistake; Melos considers neutrality to be its best option.

Like Plataea, Melos rejects the alliance offered by a threatening power. Plataea hoped for aid from Athens, yet this was compromised by the fact that Plataea was land-locked and Athens' power lay on the sea. A comparable situation arises for Melos, which hopes for assistance, yet as an island cannot be confident in aid from the land power, Sparta.[78] In these three situations—Corcyra, Plataea, and Melos—we find that neutrality is not a viable option for one reason or another. The Melian episode has the effect of forcing the reader to ask whether neutrality can ever exist. Under what circumstances would it be possible for any city to opt out of the struggle of the Peloponnesian War?[79]

In a practical sense, cities were able to remain neutral. In his work *The Concept of Neutrality in Classical Greece*, Bauslaugh provides several examples, such as Argos, that prove the point.[80] Thucydides even comments on the advantages Argos gained from alliances with both sides (ἀμφοτέροις δὲ μᾶλλον ἔνσπονδοι ὄντες ἐκκαρπωσάμενοι—5.28.2).[81] Yet before the war Corcyra had a navy; Argos had an army. The question is not whether neutrality can be a viable policy, but rather whether it is possible or advisable for a weak, small polis to claim neutrality.[82] The Melians' only hope—given that their only recource is debate—is to argue in a way that will persuade Athens. The Athenians insist upon arguments in terms of expediency, yet, as we have seen, the Melians fail to abide by this stipulation: instead we find Melos appealing to morality. Thucydides' account of the war thus far has made clear that for Melos to persuade Athens, it has to articulate clear advantages for Athens. As Bauslaugh argues, the Melians are now confronted with a "newly evolved ethos of hegemonial, imperial Greek states that refused to accept any restraints on the pursuit of self-interest."[83]

The view of the retrospective reader instructs us in assessing the validity and wisdom of Melian and Athenian argument and action. In fact, it turns out that we cannot evaluate what happens in the Melian episode—what goes wrong and why, the Melians' failure to see the difference between diplomatic discourse and actual motivation, the Athenians' selective vision of past and future—without setting this episode in the context of the rest of the *History*. Everything demonstrated in the first five books puts the reader in an epistemological position superior to that of the Melians and the Athenians. In earlier situations in the *History* (the Corcyrean episode, for example), Thucydides guides, instructs, and makes connections for the reader.[84] By the end of book 5, Thucydides has set a more challenging project for the reader. The Melian episode may have many goals, but one of these is to test the reader regarding what the

History itself teaches.[85] One of the retrospective reader's tasks is to examine lessons from the rest of the *History* and apply them in this new context. Thucydides' world suggests not only the interconnectedness of cities, but also the ways in which conflict and argument found in one setting may be relevant to new situations. Neutrality may exist in late fifth-century Greece, but in the world constructed by Thucydides, only those who have learned the lessons of history have a chance of pursuing such a policy successfully.[86]

As previously noted, like Corcyra and Plataea, Melos is not central to the outcome of the war itself. Thucydides uses these three cities for a variety of purposes. Corcyra in part is valuable for introducing "participatory history." Plataea offered an example of punctuated history in which the reader must trace action to later consequences. Melos makes clear that the retrospective reader's task in part is to explore each episode in the context of lessons learned elsewhere—learned at least by the reader if not by the participants involved. Just as Plataea was cut off by siege from the world of diplomatic discourse (such as Diodotus' arguments in the Mytilenian debate), so too Melos may be seen as being naïve due to its previous neutrality. Melos' disengagement has prevented it from learning how cities argue and behave. On this point, the reader has a superior appreciation of true motivation and the importance of the past.

PART THREE

ARGUMENT AND REVERBERATION:
COMPARISON, MAXIM, AND METAPHOR

6

THE COMPARISON OF CITIES AND
INDIVIDUALS

In this chapter we explore the comparison of cities and individuals. The previous three chapters focused on specific city-states; the goal was to demonstrate how Thucydides challenged the reader to become engaged in participatory history (Corcyra), to link action to consequence and juxtapose speech with action (punctuated history centering on Plataea), and to extrapolate from a relatively isolated event (the Melian episode) to other lessons found in the *History*. In chapters 6 through 8, our attention now turns to comparisons, maxims, and metaphorical expressions found predominantly in speeches. The challenge to the reader is similar in several respects to that of participatory and punctuated history. First, Thucydides presents speeches in a non-authoritative manner with the goal of engaging the participation of the reader; he generally does not comment in his own voice on the validity of the arguments presented. Second, like punctuated history, the reader must juxtapose and compare different sections of the *History*; that is, part of the reader's participation consists of recalling earlier passages where a similar argument applies to a different situation. A third and related point is that while it is the distant or retrospective reader's experience that especially helps us to appreciate these overarching connections, because much of this figurative language appears in speeches, the immediate, engaged element is never totally absent.

We also encounter a different sort of challenge: the task of comparing local or domestic politics with international (or interstate) relations and conflicts. In both speech and narrative, Thucydides explores the analogy of cities and individuals. This comparative model proposes that a city is like an individual person in significant ways. Indeed, speakers in Thucydides pass with great ease from the private realm to the public, from the small-scale perspective to the large, invoking such ideas as imperial slavery and imperial tyranny. What we know about human beings and human nature at the level of the individual may potentially be transferred to the larger scale interaction between communities, helping us to learn about the motivation and behavior of cities. While the comparison of cities and individuals was not invented by Thucydides, this rhetorical theme—evidently common in late fifth-century Greece—has become a subject for historical analysis in the *History*.

The first part of this chapter surveys eight passages where this comparison is explicitly made. Cities are likened to individuals in both speech and narrative of Thucydides' work. Although, at times, the comparison is merely asserted, Thucydides continues to probe this idea. The second half of this chapter considers the implications of comparing cities with individuals. In part, this model helps the historian and his readers to analyze the past. The actions and motivations of cities may best be understood by analogy with the actions and motivations of individuals. In addition, a possible means for resolving conflict between cities is also suggested. If cities, like individuals, may be thought of as moral agents, this comparison implies that when the interests of cities collide, considerations of justice may be relevant to resolving such conflicts.[1]

The idea that cities are like individuals is first articulated by Archidamus. In book one, the Spartan king asserts the possibility of resolving accusations made both by cities and by individuals.

"ἐγκλήματα μὲν γὰρ **καὶ πόλεων καὶ ἰδιωτῶν** οἷόν τε καταλῦσαι· πόλεμον δὲ ξύμπαντας ἀραμένους ἕνεκα τῶν ἰδίων, ὃν οὐχ ὑπάρχει εἰδέναι καθ᾽ ὅτι χωρήσει, οὐ ῥᾴδιον εὐπρεπῶς θέσθαι."

"For charges—*both by cities and by individuals*—are capable of resolution. But once we have all gone to war—for the sake of certain individual parties—and it is impossible to know how it might turn out, it will not be easy to settle matters honorably. (1.82.6)."[2]

Archidamus is responding to the Corinthians and Athenians who have just spoken. At issue is whether—given recent Athenian actions—Sparta and her allies should go to war. The Corinthians charge that the Athenians have been enslaving Greece (1.68.3–4); the Athenians respond that this gathering has no authority to judge its actions (1.73.1). Archidamus asserts that it is possible to resolve such charges (*enklemata*) made by cities. He goes on to say that if the confederacy under Sparta (*ksumpantas*) initiates war for the benefit of a few individual states (ἕνεκα τῶν ἰδίων— Corinth and Megara, that is), it will become difficult to resolve conflict between the two alliances under Sparta and Athens.

Yet this is only half the equation. Archidamus states that the accusa-tions of both cities and individuals are capable of resolution–καὶ πόλεων καὶ ἰδιωτῶν.[3] That is, he generalizes beyond the immediate circum-stances to express a principle, which works at two levels: the small scale perspective of individuals within a city (what we might call the domestic or intrapolitical realm), and the larger scope of relations between cities (the international sphere). Archidamus initiates the idea that cities and individuals may profitably be compared. Here the point of similarity is the issue of answering accusations, yet Thucydides returns to this comparison in different contexts in order to probe the analogy. Rather than focusing on the debate in book one, I will link this passage to other sections of Thucydides' *History* where the comparison of city and individual is further developed.

Later in the first book, the Corinthians address the cities of the Peloponnesian League, some of whom are reluctant to go to war.

"ὥστε πανταχόθεν καλῶς ὑπάρχον ὑμῖν πολεμεῖν καὶ ἡμῶν κοινῇ τάδε παραινούντων, εἴπερ βεβαιότατον τὸ ταὐτὰ ξυμφέροντα **καὶ πόλεσι καὶ ἰδιώταις** εἶναι, μὴ μέλλετε Ποτειδεάταις τε ποιεῖσθαι τιμωρίαν οὖσι Δωριεῦσι καὶ ὑπὸ Ἰώνων πολιορκουμένοις."

"From every point of view, then, since you have good reason to go to war and we recommend this for our common advantage, if indeed identity of interest is the surest guarantee *for both cities and individuals,* do not hesitate to bring aid to the Potidaeans, who are Dorians and are besieged by Ionians." (1.124.1)

Archidamus had suggested that war would advance the interests of only certain cities (1.82.6 cited above). The Corinthians answer that view here by pointing out that Athenian expansion threatens all cities. There is no safety when a tyrant (that is, Athens) is on the loose.[4] War is in everyone's interest (*koine*) provided that identity of interest (ταὐτὰ ξυμφέροντα) is the surest guarantee for cities and individuals.[5] This shared interest—secu-rity in general and the rescue of Potidaea in particular—is the goal not only of Corinth but of all the Peloponnesian cities. The Corinthians are con-cerned in this context with the advantages of each city, but again a more general principle is put forth. The second half of the equation (the coin-cidence of advantage for individuals) is not explored.

Pericles links cities and individuals at the conclusion of two of his speeches. At the end of book one, Athens considers the prospect of war.

Pericles recognizes the risks, but argues that from such risk comes great honor.

"εἰδέναι δὲ χρὴ ὅτι ἀνάγκη πολεμεῖν, ἢν δὲ ἑκούσιοι μᾶλλον δεχώμεθα, ἧσσον ἐγκεισομένους τοὺς ἐναντίους ἕξομεν, ἔκ τε τῶν μεγίστων κινδύνων ὅτι **καὶ πόλει καὶ ἰδιώτῃ** μέγισται τιμαὶ περιγίγνονται."

"We must recognize that we are forced to go to war—but if we accept more willingly, we will find our opponents less committed—and that from the greatest dangers emerge the greatest honors *for both the city and the individual*." (1.144.3)

This war is not, Pericles insists, of the Athenians' choosing. Yet if the Athenians bravely engage in it, they accomplish two things: dampened enthusiasm on the other side, and—from such danger—the greatest honors, just as individuals win the greatest honors from the greatest dangers.

After the war has begun, in spite of the plague and the devastation of the Attic countryside, Pericles argues that the Athenians must maintain their original policy. It is important for Athens to respond to these afflictions with intelligence and proper action.

"... οἵτινες πρὸς τὰς ξυμφορὰς γνώμῃ μὲν ἥκιστα λυποῦνται, ἔργῳ δὲ μάλιστα ἀντέχουσιν, οὗτοι **καὶ πόλεων καὶ ἰδιωτῶν** κράτιστοί εἰσιν."

" . . . in response to adversity, *those cities and individuals* who are hurt least in judgment and who resist most in action are the strongest." (2.64.6)

The strongest individuals and the strongest cities derive that strength from comparable behavior. These are the final words of Pericles in the *History*.

In his first two books Thucydides asks to what extent a city is like an individual, and in what ways a city behaves as an individual does. We find the idea proposed in these speeches; Thucydides himself makes no definitive judgment. The behavior of the community and of the individual is said to be similar with respect to the arbitration of disputes, the path to security, the winning of honor, and the appropriate response to adversity. We find an almost formulaic phrase, "both of cities and of individuals," signaling the comparison (with variation of number and case ending): καὶ πόλεων καὶ ἰδιωτῶν.

In book 3 the same comparison is introduced in somewhat different language. As they plot rebellion against the Athenians, the Mytilenians approach the Spartans at Olympia. Realizing that their actions may be suspect, they seek common ground with the Spartans by comparing friendship among private citizens (φιλίαν ἰδιώταις) with an alliance between cities (κοινωνίαν ἰδιώταις).

> "εἰδότες οὔτε **φιλίαν ἰδιώταις** βέβαιον γιγνομένην οὔτε **κοινωνίαν πόλεσιν** ἐς οὐδέν, εἰ μὴ μετ᾽ ἀρετῆς δοκούσης ἐς ἀλλήλους γίγνοιντο καὶ τἆλλα ὁμοιότροποι εἶεν."

"We know that *friendship between individuals* and *alliance between cities* can in no way be permanent unless they are formed by those who recognize one another as honorable and are like-minded in other respects." (3.10.1)

In attempting to link themselves to the Peloponnese, the Mytilenians explain that they previously helped the Athenians out of fear, not friendship. They now wish to free, rather than enslave Greece (3.12–13). Due to this shared goal, the Peloponnesians may trust in an alliance with Mytilene, an alliance comparable to friendship among individuals.

After the Athenians put down the Mytilenian revolt, Diodotus argues that appropriate penalties be brought against such rebellious cities. Yet Athens must recognize the inevitability of mistaken judgments, since individuals and states share the same propensity to error.

> "πεφύκασί τε ἅπαντες **καὶ ἰδίᾳ καὶ δημοσίᾳ** ἁμαρτάνειν, καὶ οὐκ ἔστι νόμος ὅστις ἀπείρξει τούτου."

"Everyone *both privately and collectively* tends by nature to make mistakes, and there is no law that will prevent this." (3.45.3)

The phrase καὶ ἰδίᾳ καὶ δημοσίᾳ has various applications: here, the latter term *demosia* evidently refers to the actions of cities such as Mytilene. Diodotus endeavors to offer an explanation not only of why Mytilene behaved as it did, but also of what other subject cities are likely to do.

In chapter 7, I will examine at length Diodotus' argument (3.42–48). Yet it is worth noting at this point that the fullest argument for linking cities and individuals derives from an examination of individual behavior. In the past, Diodotus maintains, individuals broke laws. Yet when harsher penalties were enacted, crimes were still committed. Even with the

strongest possible punishments, individuals would behave without regard
for the likely consequences; indeed, no one risked a crime he did not think
he could succeed with (3.45.1–4). Diodotus begins at the small-scale perspective with how individuals behave. He then applies the same logic to
communities. Cities no less than individuals (καὶ οὐχ ἧσσον τὰς
πόλεις) are affected by unexpected luck (3.45.6). Like individuals, cities
are subject to the enticements of chance, desire, and hope.[6]

When the focus shifts to Sicily in the next decade, Euphemus of
Athens attempts to persuade Camarina not to join Syracuse. It is not
inconsistent, he argues, for the Athenians to enslave the Chalcidians in
Euboea, yet to allow the people of Leontini independence (6.84). With
great candor, he describes Athenian motivation in terms of advantage and
trustworthiness.

"**ἀνδρὶ δὲ τυράννῳ ἢ πόλει ἀρχὴν ἐχούσῃ** οὐδὲν ἄλογον ὅτι ξυμφέρον
οὐδ᾽ οἰκεῖον ὅτι μὴ πιστόν."

"For a man who is a tyrant or for a city possessing an empire, there is nothing
unreasonable that is advantageous; ties of blood mean nothing if they cannot be trusted." (6.85.1)

These principles operate at the level both of the individual (ἀνδρὶ δὲ
τυράννῳ) and of a city (πόλει ἀρχὴν ἐχούσῃ).

These seven passages comparing cities and individuals appear in
speeches. In his own voice, Thucydides expresses this analogy in book
three. In describing the civil war at Corcyra, Thucydides examines the
judgment of cities and individuals in peacetime.

ἐν μὲν γὰρ εἰρήνῃ καὶ ἀγαθοῖς πράγμασιν **αἵ τε πόλεις καὶ οἱ
ἰδιῶται** ἀμείνους τὰς γνώμας ἔχουσιν διὰ τὸ μὴ ἐς ἀκουσίους
ἀνάγκας πίπτειν.

For in peace and prosperity, *both cities and individuals* have judgments that
are better, because they do not meet with pressures over which they have
no control.[7] (3.82.2)

Thucydides goes on to discuss individuals in Corcyra who in the midst of
civil war choose revenge over self-preservation (3.82.7).

From these eight passages we can make several observations. Various
speakers endorse specific action by arguing that honor, power, or security,

for example, are attained in the same ways for both cities and individuals. The principles expressed have two applications: to individuals within a community, and between cities themselves. The comparison could work in either direction; most frequently, however, the impulse appears to be to seek understanding of the international arena (the nature and behavior of cities) by reference to knowledge of the intrapolitical or domestic arena (that of individuals). The half of the equation focusing on the polis is often further developed by indicating the consequences for Corinth, Athens, or Mytilene. Thucydides himself expresses the analogy only once in his own voice, but such repetition indicates the historian's fascination with the comparison. It is generally the case that the "winning" argument makes use of the analogy: of the seven instances, only Archidamus and Euphemus fail to persuade their audiences.

While the second half of the equation concerning individuals must be supplied by the reader, the motivations and behavior of individuals are still of interest to Thucydides. Archidamus has neglected the aspect of individuals' accusations (1.82.6) because he is attempting to deal with the issue at hand, namely, whether the Peloponnesian allies should go to war against Athens. It is possible to deduce the other side: the analogy with war between cities would presumably be civil war (*stasis*) between citizens within a city, and the subsequent difficulty of judging accusations after citizens have been split into warring factions. We have already noted that early in the *History* Thucydides focuses on action and speech performed by cities as political units. This is indicated by his choice to have cities speak as a whole: "the Corinthians say . . . ," "the Thebans say . . . ," "the Plataeans say . . ."[8] Apparently one of Thucydides' early goals is to establish this sort of political history. It is possible to view the city-individual analogy as one productive avenue for understanding cities: speakers—and Thucydides himself—suggest that the behavior of cities may be analogous to that of individuals.[9]

Comparing cities with individuals is surely not original with Thucydides. Not only is it fully developed a generation later in Plato's *Republic* where the search for justice in the individual is sought by constructing justice in the city,[10] but it also underlies the thought and ideas found in a number of Thucydides' contemporaries. In Aristophanes' *Acharnians*, Dicaeopolis proves himself equal to his name: this lone individual (with his household) becomes a "just polis" as he makes a personal peace with Sparta and her allies. Here the smaller acts like the larger, as a man takes on the status of a political community. Knox remarks that when Sophocles' *Antigone* is called *autonomos* (*Antigone* 821), this word is generally applied to cities, that is, to independent communities living under their own laws. The tragedian likens his heroine to a sovereign state by describing her in terms more commonly used to characterize a polis.[11]

In fifth-century Athens, the comparison of cities and individuals undoubtedly became a conventional topos for writers and thinkers, as specific terms and metaphors appropriate to one arena were applied to the other.[12] It is worth emphasizing that it is from a democratic society that this model arises. In fact, there should no surprise that in the rhetoric and literature of Classical Athens the private citizen—*idiotes*—should be elevated to the status of the city itself.[13] By juxtaposing city and individual for his own purposes, Thucydides has given us a model that evolves and expands over the course of the *History*.

I would now like to speculate upon the significance of the city-individual comparison. The consequences are both analytical and practical, but first, let us recall the sort of dynamic set up for the reader. We have already examined how Thucydides praises the capacities of historians and statesmen to see likenesses and to foresee the probable course of events. Thucydides uses the verb *eikazein* and related words, which mean "to compare," and "to make conjectures on the basis of comparisons."[14] In the passages cited above, Thucydides is challenging his reader to engage in this very activity, to compare cities and individuals and to examine the possible points of similarity and difference.

Yet because Thucydides has not presented this claim in an authoritative manner—that is, because all but one of these passages occur in speeches and receive no direct comment by the historian—the reader finds himself in the position of interpreter.[15] We cannot say definitively what Thucydides' own views on the validity of the comparison are. Other than his remark at 3.82.2, Thucydides does not explicitly endorse the idea of comparing cities and individuals—this is left to the reader. Each passage appears in a different speech so that (similar to punctuated history) the reader must recall and juxtapose earlier episodes that employ this memorable catchphrase and ask: What aspects of the city-individual comparison were significant in the earlier sections? What is emphasized in this context? It is the task of the reader (and re-reader) in a retrospective (or more contemplative) mode to construct such overarching connections.

This comparative model is valuable in part for providing an analytic tool for understanding the past. The reader may return to this model as a basis for exploring a multitude of issues. Are cities, like individuals, unified in some sense?[16] Do cities, like individuals, have a particular character?[17] When a city is likened to a tyranny, in what ways is this analogy valid?[18] As a political scientist, Thucydides has offered a potentially productive avenue of approach to these questions. The statements linking city and individual are not, as we have seen, limited to specific contexts. Instead general principles are articulated that seek to link the behavior of individuals within a community to that of cities toward one another. The task of the reader is to examine critically the wide range of proposed similarities, both in the specific context in which they are introduced and with potentially broader application.

One is tempted to make a stronger claim for the importance of this analogy. It could be said that the validity of portraying the city of Athens as a tyrant, for example (discussed in chapter 8), can only be determined after evaluating the city-individual analogy. That is, the analogy of city and individual is of a higher order, which allows such subordinate ideas as a city's character and behavior to be explored at all. This analogy then possesses critical significance, because of the many key inquiries that depend upon it. The next two chapters will explore general principles and metaphors that are tied to the city-individual comparison in a less explicit manner. But first, I turn to the question of justice in international relations.

The reader's assessment of the strength of the city-individual comparison will determine whether the idea of justice in international relations should be considered in a new light. This recurring issue might also be seen as deriving from the city-individual comparison. I would like to sketch out the potential implications of the comparison, both for judging events that occurred during the Peloponnesian War and for its value toward international relations after 404 BCE.

The ethical implications of the comparison arise in the following way. Individuals within communities may settle their disputes by going to court before impartial judges. To the extent that cities are like individuals, the resolution of disputes between cities might follow a path analogous to the resolution of individual disputes. Hornblower has suggested that the city-individual comparison implies that cities may be thought of as moral agents.

> It is passages like this [Archidamus on resolution of charges at 1.82.6] which convince me that it came naturally to Th. to speak of states as moral agents and that he thought that moral judgments could be made about them: he uses the same vocabulary about both, and brackets them as here.[19]

It would follow that the principles prevailing in a domestic court system might apply to the arbitration of conflict between Greek cities. It may then be possible to judge the decisions and actions of cities by the standards of right and wrong as they exist within communities of individuals. If the reader thinks that in international affairs justice is only relevant between equal powers but that the weaker must follow the dictates of the stronger, then the Athenians' action against Melos, for example, might not only be understood but also approved of. If, however, the reader believes that, in fact, cities are like individuals to the extent that they have an obligation to behave fairly and justly toward all other cities, then those same actions would be condemned on moral grounds.[20]

Of course, the idea that cities act justly toward one another is strongly opposed in the *History*, most consistently by the Athenians. Diodotus argues that in domestic affairs citizens may look to justice, but in foreign policy expediency is the only criterion (3.44, 3.46–47).[21] This viewpoint, however, is only a part of the dialogue. Thucydides allows two views to be expressed. Each speech presents a particular perspective; the situation is dynamic. Because the issue is not resolved wholly one way or the other, the reader is forced to consider arguments in different situations and is left to inspect the consequences of following one course of action rather than another. The argument that cities might be constrained by moral values is developed throughout the *History* and is worth pursuing. By building upon the model of city and individual, we may investigate the two sides of the argument about cities' appropriate behavior toward each other and the implied consequences.

Beyond its use for assessing the past, the comparison may suggest a practical application for future conflict. What are the paths toward negotiating international conflict? The war itself leads to a variety of models for interaction between cities. There is the "overseer" model, when the Athenians debate the fate of another city, Mytilene (3.36–49). Athens not only has the final say, but the people who are judged are not allowed to speak. Second, there is third-party arbitration. The Plataeans and the Thebans trade accusations and defend themselves before the Spartan "judges" (*dicastai*–3.52.3), who ultimately fail to render an impartial verdict. As Thucydides says, the decision was determined by Thebes' strategic importance to Sparta (3.68.4). A third possibility is the "street fight" model offered in the Melian Dialogue. Both Athenians and Melians manage to voice their viewpoints, the stronger city attempts to set the rules of discourse, but ultimately neither side changes the other's mind (5.84–116). Not only is each model profoundly disturbing, but none functions as a satisfactory prototype for resolving future disputes between cities.

In accordance with the city-individual analogy, however, conflict between cities might best be resolved by looking at an *intra*-political model, one of arbitration between individuals within a community. The fullest one offered is that of the Athenian *politeia* articulated by Pericles in the Funeral Oration, where it is said that Athenians help victims of injustice, resolve private quarrels in accordance with the law, and—most importantly—all citizens are equal before the law. The Athenian constitution is even called a "model" for others (*paradeigma*–2.37). If we view Athens as a microcosm—a model for all Greece—and if we consider its constitution as an exemplar for some sort of international forum, one comes to see the practical value for future readers in examining the city-individual comparison.[22] If no effective method of resolving disputes is found, the alternative is war. Thucydides offers no blueprint for how cities could peacefully resolve their disputes, nor the means of enforcing such a scheme. But to say that the Peloponnesian War and others like it are inevitable and that arbitration between cities remains impossible is nihilistic and diminishes the enormous potential that underlies Thucydides' exposition.[23]

Again, I think the reader is challenged. What Thucydides has done is to construct a situation in which it is the reader's task to assess the practical possibilities for his or her own time and situation. The city-individual comparison offers a point of reference for considering such a possibility. As Thucydides has structured his narrative, the final act of the Athenians— before war begins—is to call for arbitration where the parties involved are on an equal footing (ἐπὶ ἴσῃ καὶ ὁμοίᾳ–1.145). While it is possible to read Pericles' words as cynically manipulative, the sequence offered by Thucydides indicates that lack of success in the field of arbitration led to the war itself. It may be that Thucydides is suggesting international negotiation in the early fourth century as a peaceful and less disruptive *modus vivendi*.[24]

One of Thucydides' goals in his *History* of the Peloponnesian War is to explore the nature of the polis.[25] As an early political scientist, Thucydides not only considers the leaders of communities, but he also examines the community as a unified whole. He returns time and again to certain key questions, such as how a polis or city behaves, in what sense a city is unified, and whether it is legitimate to speak of the character of a city. That is, there are two aspects of a city: internal politics concerning the affairs of individuals within a community, and external politics that require dealing with other states. Thucydides' comparison of city and individual suggests that these two spheres are not utterly distinct. Certain principles may apply both to the individual within a city and to the polis vis-à-vis other cities. The validity and the application of comparing cities and individuals must be determined by the reader. I have suggested that one value of this comparison is purely analytical: the reader uses the model as a point of departure in seeking to understand why events occurred as they did in the late fifth century.[26]

The possibility of a practical application of the comparison should not be dismissed. Of course, Thucydides tells a story of failed negotiation with war ensuing. Yet his history seeks to do more than help the reader understand the past; the author claims utility for his own work as well (1.22.4).[27] Thucydides emphasizes the upheaval and human suffering involved in the Peloponnesian War, and, given the constancy of human nature, the same sort of conflicts between cities would likely recur. It was in the interests of the Greek cities of the early fourth century (Thucydides' immediate audience) to seek a less violent means of resolving potential disputes. No satisfactory model was found to resolve the international conflict of the Peloponnesian War, yet, as Thucydides says, in peacetime cooler heads prevail (3.82.2).[28]

To those who remain convinced that such hopes constitute pure fantasy, a review of the evidence is worth pondering. First of all, the recurrent analogy itself asks the reader to consider the similarities between cities and individuals in a variety of situations.[29] Second, the ubiquitous use of legal and judicial language throughout the *History* is applied in most cases to cities' interactions with one another.[30] Finally, the conflict between cities has an analogue in the political tension played out within the polis between the competing claims of public and private goals. Pericles argues that citizens must sacrifice private interest for the good of the whole city (2.60–61). It is possible to extend this idea by thinking of Greece as a whole, sharing common interests—at the very least, to avoid the suffering occasioned by war—that overshadow the particular interests of individuals cities.[31]

Indeed, Thucydides begins the history itself with a look at more distant history, when Greeks united for mutual benefit against Troy and later against Persia.[32] Price's recent book, *Thucydides and Internal War*, argues that Thucydides views the Peloponnesian War as a *stasis* ("civil war") between Greeks. At one point, he argues that Thucydides "through his syntax . . . demonstrates that cities are organisms as much afflicted by *stasis* as individuals."[33] This provocative idea leads us back to the comparison's practical value. It is worth pursuing the city-individual comparison for its many possible applications: to understanding how cities act, to judging decisions which took place during the war, and also to approaching the most difficult problem of how cities should behave toward one another in the future. The next two chapters will build on potential extensions of the city-individual comparison, as we examine maxims and metaphors that also apply to both cities and individuals.

7

MAXIMS AND ASSIMILATION IN THE

MYTILENIAN DEBATE

We now turn to maxims (*gnomai*) employed in the speeches of Thucydides. Dover remarks upon their frequency and function: "Most of [Thucydides'] speakers make extensive use of generalizations about the behavior of states and mankind to explain, predict or justify recommendations." Negotiations are made, armies and navies are sent, and the issues of war and peace are determined by arguments based, in part, on generalizations about human motivation and behavior. Of particular interest is how these general rules, once expressed, are applied to specific situations or conflicts. As Wassermann puts it: "this intertwining of the concrete and particular issue with general ideas (and their popularized reflections in catchwords) is one of the characteristics of an age in search for the facts as well as the truth and the laws behind the facts."[1]

Such maxims are founding overwhelmingly in speech. Meister notes that of the approximately two hundred maxims in Thucydides, only two appear in the narrative.[2] This chapter will make a brief survey and then examine the two speeches in the Mytilenian debate (3.37–48) in which maxims build implicitly on the idea of comparing cities and individuals (explored in the previous chapter). We find that speakers, while discussing one relationship (international conflict between cities, for example), turn to the ways in which individuals relate to one another in order to support their arguments. Analysis of maxims will help us to recover the underlying assumptions by which arguments assimilate one realm to another. As we shall see, Diodotus is particularly effective in arguing from the psychology of the individual to the behavior of cities.

MAXIMS AND UNIVERSAL PRINCIPLES

Among generalizations, I would distinguish between maxims and universal principles. I label as "maxims" those proverbial statements drawn from experience or common sense, which describe general modes of behavior or serve as rules of conduct (often introduced with *gar* or *te*).[3] Universal principles also articulate general rules of behavior (they are *also* maxims), but in addition include a reference to something which happens "at all times," "in all situations," or "for all people" (signaled by *aiei* or a form of *pant-*).[4]

For example, in the Corcyrean debate, the Corinthians attempt to dissuade the Athenians from accepting the Corcyreans as allies by arguing that the Athenians will set a precedent for interference in others' internal affairs.[5] A crucial point in the debate is whether war is imminent. The Corinthians assert:

"τό τε γὰρ ξυμφέρον ἐν ᾧ ἄν τις ἐλάχιστα ἁμαρτάνῃ μάλιστα ἕπεται."

"For advantage follows the one who makes the fewest errors of judgment." (1.42.2)

It is hard to argue with such an obvious statement: of course, we think, advantage results from avoiding mistakes. Whereas the Corcyreans attempted to instill fear in the Athenians that war is coming, the Corinthians argue that war is not certain. The implication here is that it would be advantageous to Athens not to miscalculate (ἐλάχιστα ἁμαρτάνῃ) by assuming that war is inevitable.[6]

But the maxim itself is more abstract and has to do with the general connection between miscalculation and advantage. Given the context of the speech, this maxim refers to a decision by the city of Athens, yet it is easy to see this idea as referring to an individual: "He who errs least gains the most," or something of the sort.[7] In fact, such an adage most likely originated with reference to the wise individual; what Thucydides has apparently done is to transfer this maxim to an international context with relevance to the city of Athens and its potential intervention into what the Corinthians regard as their own affair.

Of course, any maxim must first be examined in its specific context. Does the principle apply to this particular argument—in this case, is anticipating the war a miscalculation?[8] But then, to the extent that a more general assertion is expressed, Thucydides suggests application of this maxim upon a broader field of play. Does this maxim illuminate other situations elsewhere in the *History*? Might the connection between mistake and advantage have some sort of general validity that helps to explain previous or later events?[9] Because of maxims' potential to illuminate multiple situations, the reader faces the challenging task of considering its relevance both in its immediate context and elsewhere.[10]

Later in book 1, Archidamus counsels against precipitous engagement. The Spartans should not count on the Athenians making mistakes; rather they should rely upon their own abilities. Archidamus then expresses another maxim.

"πολύ τε διαφέρειν οὐ δεῖ νομίζειν ἄνθρωπον ἀνθρώπου, κράτιστον δὲ εἶναι ὅστις ἐν τοῖς ἀναγκαιοτάτοις παιδεύεται."

"We must not think there is much difference from one man to the next, but the strongest is the one brought up in the severest discipline." (1.84.4)

In introducing the idea of being raised by "severe discipline," Archidamus may be seen as referring to the rigorous training of the Spartans collectively.[11] As was true in 1.42.2 (cited above), the idea easily applies to the individual ("the strongest individual . . .") and likely derives from the plane of an individual's existence. Here the maxim—stated generally—refers to the Spartans' superiority due to their cultural upbringing.[12]

Universal principles differ from regular maxims only by the extent of their application. At the first Peloponnesian Congress, for example, the Athenians describe how they acquired their empire, emphasizing that they have done nothing remarkable or "contrary to human nature" (οὐδ' ἀπὸ τοῦ ἀνθρωπείου τρόπου) by accepting the empire when it was offered (1.76.2). A universal principle is introduced to explain their domination:

"ἀλλ' αἰεὶ καθεστῶτος τὸν ἥσσω ὑπὸ τοῦ δυνατωτέρου κατείργεσθαι."

"But always it has been established that the weaker is held down by the stronger." (1.76.2)

This is not a moral argument; the Athenians' assertion concerns power. In this context, Athens, a city, is stronger than the other cities in the Aegean. Yet as Andrewes argues, "The Athenians' statement at Sparta goes far beyond any topical need to answer the Corinthians or advise the Spartans."[13] In particular, this formulation again has potentially broader application: the Athenians say that it has always been the case that the weaker is subject to the stronger. The form of expression implies that this principle explains past events and presumably will continue to operate in human society. The particular application here is to cities (Athens is stronger than the imperial Aegean cities), but this universal principle could also characterize relations between individuals.

Both Archidamus and Pericles employ universal principles. As the Peloponnesian forces invade Attica in 431 BCE, the Spartan king anticipates the effect that the destruction of crops and property will have on the Athenians.

"πᾶσι γὰρ ἐν τοῖς ὄμμασι καὶ ἐν τῷ παραυτίκα ὁρᾶν πάσχοντάς τι ἄηθες ὀργὴ προσπίπτει."

"For anger falls upon all people seeing suddenly, before their eyes, that they are suffering something unaccustomed." (2.11.7)

Again there are no qualifications here. The rule applies across the board: literally, "anger falls upon all people (*pasi*)." The Spartan king goes on to speculate that it is likely that the Athenians will be provoked to battle, rather than watch their property being destroyed.[14]

Pericles' principle applies to everything that is a part of nature (*physis*). Even though the Athenian empire has the greatest name among men and will leave an undying memorial, its power will not last forever.

"πάντα γὰρ πέφυκε καὶ ἐλασσοῦσθαι."

"For everything must naturally be diminished, too." (2.64.3)

Here Athens, a strong city, is subject to a law that governs all organisms; such a formulation could easily apply to individual persons (who suffer from the physical and mental decline of old age) as well as to other living things.[15]

When speakers invoke a maxim or universal principle, they either begin with a general statement and then turn to the argument at hand, or, alternatively, begin with a specific proposal and then support it with a maxim or universal principle.[16] While there is nothing inherent in such assertions that necessarily leads to the city-individual comparison, due to their general nature maxims and universal principles lend themselves to easy application in multiple situations. Arguments concerning past events and predictions about the future seek specific confirmation (or correction) in the narrative, yet maxims and universal principles—because they are stated so abstractly—may find potential instantiation or contradiction many times in the *History*. Internal and external politics—individual interaction within a community and cities vis-à-vis other cities—are repeatedly probed in Thucydides' work, making it inevitable that such general rules will be invoked in many contexts.

Maxims are documented from the time of Homer and Hesiod. Thucydides' innovation is to apply them so extensively to politics, not only domestic affairs but also international alliance and conflict. That is, Thucydides is engaged in exploring truths that pertain to any human society or interaction.[17] I would point out that in Thucydides' *History* it is not simply a question of a general law on the one hand and a particular situation on the other. What Thucydides has done is to challenge politicians, generals, citizens—and his reader—to determine *when* the general rule applies and *to which particular situations* the rule holds valid. We note that maxims appear overwhelmingly in speeches which generally require critical assessment by the reader; the effect of introducing maxims is to stimulate further engagement from the retrospective reader.

This survey has shown how natural it is in the rhetorical world of Thucydides to articulate ideas with respect to the behavior and motivation of cities. Often it appears that speakers appeal to how individuals react and behave and then elevate those ideas to the level of city-state interaction. It is certainly possible, however, that the comparison may work in either direction. We may be able to learn something of individual encounters by examining the actions of cities—this, of course, anticipates the argument in book 2 of Plato's *Republic* (368–69) where Socrates proposes that it is easier to see justice on the large scale (in the *polis*) than at the level of the individual. While I will not pursue this idea here, we may also learn something about individuals—Pericles, Brasidas, and Alcibiades, for example—from studying cities such as Athens and Sparta.[18]

THE MYTILENIAN DEBATE

We now turn to the maxims and universal principles employed by Cleon and Diodotus in the Mytilenian Debate. As we shall see, Diodotus is extremely skilled at integrating maxims and universal principles into extended sections of his argument. He also employs the parallelism between cities and individuals and explicitly marks out the interconnection between individuals acting within a community and cities involved in international politics. While the focus is on Mytilene, a city that has just revolted from Athens, the underlying argument for Diodotus' policy recommendations is based to a large degree on individual behavior and interaction within a polis. He may begin in the international realm, move to the world of individuals within the polis, and then back to cities: this crossing back and forth is repeated a number of times, thus apparently reinforcing the overall validity of the city-individual comparison itself. In context, Diodotus' arguments apply to the behavior of cities, but because the movement between a community and the international realm is transparent, the two arenas' similarities are clearly demonstrated, even without explicit phrases such as "of both cities and for individuals" (καὶ πόλεων καὶ ἰδιωτῶν).

We start, however, with Cleon. In his speech regarding Mytilene, Cleon employs a number of maxims. He begins with broad political generalizations: a democracy is incapable of ruling others (3.37.1)[19]; an empire is a tyranny which rules over those who plot against it (3.37.2)[20]; a city benefits from following laws which do not change rather than good laws which are not enforced (3.37.3). Cleon then expresses a maxim contrasting lack of learning with cleverness.

"ἀμαθία τε μετὰ σωφροσύνης ὠφελιμώτερον ἢ δεξιότης μετὰ ἀκολασίας, οἵ τε φαυλότεροι τῶν ἀνθρώπων πρὸς τοὺς ξυνετωτέρους ὡς ἐπὶ τὸ πλέον ἄμεινον οἰκοῦσι τὰς πόλεις."

"Ignorance combined with self-control is more beneficial than cleverness combined with intemperance; compared with more intelligent men, the less gifted usually run their cities better." (3.37.3)

Cleon warns of the dangers of intelligent men, who are "wiser than the laws" (3.37.4).[21] The overall thrust of this opening section is to question the need for further discussion regarding the Mytilenian revolt.

The next section deals with punishment: again Cleon introduces a maxim concerning the danger of delaying punishment.

"ὁ γὰρ παθὼν τῷ δράσαντι ἀμβλυτέρᾳ τῇ ὀργῇ ἐπεξέρχεται, ἀμύνεσθαι δὲ τῷ παθεῖν ὅτι ἐγγυτάτω κείμενον ἀντίπαλον ὂν μάλιστα τὴν τιμωρίαν ἀναλαμβάνει."

"For the sufferer [if he waits] proceeds against the perpetrator with a duller passion, but revenge coming as soon as possible after the injury exacts the most equivalent repayment." (3.38.1)

The statement here appears to be made with respect to the individual (ὁ γὰρ παθών), but the application is to Athens, the city which has "suffered" from Mytilene's revolt. Cleon then goes on to castigate Athenians who focus more on the future than what has actually happened (3.38.4). While in section 3.37 Cleon focuses on how decisions are made by Athenians (within their city), section 3.38 examines how another city— Mytilene—has injured Athens, an instance of city-city interaction.[22]

Cleon also uses maxims to support fine verbal distinctions. He insists that what the Mytilenians have done is a "plot" or "insurrection" (*epebouleusan, epanestesan*) against the Athenians rather than merely a "revolt" (*apestesan*).

> "τί ἄλλο οὗτοι ἢ ἐπεβούλευσάν τε καὶ ἐπανέστησαν μᾶλλον ἢ ἀπέστησαν (ἀπόστασις μέν γε τῶν βίαιόν τι πασχόντων ἐστίν)."

> "What else did they do but plot and raise an insurrection against us rather than revolt (for revolt comes when someone suffers violence [which the Mytilenians have not])." (3.39.2)[23]

The reader should note that in the earlier narrative Thucydides has undercut Cleon's distinction, for he uses both the noun and verb forms for "revolt" (*apostasies, aphistamai*) rather than the more insidious "plot" or "insurrection" (*epebouleusan, epanestesan*–3.2.1–3, 3.5.2, 3.35.1, 3.36.2, 3.50.1).[24] Cleon's claim does raise the question, though, of the Mytilenians' prior situation: if they were not suffering violence (βίαιόν τι) from the Athenians, what drove them to revolt (which in turn leads us back to their speech at 3.9–14)? Regarding the Mytilenians' plot, Cleon emphasizes that they *decided* to use violence against the Athenians. If the Mytilenians had no choice, their actions would have been understandable and forgivable. But they acted deliberately.[25]

> "ἄκοντες μὲν γὰρ οὐκ ἔβλαψαν, εἰδότες δὲ ἐπεβούλευσαν· ξύγγνω-μον δ' ἐστὶ τὸ ἀκούσιον."

> "For they did not harm us involuntarily, but knowingly they plotted against us. But [only] what is involuntary is pardonable." (3.40.1)

Indeed, rather than being forced into military resistance, it was the Mytilenians' good fortune (*eupragia*) which led them to such arrogant behavior (*hubris*–3.39.4).[26] Ultimately, according to Cleon, the question comes down to how Athens should respond. The Athenians must not show kindness or flexibility. In discussing the advantages of firm behavior, Cleon argues:

"πέφυκε γὰρ καὶ ἄλλως ἄνθρωπος τὸ μὲν θεραπεῦον ὑπερφρονεῖν, τὸ δὲ μὴ ὑπεῖκον θαυμάζειν."

"For even in other circumstances, man naturally despises conciliation and admires firmness." (3.39.5)

Cleon is concerned with how allies—that is, cities—will respond to Athens' attitude. His argument, however, is based on the idea of "man by nature" (πέφυκε...ἄνθρωπος) as he insists upon unyielding action.[27] These maxims operate on the assumption that familiar adages regarding human behavior are pertinent to the arena of international conflict.

The lesson Cleon draws is that the Athenians must show no weakness. In fact, he lists three things as presenting the greatest peril to empire: compassion, taking pleasure in argument, and "evenhandedness" (epieikeia–3.40.2–3).[28] A triple maxim outlines the appropriate times for each of these responses—none of which applies to the Mytilenians.

"ἔλεός τε γὰρ πρὸς τοὺς ὁμοίους δίκαιος ἀντιδίδοσθαι, καὶ μὴ πρὸς τοὺς οὔτ᾽ ἀντοικτιοῦντας ἐς ἀνάγκης τε καθεστῶτας αἰεὶ πολεμίους· οἵ τε τέρποντες λόγῳ ῥήτορες ἕξουσι καὶ ἐν ἄλλοις ἐλάσσοσιν ἀγῶνα, καὶ μὴ ἐν ᾧ ἡ μὲν πόλις βραχέα ἡσθεῖσα μεγάλα ζημιώσεται, αὐτοὶ δὲ ἐκ τοῦ εὖ εἰπεῖν τὸ παθεῖν εὖ ἀντιλήψονται· καὶ ἡ ἐπιείκεια πρὸς τοὺς μέλλοντας ἐπιτηδείους καὶ τὸ λοιπὸν ἔσεσθαι μᾶλλον δίδοται ἢ πρὸς τοὺς ὁμοίους τε καὶ οὐδὲν ἧσσον πολεμίους ὑπολειπομένους."

"For *compassion* is a just return to one's peers, not to those who feel no pity in return and whose position is both necessarily and permanently hostile; the orators who charm by their words will carry their contest even in less important situations, but not where the city will pay a heavy penalty for *brief enjoyment*, while they themselves will receive fine treatment for fine speaking; and *evenhandedness* is given to those who are sure to be friendly even in the future rather than to those who remain as they were, no less enemies than before." (3.40.3)

The Mytilenians do not even deserve human decency. We might see this triple maxim applying more naturally (or originally) to individuals, yet the reference again is to Athens' attitude toward the city of Mytilene.

Finally, Cleon insists that by punishing all adult Mytilenian males, the Athenians will be acting both justly and to their own advantage (τά τε δίκαια ἐς Μυτιληναίους καὶ τὰ ξύμφορα ἅμα ποιήσετε–3.40.4). Because the Mytilenians are an example of those who have acted without reason (μὴ ξὺν προφάσει) and under no compulsion (μὴ ξὺν ἀνάγκη–3.40.6—another maxim!),[29] the only reasonable solution is to make an example (*paradeigma*) of the Mytilenians to show other allies that whoever revolts will be punished by death (3.40.7). Obviously Cleon's recommendation carried the assembly on the day before; even after revisiting the issue, the vote will be quite close (3.49.1). To a large extent, Cleon's argument gains strength from ten maxims, applied to Athens' interstate conflict with Mytilene.

Diodotus' speech employs maxims and universal principles to recommend that only the leaders of the Mytilenian revolt should be held responsible. Of particular interest is the way in which individual psychology is used to explain the behavior of a city within the Athenian empire. The repeated "transposition" between one realm and the other indicates how tightly the various stages of Diodotus' argument are interwoven.[30] While my focus will be section 3.45, I would first make several observations on the opening paragraphs.

To start, in section 3.42 Diodotus employs a handful of maxims, arguing that careful deliberation—without fear of personal attack—is in the best interests of the city. Indeed, "haste and anger are the two things most opposed [*enantiotata*] to good counsel [*euboulia*]" (3.42.1). Anyone who says arguments are not the "teachers of action" (διδάσκαλοι πραγμάτων) is either stupid or seeking private gain (3.42.2). That is, Diodotus begins by rejecting Cleon's insistence on swift, unreflective action.

Second, Diodotus emphasizes his opposition to Cleon—and his rejection of Cleon's argument that justice and advantage coincide—by repeated use of "opposite" or "contrary" (*enantion*). As we saw above, haste and anger are the two things "most opposed" (*enantiotata*) to good counsel (3.42.1). Section 3.43 begins by pointing out that Athens is "doing exactly the opposite" (ὧν ἡμεῖς τἀναντία δρῶμεν) of the behavior of a wise city seeking advantage. And in section 3.44, Diodotus argues that the dispute is not about injustice but about what is best for the city (οὐ γὰρ περὶ τῆς ἐκείνων ἀδικίας ἡμῖν ὁ ἀγών, εἰ σωφρονοῦμεν, ἀλλὰ περὶ τῆς ἡμετέρας εὐβουλίας); although Cleon claims his policy will lead to fewer revolts in the future, Diodotus maintains the opposing opinion (τἀναντία γιγνώσκω–3.44.2).[31] We will return to the question of justice and advantage; let us now examine Diodotus' intricate argument against the deterrence theory of punishment in 3.45.

I divide paragraph 3.45 into seven sections (A–G). At the end of each passage I indicate the level at which each section is operating: either the argument concerns *individuals* within a polis (the intrapolitical realm); the argument concerns interaction among *cities* at the international realm; or the argument expresses a universal principle that embraces both *cities and individuals*.

A. Diodotus begins at the level of the individual with a discussion of legal systems and the laying down of the death penalty. Such penalties, however, do not eliminate crime.

"ὅμως δὲ τῇ ἐλπίδι ἐπαιρόμενοι κινδυνεύουσι, καὶ οὐδείς πω καταγνοὺς ἑαυτοῦ μὴ περιέσεσθαι τῷ ἐπιβουλεύματι ἦλθεν ἐς τὸ δεινόν."

"Yet people inspired by hope still take risks, and no one has yet faced danger without conviction that he would succeed in the attempt." (3.45.1: *individuals*)

Even when a city employs the death penalty, people—led on by hope (τῇ ἐλπίδι ἐπαιρόμενοι)—engage in risky enterprises.

B. At this point, Diodotus moves to the international issue at hand: the actions of a city trying to revolt.

"πόλις τε ἀφισταμένη τίς πω ἥσσω τῇ δοκήσει ἔχουσα τὴν παρασκευὴν ἢ οἰκείᾳ ἢ ἄλλων ξυμμαχίᾳ τούτῳ ἐπεχείρησειν;"

"And did any city in revolt ever undertake this with what seemed inferior resources, whether its own or through alliance?" (3.45.2: *cities*)

Diodotus begins with legal systems within cities and notes that individuals continue to break laws even against the threat of the death penalty. Then he applies that observation about individuals within a city to the international situation: a city in revolt.

C. This leads to an explicit link between the behavior of cities and of individuals.

"πεφύκασί τε ἅπαντες **καὶ ἰδίᾳ καὶ δημοσίᾳ** ἁμαρτάνειν, καὶ οὐκ ἔστι
νόμος ὅστις ἀπείρξει τούτου, ἐπεὶ διεξεληλύθασί γε διὰ πασῶν τῶν
ζημιῶν οἱ ἄνθρωποι προστιθέντες, εἴ πως ἧσσον ἀδικοῖντο ὑπὸ τῶν
κακούργων."

"Everyone *both individually and collectively* tend by nature to make mistakes,
and there is no law that will prevent this, since people have tried every
kind of punishment in succession, on the chance of lessening their injuries
at the hands of criminals." (3.45.3: **cities and individuals**)

Obviously in context, the issue would be a city—Mytilene—"making a
mistake" (*hamartanein*). But this statement, expressed as a universal principle, applies to both individuals and cities (ἅπαντες καὶ ἰδίᾳ καὶ
δημοσίᾳ). Human nature explains this tendency to err, manifesting itself
at the level both of the individual and of the community.[32]

D. The argument now returns to individuals within a polis, exploring
factors that argue against the deterrence of capital punishment.

"καὶ εἰκὸς τὸ πάλαι τῶν μεγίστων ἀδικημάτων μαλακωτέρας
κεῖσθαι αὐτάς, παραβαινομένων δὲ τῷ χρόνῳ ἐς τὸν θάνατον αἱ
πολλαὶ ἀνήκουσιν· καὶ τοῦτο ὅμως παραβαίνεται. ἢ τοίνυν
δεινότερόν τι τούτου δέος εὑρετέον ἐστὶν ἢ τόδε γε οὐδὲν ἐπίσχει,
ἀλλ᾽ ἡ μὲν πενία ἀνάγκῃ τὴν τόλμαν παρέχουσα, ἡ δ᾽ ἐξουσία ὕβρει
τὴν πλεονεξίαν καὶ φρονήματι, αἱ δ᾽ ἄλλαι ξυντυχίαι ὀργῇ τῶν
ἀνθρώπων ὡς ἑκάστη τις κατέχεται ὑπ᾽ ἀνηκέστου τινὸς κρείσσον-
τος ἐξάγουσιν ἐς τοὺς κινδύνους."

"Indeed, it is likely that long ago milder punishments were inflicted for the
greatest crimes, but when the laws were broken in the course of time, there
were many elevations to the death penalty. Yet this, too, was disregarded.
Either something still more frightening than this [the death penalty] must
be discovered or there is this [the death penalty], which is no restraint at
all; but while poverty brings about boldness through compulsion, abundance brings about ambition through insolence and pride, and other
chance circumstances due to human passion (depending on how each of
these is ruled by some irresistible force) will lead men into danger."
(3.45.3–4: **individuals**)

Diodotus speculates about the past. He surmises that long ago lighter punishments were likely (*eikos*) meted out for the greatest crimes; punish-

ments then became progressively harsher, eventually leading to the death penalty. Yet crimes were still committed, because of the effects of poverty, insolence, and the unpredictable effects of passion. These emotional and material factors refer most directly to individuals who break the law without regard for the death penalty.[33]

E. Next Diodotus forcefully strengthens the link between section D concerning individual criminals and the issue at hand—cities revolting—by invoking a second universal principle.

> "ἥ τε ἐλπὶς καὶ ὁ ἔρως ἐπὶ παντί, ὁ μὲν ἡγούμενος, ἡ δ᾽ ἐφεπομένη, καὶ ἡ μὲν τὴν ἐπιβουλὴν ἐκφροντίζων, ἡ δὲ τὴν εὐπορίαν τῆς τύχης ὑποτιθεῖσα, πλεῖστα βλάπτουσι, καὶ ὄντα ἀφανῆ κρείσσω ἐστὶ τῶν ὁρωμένων δεινῶν."

> "*In all situations* [ἐπὶ παντί], hope and desire—the one leading while the other follows, the one thinking up the scheme while the other holds out the ready assistance of fortune—do the greatest damage which, although invisible, is still more powerful than visible dangers." (3.45.5: **cities and individuals**)

Diodotus states that hope and desire are influential "in all situations" (ἐπὶ παντί).[34] Just as an individual—not expecting to be caught—may hope for success, so also a city (specifically Mytilene) desiring freedom may revolt; both are impelled by the same factors.[35] As always, such general statements trigger associations with passages elsewhere in the *History*. The idea of hope (*elpis*) may lead us back to the Mytilenians early in this book: they had an expectation that the time was right to break away due to Athenians suffering from the plague and the promised aid from the Spartan navy (3.13.3); later they are hopeful that they need not engage in negotiations with the Athenians (3.25.2) although they are soon forced to come to terms (3.27.1).[36] My primary goal, however, is to explore Diodotus' method of argumentation that builds on the city-individual comparison.

F. Diodotus again explicitly links the intrapolitical and international realms.

> "καὶ ἡ τύχη ἐπ᾽ αὐτοῖς οὐδὲν ἔλασσον ξυμβάλλεται ἐς τὸ ἐπαίρειν· ἀδοκήτως γὰρ ἔστιν ὅτε παρισταμένη καὶ ἐκ τῶν ὑποδεεστέρων τινὰ προάγει, καὶ οὐχ ἧσσον τὰς πόλεις, ὅσῳ περὶ τῶν μεγίστων τε, ἐλευθερίας ἢ ἄλλων ἀρχῆς."

"And on top of these, fortune plays no less a part in creating confidence; for sometimes she comes unexpectedly to one's aid, and leads men to take risks even in unfavorable circumstances, *and this is no less true for cities*, inasmuch as they are playing for the highest stakes—either for freedom or for the power over others." (3.45.6: **cities and individuals**)

The psychological portrait that Diodotus has sketched out regarding the bold optimism of individuals is now transposed to cities that seek freedom or power over others.[37]

G. Diodotus concludes this section with a look at individuals and a broad statement about human nature, the strength of laws, and prevention.

"καὶ μετὰ πάντων ἕκαστος ἀλογίστως ἐπὶ πλέον τι αὐτὸν ἐδόξασεν. ἁπλῶς τε ἀδύνατον καὶ πολλῆς εὐηθείας, ὅστις οἴεται τῆς ἀνθρωπείας φύσεως ὁρμωμένης προθύμως τι πρᾶξαι ἀποτροπήν τινα ἔχειν ἢ νόμων ἰσχύι ἢ ἄλλῳ τῳ δεινῷ."

"And each individual, when acting with the rest of a community, irrationally believes that his own powers are somewhat greater. Put simply, it is impossible and most simple-minded if anyone believes that when human nature is fervently set upon a certain course, there is some deterrent to stop it by force of law or any other threat." (3.45.6–7: **individuals**)

Diodotus' sophisticated sequence of thought has crossed the polis-individual boundary time and again. To understand the motivation and behavior of cities such as Mytilene within the Athenian empire, he appeals to ideas concerning individual motivation, especially those factors that lead to reckless criminal activity. In Diodotus' argument, poverty, hope, and desire affect not only the individual but also cities.

Diodotus then applies his conclusions more broadly to Athens' concern for the future: other allies who may revolt (τοῖς ἀποστᾶσιν).[38]

"Οὔκουν χρὴ οὔτε τοῦ θανάτου τῇ ζημίᾳ ὡς ἐχεγγύῳ πιστεύσαντας χεῖρον βουλεύσασθαι οὔτε ἀνέλπιστον καταστῆσαι τοῖς ἀποστᾶσιν ὡς οὐκ ἔσται μεταγνῶναι καὶ ὅτι ἐν βραχυτάτῳ τὴν ἁμαρτίαν καταλῦσαι."

"Therefore, we must neither choose inferior policies by trusting in the death penalty as a safeguard nor make it hopeless for rebels to have any

possibility of repenting and atoning for the mistake as soon as possible."
(3.46.1)

Indeed, if the Athenians are concerned about other cities revolting from their imperial control, the time to act is not after the revolt but before these cities make such an attempt (3.46.6). Again, the argument used to recommend Athenian foreign policy originates at the level of an individual's behavior understood from a psychological point of view. These conclusions are then applied to Athens' relations with other cities.[39]

The whole question of collective psychology—especially the emotions of the group or community—is naturally relevant to this inquiry. Groups of citizens are said to experience feelings, such as hope, fear, or anger.[40] The idea that a city—or an entire citizen body—could feel fear, for example, is of critical importance, since fear is cited as one of the motives which led the Athenians to acquire their empire, and (along with Athenian growth) was a critical factor in causing the Peloponnesian war itself (1.23.6, 1.76.2, 1.88).[41] We note that two of these statements (1.23.6, 1.88) are made in Thucydides' own voice: not only speakers, but also the historian himself attributes emotions to entire communities.

Yet while the psychology of cities and individuals may be similar, the moral situation is not comparable, at least according to Diodotus' argument. Several striking passages concerning justice reject similarities between the domestic (or intrapolitical) and international realms. Determining appropriate action toward Mytilene is not, Diodotus asserts, like judging an individual in a lawcourt; the goal is to find Athenian advantage.[42]

"ἡμεῖς δὲ οὐ δικαζόμεθα πρὸς αὐτούς, ὥστε τῶν δικαίων δεῖν, ἀλλὰ βουλευόμεθα περὶ αὐτῶν, ὅπως χρησίμως ἕξουσι."

"But we are not judging them in court to get justice, but deliberating as to how they might be useful to us." (3.44.4)

Although Diodotus argues that psychological factors influencing an individual are relevant to understanding cities, *with respect to morality* Athens' relationship with Mytilene is not wholly analogous to individual interaction within a city. Even if the Mytilenians have committed injustice, the Athenians may do better to pretend they do not notice it.[43] That is, Diodotus maintains that the Athenians cannot do what Cleon claims:

"καὶ τὸ Κλέωνος τὸ αὐτὸ δίκαιον καὶ ξύμφορον τῆς τιμωρίας οὐχ εὑρίσκεται ἐν αὐτῷ δυνατὸν ὂν ἅμα γίγνεσθαι."

"And Cleon's punishment in which justice and expediency are one and the same, both at the same time, is exposed as an impossible combination." (3.47.5)

Diodotus is not wholly consistent on the question of international justice. While clearly insisting that the Athenians should be guided by expediency rather than justice, he does advocate that Paches send only the guilty (*adikountas*) to Athens to be judged and let the others go (3.48.1). Why?[44] Because even Diodotus acknowledges that justice may be relevant to foreign policy—or at least to other cities' perception of Athenian action against Mytilene. After remarking that Athens enjoys the favor of the people (*demos*) in imperial cities (3.47.2), Diodotus hypothesizes that if Athens were to destroy the *demos* of Mytilene as well—which initially took no part in the revolt—the Athenians would commit an injustice:

"ἀδικήσετε τοὺς εὐεργέτας κτείνοντες."

"In killing your benefactors you will commit an injustice." (3.47.3)

At this point Diodotus employs language from a polis-based system of justice where guilt, innocence, free will, and justice are significant factors.[45] If all adult males in Mytilene are executed, the popular elements in other cities would be alienated, because the same punishment has been applied equally to guilty and innocent (τὴν αὐτὴν ζημίαν τοῖς τε ἀδικοῦσιν ὁμοίως κεῖσθαι καὶ τοῖς μή–3.47.3). At the very least, the perception of unjust punishment—both guilty and innocent suffering the same fate—will backfire with respect to attitudes on Athens' foreign policy.[46] To this extent, even Diodotus acknowledges that moral issues should influence how one city behaves toward another. Morality is therefore not inapplicable or nonsensical in international relations; in certain instances, however, a city's advantage should be the overriding factor. While justice is significant in dealing with individuals within a city, in international conflict moral obligations between two cities are of secondary importance.

Diodotus does not slavishly follow a formula. He makes fine distinctions between motive, action, and advantage on the one hand and the more complex issue of justice between cities on the other. Ostwald has called Diodotus' speech "one of the most profound and important speeches in

Thucydides' *History*."[47] As we saw in chapter 6, while other speeches articulate the city-individual analogy, both halves of the equation are generally not developed. The implications of Diodotus' speech are significant in
large part because the city-individual comparison is so extensively pursued, covering areas of deliberation, criminal behavior, and psychology at
both levels.

The issue of international justice was addressed briefly in the previous
chapter.[48] Without attempting to resolve this issue, it can be said that
Diodotus offers a sophisticated, nuanced approach to this problem.
Elsewhere we encounter differing views: the Athenians deny the relevance of justice (e.g., 1.73–77, 5.89, 5.107), while the Corinthians and
Plataeans argue its importance (e.g., 1.68, 3.53–59). Rather than seek
consistency, we may do better to note the tensions that Thucydides has created concerning the recurrent issue of morality in international politics. It
is striking that within Diodotus' single speech we receive such contradictory signals.

Conclusion

Thucydides makes the bold move of speaking of the collective—this has
rightly been called "the invention of political history," the course of
human events told in terms of the communities involved.[49] In ways somewhat evocative of the atomist Democritus, Thucydides moves effectively
between the microcosm and the macrocosm.[50] Ideas, terms, and descriptions that originally derive from the situation and behavior of an individual are transferred to the polis. Indeed, the city-individual comparison
manifests itself most strikingly at the rhetorical plane in speeches. The city
has been assimilated to multiple features of the individual, including motivation, behavior, and character.[51]

The Mytilenian debate is significant for many reasons; I will mention
three. First, it makes extensive use of maxims with both local and more distant application; second, in many cases these maxims derive—directly or
indirectly—from city-individual analogy; and third, it anticipates issues
(responsibility, punishment, and what actually motivates a city) which are
addressed in the Plataean debate (chapter 4).

I suggest we think of an overarching idea: a city thought and spoken of
in similar ways as an individual. Each comparison or maxim which applies
to cities is based on this premise to some degree. As we shall see in chapter 8, even metaphors (such as "the tyrant-city") are supported by this larg-

er idea and operate on the assumption that it is a legitimate and productive way of thinking. We should, of course, beware of oversimplification. Thucydides presents a complex world where it is impossible to reduce all that is said and done to a system. Certain manifestations of the city-individual comparison derive from the household (slavery, for example); others from the more public interaction of citizens (such as bringing charges against someone).[52] Still it needs to be recognized that the singular comparison of cities and individuals is a part of the rhetorical world of Thucydides and such discourse provides insight into the most difficult of political problems: the motivation and behavior of cities.

In Thucydides' *History*, speakers begin with the behavior and motivation of an individual and apply that knowledge to foreign affairs. The task of the reader is to determine where the application remains valid, where it illuminates an obscure action, and when it oversimplifies a more complex situation. Thucydides does not regularly expand upon an argument in explicit terms or answer such questions overtly. Rather his speakers introduce maxims and universal principles, as Thucydides presents the reader with the task of applying these arguments both to the immediate context and to other situations throughout the *History*.[53] The value of studying the Mytilenian debate is that we are able to appreciate how wide-ranging and integral the city-individual comparison remains. We might even say that Thucydides uses Diodotus' speech to show the reader how such an argument comparing cities and individuals might work in some detail. Diodotus' speech—and the other examples cited above—do not necessarily imply that Thucydides believes such rhetorical claims are legitimate in every case. Sometimes undoubtedly Thucydides finds himself in agreement, at other times he may distance himself. It is clear, though, that he is fascinated with the possibility of understanding a city by reference to the concerns, motivations, actions—and psychology—of the individual.[54]

8

ATHENS THE TYRANT-CITY AND THE
FUNCTION OF POLITICAL METAPHOR

Chapter 6 explored the explicitly stated city-individual comparison. Chapter 7 demonstrated how the city-individual analogy might be applied to a specific action in foreign policy (Diodotus' proposal). In neither case do we think of Thucydides unreservedly endorsing these comparative links; instead, he introduces them in speeches and offers a view of possible similarities for the reader's consideration. This chapter examines metaphors and other comparative language. Like maxims, many of Thucydides' metaphors and comparative expressions derive to some degree from the city-individual analogy. And, like maxims, most of this figurative language appears in speech rather than narrative. I will limit my examination to metaphors and comparative language from the first two books of the *History* (esp. 1.1–2.65) with a focus on domestic and international politics.

Thucydides' portrait of the city of Athens consists in part of at least eleven political metaphors and comparisons. For example, Athens is described as a tyrant and an enslaver. Such metaphorical language may at first glance appear simplistic, yet Thucydides evidently has chosen to offer such metaphors for a number of purposes. First, these expressions may reflect the political rhetoric of the time. Regarding the extremely difficult question of the historicity of Thucydides' speeches, I do not think there is one answer for every speech. Some speeches undoubtedly reproduce some of the actual language and arguments used on particular historical occasions. Bosworth has recently argued that of all the speeches in the *History*, the Funeral Oration of Pericles would have been heard by the most Athenians and was the one most likely heard by Thucydides himself.[1] This raises the question: might Thucydides' version be pretty close to what Pericles actually said? Or could it at least echo many of the sentiments of the great statesman? Pericles' expressions were certainly memorable and it is at least plausible that Thucydides would preserve his more remarkable metaphors and figures.[2] In addition, interesting work by Tompkins and Debnar has examined the different styles used to represent different figures and cities when they make speeches.[3] I do not expect to resolve this issue with this brief discussion. But given Thucydides' claim to "hold as close as possible to the overall sense of what was actually said" (1.22.2), the formulations examined here most likely reflect to some degree the political rhetoric that was current at the time (and we can only deal with likelihood in questions such as these).

A second reason for Thucydides' introduction of metaphorical and figurative language may be to unify the complex action of the *History* and guide the challenging task of analysis performed by the reader. That is, the use of metaphor may provide a basis for historical understanding. Given all the detail in Thucydides' work—the at-times bewildering recounting of armament, strategy, geography, alliance, individual personality, etc.—these political metaphors offer an anchor for the reader's understanding of the character and behavior of Athens and, more broadly, of the events of the Peloponnesian War.[4] Ultimately these metaphors may lead us to a more profound understanding of politics and the ways in which domestic and international politics might illuminate each other.

A third goal may be that such language offers an explicit invitation for Thucydides' audience to link and juxtapose various sections of the *History*. The reader is invited to compare Athens, the tyrant-city—which appears in speech—with historical tyrants referred to in the narrative. Thucydides very often leaves implicit possible connections and reverberations between early and later passages and between speech and narrative. We have seen, though, that with the city-individual comparison, Thucydides employed several times what almost amounts to a formulaic expression (καὶ πόλεων καὶ ἰδιωτῶν —"of both cities and of individuals") to help the reader easily recognize the recurring idea. Connections and parallelism between argument and conflict are sometimes explicit, but more often they lie implicit. I would argue that political metaphors such as "Athens the tyrant-city" offer explicit comparisons for the reader to examine and assess.[5] One of Thucydides' motivations for introducing such metaphors may be to train the reader in juxtaposition, comparison, and extrapolation—the activity of *eikazein*.[6] My goal is to provide a context for understanding not only the metaphor of the tyrant-city in Thucydides but also the function of such metaphorical and comparative language more broadly.

Let me briefly characterize Thucydides' metaphors and related comparisons. These formulations are political in the sense that they describe the city of Athens either with respect to internal politics (among citizens within Athens) or interstate politics (Athens' relations with other cities). In 1.1–2.65, the city of Athens is described as a tyrant, a slave-master, and an education, for example. To state the obvious, by portraying Athens in this way, these metaphors set up comparisons employing strong—indeed striking and memorable—language. The comparative aspect of these metaphors invites juxtaposition and comparison between the city of Athens and other familiar facts of life: tyranny, slavery, educating young men, and so on. Drawing on the insights of Lakoff and Johnson, this chapter argues that the obvious discrepancies between, say, imperial tyranny and individual tyrants prove a point: because there is no comprehensive correspondence between Athens and actual tyrants, Thucydides signals the reader that such formulations may offer some insight into political motivation and action, but such metaphors should not be accepted whole-sale.[7] Indeed, it is in the nature of metaphor to suggest only partial corre-spondences. This does not, however, diminish their power to illuminate: in fact, it may well be this partial correspondence that gives Thucydides' political models their dynamism.

Many of these metaphors are introduced only in speeches. This fact raises more questions for Thucydides' readers. What is the relative status of speech as opposed to narrative? Should we think of narrative as rela-tively more authoritative or dependable than what is said in speeches? Does an idea in speech ever reflect Thucydides' own opinion? These are difficult issues and, as we have already seen, Thucydides' narrative is not always authoritative—at times, it may be used to manipulate the reader's reactions.[8] Here, too, there is no single answer for all speech and all nar-rative, a narrative that contains quite different types of presentation. At times, the narrative may confirm what is said in speech; elsewhere it may provide an illustration of a general idea; in some cases, the narrative appears to correct what is claimed by making clear how inaccurate a par-ticular statement or prediction has been.[9] There remains a tension between what is said in speech and what is described as happening in the narrative. For the following analysis, it is significant that political metaphors appear predominantly in speeches; this may be seen as an invitation to the reader to become actively engaged in exploring both the comparison expressed within the speech itself and also in examining those links between what is said in the speech and what is presented in the narrative.

Athens as Tyrant-City

I begin with the metaphor of Athens as tyrant-city, a model introduced five
times in speeches. At the Peloponnesian Congress where the metaphor is
first proposed, the Corinthians twice label Athens a "tyrant-city."[10] They
warn that, without a united front, Athens will conquer Greece city by city
(1.122.2). Their ancestors freed Greece, yet now such freedom is in jeop-
ardy.

"τύραννον δὲ ἐῶμεν ἐγκαθεστάναι πόλιν, τοὺς δ' ἐν μιᾷ μονάρχους
ἀξιοῦμεν καταλύειν."

"We are allowing the establishment of a tyrant-city, yet we believe that
monarchy in a single city should be put down." (1.122.3)

The Corinthians argue that Sparta's opposition to rule by one man over a
city should extend to rejecting one city's domination of many cities. The
comparison between the two political realms is obvious: in internal politics the Spartans oppose tyranny, yet in international politics they apparently will allow a "tyrant-city" to dominate.[11] This is the immediate
relevance of the model. At the close of their speech, the Corinthians
reassert the risk Athens poses to all Greeks. War against Athens, they
argue, is in the common interest of all (1.124.1), for only by going to war
now will they enjoy future security:

"καὶ τὴν καθεστηκυῖαν ἐν τῇ Ἑλλάδι πόλιν τύραννον ἡγησάμενοι ἐπὶ
πᾶσιν ὁμοίως καθεστάναι, ὥστε τῶν μὲν ἤδη ἄρχειν, τῶν δὲ δια-
νοεῖσθαι, παραστησώμεθα ἐπελθόντες, καὶ αὐτοί τε ἀκινδύνως
τὸ λοιπὸν οἰκῶμεν καὶ τοὺς νῦν δεδουλωμένους Ἕλληνας
ἐλευθερώσωμεν."

"And understanding that a tyrant-city has been established in Greece
against all alike, ruling over some already and plotting against others, let
us attack and overthrow it, and let us live in security for the future and free
those Greeks now enslaved." (1.124.3)

In this speech—when Athens is viewed from the "outside" by non-
Athenians (in this case, the Corinthians)—the Athens-as-tyrant
metaphor is used to capture particular facets of tyranny: danger, threat to
freedom, expansionist tendencies, and the "enslavement" of others.

The city-as-tyrant metaphor recurs in the third speech of Pericles, who emphasizes the danger posed to Athens by subject allies. In admitting that the empire is "like a tyranny," Pericles qualifies the comparison, by asserting not identity, but likeness.

"ὡς τυραννίδα γὰρ ἤδη ἔχετε αὐτήν, ἣν λαβεῖν μὲν ἄδικον δοκεῖ εἶναι, ἀφεῖναι δὲ ἐπικίνδυνον."

"For you now hold your empire like a tyranny, that seems unjust to acquire, but to let it go is dangerous." (2.63.2)

Here Pericles notes two similarities between empire and tyranny. In this context—that of endorsing a continuation of Athens' imperial strategy— Pericles acknowledges both moral and strategic considerations, yet he stresses the risk associated with abandoning Athenian control over other cities.[12]

In the Mytilenian debate Cleon returns to the danger Athens faces from its allies and asserts an equivalency between tyranny and empire:

"οὐ σκοποῦντες ὅτι τυραννίδα ἔχετε τὴν ἀρχὴν καὶ **πρὸς ἐπιβουλεύοντας αὐτοὺς καὶ ἄκοντας ἀρχομένους**, οἳ οὐκ ἐξ ὧν ἂν χαρίζησθε βλαπτόμενοι **αὐτοὶ ἀκροῶνται ὑμῶν**, ἀλλ᾽ **ἐς ὧν ἂν ἰσχύι** μᾶλλον ἢ τῇ ἐκείνων εὐνοίᾳ **περιγένησθε**."

"You do not see that the empire you possess is a tyranny over *those who plot against us and who are ruled unwillingly*, whose *obedience* does not result from the favors you bestow to your detriment, but *from the superiority you enjoy by your own strength* rather than their goodwill." (3.37.2)

At issue here once again is the relationship between subject allies and Athens. Cleon argues that obedience comes from Athenian strength, not from their allies' loyalty—they are ruled "unwillingly" (*akontes*). He then discusses how best to deal with revolt.[13] The fifth instance of the comparison, expressed somewhat differently, occurs when Euphemus addresses the Camarinians on the connection between logic and imperial advantage.

"ἀνδρὶ δὲ τυράννῳ ἢ πόλει ἀρχὴν ἐχούσῃ οὐδὲν ἄλογον ὅτι ξυμφέρον οὐδ᾽ οἰκεῖον ὅτι μὴ πιστόν· πρὸς ἕκαστα δὲ δεῖ ἢ ἐχθρὸν ἢ φίλον μετὰ καιροῦ γίγνεσθαι."

"For a man who is a tyrant or a city possessing an empire, there is nothing irrational that is advantageous, ties of blood mean nothing if they cannot be trusted, as it is necessary in each situation to become friend or foe according to the circumstances." (6.85.1)

Euphemus specifically links the individual tyrant to a city holding an empire with respect to motivation: seeking advantage has priority over previous alliances (or "friendships"). When the empire is viewed as a tyranny from "within"—by the Athenians themselves—we find an acknowledgment that the empire may be unjust; it is dangerous to relinquish power; the Athenians rule over unwilling subjects; and their chief motivation is advantage.[14]

How would Thucydides' contemporaries have understood the city-as-tyrant metaphor? Clearly, a Greek ca. 400 BCE would be able to juxtapose the idea of a city-as-tyrant with experience of historical tyrants from personal memory, family stories, or common knowledge.[15] Yet Thucydides has made it clear that he is critical of many such preconceptions (see 1.20, 6.54.2, for example). Another option available to Thucydides' readers is to compare the city-as-tyrant metaphor which appears in speeches with Thucydides' narrative discussion of actual tyrants. Thucydides has chosen to return repeatedly to both imperial and individual tyranny in various contexts. In fact, it is striking that many of the retrospective passages feature tyranny, including those on prehistory (the Archaeology and Sicily—1.13–20, 6.1–5), the purification of Delos (3.104), and the Peisistratids in book 6 (6.53–59).[16] Even by limiting our analysis to Thucydides' discussion of archaic tyranny in the Archaeology, we learn that certain distinctive aspects of actual tyrannies in part coincide with—and in part differ from—the metaphorical tyrant-city of Athens.[17]

When Thucydides first discusses tyranny in his own voice, we encounter a power matrix built on ships, tribute, and power (1.13). Polycrates, the tyrant of Samos, "on the strength of his navy brought other islands under his control" (1.13.6).[18] In addition, archaic tyranny is associated with a lack of joint ventures (1.15.2–1.17)[19]; we also hear of Spartan opposition to tyranny (1.18.1). There are obvious similarities based on correspondences between Thucydides' description of archaic tyrants and the fifth-century Athenian empire itself which has been metaphorically labeled a tyranny: sea power, tribute, and control of previously autonomous cities.[20]

Yet the contrasts are equally striking.[21] Actual tyrants are characterized as follows:

"τύραννοί τε ὅσοι ἦσαν ἐν ταῖς Ἑλληνικαῖς πόλεσι, τὸ ἐφ᾽ ἑαυτῶν μόνον προορώμενοι ἔς τε τὸ σῶμα καὶ ἐς τὸν ἴδιον οἶκον αὔξειν δι᾽ ἀσφαλείας ὅσον ἐδύνατο μάλιστα τὰς πόλεις ᾤκουν, ἐπράχθη δὲ οὐδὲν ἀπ᾽ αὐτῶν ἔργον ἀξιόλογον, εἰ μὴ εἴ τι πρὸς περιοίκους τοὺς αὐτῶν ἑκάστοις."

"The tyrants in the Greek cities, who looked no further than the personal interests of individual well-being and the enrichment of their households, ran their cities with the maximum security, and accomplished nothing impressive except against neighboring peoples." (1.17)

These tyrants' goals are personal comfort and safety; they avoided risk and accomplished "nothing impressive" (οὐδὲν . . . ἀξιόλογον). On these points, of course, we find a sharp contrast to the Athenian empire's *polypragmosyne*, risky wide-ranging adventures, and enduring monuments.[22]

As the metaphor refracts, we are drawn in different directions. Thucydides has chosen to return repeatedly to both imperial and individual tyranny in various contexts—in both speech and narrative—yet he never offers his own definitive judgment. Thucydides' presentation raises the question: was Athens' empire like a tyranny? The answer is at best a qualified "yes," for (as noted above) not every aspect of the "tyranny" of the Athenian empire coincides with the qualities and habits of historical tyrants.[23] Indeed, it could be said that Thucydides has included *sufficient* detail in his narrative about actual tyrants to make it clear that there is no comprehensive, one-to-one correspondence between metaphorical and actual tyranny. Commenting on these significant contrasts, Connor concludes that Thucydides' account "seems to discourage an unqualified acceptance of the parallelism between tyrannies and the Athenian empire. . . . The contrasts are striking ones, and quite likely to be deliberate."[24] Thucydides has moved the interpretive onus to the reader, who must determine in what respects and to what degree this and other such comparisons are valid and appropriate.[25]

In their analysis of metaphor, Lakoff and Johnson offer an illuminating perspective on Thucydides and his frequent metaphors. First, according to Lakoff and Johnson: "The essence of metaphor is understanding and experiencing one kind of thing in terms of another."[26] The term "tyrant" originally designates a single ruler of a certain type within a city-state, that is, a situation concerning internal politics.[27] It is not immediately obvious that we think of tyranny when considering Athenian foreign policy. These two situations—a tyrant within a city and Athens' relations with other cities—are dissimilar in many ways, as already noted. What the metaphor suggests is that in spite of those differences, there may exist similarities—often at a different plane of interaction (between cities rather than between individuals)—which illuminate our understanding.[28] Lakoff and Johnson observe that "there is directionality in metaphor, that is, that we understand one concept in terms of another."[29] The Athens-as-tyrant model is designed to make us think of international relations between cities as analogous to certain aspects of internal politics, such as unwilling subjects who may plot against the tyrant but also respect the tyrant's strength.

Second, metaphors are built out of the cultural context.[30] It should not be surprising that speakers in Thucydides' *History* use models which draw on experience familiar to the Greeks of the fifth century—tyranny, slavery, and other relationships—to debate domestic politics and international relations.

Third, "metaphorical structuring . . . is partial, not total."[31] This means that because it is in the nature of metaphor to agree with its referent *in only certain respects,* there will be significant differences between the two situations being compared. Lakoff and Johnson remind us that if the similarity between the metaphor and the reality were total, "one concept [the city of Athens, in this case] would actually *be* the other [a tyrant], not merely be understood in terms of it."[32] Yet even if we recognize that imperial tyranny and archaic tyrants are not identical, the differences between them do not necessarily mean that Thucydides wholly rejects the metaphor itself. In fact, this may be the wrong way of describing Thucydides' purpose. It is not so much a question of whether Thucydides endorses the idea of Athens-as-tyrant; what he has done is deliberately introduce in speeches a recurrent phrase applied to Athens and its empire. Yet the narrative makes clear that Athens does not coincide with every aspect of historical tyranny. By introducing such metaphors, Thucydides invites the reader to discover how and to what degree this metaphor becomes valuable in understanding the political situation. Because metaphors work only partially, the reader is implicitly asked to explore how and when the comparison may be legitimate and valuable.[33] Thucydides employs metaphors to elicit forcefully the reader's critical engagement.

Fourth, according to Lakoff and Johnson, all metaphors are incomplete. No single metaphor "is sufficient to give us a complete, consistent, and comprehensive understanding [of a concept]. . . . Different metaphors, each of which partially structures a concept . . . [may] jointly provide a coherent understanding of the concept as a whole.[34] As we shall see, Thucydides introduces a multitude of metaphors to illuminate Athenian motivation and action.

Fifth, in a set of metaphors, we may speak of "coherence." That is, there may be overlap between two or more metaphors. Although two metaphors may not be consistent (forming a single image), as Lakoff and Johnson put it, "they nonetheless 'fit together,' by virtue of being subcategories of a major category and their sharing a major common entailment. There is a difference between metaphors that are *coherent* (that is, 'fit together') with each other and those that are *consistent*" (emphasis in original).[35] As we shall see below, tyranny and slavery form part of a coherent set of metaphors that mutually reinforce one another in certain respects.[36]

Sixth and finally, regarding the purpose of metaphor: "A metaphor works when it satisfies a purpose, namely, understanding an aspect of the concept."[37] The city-as-tyrant metaphor will be successful to the extent that it sheds light on Athens' relationships with other cities. By examining Lakoff and Johnson's work on the nature and function of metaphor in general, we apprehend that Thucydides' tyrant-city metaphor behaves to a great degree in typical fashion. Indeed, Lakoff and Johnson conclude that human thought processes are largely metaphorical.[38] To this extent, Thucydides is engaged in nothing unusual. The differences between actual and metaphorical tyranny should not surprise us, nor should the presence of competing models to which we now turn. What is of special interest is that Thucydides uses metaphor to guide the reader's exploration of political and historical argument and conflict.

OTHER POLITICAL METAPHORS FOR ATHENS IN 1.1–2.65

Before speculating further upon the purpose and effects of Thucydides' employment of metaphor, let us examine other metaphors and comparative expressions from the first two books of the *History*. Six of these, including the city-as-tyrant metaphor, are introduced to characterize Athenian foreign policy. The first three recur in various contexts.

1. *Athens, the city-as-tyrant* (discussed above).

2. *Athens, the city-as-defendant.* A second array of metaphors—found in speeches throughout the *History*—derives from what we might call the courtroom model. This model, triggered by language from the Athenian domestic system of justice, suggests that one city may "prosecute" another,

bringing "charges" against a "defendant-city," with "judges" determining guilt and innocence. Like the tyranny metaphor, metaphorical language deriving from the courtroom is taken from a phenomenon within a polis (in this case, Athens) that originally describes how citizens relate to one another in judicial matters: once again internal politics leads to a metaphor applied to international relations.

Courtroom metaphors in the first book assign the role of defendant almost exclusively to Athens.[39] For example, the Corinthians, insisting upon the injustice of the Athenians, bring forth "charges" (*enklemata*):

"ὅσῳ καὶ μέγιστα ἐγκλήματα ἔχομεν ὑπὸ μὲν Ἀθηναίων ὑβρι-
ζόμενοι, ὑπὸ δὲ ὑμῶν ἀμελούμενοι. καὶ εἰ μὲν ἀφανεῖς που ὄντες
ἠδίκουν τὴν Ἑλλάδα, διδασκαλίας ἂν ὡς οὐκ εἰδόσι προσέδει."

"To this extent we have the greatest charges (*enklemata*) that we have been outraged by the Athenians, and neglected by you. For if they were somehow acting unjustly (*edikoun*) toward Greece without being noticed, there would be a need to instruct those who do not know." (1.68.2–3)[40]

While the Athenians adopt much judicial language in their discussion of international relations, they reject the idea of other cities judging them.[41]

"αἰσθανόμενοι δὲ καταβοὴν οὐκ ὀλίγην οὖσαν ἡμῶν παρήλθομεν οὐ
τοῖς ἐγκλήμασι τῶν πόλεων ἀντεροῦντες (οὐ γὰρ παρὰ δικασταῖς
ὑμῖν οὔτε ἡμῶν οὔτε τούτων οἱ λόγοι ἂν γίγνοιντο)."

"While perceiving that the denunciation is not insignificant, we have not come to answer the charges [*enklemata*] of cities (for you are not judges [*dicastai*] before whom we or they could plead)." (1.73.1)[42]

The issues raised by courtroom metaphors are monumental. Thucydides makes recurrent use of such expressions; the reader is repeatedly confronted with international conflict described in the language of the Athenian court system. The ubiquity of forensic language and disputes over its applicability in particular situations force us to confront many questions, the biggest of which is the relevance of justice to international conflict.[43]

Because such forensic language is applied to international relations throughout the *History*, a challenge is posed to the reader. Are justice, guilt, responsibility, equality, and fairness relevant to foreign policy? When there is a dispute between cities, is there any forum which might adjudicate or resolve such conflicts? Whether or not the courtroom model itself has such validity, the metaphorical language forces the reader to explore these questions. No issue is more important, as Thucydides shows. In the last episode before war begins, Pericles offers to go to arbitration—one model of adjudication between cities (δίκας . . . δοῦναι κατὰ τὰς ξυνθήκας—1.144.2; cf. 1.145). Obviously, if some sort of resolution of international conflict is not successful, war is the alternative.[44]

3. *Athens-as-enslaver.* Slavery originally refers to the ownership and authority of a master over a slave—that is, it originates in the household (*oikos*)—yet Peloponnesian propaganda consists of the theme of Athens "enslaving" other cities; in fact, on the eve of the Peloponnesian War, the Corinthians claim that much of Greece is "enslaved."

> "νῦν δὲ τί δεῖ μακρηγορεῖν, ὧν **τοὺς μὲν δεδουλωμένους** ὁρᾶτε, τοῖς δὲ ἐπιβουλεύοντας αὐτούς;"

"But now what need is there of long speeches? Do you see that *some states have been enslaved* and that the Athenians are plotting against others?" (1.68.3)

I would make two observations. First, the slavery metaphor makes up part of the freedom/slavery polarity. Given this, we might consider to what extent the slavery model is truly metaphorical. By the late fifth century, different senses of freedom existed (personal, political, etc.).[45] To speak of the freedom or slavery of cities may be obvious and straightforward, without stretching the meaning of terms, as metaphor does. For the purposes of this survey, nevertheless, I introduce the language of imperial slavery as being on a par with the other expressions examined here, for it offers another recurrent perspective on Athenian foreign policy.

Second, the idea of one city enslaving another is not expressed exclusively in Thucydidean speeches; it is also found in Thucydides' own narrative. Note the following passage from the Pentecontaetia where a distinction is apparently made:

> Πρῶτον μὲν Ἠιόνα τὴν ἐπὶ Στρυμόνι Μήδων ἐχόντων πολιορκίᾳ εἷλον καὶ **ἠνδραπόδισαν**, Κίμωνος τοῦ Μιλτιάδου στρατηγοῦντος. ἔπειτα Σκῦρον τὴν ἐν τῷ Αἰγαίῳ νῆσον, ἣν ᾤκουν Δόλοπες, **ἠνδραπόδισαν** καὶ ᾤκισαν αὐτοί. . . . Ναξίοις δὲ ἀποστᾶσι μετὰ ταῦτα ἐπολέμησαν καὶ πολιορκίᾳ παρεστήσαντο, πρώτη τε αὕτη πόλις ξυμμαχὶς παρὰ τὸ καθεστηκὸς **ἐδουλώθη**, ἔπειτα δὲ καὶ τῶν ἄλλων ὡς ἑκάστῃ ξυνέβη.

First, under the command of Cimon son of Miltiades, [the Athenians] besieged and captured Eion on the Strymon river, which was held by the Persians, and *enslaved* [*endrapodisan*] the inhabitants. Next, they *enslaved* [*endrapodisan*] the island of Skyros in the Aegean, occupied by Dolopians, and settled it themselves. . . . After this they fought against the Naxians who had revolted and forced them back in by besieging them. And this was the first allied city *enslaved* [*edoulothe*], contrary to what has been arranged, but afterward this also happened to the others according to individual circumstances. (1.98)

Hornblower comments on the use of two terms, *andrapodizo* and *douloo*, noting the

important distinction in terminology: Eion and Skyros were "enslaved," ἠνδραπόδισαν, in the literal sense that their inhabitants were individually sold into slavery; Naxos was "enslaved," ἐδουλώθη, in the different (it would be wrong to say "figurative") sense that she was deprived of her political liberty.

He concludes: "the concept of enslavement, δουλεία, is rather loosely used."[46] I would differ from Hornblower's analysis by at least wondering whether one city "enslaving" (*douloo*) another is yet one more metaphor, designed to stimulate the reader's exploration of similarity and difference between the familiar domestic institutions and Athens' control over other cities.

The next three comparisons, all voiced by Pericles, appear only once.[47]

4. *Athenians-as-islanders*. Athenian war strategy is best captured by the model of the Athenians thinking of themselves as islanders. As Pericles advises:

"μέγα γὰρ τὸ τῆς θαλάσσης κράτος. σκέξασθε δέ· εἰ γὰρ ἦμεν νησιῶται, τίνες ἂν ἀληπτότεροι ἦσαν; καὶ νῦν χρὴ ὅτι ἐγγύτατα τούτου διανοηθέντες τὴν μὲν γῆν καὶ οἰκίας ἀφεῖναι, τῆς δὲ θαλάσσης καὶ πόλεως φυλακὴν ἔχειν, καὶ Πελοποννησίοις ὑπὲρ αὐτῶν ὀργισθέντας πολλὰ πλέοσι μὴ διαμάχεσθαι."

"For the power of the sea is great. And consider: if we were islanders, who would be less liable to attack? And now we must hold as closely as possible to this plan: we must give up land and dwellings, guard the sea and the city, and above all not fight against the more numerous Peloponnesians even if we are angered by them." (1.143.5)

Pericles' strategy itself is based on an idealization: if the Athenians were islanders, they could rely wholly on their navy. As Parry puts it: "The Athenians do not merely use sea-power to build their realm; they become almost entirely identified with seapower; they 'become nautical.'"[48] Thinking of Athenians-as-islanders is a comparison designed to promote Athens' military strategy against Sparta and her allies. Like the metaphors and comparisons previously analyzed, the idea of Athenians-as-islanders occurs in a speech, yet it appears only once. Imagining Athenians-as-islanders is, however, part of the more extensive opposition of land and sea which is developed throughout the *History* and provides a key to historical analysis.[49] Athenian strategy—and the idea of Athenians-as-islanders that is designed to capture it—must be understood with reference to this larger polarity. Thucydides places this formulation in Pericles' first speech immediately before the war narrative begins. The reader is now in a position to test Pericles' strategy with this easily memorable template: if Athens were an island, then its ships could protect its territory. Connor notes the danger: "Athens is not an island and will find it difficult to pretend to be one."[50]

5. *Athens-as-model.* In the Funeral Oration, Pericles asserts that rather than copying other cities' laws,[51] the Athenians themselves set the standard: Athens is a model (*paradeigma*) which other cities emulate.

"Χρώμεθα γὰρ πολιτείᾳ οὐ ζηλούσῃ τοὺς τῶν πέλας νόμους, παράδειγμα δὲ μᾶλλον αὐτοὶ ὄντες τισὶν ἢ μιμούμενοι ἑτέρους."

"We have a form of government that does not emulate the practice of our neighbors; rather we set an example [*paradeigma*] to some, rather than imitating others." (2.37.1)[52]

The specific context of this assertion is a constitutional one: other cities with a democratic form of government are following Athens. In this sense, the Athenian constitution (*politeia*) is a model (*paradeigma*) which is imitated by others (*mimoumenoi*).

To Thucydides' readers, a second meaning may lie here. The context of this section of the Funeral Oration deals with the city and its laws; the idea of comparison (*eikazein*) is signaled by use of the term *paradeigma*. Active application by others is also suggested by *mimoumenoi*: Athens does not imitate; it is rather the case that others copy by following Athens. Given the various political models describing Athens—tyrant, enslaver, etc.—it is possible to see a broader application for the term *paradeigma* used here.

Athens may in some sense be the model *par excellence* in more than a constitutional sense. Just as Naxos may be seen as paradigmatic for cities which attempt to revolt yet become subject "allies" (1.98), and Corcyra was paradigmatic for understanding civil war during the Peloponnesian War (3.70–85), so Athens may be paradigmatic for other cities in the following sense. A great deal of the *History's* metaphorical language is attached to Athens, more than to any other city. Thucydides may have applied such metaphors and comparisons to Athens, not only so that we learn about Athens and its relations with other cities, but also to consider more generally possible ways of viewing Greek cities, especially their relationships with other city-states. Athens is associated not only with the dominance of a tyrant and a slave holder, but may also positively influence other cities, as the next model suggests.

6. *Athens-as-education*. Later in the Funeral Oration, Pericles claims:

"Ξυνελὼν τε λέγω τήν τε πᾶσαν πόλιν τῆς Ἑλλάδος παίδευσιν εἶναι."

"In sum, I say that the whole city is an education [*paideusis*] of Greece." (2.41.1)

Once more a memorable expression appears.[53] Education (*paideusis*) normally takes place within a city, yet here the idea is applied to Athens (as educator) and to the other cities of Greece (which may learn). *Xunelon* ("in sum") looks back, although there are various opinions as to how far the summation extends. The retrospective glance may reach to section 2.40 where Pericles discusses the Athenians' love of beauty, their philosophical inclinations, the contributions of both rich and poor, and Athenian "bravery with calculation."[54] Or we might take the recapitulation more extensively, as Rusten argues, "summing up the praise, first of the city's institutions in 37–9 (with παίδευσις here, cf. παράδειγμα in 37.1), then of the Athenian character in 40."[55] This latter view suggests that what Athens might teach the rest of Greece is more than laws and constitutions in the narrow (and modern) sense of politics; Athens is also worthy of emulation in teaching others the best way for citizens to relate to one another in terms of freedom, tolerance, and even opportunities of leisure. Athens-as-educator does not reject the tyrant and enslaver metaphors, but may better be seen as a competing metaphor.[56]

The emphasis upon learning in this metaphor may be directed not only to Pericles' Athenian audience but also to Thucydides' readers. In the passage which follows, Pericles dismisses the need for a "Homer to sing our praises" (2.41.4). Havelock has argued that Plato finds himself up against the Homeric "encyclopedia" and the near-monopoly on knowledge and education residing in Homer's epics; we may find a similar tension at work here between Thucydides' new sort of political history and more traditional modes of education.[57] Rather than recall the words of older epic, Pericles calls upon his Athenians to "learn" from the city itself: its power, its character, its political way of life—this is modern and will not be found in Homer.[58] At another level, Thucydides may be urging his readers to learn from his portrait of Athens as presented in this innovative work, the *History*. In any case, the Athens-as-education metaphor expands upon the idea of Athens-as-*paradigma* by explicitly stating that Athens is a city we may learn from.[59]

In addition to metaphors characterizing Athenian foreign policy, several metaphors and comparisons—each occurring once—describe internal Athenian politics. These expressions are frequently brief and emphasize the intense and complex interaction among Athenian citizens or between citizens and the city of Athens itself. The first two appear in Thucydides' narrative.

7. *Attic villages as independent poleis.* One comparison describes the allegiance rural Athenians feel toward their local villages. During the evacuation in the spring of 431, they are forced to leave their homes:

οὐδὲν ἄλλο ἢ πόλιν τὴν αὑτοῦ ἀπολείπων ἕκαστος.

It was not other than leaving one's own city. (2.16.2)

This suggests what we might call a "microcosmic" political model, wherein the polis of Athens—which embraces the entire Attic peninsula—in a sense is made up of many little cities (*poleis*), each in some sense autonomous.[60] The pressure resulting from Pericles' war strategy in 431 is immediately apparent as the inhabitants, for example, of Acharnae, a large deme with three thousand hoplites (2.19.2), watch from the walls and see their land being destroyed (2.21.2). The younger men are upset and wish to go out to fight. Since his strategy entails Athenians abandoning their country residences, Pericles receives much blame for his policy (2.21.3).

The idea of Attic "cities" is significant in that it undermines Pericles' idea of the devotion of all citizens to a single object: the polis of Athens (see models 9 and 10 below). Rural inhabitants may feel as strong an allegiance toward their local communities as to Athens itself. Thucydides has chosen to place this model of potentially divided loyalty here at the beginning of the war—during the evacuation and before Pericles' Funeral Oration. The effect is that the reader may now question the validity of Pericles' vision. Of course, Pericles is promoting an ideal, in part, to counteract such "local" loyalty. Thucydides indicates the seeds of tension here, as we discover a different sort of allegiance undercutting Pericles' later idealization.

8. *The "arche" of Pericles*. In the "obituary notice" of Pericles, Thucydides employs an unusual description of Pericles' leadership by using the term "*arche*."

ἐγίγνετό τε λόγῳ δημοκρατία, ἔργῳ δὲ ὑπὸ τοῦ πρώτου ἀνδρὸς ἀρχή.

What was said to be a democracy was actually the *arche* [rule? empire? domain?] of the first man. (2.65.9)[61]

To describe Pericles' dominance in Athens as *arche* is notable. Of course, the term *arche* is used in several senses: it may simply mean "power," "authority," or "sovereignty." In Thucydides, however, it most commonly refers to the Athenian empire and its domination of other cities, that is, the reference is to international politics.[62] Although most of the metaphors examined thus far derive from internal politics, this metaphor derives from external relations yet describes domestic politics.

Note also the context. This assessment of Pericles follows his third speech which examined the Athenian empire: *arche* in the sense of "empire" was mentioned there four times (2.62.1, 2.63.1 [2x], 2.63.3). In the immediate context of the obituary notice itself, *arche* also refers to empire (2.65.7 and 2.65.11). These associations will color the reader's reaction. Thucydides has apparently chosen to describe Pericles' role in Athens by resorting to a term with a flavor of international politics. This is yet another illuminating comparison of domestic and international politics: in this case, a situation from external politics (Athenian imperialism) is applied to one from internal politics—Pericles' relationship with his fellow citizens.[63] If this interpretation is correct, our appreciation of Pericles becomes a bit more complicated. On the whole, Thucydides offers a glowing tribute to Pericles, yet if his leadership of Athens was analogous to Athens' role as an imperial city, was Pericles then in some sense an enslaver? Does he retain a touch of the tyrant? If Thucydides admires

Pericles, does this suggest that Thucydides admires aggressive power figures? These possibilities are at least suggested by the application of the
term *arche* to the Athenian statesman.

9. *Citizens-as-lovers*. The complex interaction between individual citizens and the community of Athens is built upon commitments from both
sides.[64] One metaphor for this interaction—found in the Funeral
Oration—is that citizens should think of themselves as "lovers" (*erastai*) of
Athens.

"ἀλλὰ μᾶλλον τὴν τῆς πόλεως δύναμιν καθ᾽ ἡμέραν ἔργῳ θεωμένους
καὶ ἐραστὰς γιγνομένους αὐτῆς."

"But rather gazing upon the power of the city each day, become lovers of
it." (2.43.1)

The metaphor itself derives not from internal politics, but from the relationship between lovers—either heterosexual lovers or an older and a
younger man. The lover is attracted by the beauty of the beloved: within the
metaphor, Athens—and its power—arouses the citizen. Hornblower mentions the implication of "passive and mercenary homosexuality."[65] By way of
reply, I rely upon an article by Monoson, in which she finds that this
metaphor "projects an image of active, energetic, controlling Athenian citizens."[66] While there is a hint of danger that the lover (*erastes*) of the city
will come to dominate the city (as *eromenos*), Monoson argues that in the
rest of the speech Pericles portrays the relationship between citizen and city
as reciprocal.[67] In fact, "for the metaphor [of citizen as lover] to work, that is,
for it to deliver praise of both citizens and city, it must successfully evade suggesting that the city plays this [submissive] role. It must successfully negotiate Greek views of honorable and shameful sexual behavior."[68] Monoson
concludes:

> The metaphor suggests . . . that interactions befitting free citizens and a
> free city are those of reciprocal, mutual exchange, understood on the pat-
> tern of benefaction and gratitude, which tie in with the compulsion of
> honor, not power.[69]

The concept of citizen-as-lover, stated in such striking language, appears
only once, yet the idea of such passion returns in Thucydides' narrative of
the Sicilian expedition in 415.[70] Monoson argues that the passion
Athenians feel toward the Sicilian expedition

is not the restrained, honorable love that Pericles refers to but a furious, raging *eros*. The consequences are, of course, disastrous. Thucydides is relying, I believe, on the cultural prescriptions against such eager, raging *eros* to convey the manner in which the Athenians' behavior on this occasion was troubling and dangerous.[71]

Thucydides has set up a contrast between what Pericles recommends early in the war and how in a later situation the idea—twisted and transformed—becomes more dangerous. Thucydides introduces a concept in remarkable language—citizens-as-lovers—which becomes relevant to his later account of the war after Pericles' successors attempt to guide Athens to success.

10. *The City as god.* Also in the Funeral Oration, Pericles says that he has "hymned" the city, suggesting that the city of Athens may be viewed as a god or hero.

"καὶ εἴρηται αὐτῆς τὰ μέγιστα· ἃ γὰρ τὴν πόλιν **ὕμνησα**."

"And the most important things have been said, in which I have '*hymned*' the city." (2.42.2)[72]

This metaphorical language also suggests an attitude that citizens might take toward the city of Athens, quite distinct from the lover model. Here the implication is that of a mortal worshiping a god, goddess, or cult figure.[73] Thucydides may be implicitly contrasting the reputed immortality of the city itself (which is like a god) with the death and decay found in the description of the plague (2.47–54) and Pericles' final speech (esp. 2.64.3, discussed just below).

11. *City—and empire—as biological organism.* A clear expression of an organic metaphor is found in Pericles' third speech. After describing the impressive stature of Athens and its imperial might, he asserts that even if the Athenians were to surrender, the memory of Athens would abide, for they have ruled over the most Greeks, fought in the greatest wars, and inhabited the greatest and wealthiest city (2.64). Parenthetically, he acknowledges an inevitable decay.

"πάντα γὰρ πέφυκε καὶ ἐλασσοῦσθαι."

"For everything must naturally be diminished too." (2.64.3)[74]

The primary reference may be to the Athenian empire (it will not last forever), but this metaphor may also apply to the city of Athens. Reading this maxim broadly, both city and empire are subject to nature (*pephuke*) and, like biological organisms, will necessarily become weaker and decline over time. The city of Athens is founded, grows, thrives, and withers in ways similar to a living creature.[75] In this connection—and given the context of the immediately preceding description of the plague (2.47–52)—we may consider a related implicit metaphor of the city as patient. The idea of city-as-organism, in conjunction with the plague description, lends support to the picture of the city as suffering from disease.[76]

In total, at least eleven metaphors or comparisons apply either to Athenian foreign relations or domestic politics. Each comparison teaches us something about the city—either domestically or in its relation with other cities. They are for the most part introduced early in the *History* and many continue to be developed as Thucydides' account of the war goes on. In one sense, each metaphor competes with the others, yet as we saw above, Lakoff and Johnson discuss "coherent systems" of metaphor, sets of metaphors that work together by virtue of sharing "entailments," traits held in common. Such entailments may be seen in the cluster of the tyrant, defendant, and slavery metaphors, which overlap and reinforce one another with respect to certain shared implied features: unrestrained power, dependence on force, lawlessness, injustice, danger to others, arrogance, and rule over unwilling subjects. Alternatively, the metaphors of Athens-as-model and Athens-as-education appear to reinforce one another and contribute to a more positive portrait of Athens. The important point, however, is that no single metaphor supplies a comprehensive understanding of the city of Athens. If one metaphor held the key to understanding—if the answer could be given so simply: Athens is a tyrant—Thucydides could have supplied such a metaphor in his own voice. Instead Thucydides uses speeches for the most part to introduce these various models in different contexts, and leaves the testing and examination as a task for the reader.

THUCYDIDES' USE OF METAPHORS

Thucydides' political metaphors challenge his readers in a variety of ways. One challenge concerns the status of such metaphors. Thucydides' discussion of historical tyrants is stated in his own voice more authoritatively, yet he never gives us explicit instructions as to what we should conclude concerning the idea of Athens as a city-tyrant. It may be valuable to examine the options the historian faced, for he had several choices regarding his treatment of tyranny and the Athenian empire.

The historian could have expressed the metaphor of Athens-as-tyrant in his own voice in the narrative. If he had done so, the effect would have been in some sense to privilege the metaphor, though this may have encouraged more passive acceptance on the part of the reader. Or he could have given less attention to both individual and imperial tyranny. Instead Thucydides has apparently chosen to promote the metaphor of imperial tyranny by introducing it in speeches, yet his own discussion of individual tyranny appears in the narrative. This choice is surely deliberate. Thucydides offers the Athens-as-tyrant metaphor (and most other metaphors and comparative expressions) in speeches as comparisons the reader must critically examine.[77] In offering political metaphors in speeches and discussing tyrants and slavery in the narrative, Thucydides sets up an implicit juxtaposition that lends these metaphors a dynamic, rather than a static role. The retrospective reader is asked to consider the extent to which a particular metaphor is accurate in its immediate and in more distant and comparative contexts.

In addition to placing political metaphors in speeches, I note the self-evident: metaphors are challenging by virtue of the fact that they are metaphorical.[78] That is, metaphors captivate by appealing to the imagination; yet because metaphors suggest only partial correspondences and similarities, there will never be a complete coincidence between metaphor and reality. The reader must constantly test the metaphor, checking to learn when it offers illumination and when and in what respects it is misleading or irrelevant. To a large extent, metaphors work by implication, and the reader must actively pursue any implied aspects of similarity and difference. This open-ended characteristic of metaphor means that the task of pursuing such implications is potentially limitless, leading to extensive analysis. Indeed, it has been suggested that metaphors are intellectually challenging to the point of jeopardizing one's sanity.[79]

Even if we maintain our mental equilibrium, disappointment may ensue. There is a part of us, as readers, that naturally desires to know whether Thucydides the historian viewed the metaphors positively or with great reservation. Not having a definitive answer leads to some level of frustration.[80] Yet this is a common experience when reading Thucydides in other respects. Gribble finds that even in the narrative there is often a "suggestive vagueness of the interpretative language . . . [that] seems rather to underline the desire *not* to employ the narrator's voice to impose interpretations, unless in the sense of modes of interpretation according to broad patterns of event and behaviour."[81] In analogous fashion the political metaphors introduced in speeches are characterized by a similar "suggestive vagueness," thus lending an interactive aspect to the History; it is the reader's task to examine and assess these comparative models. Such comparative phrases and formulations are not unlike the narrator's "interventions" that Gribble believes do not produce "definitive authorial judgement . . . [yet] their purpose is not to establish a definitive explanation which will render subsequent analysis of events redundant, but to suggest the underlying pattern revealed by the perspective of later events."[82] Clearly this is the sort of experience Thucydides has chosen to present us with—a far different one than if he were to comment on these models in his own voice. Instead he has given us sufficient coincidence and similarity between metaphor and subject to convince many perceptive scholars that these metaphors are viable, while introducing tantalizingly significant differences which call into question their universal validity.

To explain Thucydides' fondness for these political metaphors, we must keep in mind what he has to say regarding comparison. At a very basic level, Thucydides considers it important for the reader to recognize similarity and difference. In his statement of method regarding the History's usefulness, Thucydides speaks not only of learning accurately about past events, but also:

. . . τῶν μελλόντων ποτὲ αὖθις κατὰ τὸ ἀνθρώπινον τοιούτων καὶ παραπλησίων ἔσεσθαι. . .

. . . those events that in the future which, in accordance with human nature, will be similar [toiouton] and will resemble [paraplesion][83] past events . . . (1.22.4)

The History will prove "useful" (ophelima), Thucydides asserts, because the reader will gain an accurate knowledge of what happened in the past—and of similar sorts of events that will occur in the future. In effect, Thucydides is challenging his reader to compare events from the past with subsequent times. In fact, Thucydides himself compares events within the History, although most often this is implicit.[84]

It is not merely the fact that similarity and resemblance exist between past and later events; rather, the reader is asked to engage in the practice of testing similarity and resemblance and to become adept at recognizing such correspondences. We might even go so far as to say that Thucydides seeks to train his reader in the skills of juxtaposition, comparison, and extrapolation (*eikazein*). How best to accomplish such training? In order to practice these skills, the reader must employ his or her intellectual and imaginative capacities in testing likeness and disparity. Yet this is the very skill needed for grappling with political metaphors, metaphors that ask the reader to set the characterization and action of actual tyrants (garnered from Thucydides' narrative) in dynamic comparison with metaphors appearing in speeches. This is what has been done to a limited extent in this chapter and, I believe, this is what Thucydides intends us to do. Thucydides' political metaphors serve the function of offering a kind of guided, interactive training in the skill of juxtaposition and comparison.[85]

Conclusion

Thucydides' introduction of metaphors is important for several reasons. First, regarding the historical record, Thucydides seeks to reflect the political rhetoric of the time. Those who opposed Athens used a variety of slogans to rally support: Athens was enslaving Greece, Athens was a tyrant, and so on. Conversely, Pericles was known for his memorable phrases, and is likely to have used the sorts of expression Thucydides attributes to him in characterizing Athens' greatness and its citizens' allegiance to such a city. In fact, seven of the eleven metaphors and comparisons proposed here are voiced by Pericles, five by him alone (islanders, model, education, lover, city-as-god).[86] Ancient witnesses other than Thucydides confirm this picture of Pericles as a colorful, inventive, and memorable speaker. In the *Demoi* fr. 102, the fifth-century comic poet Eupolis describes Pericles:

"καὶ μόνος τῶν ῥητόρων τὸ κέντρον ἐγκατέλειπε τοῖς ἀκροω-μένοις."

"He alone of the speakers left a sting in his audience."

Like a wasp or bee, the effect of hearing Pericles speak may have been painful (this is part of the whimsical image), yet his words certainly stuck in the listener's memory.[87]

If we compare Pericles' expressions recorded by Thucydides with those found elsewhere, we note that Thucydides appears to have selected only the ones most directly related to domestic and international politics. From sources other than Thucydides, we learn that Pericles spoke of how "losing the youth of the city is like a year robbed of spring" (Ar. *Rhet.* 1365a34). The Samians were "like children who cry while they accept scraps [showing lack of appreciation]"; the Boeotians were compared to holm-oaks that knock each other down (with continual internal conflict—Ar. *Rhet.* 1407a).[88] These phrases and expressions are memorable but are derived from the natural world (spring, oak trees) rather than the political arena. Thucydides has evidently been selective in his presentation of Pericles by sticking to politics.

The second point concerns Thucydides' larger project of historical analysis. While it may be true that politicians and speakers repeated such slogans to crowds, Thucydides has also presented metaphors as a facet of historical analysis. Macleod remarks that "the rhetorical commonplace becomes a basis for historical analysis."[89] Generally, speeches contain the more daring use of language while in the narrative a stricter denotation of slaves, tyrants, etc. is employed. The effect of bold metaphor is to challenge the reader—not only to remember and keep track of these comparisons, but also to compare, probe, and test. To what extent are such metaphors accurate? In what situations? Do such metaphors help us better to understand the behavior of Athens and its empire or Pericles' relationship with the Athenian people? Leidl argues that "metaphor is necessary when a new field of knowledge is to be organized, when new concepts have to be designed for something which had not been talked about before."[90] To the extent that Thucydides is engaged in a new sort of enterprise ("inventing political history"), it makes sense to expand the use of familiar expressions in this fresh area of investigation.

A third aspect concerns Thucydides' audience and the various challenges Thucydides has proposed. But perhaps I should say audiences, for I think that Thucydides envisioned both auditors and readers (see chapters 9 and 10). In both cases—either those hearing the *History* read aloud or those reading a scroll, say, of book one—there would have been tremendous difficulties in cross-referencing (the sort of activity modern scholars regularly engage in, with their concordances, commentaries, and codices).[91] When Cleon calls Athens' empire a tyranny, Thucydides could reasonably expect his auditor *and* his reader to recall that Pericles said something quite similar. Both Thucydides' auditors and readers must rely upon memory in order to reconstruct this echo, yet Thucydides aids this process of recollection not only by the recurrence of metaphors, but by using *memorable* expressions. Thucydides' striking, figurative expressions keep these images active in the audience's mind.

While the Athens-as-tyrant metaphor is striking and memorable, to rely upon this one metaphor would be reductive. Indeed, as we have seen, Thucydides introduces competing metaphors. These metaphors offer "touchstones" to the reader—easily grasped and memorable—by which to judge the often bewildering world of action and argument found throughout the *History*. Such metaphors offer a framework within which we may gauge Athens with respect to both domestic and international politics. The internal political metaphors explore civic unity and interaction, suggesting possible pressures upon the loyalties of citizens within the polis; this is a prerequisite for understanding domestic tensions that may lead to conflict and civil war. The international political metaphors help the reader to assess relations between cities in terms of alliance, domination, and war. Yet in each case the interpretive onus belongs to the reader, who must determine in what respects and to what degree such metaphors are valid and appropriate.[92] While political models aid the reader, they also present challenges, as Thucydides insists upon the critical assessment of the reader.

The skill of apprehending and analyzing likeness and difference is useful not only for testing political metaphors, but also more generally for comparing different situations within the *History* and for comparing the reader's own life and times with those recounted in the *History*.[93] Thucydides' presentation of the *History*, of course, suggests comparisons which go beyond the realm of metaphor: Should we compare the portrayal of Athens in the Funeral Oration with the picture of Athens found in the description of the plague? To what extent are the interwoven situations of Mytilene and Plataea in book 3 comparable—and is the rationale Diodotus advocates for deciding Mytilene's fate the same one followed by the Spartans regarding that of Plataea (chapter 4)? Is the motivation for the Melian and Sicilian ventures the same? If so, why is Athens successful in one instance, and meets with disaster in the other (chapter 5)? In general, Thucydides does not *explicitly* tell his reader to compare such situations. Such an invitation to juxtapose, compare, and extrapolate is implicit throughout the *History*. Political metaphors are explicit in this respect: they ask the reader to set data garnered from Thucydides' narrative regarding actual tyranny, slavery, and the judicial process (domestic politics) in dynamic comparison with Athenian foreign policy and action (interstate politics). Political metaphors overtly signal the task of juxtaposition that the reader must pursue: the reader thus gains a special kind of training deemed valuable by Thucydides, namely, training in comparison and extrapolation.

PART FOUR
BIOGRAPHY AND RECEPTION

9

THUCYDIDES' LIFE AND WORK

The previous chapters have emphasized the experiences of the reader for certain episodes: the participatory engagement for the Corcyrean conflict, a retrospective attitude for the Melian episode, and the idea of figurative language guiding the reader through the intricacies of "comparison and extrapolation" (*eikazein*). At some level, every episode may be viewed alternatively through the eyes of an engaged or a retrospective reader. From an engaged perspective the reader may experience events from the vantage point of figures who were living through them; indeed, it was argued that Thucydides (like Plato) has successfully recreated the atmosphere of oral discourse and put his reader into the position of listener to a debate, not unlike the internal audience of the *History*. Yet it is also valuable to consider from a more distant vantage point what might have happened, based on what is known later. Another way of talking about the reader's experience is to say that Thucydides has produced a text that lends itself to experiential and participatory engagement, yet after an episode is read (or heard) the arguments, events, and ideas may be reread, discussed, and analyzed in a more dispassionate mode by scanning a broader swathe of the past.

These final two chapters will explore Thucydides' claims and motivations for writing history, various aspects of his own life, and a reconstruction of the *History's* reception. In considering Thucydides' goals beyond his explicit claims, speculation will be required in order to recover possible motivations for structuring his work as he did. It may also be valuable to consider Thucydides' biography: what he explicitly tells us, what we may infer, and what we know of the historical context. We also turn finally to Thucydides' actual readers and auditors. The analysis in chapters 3–8 was limited to an implied reader constructed from the text, based on the information and guidance Thucydides presents in the *History*. My hope now is to approach the difficult question of the reception of Thucydides' work by both ancient and modern audiences. How did Thucydides himself imagine his audience's engagement? In the introductory chapter I described Thucydides as sitting on the cusp of the divide between oral and written culture. This means it is virtually impossible to pigeonhole Thucydides' work exclusively in terms of either oral or literary culture: his sources for the war itself were largely oral; he self-consciously refers to the status of his work as a written document; and yet the reception of his account of the Peloponnesian War may very well have included both readers and auditors.

CLAIMS

Thucydides makes three significant claims for his work: the importance of the subject, the accuracy of the account, and its lasting value. Let us explore these in turn. In the opening paragraph of the *History*, Thucydides claims that the war between the Athenians and the Peloponnesians was "most worth recording" (*axiologotaton*–1.1.1). He argues for this by magnifying his own subject (and his accomplishment in writing about it) and by comparing his subject and work with that of others.

Almost in awe of the Peloponnesian War, Thucydides is exceedingly fond of superlatives. The disruption of the Greek world was the greatest (κίνησις . . . μεγίστη –1.1.2). The plague was the greatest in human memory (2.47.3). The scope of the war and the extent of the suffering it caused were so great that *never before* had as much suffering occurred in an equal period of time: so many cities were destroyed, so many were driven into exile, there was so much murder. All this was due to war and civil strife. As if this were not bad enough, earthquakes, eclipses, drought, famine, and disease were also more crowded into one period than in previous times (1.23.1–3).[1]

Thucydides also argues that the Peloponnesian War is the greatest war in comparative terms, by seeking to demonstrate that "his war" is of greater magnitude in terms of scope and suffering than the wars recounted by Homer and Herodotus.[2] One function of the Archaeology (1.2–19) is to demonstrate that earlier wars could not have been of the magnitude of the Peloponnesian War, due in part to lack of capital reserves, walled cities, and sufficiency large navies.[3] The great Panhellenic ventures of the heroic age and even the early fifth century were of lesser scope and consequence.

Thucydides' second claim concerns accuracy: his work is reliable. Again, he argues for this in part by comparing his accomplishment with other histories and common knowledge. In the section on method,

Thucydides asserts that his versions of speeches "hold as close as possible to the overall sense of what was actually said" (ἐχομένῳ ὅτι ἐγγύτατα τῆς ξυμπάσης γνώμης τῶν ἀληθῶς λεχθέντων); his presentation of events is offered "with the utmost possible accuracy in each case" (ὅσον δυνατὸν ἀκριβείᾳ περὶ ἑκάστου ἐπεξελθών–1.22.1–2). Thucydides emphasizes the meticulous labor that was necessary on his part due to the contradictory or biased reports he received:

> Finding out the facts involved great effort [ἐπιπόνως δὲ ηὑρίσκετο], because eye witnesses did not say the same things about the same events, but [reported] according to favoritism or [lapses of] memory. (1.22.3)[4]

Thucydides also stresses clarity and truth in his work. For example, regarding clarity (*saphes*), Thucydides' audience will include "as many as wish *to look clearly* at past events" (τὸ σαφὲς σκοπεῖν–1.22.4). With regard to truth (*aletheia*), Thucydides promises to reveal the "truest (*alethestaten*) cause of the war" (1.23.6).[5]

Thucydides claims preeminence by contrasting his own *History* with the work of others and with people's general knowledge. That is, in a polemical tone, Thucydides asserts that others have failed to reach his standards of clarity, truth, and accuracy. Indeed, others are likely to receive reports uncritically.

> οἱ γὰρ ἄνθρωποι τὰς ἀκοὰς τῶν προγεγενημένων . . . ὁμοίως ἀβασανίστως παρ᾽ ἀλλήλων δέχονται.

> For people accept what they hear from one another about the past . . . with a uniform lack of testing. (1.20.1)

Many avoid the toil needed to attain the truth (1.20.3). Thucydides' pronouncements made in his section on method (1.20–23) repeatedly contrast his own finished product with the less reliable and demonstrably false stories that people pass around.[6]

Thucydides makes a third claim: he announces that his work will have lasting value. We might assume that an accurate history of the most noteworthy war would be inherently valuable, yet Thucydides states that his work will be *useful* because human nature is constant, so that events comparable to those he recounts will take place in the future.

> ὅσοι δὲ βουλήσονται τῶν τε γενομένων τὸ σαφὲς σκοπεῖν καὶ τῶν

μελλόντων ποτὲ αὖθις κατὰ τὸ ἀνθρώπινον τοιούτων καὶ παραπλησίων ἔσεσθαι, ὠφέλιμα κρίνειν αὐτὰ ἀρκούντως ἕξει.

Yet if [my work] is *judged useful* by as many as wish to look clearly at both
past events *and those in the future which, in accordance with human nature,
will be similar and will resemble past events*, that will suffice. (1.22.4)

Below I will address the questions of how and to whom the *History* may be
useful.

Another aspect to Thucydides' claim is that the value of his work will
endure. He introduces an unusual expression, referring to the *History* as a
"possession":

κτῆμά τε ἐς αἰεὶ μᾶλλον ἢ ἀγώνισμα ἐς τὸ παραχρῆμα ἀκούειν
ξυγκεῖται.

[This work] is composed as a possession forever rather than a competition
piece to be heard for the moment. (1.22.4)

We find a suggestion here that one of the reasons Thucydides' work will
be valuable and is a "possession forever" is that it is written. He does not
use a form of *grapho* in this particular passage, but states rather that his work
will not be a competition piece *to be heard* (*akouein*) for the moment. Does
this imply that Thucydides' work must (or should) be read? I think not, but
again, I will argue this position below.[7]

MOTIVATIONS

Based on these claims it is possible to speculate regarding Thucydides'
motivations. Let us consider three: rivalry, teaching, and exile. As we have
already seen, Thucydides often asserts claims for his work in comparative
terms: his war is a greater war than any other war; his account is more accurate; this work will last forever (that is, longer than any other). Such rivalry is a defining characteristic of Greek culture. Indeed, the agonistic spirit
is a feature of most Greek artistic, political, and military endeavor, and it
certainly constitutes an essential element of Thucydides' attitude. One
way of setting himself within a tradition of greatness is to recall other prac-
titioners, and he does so by remarks concerning the Trojan War
(1.9–10)—a nod to Homer—and the four major battles that essentially

constituted the Persian war (1.23.1)—a shrug to Herodotus. After ceding lesser events to these composers, Thucydides proclaims superiority for his war and his work; indeed, he reveals his competitiveness by taking on the greatest of rivals.[8]

Rivalry is not the only motivating factor. Beyond seeking to distinguish himself from previous "writers" of war, Thucydides also views himself as a teacher who offers something of value to his listeners and readers.[9] One benefit of recounting the story of the greatest war in Greek history—that he distinguishes by his superior method, reliability, and soundness—is that the lessons learned will be more valuable than those offered by earlier or contemporary rivals.

What are the lessons? First, one goal is recognition of similar events in the audience's own time (1.22.4, quoted above; cf. 2.48.3). But there may be more. We find admiration for brilliant statesmen who may serve as role models. Themistocles is described as someone who excels at anticipating what will happen given the present circumstances: he is "best at conjecturing" (ἄριστος εἰκαστής–1.138.3). Thucydides goes on to praise Themistocles' ability to improvise (autoschediazein).

κα‹ τ‹ ξύμπαν εἰπεῖν φύσεως μὲν δυνάμει, μελέτης δὲ βραχυτάτι κράτιστος δὴ οὗτος αὐτοσχεδιάζειν τὰ δέοντα ἐγένετο.

To sum up, this man by natural ability, with rapid deliberation, was certainly supreme in improvising what was necessary. (1.138.3)

We also find admiration for Pericles, whose final words in the *History* are an exhortation that the Athenians think ahead (2.64.6).[10] Thucydides, I believe, wished to help prepare later statesmen and citizens to follow in the paths of Themistocles and Pericles. From grappling with Thucydides' account of what happened and what was said during the Peloponnesian War, readers should be in a better position to anticipate what would be likely to happen in new situations.

Given the disruption, suffering, and casualties of the Peloponnesian War, we might believe that learning the lessons of the past could in some way offer hope for avoiding future conflicts of such magnitude. The didactic element in Thucydides' work necessarily contains a kernel of optimism for a better future: this is one reason people teach. In part, Thucydides is teaching the basics of politics by offering an appreciation of rhetoric and its political consequences. In terms of military and political conflict, a reader with a keener appreciation for why people fight, why negotiations fail, and how cities interact for mutual benefit or harm may envisage—and bring about—a world with less suffering.

Some speculation is necessary if we are to speak of Thucydides' motivations for writing this work and for constructing it as he did. To add a third factor to these two probable motivating factors (competition with rivals, enlightenment for his audience), we might ponder the profound effect of exile upon Thucydides. In order to do so, I would like to place Thucydides' twenty years of exile (424–404 BCE) in the larger context of what we know of Thucydides' life and times.

BIOGRAPHY

In chapter 1, I argued that Thucydides should be seen as a transitional figure in terms of intellectual history, for he bridges the gap between the predominantly oral culture of the fifth century and the coming of a book-reading public in fourth-century Athens. The world in which Thucydides was raised consisted very much of an oral culture. Speeches were spoken and heard in the courts and the assembly; tragedy and comedy were performed before Athenian audiences; Socrates interrogated Athenians in the agora and elsewhere. During the war the so-called "sophists" had come to Athens, promising to make young Athenians effective speakers.[11] Yet by the time of Aristotle's Lyceum in the mid-fourth century (two generations later), we clearly encounter habitual readers. Thucydides (and Plato) fall into the gap between these two more clearly defined periods.

I would add that this was also a highly politicized time, politicized in the sense that every Athenian living in the mid- and late-fifth century saw the consequences of decisions and actions—of how they lived their lives—in terms of how the polis of Athens would be affected.[12] In order to influence your city and shape the course of civic affairs, it was necessary to be engaged by participating actively in public life. Citizens judged in the law courts and proposed motions, debated, and voted in the assembly; they addressed their fellow citizens and challenged their opponents; they fought in the army and rowed in the navy. Given the scale of Athenian greatness (2.64.3)—an empire whose power is comparable only to the Persian empire—there is an almost tangible thrill Thucydides conveys in having played a role in that project.[13]

I rehearse these features in order to give a sense of what Thucydides lost—and missed—when he went into exile. No longer could he address (in live, face-to-face civic discourse) his fellow Athenians, point out the proper course of action, or warn them on the spot in the assembly of a mistake. His contributions to the city of Athens as a citizen, as a soldier, as a politician, and as a speaker vanished. I surmise that a possible—indeed a likely—motivation for Thucydides' project (especially his means of presentation) was the search for a substitute that could serve in some way for that engagement in civic affairs, now no longer available to him. He could still address his fellow citizens, but it was no longer in oral, living dialogue; rather it was now with words written on papyrus with a goal both local (to Athenians and other Greeks ca. 400 BCE) and for all time.

So much for the times in which Thucydides lived. He also offers some unambiguous information about his own life. In general terms, the historian tells us that he was present at some of the speeches and some of the events: αὐτὸς ἤκουσα . . . αὐτὸς παρῆν . . . (I myself heard . . . I myself was present . . . –1.22.1–2). We immediately wonder: Which speeches and events did Thucydides witness? Was he present at Pericles' Funeral Oration? Was he involved in the Athenian expeditions to aid Corcyra in 433 or to put down the Mytilenian revolt in 427?[14]

Regarding the plague, we know that Pericles died and Thucydides survived. In his account, Thucydides relies upon what he experienced and saw with his own eyes.

αὐτός τε νοσήσας καὶ αὐτὸς ἰδὼν ἄλλους πάσχοντας.

I myself caught the plague and saw others suffering from it myself. (2.48.3)[15]

Thucydides sketches out the relationship among the plague, suffering, and memory. In his description, Thucydides recounts in detail the progression of symptoms: fever, cough, diarrhea, disorientation, lapses of memory, and so on (2.49). He also speaks of those who survived a bout of the plague: some lost their extremities, their eyes, or their genitals (2.49.8), yet—because they did not die from the plague—believed that they would live forever (2.51.6). Did Thucydides' lose the ends of his fingers or toes? Did he lose his genitals? Did he entertain the illusion that he would live—if not forever—at least a very long time? We wonder but cannot know the long-term effects of the plague upon Thucydides.

Much of Thucydides' information derives from someone's memory, largely that of his informants, who remember battles and speeches and then recount those experiences to Thucydides in accordance with their recollections.[16] Yet the historian acknowledges certain drawbacks to memory. It was hard, Thucydides tells us, for the historian and his informants to remember precisely what people said (1.22.1). Indeed, Thucydides asserts that memory may be faulty, for he also remarks that differing accounts of the same events resulted from favoritism or lapses of memory (1.22.3). To this extent, even memory of events *that someone has participated in* may be unreliable.

Particularly interesting in Thucydides' account of the plague is the connection between memory and suffering. There were two current versions of an oracle: one version stated that "A Dorian war will come, and a plague [*loimos*] with it"; a different version read "A Dorian war will come, and a famine [*limos*] with it." Disagreement ensued over which word—"plague" or "famine" (*loimos* or *limos*)—was sung (2.54.2–3). In this case, "plague" (*loimos*) prevailed and Thucydides remarks:

οἱ γὰρ ἄνθρωποι πρὸς ἃ ἔπασχον τὴν μνήμην ἐποιοῦντο.

People shaped their memories in accordance with what they suffered. (2.54.3)

Such a remark suggests that memory is pliable and may be adjusted with respect to experience.[17] This observation leads in turn to another question: To what extent might Thucydides himself have shaped his account of the Peloponnesian War in accordance with what he suffered? He suffered from the plague; he endured the ignominy of exile. How might these experiences have influenced him as a person and as an historian? Might this have affected his overall goals in writing the *History*?[18] Let us examine more closely the account of his exile.

In the so-called second introduction, Thucydides lays out his credentials for writing the *History*:

> I lived through the whole [of the war] when I was of an age to observe and had my mind engaged, in order to gain knowledge with some exactness; it also happened that I was exiled from my city for twenty years after the command at Amphipolis and, being present at the activities of both sides, especially that of the Peloponnesians because of my exile, I had leisure to observe affairs better. (5.26.5)

Thucydides refers to an exile of twenty years' duration after Amphipolis (424 BCE), access to both sides, and the leisure of an extended sabbatical—the necessary conditions perhaps for writing accurate history.[19] Thucydides says that during his exile, he had access to both sides and presumably time to test his various sources (5.26.5).

The circumstances that led to his exile (recounted in the *History*) were as follows. In the year 424, Thucydides himself played a role in the events leading up to the loss of Amphipolis. After mentioning himself as "the other general, Thucydides, son of Olorus, who wrote this history" (4.104.4), Thucydides describes his own actions upon hearing of the Spartan threat to Amphipolis:

> When [Thucydides] heard this, he sailed at once with seven ships which were on the spot, and he wanted above all to get to Amphipolis before its surrender, but otherwise to occupy Eion in advance. (4.104.5)

There were two consequences of Thucydides' quick response. First, the Spartan general Brasidas made a deal with the people of Amphipolis on more moderate terms than he would have otherwise; and second, although Thucydides arrives too late to save Amphipolis, he did save the city of Eion. The contingent nature of this sequence of events is highlighted by one of the counterfactual hypotheses analyzed by Flory.[20]

> ὁ δὲ Θουκυδίδης καὶ αἱ νῆες ταύτῃ τῇ ἡμέρᾳ ὀψὲ κατέπλεον ἐς τὴν Ἠιόνα. καὶ τὴν μὲν Ἀμφίπολιν Βρασίδας ἄρτι εἶχε, τὴν δὲ Ἠιόνα παρὰ νύκτα ἐγένετο λαβεῖν· εἰ γὰρ μὴ ἐβοήθησαν αἱ νῆες διὰ τάχους, ἅμα ἕῳ ἂν εἴχετο.

> Thucydides and his ships sailed into Eion late on the same day. And Brasidas had just taken Amphipolis and came within a night of taking Eion; if the ships had not come to the rescue quickly, it would have been his at dawn. (4.106.4)

Thucydides the general came literally one day too late to protect Amphipolis. How different things might have otherwise been in his life (and perhaps in the war). We note the emphasis on events that occur contrary to expectation (4.103.5, 4.106.1) and recall the many other times Thucydides indicates the contingency of events. This close call—a failure both personal and strategic—may have impressed upon the historian how often the course of events may have followed a different path.[21] In this section, while Thucydides includes both praise for Brasidas and some degree of exculpation for himself, there is no mention of his exile here—this gains notice only in book 5—nor is there any record of the discussion in the Athenian assembly which resulted in Thucydides' exile.[22]

THE PISISTRATIDS, NICIAS, AND THUCYDIDES

Two other episodes relevant to Thucydides' own life and work should be investigated: the Pisistratids (6.54–59) and Nicias' letter (7.8–15). In the middle of book six, soon after the Sicilian Expedition is underway, Thucydides expands upon his discussion of the mutilation of the Herms and mocking of the Mysteries in 415 (6.53–61; cf. 6.27–29). Thucydides criticizes the Athenians' investigation into these crimes on several counts, including the Athenians' failure to gain accurate information, a failure that results in part due to the unreliability of the informants.

> After the fleet sailed, the Athenians in fact had not slackened in their *investigation* (*zetesin*) of the acts committed regarding the Mysteries and the Herms, but *not testing the informers* [οὐ δοκιμάζοντες τοὺς μηνυτάς], they found everything grounds for suspicion, arresting and putting in prison some very upright citizens because of their own trust in scoundrels, since they felt it more essential to *investigate exhaustively* (*basanisai*) the affair and make discoveries than to let anyone accused, however worthy he seemed, *escape examination* (*anelengkton*) on account of an informer's baseness. (6.53.2)

We note that in this description, Thucydides employs terms that he also uses in reference to his own labor as an historian (*zetesis, basanisai, anelengkton*). Just as the historian interviews his informants, the Athenians make an enthusiastic effort to investigate previous events by gathering accusations. But in the end, because they did not "test" the informers (οὐ δοκιμάζοντες τοὺς μηνυτάς), the Athenians' efforts fail to yield any conclusive information or just rulings (6.60.5, 6.61.1)—this contrasts pointedly with Thucydides' own success as an historian.[23]

Thucydides moves from this investigation to the Athenian people's opinions about the tyranny of Pisistratus and his sons. Just as the Athenians in 415 relied on reports from informants, so they also relied for their knowledge concerning the Pisistratids on oral report: ἐπιστάμενος γὰρ ὁ δῆμος ἀκοῇ . . . ("For the people knew from hearing . . ."–6.53.3; cf. 6.60.1). Thucydides here expands upon a correction stated early in the *History:* that Hippias, not Hipparchus, was the son who succeeded

Pisistratus, the sixth-century tyrant of Athens (1.20.2). In Thucydides' account of the Pisistratids, we encounter the familiar elements of collecting information and evaluation of evidence. The evidence Thucydides draws on is in part oral, in part written. Thucydides concludes that Hippias was the elder brother by emphasizing that Hippias—not Hipparchus—had legitimate sons. Inscriptions on the Altar of the Twelve Gods and on a stele on the acropolis record no children for Hipparchus, yet five children of Hippias are mentioned (6.54–55).[24] It is no surprise that Thucydides characterizes his account as more accurate:

> In describing these events fully, I will demonstrate that neither others nor the Athenians themselves are *saying anything accurate* [ἀκριβὲς οὐδὲν λέγοντας] about their own tyrants or about what happened. (6.54.1)

When Thucydides concludes this digression and returns to the situation in Athens in the year 415, he comments that the people have now become harsh and suspicious (6.60). As far as those in prison were concerned, no reliable information had been obtained:

> There is conjecture [*eikazetai*] in both directions, but no one then or later could say anything definite [τὸ σαφές] about those perpetrating the deed. (6.60.2)

Here we note that the Athenians engage in "conjecturing" (*eikazetai*), a word denoting the activity Thucydides uses in an admiring manner for certain statesmen and historians. Yet in this case, one of Thucydides' own goals—"clarity" (τὸ σαφές)—is not achieved, evidently due to a failure of testing and extrapolation. Thucydides remarks that it is unclear whether prisoners were unjustly put to death (6.60.5). Regarding Alcibiades in particular, all that Thucydides will say is that the Athenians *thought* they had clear information about his guilt (6.61.1).[25]

Many aspects of this section deserve further reflection. Regarding the Pisistratids, Thucydides promotes the accuracy of his own account with an explicit reference to an oral source.

εἰδὼς μὲν καὶ ἀκοῇ ἀκριβέστερον ἄλλων ἰσχυρίζομαι.

> I insist with more accurate knowledge than others *through what I have heard* [*akoe*]. (6.55.1)

As Connor remarks, an oral report "can be useful if subjected to careful examination."[26] This Thucydides does, but the Athenian people have failed to do with their informants regarding the Herms and Mysteries. But there is the larger question: Why this digression? What is the connection between the charges against Alcibiades in 415 and the Athenians' faulty beliefs about Hippias and Hipparchus? Why has Thucydides chosen to juxtapose these two episodes?

Among other links, scholars have pointed to the shared themes of passion (*eros*) and tyranny.[27] In addition I would like to emphasize the Athenians' readiness to listen to and believe false accounts. The Athenian people heard Hipparchus was tyrant and they believed it, just as they listened to possibly false accusations against Alcibiades and others in 415 and were persuaded without effective testing. In both cases, we find the Athenians accepting misleading or false reports. A third yet implicit point of comparison, I believe, concerns the circumstances of Thucydides' own exile. After Brasidas took Amphipolis in 424, Thucydides was undoubtedly attacked in the Athenian assembly—according to Marcellinus' biography of Thucydides, it was Cleon who denounced him.[28] Although the grounds for his exile were presumably presented in speeches made in the assembly, Thucydides does *not* maintain that oral reports are necessarily inaccurate—much of the *History* is based on oral report. Indeed, regarding the Pisistratids, Thucydides appears to assign as great weight to his oral source (6.55.1) as to the inscriptions in Athens. Thucydides, however, has tested and compared these reports and evidence. On the other side, as Thucydides has demonstrated, *regarding what it hears* the Athenian people—in its democratic institutions of the assembly and the courts—repeatedly fails to engage in the sort of critical evaluation that Thucydides has engaged in for his own work.

The Athenian assembly also plays a role later in the Sicilian Expedition. In the winter of 414–413 BCE, Nicias sends a report to the assembly by letter.[29] It is of great interest that Thucydides records Nicias' motivations for writing a letter rather than sending an oral report by messenger. Nicias feared that an oral report would distort his message.

> Because [Nicias] was afraid that the men he sent would not report the facts, *whether because of incompetence in speaking, failure of memory, or speaking to please the crowd* [ἢ κατὰ τὴν τοῦ λέγειν ἀδυνασίαν ἢ καὶ μνήμης ἐλλιπεῖς γιγνόμενοι ἢ τῷ ὄχλῳ πρὸς χάριν τι λέγοντες], he wrote a letter believing that this would be the best way for the Athenians to learn his opinion—with no lapses in the transmission—and to deliberate about the true situation. (7.8.2; cf. 7.14.4)

This letter is only partially effective, for the Athenians leave Nicias in command (against his wishes); this in turn leads to a disastrous outcome in Sicily. What is emphasized here are the *disadvantages* of oral communication: the lack of proficiency in speaking, lapses of memory, and the temptation to curry favor with a large audience. But we also might see this passage (in which Thucydides infers Nicias' motivations) as providing a *positive* model for the advantages of written communication found lacking in oral report: a "triad" of skill, fixed remembrance, and objectivity counteracts the fallibility of memory and any inclination to play to a crowd of listeners. Harris argues: "we may gain the impression here that both Nicias and Thucydides had made a discovery"—namely, the superiority of writing over trusting to a messenger's memory and later oral report.[30]

It is worth comparing Thucydides' situation with the circumstances of Nicias in Sicily. Nicias was away from Athens; Nicias was concerned about unreliable speeches made in the assembly; when Nicias wrote his letter in 414, he was writing to guarantee objectivity. He used a written document to combat the sort of speeches often heard in the Athenian assembly. Thucydides found himself in somewhat the same position after his exile: he too relies on writing to convey the truth, but writing alone does not confer accuracy. The reader (and audience) can rely upon the *History*'s accuracy due to Thucydides' research, testing and questioning of sources, comparing of evidence, and laboring for untold hours.[31] Although Thucydides began his *History* at the start of the war, he apparently came to appreciate how he might use the written word in order to speak to and correct his fellow Athenians, whom due to years of exile he has been unable to address.[32] In the final chapter I will attempt to reconstruct that audience.

10

Ancient and Modern Audiences

Throughout most of this book I have referred to the experiences of the "engaged" and "retrospective" readers. Yet these "readers" are artificial constructions implied by Thucydides' *History*. Nevertheless, I have deemed them useful for analyzing how Thucydides structures his presentation and challenges those who encounter it. It is now time to turn to the question of actual audiences—real flesh-and-blood readers and auditors—both in the ancient Greek world and in our contemporary world. This chapter seeks to reconstruct Thucydides' intended audience in antiquity and then turns to modern readers and an example of the *History's* relevance to us today.

Reading Aloud: Oral and Written

There is a complex interplay between the written and oral aspects of Thucydides' work that is central to reconstructing the circumstances of the *History's* reception. Oral sources of both speech and action are of tremendous importance for creating the *History*.[1] Yet Thucydides emphasizes that the *History* is a written document. Thucydides inserts "signatures" as he brings a year of the war to an end with a near-formulaic sentence twelve times in the *History*: for example, "And a second year finished for this war which Thucydides wrote down" (ὃν Θουκυδίδης ξυνέγραψεν–2.70.4).[2] The repeated appearance of this basic expression serves not only as a regular reminder of the authorship of this work, but also highlights the fact that this is a written document. Because the *History* is explicitly proclaimed as written, it comes to share in those advantages in Nicias' triad spelled out in the previous chapter. Indeed, Thucydides may be suggesting that the value of his work—that it will endure as a "possession forever"—is based on its reliability and its status as a written document.[3]

Scholars have not reached a consensus on the identity (and narrowness) of Thucydides' intended ancient audience. Crane argues that Thucydides "created a work designed primarily for—indeed, only fully comprehensible by—the reflective reader."[4] Thomas, however, cautions that the difficulty of Thucydides' style does not necessarily imply a text for readers alone: "His complex, antithetical style is closely akin to that of the contemporary Sophists, for example Antiphon and Gorgias, and they certainly set great store by performance and recitation."[5] It is true that modern readers and scholars gain enormous insight in approaching Thucydides' *History* as a written document in book form, armed with concordances and commentaries. Yet I think Thomas' view better captures the times in which Thucydides lived. Purely from a practical point of view, the sort of examination modern scholars engage in—silent reading of a codex and flipping back and forth to check cross-references—would have been tremendously complicated by a work consisting of cumbersome papyrus rolls. We might instead imagine a group listening together and discussing passages (and sharing recollections of earlier passages) in order to come to grips with Thucydides' work.[6]

Although Thucydides refers to the written status of his work, he clearly expects it to be heard. He candidly acknowledges the *aural* effect of his type of history:

καὶ ἐς μὲν ἀκρόασιν ἴσως τὸ μὴ μυθῶδες αὐτῶν ἀτερπέστερον φανεῖται.

And the results, by my avoiding patriotic storytelling, will perhaps seem the less enjoyable *for listening*. (1.22.4)[7]

Again I believe there is a link with Nicias' letter. Nicias wrote a letter to guarantee the triad of skill, fixed remembrance, and objectivity. But when that letter arrived in Athens, it was *read aloud* by a secretary (*grammateus*) and *heard* by the Athenians:[8]

ὁ δὲ γραμματεὺς ὁ τῆς πόλεως παρελθὼν ἀνέγνω τοῖς Ἀθηναίοις δηλοῦσαν τοιάδε. . . . Ἡ μὲν τοῦ Νικίου ἐπιστολὴ τοσαῦτα ἐδήλου, οἱ δὲ Ἀθηναῖοι ἀκούσαντες αὐτῆς τὸν μὲν Νικίαν οὐ παρέλυσαν τῆς ἀρχῆς.

The secretary of the city came forward and read it to the Athenians, disclosing the following. . . . So much the letter of Nicias disclosed, but when the Athenians heard it, they did not release Nicias from his command. (7.10, 7.16.1)

I would suggest that circumstances somewhat analogous to these may have existed for the reception of Thucydides' own work. In a group setting, one of those present would read aloud from the text of Thucydides' *History*; the rest would listen. Naturally there would have been the opportunity for someone to go back and reread (alone and silently or aloud to those present) difficult passages that required a second or third perusal, but the experience for the majority would be aural.[9]

Thucydides' Ancient Audience

Several contrasts developed in the *History* help us in our search for the identity of Thucydides' audience. For one of these significant contrasts, Thucydides opposes the pleasure of listening to certain works to the usefulness and truth of his own. As he concedes, his own work will appear *ater-pesteron*— "less likely to give pleasure." Yet it may be judged "useful" (*ophelima*–1.22.4). Earlier he criticizes the logographers who compose work "more attractive for listening than truthful" (ἐπὶ τὸ προσαγω-γότερον τῇ ἀκροάσει ἢ ἀληθέστερον–1.21.1; cf. 6.8.2). Not only is Thucydides' work less than delightful to listen to but he emphasizes the difficulties he had to overcome, obstacles his audience also confronts.

This leads to a second contrast. In addition to promoting usefulness and truth over pleasure, Thucydides suggests that his target audience will be small. In several passages, Thucydides distinguishes between the few and the many. For example, while "the many" are likely to receive reports uncritically or avoid the toil needed to attain the truth, Thucydides insists upon the extensive labor he has expended on analyzing his sources.

> οὕτως ἀταλαίπωρος **τοῖς πολλοῖς** ἡ ζήτησις τῆς ἀληθείας, καὶ ἐπὶ τὰ ἑτοῖμα μᾶλλον τρέπονται.

> The search for truth is so devoid of effort *for the many*, that they would rather turn toward what is readily available. (1.20.3; cf. 1.1.3, 1.20.1, 1.22.3)

In part, these statements are polemical and serve to emphasize Thucydides' own critical examination of evidence. Edmunds has explored these dichotomies—pleasure vs. utility; the few vs. the many—and reads this latter contrast in political terms: "The words Thucydides uses to describe those who are content with untruth [*to plethos, hoi polloi*] are unmistakably political."[10] Thus far our reconstruction posits that Thucydides' *History* was read aloud and heard by a select group—perhaps of elite political and social standing—seeking valuable history as opposed to a multitude in pursuit of delight.[11]

While Thucydides clearly recognizes the potential of written report and proclaims his own work to be of that status, there is no compelling reason to think that Thucydides felt access by a silent reader was superior to that of a critical listener. In addition to the model of Nicias' letter (read aloud to the Athenian assembly) and Thucydides' own explicit remarks on those who "hear" his work, there is a third type of contemporary evidence that may bear on this question: the reception of Plato's dialogues.

THUCYDIDES AND PLATO

Here I return to parallels between the historian Thucydides and the philosopher Plato suggested in chapter 1. Both were raised in a culture dominated by oral discourse; for somewhat different reasons both turned to composing works meant to be read and, I think, read aloud. I have argued that the works of both Thucydides and Plato sought the engagement of the reader—and both did so successfully, in part, because the arguments were not presented as authoritative by the author. The judgment of the reader is invited. I believe another major parallel may exist between Thucydides' and Plato's work—that of reception.

Plato's works appear less than a generation after Thucydides' *History*. While we can only speculate regarding the reception of both these writers, there is evidence in Plato (and later testimonia) that Plato's works were meant to be heard and interacted with along the lines I have suggested for Thucydides' *History*. If the circumstances sketched out above are correct, those in the group may listen, but would also have the option of responding by joining in the debate, making a pointed objection that one of Thucydides' speakers (or one of Socrates' interlocuters) fails to make, or proposing a better argument or strategy. As teachers know quite well from classroom experience, the words of Thucydides' and Plato's texts—both in substance and style—are ideal prompts for discussion. It is not going too far to imagine an interactive social setting, in some ways comparable to the Athenian assembly, in which Athenian (and other) citizens would listen critically (as they would to Nicias' written report from Sicily) and then engage in serious oral debate on the difficult issues at hand. This practice apparently reflected Athenian culture at large.

Plato's works would very likely have been read aloud and discussed. Socrates describes how he heard someone else reading aloud from Anaxagoras' book (Plato *Phaedo* 97b–c); Diogenes Laertius recounts that both Antisthenes and Plato read aloud from their own written works (Diogenes Laertius 3.35, 3.37; cf. Xenophon *Memorabilia* 1.6.14); in Plato's *Parmenides*, Zeno reads aloud from his written works to a gathering.

ἀναγιγνώσκειν οὖν αὐτοῖς τὸν Ζήνωνα αὐτόν...τὸν οὖν Σωκράτη ἀκούσαντα πάλιν τε κελεῦσαι τὴν πρώτην ὑπόθεσιν τοῦ πρώτου λόγου ἀναγνῶναι, καὶ ἀναγνωσθείσης, " πῶς, " φάναι, " ὦ Ζήνων, τοῦτο λέγεις; εἰ πολλά ἐστι τὰ ὄντα, ὡς ἄρα δεῖ αὐτὰ ὅμοιά τε εἶναι καὶ ἀνόμοια, τοῦτο δὲ δὴ ἀδύνατον· οὔτε γὰρ τὰ ἀνόμοια ὅμοια οὔτε τὰ ὅμοια ἀνόμοια οἷόν τε εἶναι; οὐχ οὕτω λέγεις;" "οὕτω," φάναι τὸν Ζήνωνα.

So Zeno himself read aloud to them. . . . Socrates listened to the end, and then asked that the first proposal of the first argument be read again. When this had been done, he said: "Zeno, what do you mean by this? That if the things which exist are many, they must be both like and unlike, which is impossible; for the unlike cannot be like, nor the like unlike? Is not that your meaning?" "Yes," said Zeno. (Plato *Parmenides* 127c–e)[12]

The historicity of this dialogue is not at issue—whether Zeno actually read at Pythodorus' house or whether Socrates was present. The important point is that in the first half of the fourth century (when Thucydides' and Plato's works would have been first available), this sort of interaction was not exceptional.[13] Not only does Zeno read aloud but Socrates also requests that Zeno read a particular passage for a second time, provoking an extended discussion. Looking at such evidence, Thomas comments: "A single text may be read aloud to a gathering of people and discussed. . . . Perhaps we are also glimpsing the peculiarly communal way in which ideas were presented in classical Athens, which meant that reading to a group was quite natural."[14]

So who actually read, heard, and discussed Thucydides' work? In an article on the fourth-century and Hellenistic reception of Thucydides, Hornblower surveys the various students, thinkers, and writers who were influenced by Thucydides' *History*. In addition to Xenophon (who continued the *History*) and Demosthenes, Hornblower argues that Thucydides was studied in the Academy and the Lyceum. The best case for influence—and imitation—is found by comparing Thucydides' account of the

Corcyrean civil war (3.82–83) with Plato's discussion of constitutional change in *Republic* book 8 of the *Republic* —in particular, the section on the transformation of language as the soul changes from an oligarchical to a democratic soul. In the *Republic*, the desires competing for the young man's soul rename familiar concepts:

"Doing battle and controlling things themselves, *won't they* [the desires competing for the young man's soul] *call reverence foolishness and moderation cowardice* [τὴν μὲν αἰδῶ ἠλιθιότητα ὀνομάζοντες . . . σωφροσύνην δὲ ἀνανδρίαν καλοῦντές], abusing them and casting them out beyond the frontiers like disenfranchised exiles? *And won't they persuade the young man that measured and orderly expenditure is boorish and mean* [μετριότητα δὲ καὶ κοσμίαν δαπάνην ὡς ἀγροικίαν καὶ ἀνελευθερίαν οὖσαν πείθοντες], and, joining with many useless desires, won't they expel it across the border?"

"They certainly will."

"Having thus emptied and purged these from the soul of the one they've possessed and initiated in splendid rites, they proceed to return insolence, anarchy, extravagance, and shamelessness from exile in a blaze of torchlight, wreathing them in garlands and accompanying them with a vast chorus of followers. They praise the returning exiles and give them fine names, *calling insolence good breeding, anarchy freedom, profligacy magnificence, and shamelessness courage* [ὕβριν μὲν εὐπαιδευσίαν καλοῦντες, ἀναρχίαν δὲ ἐλευθερίαν, ἀσωτίαν δὲ μεγαλοπρέπειαν, ἀναίδειαν δὲ ἀνδρείαν]. Isn't it in some such way as this that someone who is young changes, after being brought up with necessary desires, to the liberation and release of useless and unnecessary pleasures?"

"Yes, that's clearly the way it happens." (Plato *Rep.* 560c–561a)[15]

In Plato, we find a type of civil war (*stasis*) in the soul of the young man. In Plato's apparent model—book 3 of the *History*—Thucydides describes civil war (*stasis*) in the city of Corcyra. Again language and what it refers to undergoes a transformation.

καὶ τὴν εἰωθυῖαν ἀξίωσιν τῶν ὀνομάτων ἐς τὰ ἔργα ἀντήλλαξαν τῇ δικαιώσει. τόλμα μὲν γὰρ ἀλόγιστος ἀνδρεία φιλέταιρος ἐνομίσθη, μέλλησις δὲ προμηθὴς δειλία εὐπρεπής, τὸ δὲ σῶφρον τοῦ ἀνάνδρου πρόσχημα, καὶ τὸ πρὸς ἅπαν ξυνετὸν ἐπὶ πᾶν ἀργόν· τὸ δ' ἐμπλήκτως ὀξὺ ἀνδρὸς μοίρᾳ προσετέθη, ἀσφαλείᾳ δὲ τὸ ἐπι

βουλεύσασθαι ἀποτροπῆς πρόφασις εὔλογος. καὶ ὁ μὲν
χαλεπαίνων πιστὸς αἰεί, ὁ δ' ἀντιλέγων αὐτῷ ὕποπτος.
ἐπιβουλεύσας δέ τις τυχὼν ξυνετὸς καὶ ὑπονοήσας ἔτι δεινότερος·
προβουλεύσας δὲ ὅπως μηδὲν αὐτῶν δεήσει, τῆς τε ἑταιρίας δια-
λυτὴς καὶ τοὺς ἐναντίους ἐκπεπληγμένος.

And men inverted the usual verbal evaluations of actions according to
their perception of what was justified.[16] Irrational recklessness was now
considered courageous commitment, hesitation while looking to the
future was high-styled cowardice, moderation was a cover for lack of man-
hood, and circumspection meant inaction, while senseless anger now
helped to define a true man, and deliberation for security was a specious
excuse for dereliction. The man of violent temper was always credible,
anyone opposing him was suspect. The intriguer who succeeded was intelligent, anyone who detected a plot was still more clever, but a man who
made provisions to avoid both alternatives was undermining his party and
letting the opposition terrorize him. (Thuc. 3.82.4–5)

Rutherford calls this "probably . . . the best candidate for actual imitation
of the history by Plato." To be sure, the relationship between Plato and
Thucydides is not a simple one. Yunis has recently argued that Plato's
Gorgias and *Republic* contain a critique not only of Pericles, but specifical-
ly of the Thucydidean Pericles.[17] As far as Aristotle is concerned,
Hornblower mentions both Aristotle's *Politics* and the *Constitution of the
Athenians* making use, in particular, of Thucydides' account of the oligarchical revolution in book 8.[18] All of this suggests that Thucydides' work
was read, studied, and responded to by Plato, Aristotle, and their students.
    The goal was not purely theoretical. In an article on the Academy,
Baltes maintains that these fourth-century schools were more than think-
tanks. Neither the Academy nor the Lyceum was divorced from the world
of active politics. As Baltes suggests:

Plato sought to win over Dionysius II of Syracuse for philosophy, and to
fashion from him the Platonic ideal of a philosopher king. Aristotle was
engaged as tutor for Alexander the Great. Various members of the
Academy had freed their homelands from tyranny, others gave new constitutions to cities which requested them, and again others accepted public office, and so on. We see that it was not feeble theoreticians who lived
together in the Academy at that time—they exerted powerful influence

outside. The philosophy, then, of Plato and his associates was no bloodless affair, but an extremely living thing.[19]

A primary goal of both Thucydides' *History* (and Plato's dialogues) may well have been to provoke discussion *and action* from the audience.[20] This scenario envisions a sort of "feedback" loop: oral reports constitute the primary raw material of Thucydides' *History* (just as Socrates' conversations inspired Plato's dialogues); the work itself is superior to oral reports, because it results from testing, years of work, and the permanence of writing; but access and reaction to the *History* may have been largely oral for those who heard it and could respond to it in spoken discourse—in the philosophical schools and elsewhere.[21] Remember Thucydides' original characterization of the Peloponnesian War: it is "most worth recording" (*axiologotaton*–1.1.1), or strictly speaking, it is the war "most worthy of *logos*." Given the historical context, he may mean that this war is most worthy of speech, discussion, and analysis—both written and spoken. Ultimately, then, it is valuable to distinguish between the status of the *History* as a written document and its intended audience which may have included both readers and auditors.

Given the political affinities of those reading (and hearing) Thucydides' work, I would not claim that writing itself is inherently opposed to democracy. On the connection between writing and politics, I find myself in agreement with Steiner: "It was not writing per se that was anti-democratic; it was rather that the written text was the vehicle of choice for individuals who rejected or were excluded from democratic politics." To be sure, exile "excluded" Thucydides from participation in Athenian politics; he turned instead to a self-consciously written history. It is perhaps not surprising that students of Thucydides would have included the so-called political "dissenters" that Ober examines: Xenophon, Plato, Aristotle, and other critics of Athenian democracy.[22]

TYPES OF ORAL DISCOURSE

It must be acknowledged that Thucydides employs an unusual expression to describe what he has produced. He contrasts his "possession forever" (κτῆμά τε ἐς αἰεί) with a "competition piece to be heard for the moment" (ἀγώνισμα ἐς τὸ παραχρῆμα ἀκούειν). This may appear to suggest that the permanence of writing allows the *History* to transcend the momentary existence of a competitive speech. How are we to understand the term *agon-isma* which Thucydides employs to characterize other work but not his?

At this point, we need to distinguish among different types of oral per-formance. One type was the display piece, the *epideixis* of the sophist—for example, a performance by Prodicus of the choice of Heracles or an epi-deictic speech by Gorgias or Protagoras. The goal of *epideixis* was to impress and dazzle the audience, not to elicit discussion on the part of the listeners. Thomas sees this as Thucydides' target.

> It was perhaps this agonistic, display-oriented mode of exchanging and discussing ideas against which Thucydides reacted so energetically when he declared that his work was going to be no mere *agonisma*, no competi-tive piece for the immediate pleasure of the listeners. (I 22.4).[23]

This sort of display-oriented speech, I would argue, is quite different from the sort of engagement Platonic dialogues elicit, which probably were read aloud and discussed. Just as it is legitimate to distinguish between sophis-tic *epideixis* and Platonic dialogue (although both are examples of oral per-formance texts that were read aloud), in a similar way—by using the term *agonisma* (competition piece)—Thucydides may be distancing his work from such display pieces.[24]

Yet Thucydides might still expect that his work be read aloud. The dif-ference would be the anticipated reaction from the audience. Unlike *epi-deixis* or competitive oratory, Thucydides would expect parts of his work to be read aloud, with oral response and debate to follow. Indeed, this dis-tinction between *epideixis* and serious discussion appears in book 3 of Thucydides' *History* when Cleon condemns the Athenian assembly for the pleasure (*hedone*) it takes in listening: they are like spectators of sophists rather than being engaged in "deliberating about the city."

> " ἁπλῶς τε ἀκοῆς ἡδονῇ ἡσσώμενοι καὶ **σοφιστῶν θεαταῖς ἐοικότες** καθημένοις μᾶλλον ἢ **περὶ πόλεως βουλευομένοις**."

> "In short, overcome by the pleasure of listening, [you are] *like men seated for entertainment by sophists* rather than *for deliberating about the city*." (3.38.7)

In this *one* instance, Thucydides may well find himself in agreement with Cleon, who argues against the mere "enjoyment" of listening when more serious matters are at stake.

THE DIFFICULTY OF THUCYDIDES

The question also arises about what was actually read—was it Thucydides' *History* cover to cover (scroll by scroll) or is it more likely that excerpts were read? This topic relates to the difficulty of Thucydides' work. In order to infer what may have been read to a particular audience, we should begin by acknowledging the extreme difficulty of at least some of the passages in Thucydides. Dionysius of Halicarnassus comments upon the fact that certain sections are almost impossible to understand.

> I shall pass over the fact that if people spoke like this, not even their fathers or mothers could bear the unpleasantness (*aedian*) of listening to them: they would need an interpreter, as if they were listening to a foreign tongue . . . for the number of men who can understand the whole of Thucydides can easily be counted, and even these cannot understand certain passages without *a linguistic commentary* [ἐξηγήσεως γραμματικῆς].
> (Dionysius of Halicarnassus *On Thucydides* 49, 51)[25]

So says Dionysius who comes four centuries after Thucydides, yet he is a native speaker of Greek. Of course not all of Thucydides' work is equally difficult. We might distinguish between passages such as the archaeology and maybe the Melian dialogue from tougher going found in the Funeral Oration and elsewhere. In fact, this is what Dionysius does. He judges the description of civil war (*stasis*) in Corcyra (3.82.3) to be "tortuous and difficult to follow" (29), while he praises the exchange between the Plataeans and the Spartan King Archidamus (2.71–75) for its "purity, lucidity, and brevity" (36).

Once again I propose a possible analogy with Plato's work. In his book *Plato and the Socratic Dialogue*, Kahn makes a compelling argument about the varying degrees of difficulty of Plato's dialogues. He points to the early work of Plato, such as *Protagoras*, *Meno*, and *Symposium*, as:

> sustained protreptic to philosophy. As the choice of interlocutors indicates, *Plato's intended audience for these dialogues includes* not only professional philosophers and beginners in philosophy but also *the general public, and in particular the young men in search of themselves*, in search of knowledge, or in search of a career, men who in the fifth century would have sat at the feet of the sophists and who in Plato's own day might be tempted by the lessons of Isocrates or Antisthenes [my italics].[26]

Kahn goes on to argue that the *Phaedrus* may perhaps be the last work that Plato "designed for this wider public." The works which follow, such as the *Parmenides* and the *Theaetetus*, are "works of philosophy written for philosophers."[27] Kahn thus contends that not all Plato's works are of comparable difficulty, nor are they all intended for the same audience. We might imagine a similar situation for the *History*. For a less experienced audience, excerpts from the more accessible passages from Thucydides might have been read aloud and discussed. For those with more experience, readings might include the description of the Corcyrean civil war. So if we ask: who is Thucydides' audience?—there is not necessarily a single answer. What was read and discussed could well have depended upon the experience of the audience and its familiarity with Thucydides' ideas and style.[28]

We might even think of Thucydides' work—at least much of it—necessitating discussion *because* of its difficulty. Consider the sorts of readers' tasks I have described in chapters 3–8: connecting events early in book 2 (the Theban invasion of Plataea) to speeches that reassess those events midway through book 3; interpreting the Melian Dialogue in terms of lessons learned elsewhere in the *History*; comparing Athenian imperial behavior with that of actual tyrants, and so on. In addition, readers must negotiate between competing views of the past, especially when confronting passages that suggest certain events may be inevitable as well as those that apparently emphasize how contingent events are—where wind, a reversed decision, or a fortuitous arrival (or an arrival one day too late!) not only affect the course of events, but demonstrate that such a sequence of events might have turned out differently. These challenges are all demanding, especially so when we imagine the difficulties (and unfamiliarity) of reading a text in the early fourth century. It may well be that Thucydides' goal was to provoke discussion—yet if serious discussion was to take place, it might have required auditors working as a group and pooling their recollections in order to debate these profound problems.

My hope is that the analogy between Plato and Thucydides sheds some light on how Thucydides' work may have been experienced in the early fourth century. For both writers, then, a distinction should be made between the status of the *History*—or the dialogues—as written documents and their intended reception. The difficulty of engaging with such texts (consisting of writing on papyrus rolls without word division or punctuation) may favor imagining the original reception as a group listening together, discussing passages, and sharing recollections of earlier passages, of juxtaposing, comparing, and extrapolating—*eikazein!*—from different sections of the *History* (or the dialogues) as a means of coming to grips with Thucydides' (or Plato's) work.

One final idea concerning Thucydides and his audience. There are, I think, cues in the text of Thucydides that support this "hybrid" reception model.[29] These markers guide the reader's and auditor's responses; that is, Thucydides shows what is worth pursuing, comparing, and discussing. Such cues include striking metaphors, such as "Athens-the-tyrant-city," polarities (such as land and sea or freedom and slavery), maxims, and recurrent themes—all these provide a kind of unity to Thucydides' work. Markers of this sort would facilitate the apprehension of cross-references in non-contiguous passages; suggest how both auditors and readers might connect early and later sections of the *History*; and invite both reader and auditor to appreciate deliberate juxtapositions. One of Thucydides' achievements is to have created the type of work that remains accessible to a listening audience, yet promises greater potential for those who read and reread it—and hear and rehear it. Both readers and auditors are invited to return for a more profound appreciation of this "possession forever" (1.22.4).

THUCYDIDES' MODERN AUDIENCE

So where does all this leave us in the modern world? My hope is that this discussion has been valuable in providing a plausible reconstruction of Thucydides' original intended audience. And yet I believe he is much more ambitious, for he also includes us as his audience. What does our task consist of? In part, our goal is to reflect upon the experiences of the engaged and retrospective reader, in part, to ponder the circumstances of an actual audience in late fifth- or early fourth-century Greece; but our task is also to be engaged actively with respect to our own world. One challenge Thucydides throws out for his reader—and auditor—is to apprehend events and arguments of later times that are comparable to the events and arguments of the Peloponnesian War. We too must engage in comparison and extrapolation (*eikazein*).

Thucydides states that his work will be valuable (*ophelima*—1.22.4), yet what sort of "use" is this work? Is it valuable only in terms of learning about the past or is there a practical application? Rood wisely comments:

> Scholars have long noted the fact that [Thucydides] does not say what sort of advantage the narratee is meant to gain: is it simply a better understanding of

the world or is it an understanding that has practical use? Thucydides' lack of
precision is itself revealing. He leaves it to readers to make of his history what
they will.[30]

I, too, would like to keep the question open. If Thucydides had a narrow
view of the *History's* value, he could easily have indicated as much. We
need not rule out practical lessons for citizens and leaders. It is true that
much of our analysis has focused on the apprehension of what happened—
or what might have happened—and how to understand it. While finding
a straightforward application of a Thucydidean lesson to a specific contemporary problem is hard to imagine, other works of history have clearly
influenced statesmen. Frankel has recently written about the influence of
Barbara Tuchman's *The Guns of August* (1961—about the start of World
War I) upon Kennedy's decision-making and diplomacy during the Cuban
Missile Crisis in 1962.[31] I propose exploring a more recent set of events that
reverberates in a variety of ways with Thucydides' *History:* the diplomatic
dispute that led up to the 2003 U.S.-Iraq War.

A recurring situation in Thucydides presents a powerful state attacking
a smaller, weaker state. In a few cases, before the attack negotiations under
threat of force take place. The Athenians' conflict with Melos immediately
comes to mind (5.84–116) as does Archidamus' negotiations with Plataea
(2.71–78). These scenarios suggest several similarities to the build-up
before the war against Iraq in 2003. My analysis will be limited to the
rhetoric in both the ancient and modern situations, specifically, the ultimatum and rationale presented by the larger power, and the response by
the weaker power in light of available options. I would anticipate four
areas worthy of comparison between the ancient and modern confronta-
tions: the situation, the outcome, the rhetoric employed, and—once we
step back—a method of analysis.

MELOS, PLATAEA, AND CORINTH

I begin with a few highlights of events involving Melos, Plataea, and
Corinth. When the Athenians arrive at the island of Melos in 416 BCE,
before doing any damage to the land, they send ambassadors to speak to
the Melians in charge. As we saw in chapter 5, the Athenians make clear
their demands to the Melians: submit by joining the Athenian empire or
suffer attack (5.91.2). The rationale put forth by the Athenian ambassadors covers quite a range. They assert their own power (5.89); they

would become safer (5.97); the Athenians also suggest the advantages to the weaker state, for the Melians would avoid suffering (5.93). The Melians however insist they are confronting injustice (5.104) and ultimately refuse to submit to Athens, basing their rejection upon the seven hundred years of freedom they have enjoyed (5.112).

Earlier in the History—in 429 BCE—a coalition of Peloponnesian allies marches on the city of Plataea. Again just as this force is about to ravage the land, the Plataeans send ambassadors to make a plea (2.71.1). But again, in spite of various options offered by Archidamus, the Plataeans reject Archidamus' overtures largely upon the Athenians' promise of assistance.

In both scenarios—Melos and Plataea—the weaker and the stronger powers address one another in order to avoid bloodshed. The result, however, is the same: the negotiations are unsuccessful and the weaker power is attacked and subdued. We do find several contrasts in the negotiations: one of these is the Athenian exclusion of moral appeals in the Melian dialogue, while both the Plataeans and Archidamus insist on the justice of their causes. The greatest surprise is the decision by the weaker state to reject the stronger's demands. Yet we find such responses even in modern times. Before venturing there, it may be valuable to move backward in time and examine briefly the Corinthians' speech to the gathering of Peloponnesian allies in 432 just before the war begins (1.119–124—I do realize my analysis is moving backwards in time).

The primary thrust of the Corinthians' remarks is to convince the Spartans and their other allies that the time has come for war. The Corinthians appeal to the allies' "common interests" (τὰ κοινὰ προσκοπεῖν–1.120.1, 1.124.1); cities away from the sea no less than coastal states are threatened by Athens, the tyrant-city (1.120.2, 1.122.3, 1.124.3). After these justifications for war, the Corinthians insist that they must not delay or disaster will ensue (1.124.1–2). The Corinthians' final call is for freedom—to rescue those Greek cities already enslaved and to prevent further Athenian aggression. The alternative, they say, is "outright slavery" (1.122.2, 1.124.3).

So much for the Corinthian argument. It is not a case of a stronger power threatening a weaker one during wartime; rather this is an internal discussion by a coalition with one member, Corinth, urging the others to make war. Following his presentation of the Corinthian argument, the allies vote to go to war. The historian then comments:

Once they voted for war, it was still impossible for them to commence, for they were unprepared; but it was resolved that the different cities procure what was needed without delay . . . in the meantime they sent embassies to Athens bringing *charges* (ἐγκλήματα), in order to obtain *the greatest pretext* [μεγίστη πρόφασις] for war if the Athenians would not yield. (1.125.2–126.1)[32]

These comments of Thucydides may be relevant to our analysis of the 2003 War.

The U.S.- Iraq Conflict (2002–2003 CE)

I turn now to the escalation in the years 2002–2003 that led to the U.S.-Iraq War. At the time of writing (2006), the war continues between factions and between U.S. troops and various groups, yet I will limit my discussion to the rhetoric put forth before the war itself began. First, a few disclaimers. The situations described in Thucydides are not exactly parallel to the modern scenario—I realize this. Before the March 2003 war, there was Iraq's invasion of Kuwait, the 1991 Gulf War, UN sanctions, the establishment of no-fly zones, the oil-for-food program, weapons inspections, and the attacks of 11 September 2001. In addition, the negotiations in 2002–2003 took place over many months in different venues with various spokespersons. Not for a minute do I assume that the United States is identical to Athens (or Sparta) or that Iraq is just like Melos or Plataea.

And yet Thucydides does invite us to examine similar situations in later times which are comparable to both words and deeds from the Peloponnesian War—not only what is said, but what "ought to be said" in a given situation (τὰ δέοντα μάλιστ᾽ εἰπεῖν—1.22.1). My goal, then, is to consider parallels from Thucydides' work by examining the public rhetoric used before the war. I will focus on two speeches: President Bush's address to the United Nations (12 September 2002) and Secretary of State Colin Powell's UN speech (5 February 2003). In order to provide a context, I offer a timeline indicating some of the significant events before the war began on 20 March 2003.

2002–2003 *Timeline*

Summer 2002 to March 2003: Movement of U.S. and Coalition Weapons, Ships, and Troops into the Persian Gulf.

12 September 2002: President Bush's address to the United Nations.
8 November 2002: UN Resolution 1441.
November 2002–March 2003: UN Inspectors in Iraq.
8 December 2002: Iraq sends 12,000 pages of documents to the UN.
5 February 2003: Secretary of State Colin Powell's speech to the UN.
February and March 2003: Responses of the Iraqi government.
17 March 2003: UN Resolution authorizing force is withdrawn.
17 March 2003: U.S. ultimatum that within 48 hours Saddam Hussein
and his family unconditionally surrender or leave Iraq.
20 March 2003: The war begins.

President Bush's Speech to the United Nations (12 September 2002)

Bush's speech addresses a double audience, for it is aimed in part at the
Security Council and General Assembly, in part at Iraq. Early on Bush
asserts that all nations have been threatened.

> *Our common security is challenged by regional conflicts.* . . . Above all, our
> principles and our security are challenged today by outlaw groups and
> regimes that accept no law of morality and have no limit to their violent
> ambitions. . . . This threat hides within many nations, including my own.
> In cells and camps, terrorists are plotting further destruction, and building
> new bases for their war against civilization. *And our greatest fear is that ter-*
> *rorists will find a shortcut to their mad ambitions when an outlaw regime sup-*
> *plies them with the technologies to kill on a massive scale.* [my italics, as
> below][33]

Bush emphasizes the link between terrorists and "an outlaw regime" and
then claims that these dangers reside in Iraq alone.

> In one place—in one regime—we find all these dangers, in their most
> lethal and aggressive forms, exactly the kind of aggressive threat the
> United Nations was born to confront.

Bush then looks to the past, both Iraq's previous aggression against Kuwait
and previous UN resolutions that demanded Iraq

> stop development of all weapons of mass destruction [W.M.D.] and long-

range missiles . . . [and allow] UN inspectors immediate and unrestricted access to verify Iraq's commitment to rid itself of W.M.D.

Bush claims that efforts thus far have been unsuccessful:

> Saddam Hussein has defied all these efforts and continues to develop weapons of mass destruction. The first time we may be completely certain he has nuclear weapons is when, God forbids, he uses one. We owe it to all our citizens to do everything in our power to prevent that day from coming.

According to Bush, if Iraq wishes to enjoy peace, the Iraqi regime must

> immediately and unconditionally forswear, disclose, and remove or destroy all W.M.D., long range missiles, and all related material . . . [and] immediately end all support for terrorism.

While hoping that the UN will meet "our common challenge," Bush's speech concludes with a threat of unilateral action:

> But the purposes of the United States should not be doubted. The Security council resolutions will be enforced—the just demands of peace and security will be met—or action will be unavoidable.

As I mentioned above, President Bush is addressing more than one audience. The result is that some of what he has to say may recall what the Athenians said to the Melians (the demand for certain actions under threat of force) while other sections of his speech may echo the Corinthians' insistence on war (common interests are threatened, a dictator or tyrant is plotting against everyone else).

UN Resolution 1441 (8 November 2002)

On 8 November 2002, the United Nations voted to pass UN resolution 1441, insisting that Iraq allow weapons inspectors into their country and give full cooperation. The key provisions concerned Iraq's previous failure to meet its obligations, yet Iraq is offered a final chance to comply.

> Iraq has been and remains in material breach of its obligations. . . . Iraq will be afforded, by this resolution, a final opportunity to comply with its disar-

mament obligations under relevant resolutions of the Council.[34]

Iraq is given thirty days to make a full declaration to UNMOVIC (United Nations Monitoring,· Verification, and Inspection Commission), the IAEA (International Atomic Energy Agency), and the UN Security Council of:

> a currently accurate, full, and complete declaration of all aspects of its programmes to develop chemical, biological, and nuclear weapons. . . . Iraq shall provide UNMOVIC and the IAEA immediate, unimpeded, unconditional, and unrestricted access to any and all . . . areas, facilities, building, equipment, records, and means of transports and to officials or other persons.

Secretary of State Colin Powell's Speech to the UN (5 February 2003)

In response to the demand for a full declaration, on 8 December 2002 the Iraqi government sent 12,000 pages of documents to the UN. The inspection agencies evaluated these materials and then (following the inspectors' assessment), U.S. Secretary of State Colin Powell addressed the UN in a speech on 5 February 2003. He begins by recalling that the purpose of Resolution 1441 (from 8 November 2002) was:

> to disarm Iraq of its weapons of mass destruction. . . . [and to offer Iraq] one last chance . . . to come into compliance or to face serious consequences.[35]

Powell states that he has asked to address the UN on February 5th session for two purposes: "First, to support the core assessments made by Dr. Blix and Dr. ElBaradei."[36] His second goal was:

> to provide you with additional information, to share with you what the United States knows about Iraq's weapons of mass destruction as well as Iraq's involvement in terrorism. . . . What you will see is an accumulation of facts and disturbing patterns of behavior. . . . The facts of Iraq's behavior demonstrate that Saddam Hussein and his regime have made no effort—no effort—to disarm as required by the international community.

Powell describes the various sources he has made use of in order to reach his conclusions: audio-tapes, video film, satellite photos, and human intelligence sources among others.

His particular concern is not only that weapons of mass destruction were being developed by Iraq but also that connections exist between Iraq and terrorist organizations:

> Our concern is not just about these illicit weapons; *it's the way that these illicit weapons can be connected to terrorists and terrorist organizations that have no compunction about using such devices against innocent people around the world.* . . . Iraqi officials deny accusations of ties with al Qaeda. These denials are simply not credible.

In contrast to the denials of the Iraqi government that Powell labels as "not credible," he emphasizes the credibility of his own information:

> My colleagues, every statement I make today is backed up by sources, solid sources. These are not assertions. What we are giving you are facts and conclusions based on solid intelligence. . . . Ladies and gentlemen, these are not assertions. These are facts corroborated by many sources, some of them sources of the intelligence services of other countries.

Powell returns to what he interprets as the original purpose of Resolution 1441 and issues a call to action:

> My colleagues . . . we wrote 1441 not in order to go to war. We wrote 1441 to try to preserve the peace. We wrote 1441 to give Iraq one last chance. Iraq is not, so far, taking that one last chance. . . . We must not shrink from whatever is ahead of us. We must not fail in our duty and our responsibility to the citizens of the countries that are represented by this body.

U.S. ULTIMATUMS

In both February and March 2003, the U.S. issued ultimatums, both to its European allies and to Iraq. With a clear reference to France, Powell spoke to reporters on 20 February 2003:

> It is not a satisfactory solution to continue inspections indefinitely because certain countries [like France that oppose swift military action against

Iraq] are afraid of upholding their responsibility to impose the will of the international community.[37]

. Almost a month later, on 17 March 2003 the U.S. insisted that within 48 hours Saddam Hussein and his family surrender unconditionally or leave Iraq. This day (17 March 2003) was also the same day that—before a vote—the United States withdrew its request for a UN Resolution authorizing force against Iraq. The war began three days later on 20 March 2003.

Allow me to make a few observations. First, the ultimatum made by the U.S. United States shifts over time. Originally they insisted that Iraq allow weapons inspectors in and fully comply with UN resolutions; then the ultimatum became either Saddam and his relatives surrender or depart from Iraq within two days. Second, the rationale arguing for such actions covered a broad range. We might consider four major categories of argument: (1) *violation of UN resolutions* (non-compliance and material breach of UN Resolutions; access denied to UN weapons inspectors); (2) *the danger posed by Iraq* (both in term of its weapons of mass destruction and its links to terrorism); (3) *regime change* (Saddam Hussein's tyrannical rule was a threat to the Iraqi people and their neighbors; the flip-side was that removing Saddam Hussein would lead to the liberation of the Iraqi people); and (4) other reasons including "history calls the U.S. to action"; the war would serve as a warning to other terrorists; removing Saddam Hussein would transform the region; it would also conclude the 1991 war; "because the U.S. could"; and in order to preserve peace. A valuable inventory of twenty-one reasons voiced by various U.S. officials endorsing war against Iraq has been compiled by Devon Largio, a student at the University of Illinois.[38]

Iraqi Reponses

During fall 2002 and winter 2003, the Iraqi government made various responses, which were to a large degree reactive. They also addressed multiple audiences: others in the Arab world, the UN, and the U.S. The Iraqis claimed they were complying with UN demands, they were giving full access, they did not have weapons of mass destruction (W.M.D.), and they had no connections to Al Qaeda.

For example, in an interview with Dan Rather in Baghdad on 26 February 2003, Saddam Hussein said:

We have never had any relationship with Mr. Osama bin Laden, and Iraq has never had any relationship with Al Qaeda. And I think that Mr. Bin Laden himself has recently, in one of his speeches, given such an answer—that we have no relation with him.[39]

Saddam also spoke of the need for the Iraqis to protect themselves:

It is our duty, it is our responsibility to defend our country, to defend our children, to defend our people, and we are not going to succumb, neither to the United States nor to any other power.

Echoing a sentiment of the Melians, he refers to the long history of Iraq:

We hope that war will not take place, but if war if forced upon us, then Iraq will continue to be here. . . . This country . . . the cradle of the first civilizations for humanity, will not finish just like that, even though a huge power may want it to be like that.

In the end, Saddam insisted that the Iraqis would fight for their freedom and dignity:

We do not compromise our independence, or our dignity and our freedom. And at the same time, we will continue to commit ourselves to what has been decided by the Security Council.[40]

Ancient and Modern Conflicts

There are at least four features of Thucydides' *History* deserving attention that may be relevant to the recent U.S.-Iraq conflict, some specifically regarding the Melian and Plataean conflicts, some with regard to rhetoric and analysis more generally.

First regarding the *situation* itself, with Melos and Athens—and Plataea and the Peloponnesian allies—we encounter a stronger state threatening a weaker state, yet before an attack there is diplomatic negotiation. Before the 2003 invasion of Iraq, President Bush was evidently persuaded to follow the "diplomatic" route.

Second, we find a similar *outcome*, in which the weaker state rejects the ultimatum. We should perhaps not be surprised when the weaker resists the stronger's demands. As Chuter points out in his discussion of twentieth-century ultimatums, others have threatened force for various ends:

> The concept of military force [has been] exercised or threatened to bring
> about the political collapse of a state, or the destruction of the morale of
> its people, or even a modification in the policies of its government.[41]

But the odds that the threat of force will achieve those political goals are
not promising. Chuter identifies four criteria that must be met for success:

> First, the identity of the decisive authority has to be established. Second,
> exactly the right amount and kind of pressure has to be applied to achieve
> the desired political effect. Thirdly, there has to be a transmission mecha-
> nism to convey this pressure to the authority. Finally, the desired conces-
> sion must be within the power of the authority to grant without
> encompassing its own destruction. Any plan which is deficient in any of
> these respects will fail.[42]

In the modern scenario, while the UN might be seen as a decisive authority, in retrospect, it was difficult to apply the right amount of pressure by
an effective "transmission mechanism." Finally though, the latest ultimatum to Saddam Hussein (surrender or leave) in fact dictated his own
destruction. According to Chuter, an offer that entails self-annihilation
precludes any chance for success.

In addition, in the case of both Melos and the 2003 Iraq war, we might
well consider the lack of flexibility on both sides. In the Melian conflict,
violence was perhaps inevitable, because "neither side [was] willing to give
in."[43] For the 2003 Iraq war, Hans Blix has said that factors such as pride
may have strongly affected Saddam Hussein, who viewed himself as a suc-
cessor of a glorious past. "Saddam Hussein saw himself as a modern King
Nebuchadnezzar, and had enormous pride in himself and in Iraq."[44] In
Blix's view, Saddam Hussein was defiant and willing to call what he
thought was the United States' bluff. Blix also notes "the unchanging
mindset of the West" leading up to the invasion itself.[45]

Beyond these specific parallels of situation and outcome, the *rhetoric*
employed by speakers in Thucydides continues to find its way into diplomatic discourse—what was said *and* what should have been said, as Thucydides
puts it (1.22.1). There seems to be little question that similar types of arguments are employed today to persuade a state to acquiesce to demands and to
get other states to go to war. The echoes of Thucydidean rhetoric include violation of previous treaties and resolutions (1.68), the claim that all concerned

are in danger (1.120), the threat of an evil dictator or tyrant (1.122, 1.124), and the ultimate goal of liberation (1.124). Yet in each particular situation, politicians, political organizations, and the citizens of both nations and international groups face a very difficult problem. When are such claims valid? When is the danger so great that war is the only option?[46]

It is possible to see the rhetoric found in diplomatic discourse presented by Thucydides as providing a framework, a vocabulary, and a set of appeals that may be—and are—introduced in later conflicts. It is particularly fascinating when certain arguments are *not* made in the modern scenario. Motivations and rationales—although unstated today, yet articulated by Thucydides' speakers—may signal underlying motivations for war. For example, at Melos the Athenians assert the will of the stronger (5.89, 5.105), prefer to conquer without expense (5.89), and wish to avoid looking weak (5.95). I would suggest that—although unstated by U.S. officials—Thucydides may be supplying actual motivations that do not find public expression.

This possibility leads to a fourth area of common ground: *analysis.* Allow me to explore just one of the more obvious instances: Thucydides' distinction between the stated reason for war as opposed to the underlying cause. Early in the *History* Thucydides contrasts the most visible complaints triggering the Peloponnesian War with the truest cause.

> As to the question why they broke the treaty, I write first of *their grounds of complaint and conflict* [τὰς αἰτίας . . . καὶ τὰς διαφοράς] so that no one may ever have to ask the immediate cause which plunged the Hellenes into a war of such magnitude. I consider *the truest reason, though least openly expressed in speech* [ἀληθεστάτην πρόφασιν, ἀφανεστάτην δὲ λόγῳ], was Athenian greatness and the resulting alarm among the Spartans that forced them to war. (1.23.6)

Many moderns analysts make this same distinction between professed reasons and underlying causes for the 2003 Iraq War. For example, Zizek distinguishes between three stated or openly professed reasons for the war (W.M.D. posed a threat to all; Iraq's involvement with Al Qaeda; and Saddam Hussein as a ruthless dictator threatening neighbors and the Iraqi people) and three underlying—but unstated—reasons:

> First, a sincere ideological belief that the destiny of the United States is to bring democracy and prosperity to other nations; second, the urge to brutally assert and signal unconditional U.S. hegemony; and third, the need to control Iraqi oil reserves.[47]

In similar fashion but with a different emphasis, Mearsheimer and Walt contrast the "immediate cause" with the "deeper root of the conflict":

> The *immediate cause* is likely to be Saddam's failure to comply with the new UN inspections regime to the Bush administration's satisfaction. But this failure is not the *real reason* Saddam and the United States have been on a collision courses over the past year. The *deeper root of the conflict* is the U.S. position that Saddam must be toppled because he cannot be deterred from using weapons of mass destruction. [my italics][48]

This has perhaps become a commonplace, but Thucydides' fundamental warning that the strongest cause may never be expressed continues to keep us on the alert: we must be sensitive to possible *unstated* motivations.

I acknowledge that the ancient and modern situations are not precisely parallel: there is no ancient analogue to the UN, although there were Panhellenic gatherings of various sorts. My goal has been to suggest a number of possible links between Thucydides' work and more recent events. My hope is that this sketch helps us assess the value of Thucydides' presentation and analysis when applied to more recent conflicts. During the cold war, Thucydides' account of the Peloponnesian War was seen to be relevant to contemporary conflicts, in large part due to the parallels between the two blocs: the NATO alliance of the twentieth century (characterized by both its navy and democracy) was seen as analogous to the fifth-century Athenian empire; the Warsaw Pact was comparable to the Peloponnesian alliance under Sparta. Yet since 1989 and the end of the cold war, Thucydides continues to have many applications.[49] Thucydides has asked us to compare his times with ours: it is our task to find the valid and illuminating comparisons from the past for today.

THUCYDIDES' ACHIEVEMENT

We come at last to an assessment of Thucydides' achievement as an historian, rhetorician, writer, and teacher. By looking at Thucydides' own experience, we gain a better appreciation for the historian's opportunities and motivations. In 431 Thucydides decided that the impending conflict would be a great event; he would devote himself to recording this war still yet-to-come (1.1.1). When war began, he was a military man. He soon became a general, and, to reach such a position, he must have been an active politician and effective speaker. Thucydides may well have seen himself as one of Pericles' successors. Yet seven years into the war, exile removed him from political engagement and any chance of leading Athens. Thucydides' *History* becomes, as it were, a surrogate means for addressing his fellow citizens and—given the nature of his project—future leaders, generals, and citizens. I contend that this audience would have included both readers and auditors, and that Thucydides intended his audience to respond by continuing the dialogue and arguments that the *History* presents. One of Thucydides' goals was to encourage the group—a listening *and* reading audience—to become engaged with the past (both retrospectively and as vicarious participants) and to apply those arguments and conflicts to the current day.

One final connection between Plato and Thucydides. It may be useful to distinguish between the *genesis* of their works and the *intention*. In terms of the genesis of the dialogues, Plato was inspired by the historical figure of Socrates, who did not write himself, but engaged in question and answer and serious debate on matters of concern to the city (*ta politika*). Plato's goal was in part retrospective: to recreate Socrates arguing in the agora, to bring him back to life—now on the page, yet heard by members (and potential members) of the Academy. Plato's purpose, however, was not purely retrospective. He also sought to advertise the Academy and to teach others how to *do philosophy*—there's a forward-looking aspect as well.

In a similar way, we might say that Thucydides was inspired and provoked by debate in the Athenian assembly, by diplomatic negotiation, and by military strategy. In part, these activities are the impetus for the *History*, and to some degree, we might think of Thucydides as striving to recreate the world of debate, politics, and warfare of the late fifth century. That is, like Plato, one of Thucydides' goals is backward-looking: he seeks to recapture the figure of Pericles and to record the achievements and failures of the Athenian polis and its empire. But Thucydides is also looking ahead. Like Plato, Thucydides wishes to provoke his readers and auditors, so that they also become engaged in historical analysis and the business of politics.

Ancient Athenian democracy—and modern representative systems—share the premise that in order to balance public and private interests, the citizens affected must weigh in with their judgment. Yet to participate intelligently in the affairs of their community, these citizens need valuable instruction as to what is at stake and what the potential conflicts will be.[50] There is a seed of optimism in Thucydides' work, for it encourages his readers and listeners to be engaged in critical issues, to discuss them, and to continue that debate and dialogue—guided by Thucydides' History.

Thucydides never tells us in his own voice why speeches are included in the History. Yet surely their inclusion helps to recreate the atmosphere of a political assembly's discussion, courtroom conflict, and diplomatic discourse—to say nothing of a general addressing his troops. In Thucydides' History, there are speakers—and there are internal audiences listening, either the Athenian assembly, representatives from various city-states, or the army. These audiences act in some sense as models for the audience listening to and reading Thucydides' own work.[51] In his work Thucydides seeks to explore the issues and difficulties inherent in the politics of any age, yet these issues demand our participation as well. We, too, must join in that exploration, because we, as citizens, must rethink current problems with reference to knowledge of past conflicts, their potential resolutions, and their ultimate outcomes.

NOTES

CHAPTER ONE

1. White (1984), 88. Kitto (1966, 298) labels this Thucydides' "method of immediacy." Connor (1984, 16) adds that "readers had to be led to reexperience the war, to live through it again." Orwin (1994, 4) remarks on the "vicarious experience of the events that he describes."

2. As Connor (1985, 12) puts it: "The historian's job is to investigate, compile, select, edit and present. The reader's half, the greater half, is to react, to assess, and thereby to learn." Kitto (1966, 349) describes the reader's task as "kind of collaborative, less purely intellectual and more imaginative."

3. I recognize that Thucydides began his enterprise while still in Athens and that he lived as a citizen (and general) for seven years before his exile (1.1.1, 4.104–8, 5.26). The question I am raising is whether the ultimate form of the *History* may reflect the motivations suggested here. Pondering Thucydides' possible motivations is certainly a speculative venture and brings us dangerously close to the question of composition, which I will not address.

4. Here, too, we may find shared ground with Plato and what led him to compose written dialogues. After Socrates was condemned to death by a democratic jury in 399 BCE, Plato left Athens, his polis, to go to Megara. When he returned to the city, he may well have felt that—given the consequences for Socrates—it was too dangerous to engage in the sort of dialogue and aggressive interrogations Socrates practiced upon his fellow citizens. However much Plato may have emulated Socrates, it was clearly risky to do what Socrates had done. Plato was no longer in exile, but he did set up his school outside the walls of the city, apart from where the courts and the assembly met. This is not where Socrates engaged his fellow Athenians (see *Phaedrus* 230d). Plato distanced himself geographically from the center of politics and of power. He also distanced himself by using written dialogue rather than spoken conversation to engage his fellow citizens outside the Academy. When the world had changed in ways beyond their control, both Plato and Thucydides turned instead to a larger audience and to later generations.

5. Yet Homer's narrative may not be wholly consistent: on the inevitability of events, see Morrison (1992, 1997); on causation in Herodotus, see Lateiner (1989, 189–210).

6. See Flory (1988, 49, 55). From the number of these hypotheses and the high degree of speculation, Flory infers Thucydides' "sensitivity to possible alternative sequences." See also Stahl (2003, especially 90–93).

7. It is notable that in the past decade some fascinating work along these lines has explored more recent events under the rubric "virtual history." Ferguson (1997) speaks of thinking "counterfactually" by imagining possible alternatives to what has actually happened in the past. In his introductory essay, Ferguson seeks to limit counterfactual thinking—and the idea of "virtual history"—to those cases where "options and data were actually available to figures in question at the time" and only when explicit mention is made of such a possibility in contemporary documents (12). For example, in the early days of World War Two, individuals—and the governments of several countries—anticipated a successful German invasion of England: see Roberts and Ferguson, "Hitler's England" in Ferguson (1997, 281–320). As Ferguson notes, a classic essay of this sort is Bury (1964).

8. There were actually two systems of writing; before the alphabet in the eighth century, there was a syllabic system used by the Mycenaean Greeks in the Bronze Age (1600–1200 BCE). By the 1950s scholars had deciphered these linear B tablets as Greek. Its use was evidently restricted to a group of professional scribes who kept palace inventory accounts. With the collapse of Mycenaean civilization (after 1200 BCE), this system of writing vanished.

9. Three types of evidence endorse this view of Homer's epics as growing out of an oral tradition: internal evidence such as scenes in the *Odyssey* of singers (Phemius and Demodocus) performing before audiences; stylistic evidence, such as Parry's work on noun-epithet pairs (see M. Parry 1971); and modern comparative studies of twentieth-century oral (often illiterate) singers; see Lord (2000).

10. See Robb (1994, 253).

11. Nicias' letter sent to the Athenian assembly (7.8–15) is discussed in chapters 9 and 10. On the interconnections between literacy and education and law, see Robb (1994). Certainly many fascinating questions arise concerning the Greek alphabet, literacy, and the development of democracy (the alphabet is easily learned with its small set of letters and the fact that it is phonetic); for an interesting argument in this regard, see Steiner (1994).

12. Robb (1994, 140); see 209 n8. Havelock (1963, 47–48) distinguishes between non-literacy (primary orality), craft literacy, semi-literacy, and full literacy.

13. Robb (1994, 253).

14. Havelock (1963, 38).

15. Robb (1994, 218).

16. In fact, Havelock (1963, 123) claims that Thucydides' project requires a shift in consciousness, for in an oral culture, "strictly speaking, an historical time sense is impossible." Havelock (1986, 17) posits that by the time of the fourth century, not only had "Greek literacy changed . . . the means of communication, but also the shape of the Greek consciousness." These claims regarding a different sort of consciousness must remain speculative. Havelock (1982, 10) also remarks that the speeches in Thucydides "provide a fascinating study of the interweave between oral and written styles of vocabulary and syntax." He then asserts that Thucydides "confirms by his position in the chronology of the transition the thesis that Athens was becoming 'literate' only as late as the period of the Peloponnesian War" (21).

17. Robb (1994, 235–36) says that the Platonic dialogues should be thought of as "textbooks" which put students in direct contact with the methods of Socrates and notes that the dialogues might be seen as "transitional texts."

Nightingale (1995, 5) argues that Plato is "introducing and defining a radically discursive practice, which he calls 'philosophy.'" Havelock (1963, 56 n16) remarks that "Thucydides was the first Attic author to extrapolate written memoranda into continuous written discourse, just as Plato and Isocrates were the first to adapt sustained oral teaching to the same end." He also argues that Thucydides' remark at 1.22.4 about his "possession forever," "surely identifies the permanent influence of a manuscript stylistically composed for readers, as against the more ephemeral effects of a composition designed for recitation at an oral 'competition'" (54 n8). Havelock (1986, 16) speculates about "the historians whose methods of managing prose surely offered an alternative, and perhaps a rival, to Plato's own type of discourse." See Turasiewicz (1990, esp. 85) on Thucydides' "nouvelle forme de présentation."

18. Havelock (1963, 46) argues that it is "roughly down to the death of Euripides [406]" that Greek poetry "enjoyed an almost unchallenged monopoly of preserved communication," noting that "the first magisterial composition in Attic, equaling in length the achievements of epic poetry, was the history of Thucydides. Thus, while the last half of the fifth century begins to see the acceptance of prose as a viable means of publication, acceptance does not become complete until the fourth." Plato's work comes at a time when "Greek orality was giving way to Greek literacy and . . . an oral state of mind was to be replaced by a literate state of mind" (Havelock [1986], 8). More recently Thomas (1993, 2000, 2003) has explored these problems with respect to Herodotus and his contemporaries. For proposed differences between oral and written discourse, see Ong (1982, 31–77).

19. Especially valuable have been Connor (1984, 1985), Gribble (1998), Hornblower (1994), and Rood (1998a). I will make references to Stahl (2003), the revised and somewhat expanded English version of Stahl (1966, 1973). Work by de Jong (1987, 1997, 2001, 2002), while directed at Homer, Herodotus, and Greek tragedy, has also suggested application to Thucydides' work. (For a fuller bibliography on narratology applied to ancient literature, see de Jong and Sullivan [1994], 282–83.) Because my approach focuses on the reader's experience, I have also found reader-response criticism such as Iser (1974) valuable (full bibliography in de Jong and Sullivan [1994], 284–85).

20. Blondell (2002), Hershbell (1995).

21. In addition to Flory (1988), see also Bernstein (1995), Cowley et al. (1998), Ferguson (1997), Gould (1989), Kagan (1995), Stahl (2003), and Varnadoe (1990). Some of my own work on Homeric epic along these lines has guided the current exploration; see Morrison (1997). There is also the "What If" history series; see Cowley (2001), for example.

22. Recent work offering a broader view of literacy in the ancient world includes W. V. Harris (1989), Robb (1994), and Thomas (1989, 1992, 1993, 2003). For the issue of literacy in Thucydides, see Loraux (1986b), Edmunds (1993), Marincola (1997), and Morrison (2004). Also valuable have been the volumes from the biennial Orality meetings that began in 1994, e.g., Mackay (1999) and Mackie (2004).

23. While I do explore several passages from book 6 in chapters 9 and 10, the Sicilian Expedition is intelligently discussed by Stahl (2003, 173–222).

24. Havelock (1982, 148) reminds us that "the historian of the Peloponnesian

War, while still a bard in the sense that he is a celebrant of the great deeds of heroes, is himself modernized and literate, a singer no more but now a self-styled writer." While Havelock (1963, 186) also comments, it is "only the reflective mind of the sophisticated reader, who rereads and reviews the text," I will attempt to modify this view in chapters 9 and 10.

Chapter Two

1. Hornblower (1994, 134) defines focalization as "different perspectives or points of view from which events are viewed [or more generally, I would add, are experienced] or interpreted." The point here is that we are given a view or perspective from someone other than the narrator, Thucydides, although we do encounter a complicated situation in book 4 where Thucydides the historian (narrator and primary focalizer) may present events through the perspective of an individual involved, namely, Thucydides the general (4.102–8).

2. De Jong (1987, esp. 38–110), refers to "embedded focalization" (or secondary focalization—she uses both expressions interchangeably) which in her scheme includes perception, thoughts, emotions, feelings, and indirect speech. Schneider (1974) does a superb job of showing how the report of perceptions, thoughts, and intentions constitute "a uniform principle of Thucydides' narrative" (28). For an interesting parallel situation in the history of Polybius, see Davidson (1990, 13), who says, "Polybius, then, can be seen writing through the eyes of others. . . . These different views of the same episode . . . take their own place as events within the history he is composing."

3. I fully agree with de Jong (1987, 113) that the "narrator-text does not consist of a succession of events only, but is interspersed with short 'peeps' into the minds of the characters participating in those events." For her discussion of indirect speech, see 114 ff. We may also distinguish between explicit and implicit focalization; de Jong (1987, 118) remarks that implicit embedded focalization is not marked by a verb of perceiving, thinking, or feeling.

4. Of course, it is possible to construct the readership Thucydides had in mind by considering the information he chooses to include. For example, a broad readership is implied by his decision, in ignoring parochial state calendars, to base his chronology on the natural division of summer and winter. In identifying Athenians by his use of patronymics rather than demotics, he reaches out to non-Athenian readers—as well as by including other information. All this indicates a vision of his audience as Greeks of the post-war period, not limited to the principal cities of Athens and Sparta. See Gomme HCT 1: 108 on chronology and the lack of demotics, though Gomme notes the lack of explication for Athenian constitutional practice which suggests that Thucydides expected his readers to be familiar with such institutions (24–25). Ridley (1981, 41) sees the information on Western Greece and Chalcidike as possibly reflecting where Thucydides' own interests or expertise lie; still, he argues that Thucydides was writing for all of Greece. Hornblower (1994, 164) points out that since Thucydides calculates the beginning of the war from the Spartan invasion of Athens, this would be an example of Athenian "focalization."

5. This has been noted by ancient critics as well; on such "vividness" (*enargeia*), see Walker (1993).

6. According to Davidson (1991, 15–16), reading Polybius offers a very similar experience. He distinguishes "two general tendencies. One the gaze of σύγκρισις, or comparison, takes a remote view of things, assessing, contrasting, and placing into a context . . . The other tendency of the gaze shares a lot with the gaze of comparison, but its process is much more involving, entailed the 'projection' (μεταφερέσθαι) of the sufferings of others onto one's own circumstances."

7. Thucydides explicitly connects the Corcyrean conflict with the outbreak of war and compares the battle of Pylos with that of Syracuse: 1.23.6, 1.55.2 (cf. 1.146), 7.71.7.

8. The phrase "significant reminiscence" comes from Macleod (1983, 146) where he discusses the literary technique of echo and reminiscence which "draws attention to causes and motives as well as pointing up ironies." Hornblower (1991–96, 2: 16) calls these "deliberate cross-references." Kitto (1966) says that Thucydides expects his readers to see the parallels for themselves (285) and must seize on the significance of such "to and fro" references (349). Connor (1984, 12) describes this as "the activation of the reader's own evaluative capacities." Farrar (1988, 136) says that the "many echoes and recurrent patterns . . . [are meant to] . . . challenge [the reader] to assess the genuine differences and similarities between two contexts, to think historically." Arnold (1992) comments: "The reader . . . is not likely to be allowed to remain a passive eavesdropper on historical debates" (45); Thucydides "places his readers on guard and challenges us to integrate, as he himself has, the λόγοι and ἔργα. Although we stand as rational and objective judges of arguments in the debates, the active, intellectual involvement demanded by the style of Thucydidean speeches requires us to become more participants in and less passive witnesses of not only the debates, but also the historian's analysis of the war" (57).

9. That is, the reader may also find significant parallels in more recent history and in contemporary events. We might distinguish three types of analysis: local, distant, and extra-textual. For local analysis, the focus is limited to the passage or episode in question. At this level, we wish to understand the past—what happened, why, and how it is significant—and to see how events may have been experienced from the perspectives of the participants involved. Distant analysis involves juxtaposing the issues, ideas, and events from the local passage with other sections of the *History*. Extra-textual analysis leads to setting the problems raised in the text with other contexts, including the reader's own world. This book focuses primarily on local and distant analysis; still it is valuable to ponder the play between a particular episode and extra-textual political phenomena (see chapter 10).

10. Rabinowitz (1987, 22) uses the concept of the "authorial audience" that comes close to the sense of my implied, hypothetical reader. His hypothetical authorial audience "allows us to treat the reader's attempt to read as the author intended . . . [by] the joining of a particular social/interpretive community . . . to read in a particular socially constituted way that is shared by the author and his or her expected readers."

11. Connor (1985, 9). On this recreation of the historical past, see, e.g.,

Connor (1985): Thucydides "creates the illusion that we are ourselves present, witnessing events" (10); he quotes Hobbes: "[Thucydides] maketh his auditor a spectator" (11). Connor continues: "We are as far from the historian's study as we can possibly be; we are in the war itself. We see; we hear; we even know the plans and thoughts of the participants" (15). In commenting on the vividness of the narrative, Arnold (1992, 44) quotes Plutarch *Moralia* 346A: Thucydides tries "to transform his reader into a spectator and to let the sufferings that were so dazzling and upsetting to those who beheld them have a similar effect on those who read about them." Cf. Gorgias *Helen* 9 on the tremendous power of language (here of poetry specifically): "For those who hear poetry comes fearful fright and tearful pity and mournful longing, and *at the successes and failures of others' affairs and persons the mind suffers—through speech—a suffering of its own* (ἐπ' ἀλλοτρίων τε πραγμάτων καὶ σωμάτων εὐτυχίαις καὶ δυσπραγίαις ἴδιόν τι πάθημα διὰ τῶν λόγων ἔπαθεν ἡ ψυχή [I include the Greek for the italicized section])." This translation comes from MacDowell (1993).

   12. Hornblower (1991–96, I: 33) translates *eikazein* as "form our conjectures." Gomme (HCT, I: 111—s.v. 1.9) defines it as "imaginative inference and interpretation or reconstruction of the past." Hunter (1973a, 27) offers a fuller definition for *eikazein*: "It is the ability to relate past and present experience, find their essential similarities, and then conjecture or predict what is most likely to occur under the given circumstances. It is reasoning based on probability" (see her discussion at 23–41).

   13. Cf. προαισθόμενος. . .προεώρα ("perceiving ahead of time . . . he foresaw"—1.136.1, 1.138.3). Themistocles is able to do this without preparation: note αὐτοσχεδιάζειν τὰ δέοντα (1.138.3) which Hornblower (1991–96, I: 223) translates: "to improvise the right thing to be done." On Pericles' abilities, see προγνοὺς. . . προέγνω ("knowing in advance . . . he knew before"—2.65.5, 2.65.13; cf. 2.60.1, 2.64.6). Cf. Thucydides' comparison of the small and large battles of Sphacteria and Thermopylae: . . . ὡς μικρὸν μεγάλῳ εἰκάσαι ("in comparing small to great"—4.36.3).

   14. Whether Thucydides fully anticipated in 431 the scope of the coming war, he did have reasons for suspecting a "great" war and "cites the evidence (*tekmairomenos*) . . ." (1.1.1). On contemplating the fifth century from a future (post-404) perspective, see 1.10.2.

   15. Translations throughout this book are adapted from Lattimore (1998). Of course, future historians may makes mistakes, as Thucydides acknowledges: Ἀθηναίων...διπλασίαν ἂν τὴν δύναμιν εἰκάζεσθαι ἀπὸ τῆς φανερᾶς ὄψεως τῆς πόλεως ἢ ἔστιν ("one would conjecture from the visible appearance of [the ruins of] the city that the power of Athens was double what it actually was"—1.10.2).

   16. It has been argued that Thucydides is writing for the politically active reader, i.e., the statesman; see, e.g., Macleod (1983, 146): "to educate future statesmen"; cf. Hornblower (1987, 133); Orwin (1994, 4); and White (1984, 88). Lessons of lasting value are offered to those like Themistocles and Pericles who must lead their cities against the backdrop of political uncertainty—Thucydides certainly has much to teach such readers—but I would like to broaden our conception of Thucydides' audience to include the more general reader, or perhaps we

should rather say the "citizen," an engaged reader who is also involved in his or her own world (outside the text) so that what Thucydides says finds a context for application within that reader's place and time.

17. Yunis (1991, 180); this argument is expanded and given a broader context in Yunis (1996). Yunis (1991, esp. 190–200) distinguishes the instructional rhetoric of Pericles from the demagogic rhetoric of Cleon, emphasizing how important it is that the best political leader not only recognize the best policy, but be able to explain it (note *gnonai* and *hermeneusai*–2.60.5); see Yunis (1991, 180–86 and 189 n26).

18. Yunis (1991, 199). This slippage between political and literary exchange is also found with the term "exposition" or "demonstration" (*apodeixis*). Hornblower (1991–96, I: 148) comments that Thucydides' use of *apodeixis* at 1.97.2 (where he begins his account of the growth of the Athenian empire) is "surely intended to recall the famous use of the word in the preface of Herodotus." Note that the other use of the term is political, describing Pericles' explanation of policy to the Athenians (2.13.9).

19. On the importance of decision-making, see Yunis (1991, 185, 199). Arnold (1992, 56) comments: "Without directly interceding as narrator, therefore, by including debates within the history Thucydides asks his own audience to consider the factual, ethical and psychological factors that led to crucial decisions pertaining to war—factors that were and are likely to play similar roles in the future." Given that the reader's situation is different from that of the fifth-century citizen, we need to contemplate how the experience of a citizen living through the war, engaged in debate, voting, and fighting, is significantly distinct from a modern reader experiencing Thucydides' work.

20. Of course, the decision to show the war from different sides may have been reinforced by Thucydides' exile and his access to sources in Sparta and elsewhere (5.26.5).

21. At times, Thucydides is nothing if not authoritative, magisterial even, in passing judgment, criticizing ideas, strategies, and statesmen. These well-thumbed exceptional passages include 1.20–23, 2.65, 3.82–84, 5.26.

22. Translation by Halliwell (1987, 59–60).

23. Flory (1990, 194). Hornblower (1987) argues that, in opposing "flattering traditions" (85 n50), Thucydides may be reacting to "overtly partisan use . . . of antiquarian material" (85); cf. his remark on Thucydides' lack of narrow partisanship or attachment to one city (27).

24. Athenian arguments maintaining the irrelevance of morality to foreign policy are found at 1.73–77, 2.62–64, 5.89, 5.107; cf. Diodotus at 3.44, 3.46–47 (discussed in chapter 7). De Ste. Croix (1972, 16–17) maintains Thucydides' view is that in "relations between states . . . moral judgements are virtually inapplicable . . . force [is] the sole ultimate arbiter in international affairs." Still he admits that Thucydides never makes this fundamental distinction explicit.

25. Newman (1988, 45) articulates the dialogic principle as "all dogmatic and would-be final formulations are betrayals."

26. Newman (1988, 45) remarks that "twin speeches occurring in real life called for the judgment of an audience. Set now in the record, thesis and antithesis have to be synthesized by the reader for himself." Paradoxically Thucydides has

produced a "possession for all time" by the lack of closure for arguments which continue to sound familiar to us today.

27. On Thucydides' choices for inclusion, see Hornblower (1987, 34–44).

28. Although such cross-references and juxtapositions may be multiplied endlessly, I mention several examples. Various sections in the opening 23 chapters prepare the reader for issues relevant to the Corcyrean conflict, such as sea power (Minos, Agamemnon, and the development of the trireme at 1.4, 1.9.3–4, 1.13–14); civil war (1.2.4–6, 1.12.2, 1.18.1); and motivation by fear (1.9.3; cf. 1.23.6). Looking ahead, the Corcyrean conflict anticipates the land/sea antithesis (1.35.5–noted by Hornblower [1991–96], II: 79); the strategic value of Italy and Sicily (especially in books 6 and 7); and the idea of arbitration instead of armed conflict (e.g., 1.28.4–5; cf. 1.71.5, 1.78.4, 1.144.2–1.145).

29. This of course is criticized by Dionysius of Halicarnassus, who condemns the episodic nature of Thucydides' *History*. In ch. 9, Dionysius asserts that Thucydides' seasonal division of the narrative has led to greater obscurity (*dusparakolouthetotera*): "it is surprising how he failed to see that a narrative *which is broken up into small sections* (εἰς μικρὰς κατακερματιζομένη τομάς), describing the many actions which took place in many different places will not catch 'the pure light shining from afar'" (a quotation of Pindar *Pythian* 3.75). Dionysius also objects that many episodes have been left "half finished" (*hemiteles*), concluding "the continuity [τὸ διηνεκές] of the narrative is destroyed" (ch. 13). Yet Thucydides is certainly aware of how he has organized the *History*: he not only defends his chronological framework (5.20.2–3; cf. 2.2.1); he even points out his "digressions" (*ekbole*–e.g., 1.97.2).

CHAPTER THREE

1. For the Corcyrean conflict as programmatic, see Crane (1992b, 4). I see the Corcyrean conflict as comparable to the programmatic encounter between Croesus and Solon in book 1 of Herodotus' work; see Shapiro (1996) with bibliography. For the Archaeology as programmatic, see, e.g., Connor (1984, 27) and Hornblower (1991–96, I: 8).

2. Connor (1985) and Arnold (1992). I have also found the essays on Thucydides in Macleod (1983) extremely valuable.

3. Connor (1985, 8, 10); Arnold (1992, 45). Arnold says she will explore how the "history creates such an experience" and "how the demands Thucydides places on his audience shape their reception of the text" (45).

4. I owe this formulation to Rosenbloom (1995); cf. the discussion in Turasiewicz (1990, esp. 88) on the "polyphonic mix" of Thucydides' work.

5. The difficult question is: when is a detail a telling one? That is, when is a detail intended to set up a parallel, contrast, or comparison, and when is it simply a matter of what happened with no larger significance? Of course, Thucydides is highly selective in using speeches as a way of highlighting certain issues or conflicts, but it is tougher to determine his criteria for inclusion in the narrative. For the question of what Thucydides does *not* tell us, see HCT, I: 1–29; Kitto (1966, 259–79); and Hornblower (1992b). Crane (1996) points to Thucydides' elimina-

tion of the importance of family and kinship connections: the effect is to make the polis and the individual predominant, "minimiz[ing] all social ties that mediate between individual subject and the collective city-state" (24).

6. Non-Greeks are involved as well: the Taulantians on the mainland are Illyrian by "tribe" (*ethnos*–1.24.1).

7. Epidamnus' location on the entrance to the Adriatic begins the episode (1.24.1); later the Epidamnian isthmus is indicated and Actium is located (1.26.5, 1.29.3). Distinctions among Greeks are also made: the Dorian *ethnos* at 1.24.2; kinship (*suggeneia*) is appealed to at 1.26.3. On *suggeneia*, see Hornblower (1991–96, II: 61–80).

8. Noted by Hornblower (1991–96, I: 67). Summer is mentioned later (περιιόντι τὸ θέρει–1.30.3; cf. 1.31.1). On chronology, see HCT, I: 196–98, and Wilson (1987, 31–32).

9. The speakers addressing the Athenians at 1.32ff. are unnamed, implying that the ambassadors speak for the entire communities. As White (1984) notes, while "the principal figures in this world are the individual cities, regarded as units" (64), this premise, "the unity of each city, is challenged by the civil war in Epidamnus" (68). See Strasburger (1954); Macleod (1983, 84); and Hornblower (1987, 61). The subject of civil war here is prepared for in the Archaeology: see 1.2.1, 1.12, 1.18; cf. 1.23.2.

10. ὡς λέγεται, ἀπὸ πολέμου τινὸς τῶν προσοίκων βαρβάρων ἐφθάρησαν. On the function in this passage of the expression, "it is said," Westlake (1977, 357) thinks the phrase "indicate[s] that Thucydides is using a written source, though he may have felt some uncertainty because of the vagueness or brevity of this source." Hornblower (1991–96, I: 68) guesses Thucydides' source to be "oral informants."

11. We note repeated use of participles to reveal motivation in narrative sections, especially for the battle of Sybota. Lang (1995, 53) calls participial motivation "a narrative technique which links actions and actors chainwise." She concludes that its appearance in Thucydides is a "continuing elaboration of the Herodotean narrative technique" (56). On motivation more generally, see Hornblower (1987, 78–79), who suggests that while motives and intentions may be inferred by Thucydides (who uses it as a literary device), this is not necessarily inconsistent with a truthful account. See also Westlake (1989a).

12. On justice, see discussion below. Again note the participial motivation, "believing" (*nomizontes*–1.25.3).

13. HCT, I: 159 contrasts Thucydides' political and economic motives (1.23) with the "sentimental" motivation here. Crane (1992b) calls this view into question. Hornblower (1991–96, I: 69) comments: "As so often, Th. is very confident about motive." Kagan (1995, 7–8) emphasizes the triad of motivation articulated by the Athenians regarding their empire: "honor, fear, and interest" (1.77), and argues that honor prevails as a factor for the Corinthians (37–41).

14. No ethnographic information concerning customs, courtship rituals, etc., is forthcoming, such as we might expect from Herodotus. Other omissions are noted by Hornblower (1991–96, I): no mention that Apollonia is a joint Corinthian-Corcyrean colony (76); "very little about the Corinthian northwestern expansion in 480–435 which formed the background to the Corinthian-

Corcyrean tension described in chs. 24–55" (66); Hornblower also comments on
the absence of references to the Cocytus River (which joins the Acheron) and the
reputed entrance to Hades (1.46.4): "note the absence of any of this interesting
material in Th." (91). Kitto (1966, 261) captures the process of Thucydides' deliberate elimination of possible material with the metaphor of a carver or sculptor who
pares away the "excess" and notes that (for the finished product) Thucydides wrote
only twenty pages a year.

15. Cf. the earlier involvement of the Ambracians and Leucadians (1.26.1–2;
cf. 1.30.2).

16. Wilson (1987, 33–34) explains the Corinthian intransigence as an effort
to maintain her prestige among her western allies.

17. For anger as motivation, cf. also the Corcyrean anger at 1.26.3.

18. Wilson (1987, 31).

19. Regarding the topographical description of Ephyre and Cheimerion,
Wilson (1987, 38) comments that the reader is "no doubt ignorant of this non-
Greek coastline." Still, we should conceive of Thucydides' audience broadly—
some of his readers may be from this area. Hornblower (1991–96, I: 73) says that
the naming of the Corinthian generals with patronymic at 1.29 "is hard to account
for except by assuming that Th. intended in some sense to be comprehensive."
HCT, I: 182 notes the omission of the Corcyrean commanders' names in contrast
with the Sybota narrative (1.47.1). Still, the battle is fought by "the Corinthians"
and "the Corcyreans" (1.29.3ff.), that is, each general's involvement is not specified. The Corcyreans bring 80 ships (40 more are engaged in the Epidamnian
blockade–1.29.4); the Corinthians bring 75 ships and 2,000 men (1.29.1; cf.
1.27.2).

20. As Kagan (1995, 19) puts it: "No one could have predicted that an internal quarrel in this remote city on the fringes of the Hellenic world would lead to
the terrible and devastating Peloponnesian War." Hornblower (1991–96, I: 72)
notes the "first appearance in the narrative proper" of the Spartans (the ambassadors mentioned at 1.28.1) and finds significant their ineffective role as negotia-
tors. Athens itself is implied at 1.28.3.

21. See discussion of Flory (1990) in chapter 2.

22. For what may be an analogous situation in "welcoming" the audience early
in Homer's *Iliad*—and the problems with reconstructing such an audience—see
Scodel (1997).

23. Thucydides does not, however, allow the Epidamnians to speak on their
own behalf. HCT, I: 162–63 comments that it is "as though Epidamnus were not
an independent state which might have some say in the matter itself." White
(1984, 305 n5) says that denying the use of discourse to a city is "the most drastic
step a system of rhetoric can take."

24. In this case Thucydides himself may very well have been present in the
assembly—he may have spoken himself, as noted by HCT, I: 166. Stadter (1983)
emphasizes the Athenian desire to weaken both the Corcyrean and Corinthian
navies (1.44.2). On Pericles' role and why Thucydides does not explicitly mention
him, see Plutarch *Pericles* 29; Kitto (1966, 292–94); Kagan (1969, 237–45); Orwin
(1994, 60 n60); and Bloedow (1994).

25. Thucydides has adapted sophistic practice to historical circumstance by

allowing each side to make its best case; see Newman (1988). The challenge for the Athenians—and for the reader—is to determine which argument is actually preferable in this particular situation.

26. Ober (1993, 86) lays emphasis on the term *antilogia* (1.31.4), which "reveals that the speakers will take diametrically opposed positions. By implication, there is no possibility of a genuine compromise in this dispute; either the Athenians make an alliance with Corcyra or they do not."

27. The *postscript* at 1.44 has particular relevance to the challenging problem of speech-narrative correspondence. In explicitly noting the decisive reasons for the Athenians' second choice (they believed that war with the Peloponnesians would take place, the Corcyrean navy would be useful, and Corcyra was strategically located (καλῶς... κεῖσθαι) on the trade route to Italy and Sicily [1.44.2–1.44.3]), Thucydides makes clear that these factors coincide with three points made by the Corcyreans in their speech: war would come (1.33.3); their navy would be useful (1.33.2, 1.36); and Corcyra was on an important trade route (1.36.2). This first episode with speeches offers an example of how speech can influence action, as Thucydides emphasizes Athenian motivation (in the *postscript*) with deliberate echoes of the arguments made in the Corcyreans' *speech*. The very proximity of *postscript* and *speech* allows the reader easily to juxtapose argument and coincident motivation. See Morrison (2006).

28. This decision appears also to reveal a caution on the Athenian side which is not necessarily found in the years after 431 BCE. As Thucydides later states, better judgments (*gnomai*) occur in peacetime (3.82.2; cf. 1.78.3, 1.82.6). Kagan (1995, 71) argues that the Athenians have found "an inventive policy aimed at steering a middle course that would frustrate Corinth's aims without bringing on a general war." As Stadter (1983, 133) puts it, "Rather they attempted to go between the horns of the dilemma, satisfying neither party completely." Other moderate decisions by Athens, according to Kagan (1995), occurred with respect to Potidaea, "Athenian action should be understood as a diplomatic response to a looming problem, a moderate choice between unwelcome extremes" (49), and the Megarian decree, "once again, the Athenian action should be seen as a middle path" (50). Wilson (1987, 138) says that the tone of Pericles' policy (1.140ff.) "takes a middle path between aggression and backing down. In just such a spirit the Athenians at Sybota tell the Corinthians that they are not starting a war and not breaking the treaty, but that they will not retreat from their commitment to defend Corcyra."

29. Connor (1984, 34) characterizes the major themes in these speeches as "the introduction of what is to be a major theme in the *Histories*—the conflict between right and advantage; the second is Corcyra's significance as a naval power."

30. See 1.34.2, 1.35.3–4.

31. The Corinthians feel they must respond to the idea that "we are behaving unjustly" (*adikoumen*–1.37.1). On further invocations of justice on the Corinthians' part, see 1.37.3, 1.37.5, 1.38.4. The Corinthians use the term *hamartia* in the sense of "crime" for the Corcyreans' actions, rather than simply "mistake" (1.39.2, 1.39.3): the Athenians risk joining in such unjust activities. Kagan (1969, 231) says that the Corinthians have little or no grounds for their involvement in

Epidamnus and choose instead to attack the Corcyreans' character.

32. In the Archaeology and Method (1.2–23) we find virtually no moral terms: only the "virtue" (*arete*) of the soil (1.2.4) and lack of shame (*aischune*–1.5.1). In the first section of the Corcyrean conflict (1.24–31), there are a few instances: κατὰ . . .τὸ δίκαιον (1.25.3); *enklemata* (1.26.1); and three phrases connected with potential arbitration: δίκας δοῦναι (1.28.2), *dikazesthai* (1.28.4), and *dike* (1.28.5).

33. White (1984, 65–66).

34. Connor (1984, 34–35, n37) finds the Corcyreans' portrayal of themselves as victims of injustice to be weak. Still, they must have felt that their case would have been weaker if they had not made such appeals. For the prevalence of concepts associated with the idea of justice, consider, for example, the "accusations" (or "indictments"–*enklemata*) at 1.34.2, 1.40.1, and 1.42.3. The Corinthians describe the process of arbitration as "to be determined by justice" (δίκη κρίνεσθαι–1.39.1); the "laws of the Greeks" are also appealed to (κατὰ τοὺς Ἑλλήνων νόμους–1.41.1). For a survey of such legalistic language in Thucydides, see Darbo-Peschanski (1987).

35. The Corcyreans first mention their fleet at the opening of their speech (1.33.1).

36. The Corinthians preface their remarks by saying they will show that the Athenians will not irrationally reject the offer of the Corcyreans (τὴν τῶνδε χρείαν μὴ ἀλογίστως ἀπώσεσθε–1.37.1); cf. the claim at 1.43.4: the Athenians will be acting rightly and in their own interests (τὰ ἄριστα βουλεύσεσθε ὑμῖν αὐτοῖς; see also 1.42.1, 1.42.4). The Corinthians have no response to the advantages of Corcyra's location, the importance of which the retrospective reader will appreciate in connection to the Sicilian expedition.

37. Both justice and advantage of course pertain to such international relationships.

38. The Corcyreans tell Athens, "The way the Corinthians treat us, their kinsmen (πρὸς ἡμᾶς τοὺς ξυγγενεῖς), should be taken as a warning to you" (1.34.3; cf. 1.34.1). The Corinthians respond by asserting that they are honored and loved by their other colonies, although no examples are given (1.38.1–3; Corinth is later helped by three colonies–1.46.2). Hornblower (1991–96, II: 73) comments on "kinship" (*suggeneia*), saying it was "stretched until it had become almost a metaphor for a relationship of obedience and control"; see de Ste. Croix (1972, 71).

39. On the treaty of 446/445, see 1.35, 1.36.1, 1.37, 1.40.4; cf. 1.32.2, 1.45.3.

40. On "friends" and enemies" (*echthroi* and *philoi*), see 1.33.3, 1.35.4, 1.41.1–3; cf. 1.50.1, 8.48.4. HCT I: 176 remarks: "*echthros* has wider import than *polemios* (which implies 'being at war with')."

41. In the Archaeology and Method (1.2–23) we find mention of collaborative efforts (based in part on coercion): the Greek expedition to Troy and the battle against the Persians (both Panhellenic ventures), and the Athenian and Spartan alliances.

42. Hornblower (1987, 162) calls the speeches "treacherous evidence" for Thucydides' own opinions.

43. The idea of the Corcyreans teaching the Athenians is balanced at the end

of their speech, when they boil down their argument (βραχυτάτῳ . . . κεφαλαίῳ) so that the Athenians may "learn" (mathoite–1.36.3) the importance of the Corcyrean navy.

44. The Corinthians' phrase "keep in mind first of all" (μνησθέντας πρῶτον–1.37.1) answers the Corcyreans' first "lesson" (ἀναδιδάξαι πρῶτον–1.32.1); their goal is to give Athens a clear view of the approaching situation (προειδῆτε–1.37.1). The Corinthians also introduce the idea of learning based on a model of experience: "the younger also learns from the older" (καὶ νεώτερός τις παρὰ πρεσβυτέρου αὐτὰ μαθών–1.42.1). Cf. the later need, in the Corinthians' eyes, of teaching the Spartans (didaskalias–1.68.3).

45. The Corinthians wish to have made clear (dedelotai) the grounds for their complaints and the violent, grasping nature of the Corcyreans (1.40.1).

46. "Evidence" (tekmerion–1.1.3, 1.3.3, 1.9.4, 1.20.1, 1.21.1); "clarity" (delos and cognates–1.3.1, 1.5.2, 1.10.4 [twice], 1.11.1, 1.11.2, 1.21.2; cf. saphes at 1.22.4); a "sign" (semeion–1.6.2, 1.10.1, 1.21.1); "evidence" (martyrion–1.8.1); "investigate" (skopein–1.1.3, 1.20.5, 1.21.2, 1.22.4); and "demonstrate" (apodeiknumi–1.6.6). See also Hornblower (1987), 100–107. As Ober (1993, 90) puts it, "The speakers thus claim to do just what Thucydides claims his history will do— teach about interest and power and offer an understanding of past events and the probable course of the future."

47. The "good service" (euergesia) of the Corinthians gains points with the Athenians in contrast to the Corcyreans' inability to point to past service—which they acknowledge in their opening remarks (μήτε εὐεργεσίας μεγάλης–1.32.1). On past service (euergesia), see 1.41–43 and Crane (1992b, esp. 14–17).

48. This notion of helping friends and hurting enemies is spelled out at 1.41.1 in accordance with the laws (nomoi) of the Greeks; cf. 1.41.3, 1.43.2, and see Crane (1992b, 14–17, 22). Missiou (1998) argues that the Athenians are not much swayed by such conventional notions of reciprocity.

49. Hornblower (1991–96, I: 77) translates: "instead of being wisdom, as we once thought, [our policy of neutrality] has now proved to be folly and weakness." Note the perfect tense of tunchano at 1.32.3: tetucheke ("it has turned out that . . .").

50. The Corcyreans say that this help would be gained without expense (charis is mentioned three times–1.33.1–2, 1.36.1); cf. the gratitude that will be preserved as "ever memorable proof" (μετ᾽ αἰειμνήστου μαρτυρίου–1.33.1).

51. On such contradictions, see Calder (1955, 179) and HCT, I: 169.

52. For the Corcyreans' and Corinthians' deficiencies as teachers, see Ober (1993, 87–90).

53. Ostwald (1988, 65), citing de Romilly (1988, 43–44). He also says that "growth and fear created a situation in which no viable alternative in human terms [existed] to either side but to go to war" (19). See 21–32 on the "concatenation of circumstances leading to the outbreak of war" (26). The first four steps in this chain are found in the Corcyrean conflict. Wilson (1987, 29) says that "Thucydides certainly writes as if it [i.e., the war] were commonly regarded as imminent."

54. Ober (1993, 88) remarks that "one might go so far as to suggest that Athens' making of the alliance . . . was the act that fulfilled the Corcyrean prophecy."

55. Arnold (1992, 45).

56. Certainly the reader may employ a more distant, less engaged perspective: these two perspectives may coexist in some sort of tension or alternation. For an analogous situation, see Macleod (1983, 77) who describes how the "elegant polemic" of Alcibiades in book 6 may be "satisfying perhaps to an audience, [but] must give the reader pause." Connor (1984, 36) says that "the effect of this section, then, is to intensify the discrepancy between the analysis of power in the text and the reader's knowledge of the outcome of the war"; see Connor (1984, 39) on the "reader's knowledge" of a long and difficult war.

57. See Kitto (1966, 339) on the uncertainty of the future; he also remarks: "we watch and listen as actors peer ahead into the dark," having to guess what will happen (299).

58. Farrar (1988, 145) says that Thucydides shows how things happened and why, but also suggests that it was not inevitable. Kagan (1995, 10) raises the question more generally on the origins of war: "What choices were available, and more importantly what choices did they [the participants] believe were available?" We are more likely to discover the answer by employing the open-ended perspective of 433 BCE rather than remaining at a distance and judging with hindsight. Stahl (2003, 53) wonders whether Thucydides saw any possibility of averting war and points to Archidamus' speech (1.80–85) as the last chance for peace.

59. Kagan (1995, 58); see his discussion of options at 68–74.

60. Ibid., 70. Alternatively the reader is confronted with considering what it may mean when Thucydides says the Athenians and Spartans were "forced" to go to war (1.23.6). Connor (1984, 32 n31) says of *ananke* that it is "strong pressure in one direction, not philosophical determinacy or practical inevitability."

61. Kagan (1995, 46) remarks that the "defensive alliance was a precisely crafted diplomatic device meant to bring the Corinthians to their senses without war" (see n28 above).

62. Stahl (2003, 75–77) notes that other speakers, such as Pericles and Archidamus, try to anticipate the future. For discussion of (wrongly) seeing the past as inevitable, see Gould (1989) on evolution, Varnedoe (1990) on modern art, Bernstein (1995) on literature and history, and Ferguson (1997) on history.

63. Thucydides informs the reader of the names of generals (1.46.2, 1.47.1), the contributors and number of ships (1.46.1), and the geography of the city of Ephyra and its harbor (1.46.4). HCT, I: 179 comments: "This careful description [1.46.4] of a not very important locality suggests to me autopsy or information from a special source."

64. Thucydides does not explicitly comment on the fact that the Athenians are facing the Corinthians. Wilson (1987, 45) remarks that Corinth may have "wished to put the Athenians diplomatically on the spot, as it were, by forcing them to fight against the Corinthians themselves rather than against their allies."

65. Wilson (1987, 47–48) notes the "apparent contradiction" between Thucydides' comment that there were no "breakthroughs" (*diekploi*–1.49.3), yet *diekpleontes* appears at 1.50.1; see Hornblower (1991–96, I: 92). Thucydides later makes several comments: this was the biggest sea battle ever fought between two Greek navies at that time (ναυμαχία . . . νεῶν πλήθει μεγίστη–1.50.2); it was

fought with "more enthusiasm than skill" (ἀλλὰ θυμῷ καὶ ῥώμῃ τὸ πλέον ἐναυμάχουν ἢ ἐπιστήμῃ–1.49.3; cf. 7.63.4 on skill versus enthusiasm).

66. A possible additional focalization would be the Corcyreans' pursuit of the Corinthians (1.49.5).

67. Athenian fear of a Corcyrean defeat serves as motivation (*deisantes*–1.50.5). On fear as a motivating factor, see de Romilly (1956b).

68. Hornblower (1991–96, I) comments on the "cinematic" technique of this description, for Thucydides "lets us see how individuals react" (93) and calls the upcoming section 1.52 "exceptionally vivid" (95). For the analogy with cinema, see Hornblower (1987, 192).

69. This omission is noted by Hornblower (1991–96, I: 94): there must have been a third Athenian assembly resolving to send an additional twenty ships. Hornblower's explanation is that this silence "minimize[s] Athenian aggressiveness by leaving in the reader's mind the impression of scrupulousness created by [1.]45.3." On this point more generally, see Badian (1993, 125–62, 223–36).

70. On Corcyra's "bloodthirsty" nature in demanding the killing of the Corinthian embassy (1.53.3), see Wilson (1987, 31). Yet again the Athenians try to find a third, moderate path. As de Ste. Croix* (1972, 77) points out, the Athenians and the Corcyreans could have destroyed or captured the entire Corinthian fleet on the second day, yet they refrain from doing so (see n28 above).

71. Orwin (1994, 59–60) notes that 21 of the 146 chapters in book 1 (one in seven) concern charges against the Athenians and their responses. Cf. Thucydides' comment on the goodwill toward Sparta in "freeing Greece" when war begins (2.8.4).

72. HCT, I: 190 notes that this is "normally a sign of victory, that they did not have to obtain them under a flag of truce (cf. 63.3)."

73. Of course the Corcyreans do so with the help of the second Athenian contingent.

74. Thucydides does comment more authoritatively on the Corcyreans' success (note *perigignetai*–1.55). HCT, I: 196 comments on Corinth's failure: "Corinth had neither secured the freedom of Epidamnos nor reduced Kerkyra [Corcyra] to obedience."

75. Wilson (1987, 120). Kitto (1966, 294) comments on Thucydides' decision not to anticipate the later course of events concerning Corcyra. The Corcyreans do provide Athens with fifty ships in 431 (2.25.1), 15 in 426 (3.94.1), and 15 in 413 (7.31.5; cf. 7.44.6, 7.57.7). Of more immediate significance, Wilson asks why Corinth failed to make another attack on Corcyra if Athens did not keep a permanent fleet in the area (63).

CHAPTER FOUR

1. As Cogan (1981, 4) notes, while the city of Plataea is "of little or no material consequence, Thucydides treats it with a care and emphasis reserved for only a very few events in the course of the war . . . [there must be] some crucial non-material consequence or significance." Gomme HCT, II: 3 notes that

"Thucydides says nothing of the military importance of Plataea to either side." In raising the question why Plataea is dealt with at such length, Cartwright (1997, 154) concludes it was "perhaps this very insignificance of Plataea in the scheme of things and the disproportionate hostility of the Peloponnesians to it that aroused Thucydides' interest."

2. Rusten (1989, 97) believes that Thucydides "gives it [Plataea] the foremost place only chronologically, not causally . . . yet it is paradigmatic in many ways for the Peloponnesian War: careful planning is ruined by lateness at crucial moments . . . the co-operation of minor *stasiotai* and greater powers bring to local disputes an international dimension . . . instead of concluding these disputes, the greater powers may be infected by their savagery." Gomme HCT, II: 354 speaks of Thucydides' interest "in the political and moral issues raised by Plataia's alliance with Athens, her obliteration, and the cold-blooded execution of the survivors."

3. Badian (1993, 109).

4. On what seems "more than coincidence," see Aristotle *Poetics* ch. 9, 1452a. Rusten (1989, 102) compares the rain at 2.5.2 with the second "rescue" at 2.77.6. Is there possibly an echo of the rain which saves Croesus on the pyre in Herodotus 1.86–87? Gomme HCT, II: 211 remarks: Thucydides "did not at once believe all that he was told, including a story that Plataea was saved in much the same way as Croesus had been."

5. Stahl (2003, 67) comments on the movement from disorientation to orientation.

6. Connor (1984, 53) says that Thucydides "encourages the reader to act like a contemporary with surprise at the unexpected form taken by the outbreak of the war." Stahl (2003, 66) believes this "shows the psychological interest of the author"; cf. 69 on the reader who experiences events simultaneously with the participants.

7. Many key figures are unnamed including the Plataean who, by shutting the city gate, pens the Thebans in (*tis* . . . 2.4.3); the woman who gives the axe to the Thebans (2.4.4); and the Athenian herald who arrives to find the Theban prisoners dead (with the final focalization–2.6.3). Those who are named include the leaders at the start (the Thebans Pythangellus and Diemporus; the Plataean Naucleides) and the Theban go-between Eurymachus (2.2.3; also mentioned when he dies at 2.5.7). Thucydides provides information such as the distance from Plataea to Thebes (80 stades–2.5.2) and the reasons for the slowness of the auxiliary force (in the rain, the journey is slower, and the Asopos in flood is difficult to cross–2.5.1).

8. As Hornblower (1991–96, I: 241) notes: "People in Thucydides who think things can be done 'easily' tend to be wrong." Kagan (1969, 46) comments on the oligarchic Plataeans who "more accurately estimate[d] the mood of their fellow citizens, believing they would surely attempt to resist the Thebans once the shock of the coup had worn off. Their advice was ignored."

9. Connor (1984, 52) comments that this is "as surprising to the reader as to the unwary Plataeans."

10. Hornblower (1991–96, I: 242) considers this a "paragraph of exceptionally vivid description." On 2.4.4, Brunt (1993, 403) remarks: "each phrase can be like a camera shot."

11. Connor (1984, 52 n1) comments on the technique of "postponed information": "Throughout the Plataean episode Thucydides shows a tendency to postpone the introduction of important material until very late in the narrative." Cf. Hornblower (1991–96, I: 237) regarding the fact that the invasion was made during the sacred time of the month (3.56.2, 3.65.1)—more delayed information.

12. Connor (1984, 53) remarks that the "element of the unexpected remains prominent" throughout book 2; cf. Stahl (2003, 94).

13. Rood (2004, 120) offers a valuable discussion of this passage (2.5.6). Stahl (2003, 72 n3) astutely remarks: "Is it likely that the Theban army would actually have given up its human collateral in exchange for the mere prospect of 'negotiations'?" I have suggested elsewhere (Morrison 2004, 98) that the effect is to give the reader a sense of what Thucydides' own experience as an historian must have been like when he confronted conflicting eye-witness accounts (1.22.3). It is not even clear how much of 2.5.5 is the Thebans' account: only the end—the promise to give back the prisoners—or the whole report from the herald?

14. Lateiner (1977, 100) notes that "heralds are prominent in the Plataean narrative because, in the earliest phase of the war, diplomacy was as important as warfare for achieving political objectives." Indeed, "heralds have punctuated Plataea at each major incident." See Stahl (2003, 69) on self-deception and what cannot be foreseen. Hornblower (1991–96, I: 236) finds this to be the "first event of the war proper." See the valuable discussion in Price (2001, 277–89).

15. Connor (1984, 52–53) notes that the Thebans and Plataeans were not prominent in book 1.

16. Later the issues arise whether the Thebans took Plataea by force (3.52.2, 5.17.2); regarding the Spartans' sense of guilt at the transgression (*paranomema*) of the Thebans who invaded Plataea while the treaty was still in effect, see 7.18.2 (cf. 1.85.1).

17. The invasion of Plataea is used for dating purposes: 2.10.1, 2.19.1. Rusten (1989, 216 [s.v. 2.71]) notes, "Thucydides continues in detail the story he began in 2.2–6." We are reminded that the Plataeans sent their women, children, and elders to Athens (2.72.2, 2.78.3).

18. Badian (1993, 111) thinks that Archidamus "shows himself willing to abate the rigour of that demand, evidently in accordance with a Spartan policy earlier decided upon, and to accept something less than strict fulfillment." Bauslaugh (1991, 131) notes that neutrality served useful propaganda purposes (2.77.5).

19. Pausanias, of course, is cast in a different light at 1.128–135.

20. Connor (1984, 57–59).

21. Kagan (1969, 102). Connor (1984, 54) remarks that the best strategy of the Peloponnesians is to draw Athens into land battle; see Connor (1984, 57) for his discussion of the "commander narrative" of Archidamus and Pericles in book 2.

22. Kagan (1969, 104–105, 174). Gomme HCT, II: 206 calls Archidamus' final offer "generous." Cf. Badian (1993, 111) on neutrality.

23. Kagan (1969, 105); Badian (1993, 111). Gomme HCT, II: 206 believes that while it is surprising that Athens set so much store on Plataea, Athenian strategy dictated such a move. Bauslaugh (1991, 132) surmises that the Athenians were worried that neutrality for the Plataeans might set a precedent. See Stahl (2003, 81) on Plataea being caught in the middle.

24. Rusten (1989, 217); Kagan (1969, 174).

25. See Stahl (2003, 82).

26. The situation of some working while others ate or slept is echoed when the second Athenian trireme is sent to Mytilene (3.49.2); see Gomme HCT, II: 207–8 and Hornblower (1991–96, I: 360).

27. Note the double labor (ἐν ἀμφιβόλῳ –2.76.3); cf. Rusten (1989, 21).

28. Flory (1988, 50–51) remarks: "Fire, wind, night, and the weather in general thus constitute a significant pattern in the external contingencies about which Thucydides hypothesizes."

29. The second half of this section is in fact quite difficult for the reader to follow: in addition to the many technical terms, a diagram is practically required to keep clear the tactics of siege and counter-siege operations. Would Thucydides expect his reader to draw one? Gomme HCT, II: 209 remarks: "The care with which Thucydides relates all the details proves at least a comparative novelty."

30. Also we note the contrast between the anonymous (and collective) feel to the Plataean resistance. No Plataeans are named: none of the ambasssadors to the Spartans, no speakers, no couriers to Athens are identified. Once again the effect is that the Plataeans are viewed very much as a collective, though there is a distinction between the ambassadors to Sparta and Athens and the populace. On the other side, Archidamus is the only Spartan named other than references to Pausanias.

31. Spence (1990, 93) remarks that for Athens the "navy and long walls precluded an effective siege of the city. . . . Most Greek cities could not afford to lose more than one harvest without being forced to import food to avoid starvation." Later, after the fortification of Deceleia, the city of Athens (polis) has become a fortress (phrourion–7.28.1).

32. See Connor (1984, 75 n56) on Pericles' obscure role.

33. Thucydides mentions 220 volunteers (3.20.2); cf. the account in Demosthenes 59.103 on the drawing of lots to determine who might escape so that the remaining food might last longer. On Thucydides' knowledge, see Gomme HCT, II: 283; on page 287, he remarks that all the details could have been told to Thucydides by one or more of those who escaped on their arrival in Athens, except about the half dozen turning back who believed all were lost. Thucydides would have had to wait for this information, perhaps questioning the Spartans at a later time.

34. Their success is marked at 3.24.3 by esothesan; cf. soteria at 3.20.1.

35. On the task and position of these 300, see Harrison (1959, 30 n1).

36. As Harrison (1959, 30) points out: "The considerateness [of the Peloponnesians and the Boeotians] was misguided, as events proved, since progress round the top of the wall was now possible only by passing through these towers; and the capture of two adjacent towers by a small party would mean that the wall was effectively breached."

37. Harrison (1959, 33) comments on the "smoothness and precision which characterizes the whole enterprise, making it seem almost too good to be true."

38. Lateiner (1977, 100) notices that "only here in Thucydides a herald discovers that there are no dead. The fruitless mission underlines dramatically, as does the concluding formulaic sentence, the fortunate peripety for part of the Plataean garrison."

39. See Gomme HCT, II: 280–281 on their measuring for the length of the ladders: "exactness was necessary: the ladders must be short of the top of the wall, or the defenders will be able to push them over, but only just short, or it will be difficult to get from the top rung onto the wall; and they must be put against it at an angle not so steep that it may fall backward, or, with a very slight effort, be pushed over, and not so steep that, with many men mounting at a time, it may break."

40. Gomme HCT, II: 286 comments: "the success of their flight was due primarily to this same storm." The leaders of the escape are named at 3.20.1: one is a general, the other, Theainetes, is a seer; Ammeas is the first one up the ladder (3.22.3).

41. The Spartan archon at 3.52.2 is unnamed; the Plataeans, however, are personalized: Astymachus and Lacon (3.52.5). This contrasts with those who negotiated earlier with Archidamus (2.71–74) and those who escaped.

42. Cartwright (1997, 154) remarks that in contrast to Mytilene, there is no dramatic reversal; what appears to be an advantage to Plataea (the right to speak on its own behalf—again contrasting with the Mytilenians) proves fruitless.

43. The Plataeans say that if they thought they were being given over to the Thebans, they would have chosen starvation (3.59.3).

44. Yet the original question posed by the Spartan suggests that past actions are not pertinent; see Hornblower (1991–96, I: 463).

45. Hornblower (1991–96, I: 465). Note the remark at 3.57.4 that no ally has come to help.

46. Cf. Gomme's remark at HCT, II: 212 on how "Thucydides deserts his normally strict chronological order . . . in order to finish with Plataea for this year." Alternatively, Hornblower (1991–96, I: 466) explains the omission of the subsequent status (as Athenian citizens) of the Plataeans who did escape, for Thucydides did not wish "to take away from the emotional power of his ending by recounting the hospitality and improved status accorded to the Plataians at Athens after 427."

47. Cf. 5.17.2, where the Thebans resist handing over Plataea. Connor (1984, 93) comments that "the reader, of course, already knows that the Plataeans' appeal will be unsuccessful, for every Greek was aware of the fate of Plataea . . . there is no suspense in the Plataean debate, for the outcome is well-known." This of course represents the perspective of the retrospective reader. Contrast the comment by Macleod (1983, 227) on uncertainty: "the speakers cannot even say they know for sure how badly off they are"—this coincides with how the engaged reader may experience this situation.

48. The Plataeans' speech makes explicit mention of knowledge and ignorance: if the Plataeans and Spartan judges were "not familiar" with each other (ἀγνῶτες μὲν γὰρ ὄντες ἀλλήλων–3.53.4), the Plataeans could bring in new evidence (μαρτύρια ὧν ἄπειροι ἦτε–3.53.4). As it is, they speak to those who know (πρὸς εἰδότας–3.53.4).

49. Arnold (1996, 108) remarks that the Thebans were ignorant about "the degree to which the fate of the Plataeans has already been decided."

50. Note that surrender in both cases results from lack of food (sitos–3.20.1, 3.26.4) and lack of hope (elpis–3.20.1, 3.32.3). See the discussion of parallels in

Macleod (1983, 118–22) and Connor (1984, 91–93). The rationale of Diodotus' argument (expediency "trumps" justice in foreign policy–3.44) apparently endorses the Spartans' decision concerning the Plataeans (3.68.4).

51. At one level, the Plataean debate may be thought of as a set of nested speeches, which becomes a component in the larger pattern of interwoven episodes; see Rood (1998a, 120–21) and Morrison (2006). Another example of *interwoven episodes* can be found in books 6 and 7 where several strands— Athenian, Syracusan, and Spartan—are introduced in turn. On the weaving metaphor for historical narrative, see Polybius 1.4 and 3.32.2, discussed in Walbank (1975). de Jong (2001, 589–90) describes the technique of interweaving episodes in Homeric epic as an "interlacing technique."

52. Hornblower (1991–96, I: 445) remarks that the "theme [of the Persian war] is developed in much more 'traditional' ways than is usual in a Thucydidean speech . . . it is safe to say that the elaborate appeals to tombs and ancestors are done in a style which Thucydidean speakers often reject with impatience."

53. Cf. the Thebans' words at 3.63.3–4.

54. This is contrary to the Plataean claims regarding the actions of the Spartan ancestors (3.58.4, 3.58.5). At 3.58 in particular, they invoke the *philia* of Pausanias (3.58.5); the Plataeans are not hostile, but well-disposed (not *echthrous*, but *eunous*—3.58.2). Macleod (1983, 110) cynically but realistically comments: "the past, and the values a living memory guarantees, mean nothing in war." See Cogan (1981, 15) on the hope for "Spartan willingness to consider Medism or fidelity to the Hellenic side [as] the primary distinction to be made in determining the moral character of nations." In Plato *Republic* book 1 (332d–336a) helping friends and hurting enemies is proposed as one definition of justice, though this is rejected: cf. *Iliad* 9.613–14, Thucydides 2.40.4, and discussion in Creed (1973), Missiou (1998), Pearson (1957), Seaford (1994), and Whitlock Blundell (1989).

55. The Plataeans reveal their expectation that they did not anticipate such a brief interrogation, but something more customary (οὐ τοιάνδε δίκην οἰόμενοι ὑφέξειν, νομιμωτέραν δέ τινα ἔσεσθαι—3.53.1). It is "just" (*dikaion*), they believe, that if the Plataeans do not persuade the Spartans, they should put the Plataeans back in the same situation as before they surrendered the city (3.59.3).

56. Nor have the Plataeans themselves acted unjustly in refusing to desert the Athenian alliance (οὐκ ἠδικοῦμεν—3.55.3), because the Athenians helped the Plataeans in the past—again, an appeal to conventional morality: they were helped by Athens, so the Plataeans should be loyal to them.

57. Later the Plataeans insist that it is not the followers, but the leaders who are responsible (*aitioi*–3.55.4).

58. Macleod (1983, 108) remarks that this law is "scarcely more than a law of nature . . . The very word νόμος is revealed as ambiguous." Note the Plataeans' appeal to Spartan reputation and the common laws of the Greeks: ἐς τὰ κοινὰ τῶν ῾Ελλήνων νόμιμα (3.59.1); cf. Gomme HCT, II: 341 (s.v. 3.56.2): the execution of the Theban prisoners is "a matter over which the Plataean speakers hurry, the Thebans dwell."

59. Macleod (1983, 109) comments: "The Plataeans invoke the 'law' that those who surrender in battle should be spared. But the Thebans can justly retort that the Plataeans themselves flouted it (66.2–3, 67.6). This reveals the shakiness

of such a 'law.'" On suppliants (hiketai) invoking the Spartans' fathers' graves and "we are suppliants of your good faith" (τῆς ὑμετέρας πίστεως ἱκέται ὄντες), see 3.59.2, 3.59.4.

60. Gomme HCT, II: 345 translates: "gods worshipped by us and you and all of Greece"; cf. 3.58.1, 3.58.5.

61. Cogan (1981, 12) remarks that even if Diodotus is not offering an innovation in Athenian policy, "we would still have to conclude that it is presented to us as one by Thucydides."

62. Hornblower (1991–96, I: 445) sees the Plataean speech as "exceptional in Thucydides for the detailed way it dwells on the past." The reader is made aware of several of these past actions presented earlier in the History.

63. Also the Plataeans remind the Spartans of the unpredictability of the future: ὡς ἀστάθμητον τὸ τῆς ξυμφορᾶς (3.59.1; cf. the Corinthians at 1.42.2). Macleod (1983, 111) remarks: "Not only are we reminded how useless appeals to the past are; we also see that appeals to the future, i.e., to loss of reputation (cf. 59.4 fin.) are equally so."

64. See also τὴν δύσκλειαν (3.58.2) and Spartan doxa (3.59.1; cf. 3.57.1); cf. the use of paradeigma elsewhere (cf. 2.42.3, 2.63.2, 3.40.7, 3.40.4) and the Thebans' response at 3.64.4, 3.67.6.

65. Hornblower (1991–96, I: 446) says that both speeches show a "freedom with tenses and moods," desiring "to roll together past, present, and future on the one hand, and hypothetical and actuality on the other." Rather than seeing all time collapsed, I would argue that the Plataeans are desperately trying to show that the past and future are relevant to the impending decision of the Spartans.

66. Macleod (1983, 111) comments: "The richest resources of Thucydides' style are employed as the Plataeans try in vain to make a bridge between the past and the present."

67. Gomme HCT, II: 342 calls this "a somewhat specious argument."

68. See Debnar (1996, 97) on the Thebans' reputation "for being incompetent speakers." Hornblower (1991–96, I: 454) notes that the "first three words" recall Sthenelaidas' remark at 1.86.1.

69. In book 2, there was no indication to what extent the Plataeans debated the fate of the Theban prisoners.

70. Macleod (1983, 119) asserts that, "The result is that self-interest dominates again, but it is not enlightened, so far as that is possible, by open and rational discussion, and it limits its view to the 'present war' (52.4, 56.3, 68.4)."

71. Debnar (1996, 99) thinks the "overall impression of the opening of the exordium is that the Thebans object more strenuously to the Plataeans' speaking than to their having done anything wrong or even to their having failed to do anything good."

72. The Plataeans' role as benefactors during the helot revolt is passed over.

73. Cf. the Athenian claim to have fought alone at Marathon (1.73.4; cf. the Thespians at Hdt. 9.27.2, 5).

74. Debnar (1996, 100–101) is quite explicit on the connotation: "for all the scorn they intend to convey with the word 'atticize,' the force of this taunt depends on an implicit condemnation of its model 'medize.'"

75. On consistency in action, see also Pericles and Cleon's echo (2.61.2,

3.37). Hornblower (1991–96, I: 455 [s.v. 3.62.3]) notes that the Thebans emphasize that the circumstances are different (ἐν οἵῳ εἴδει).

76. For such reverberations, see Hornblower (1991–96, I: 461).

77. Macleod (1983, 114) comments: "What is implied here is that political
rights—above all the right to vote on questions of national policy—were denied
to citizens at large."

78. In fact, the Athenians also offered to help Sparta (1.101–2). Does this
reinforce the Theban charge that Plataea only followed Athens?

79. Macleod (1983, 120) says: "Past deeds count for nothing because they
serve only to frame moral arguments, which both tend to entangle themselves and
can easily be reversed."

80. Macleod (1983, 120) argues: "If moral credit and blame are to be assigned,
there must be free will. But the speeches concerning both Mytilene and Plataea
show how difficult it is to establish free will in political action, just as in broader
terms they show the futility of moral conventions in war."

81. The Plataeans fear the Spartans will betray them in spite of their past service (προδοῦναι τοὺς εὐεργήτας–3.57.1). The Thebans have no answer to this.
Debnar (1996, 99) comments: "because the Thebans refer to their own κακία and
the Plataeans' δόξα before they appeal to the truth, however, the immediate
impression is that they acknowledge the validity of both reputations"; and later
says: "Clearly the Thebans view themselves as one of the liberators . . . [yet] the
Thebans make strange spokesmen indeed for a group from which they were excluded because of their collaboration. By referring to the oaths the Thebans once again
draw attention to their ignominious role in the Persian wars" (103).

82. See Cogan (1981, 15–17).

83. Macleod (1983, 115) argues: "This contradiction is the mirror-image of the
Plataeans": they wanted what they did in the Persian Wars to be reckoned to their
credit but what they did as Athens' allies to be excused as involuntary (55.4). The
Thebans in 65.2, when discussing their entry into Plataea, then turn the argument and
wording of 55.4 against their adversaries; and this connects for the reader the questions concerning a city's free will when there is faction within it and those when there
is pressure from outside; elsewhere he maintains that Thucydides "see[s] the historical
meaning of the rhetorical contradictions. External necessity or internal strife not only
remove moral scruples (cf. 3.82.2); they also remove the conditions for actions to be
judged morally. But that does not stop men using such judgments for their own purposes (cf. 3.82.2), as constantly happens in Thucydides' speeches" (240). This is the
first time the term *attikismon* is found extant in Greek literature. See Cogan (1981,
16) on this "neologism": "Thucydides seems to imply that this debate was either the
occasion of its invention [the slogan of Plataea as 'atticizing'] or the first instance of
its use to determine policy." Cf. Macleod (1983, 116).

84. Debnar (1996, 105) remarks: "Once again their response does not ade-
quately address the Plataeans' charge, since it makes no reference at all to the
peace or the festival. By mentioning these details the Thebans appear to concede
their opponents' point and may, in fact, admit their own impiety." Cf. Hornblower
(1991–96, I: 459).

85. Debnar (1996, 107) finds this inconsistent: "The Thebans cannot disguise
the illogic of first contending that the Plataeans' treatment of Theban prisoners

transgressed Greek law (3.66.2) and then asking the Spartans to preserve this same law by transgressing it in return (3.67.6)."

86. Such an argument has persuaded the Spartans in the past (see Sthenelaidas' claim at 1.86.1).

87. Cf. Cleon's argument against emotion (3.40) and Diodotus' analysis (3.45). Cogan (1981, 15) comments on the Plataeans' direct appeal for mercy; cf. Gomme HCT, II: 343 and Hogan (1972, 247).

88. See another echo at 3.57.1.

89. Macleod (1983, 118) comments that "the Thebans' cocksure anticipation of the future is in striking contrast to the Plataeans' hopeless attempt to revive the past in chs. 58–59."

90. Hornblower (1991–96, I: 446).

91. Macleod (1983, 113; cf. 117). Cogan (1981, 20) argues that the true significance of debate is not the result but speeches "as political events in their own right."

92. Macleod (1983, 110) makes the following distinction: "in rhetorical terms, this is a forensic speech to a body of deliberators" (who are concerned with expediency).

93. See Gomme HCT, II: 343.

94. As Macleod (1983, 104) notes: "we have already seen them [the Spartans] hear and reject such a speech in 2.71–72." Cf. also the Plataeans' hope in 429 that Athens would come to their aid and the realization in book 3 that such help was not forthcoming (3.57.4). Connor (1984, 92 n30) says this "calls attention to the Athenians' ineffectiveness in aiding Plataea or even to their unwillingness at one point (3.36.1) to explore a possible way of saving Plataea." Kagan (1969, 174) says "the fall of Plataea and its abandonment by the Athenians were inevitable," in part because it was "strategically untenable," yet notes that in 429 they "could have yielded on reasonable terms had not Athens held her to the alliance and promised help."

95. Connor (1984, 91) finds the following parallels: both cities are under siege (2.78.1, 3.18); one great power is in control while the other great power is unable—or unwilling—to render significant aid; supplies run out (3.20.1, 3.27.1); capitulation follows; then an antilogy in direct discourse; decisions are made in the immediate interests of the major power (based on advantage, not right); casualties are listed; the disposition of land is announced (and put under foreign control); a dedication (3.50.2, 3.68.3); and finally, a "rounding off" sentence (3.50.3, 3.68.4). Gomme HCT, II: 337 believes, "the sentence, τοὺς τε ἀδίκους κολάζειν, παρὰ δίκην δὲ οὐδένα, reminds one of the Athenians' μετάνοια, 36.4, of Kleon, 40.7, and of Diodotos, 48.1." See also de Romilly (1988, 146–49) and Hornblower (1991–96, I: 462). In addition to the intertwined narratives, note the reminder before the Mytilenian debate that Plataea is still under siege (3.36.1); also the goal of survival (soteria—3.20.1, 3.24.3), lack of readiness on the part of the Mytilenians (3.4; cf. the surprise attack on Plataea at 2.2), the refuge to altars— and divine protection—by both sides (3.28.2; cf. 3.59.2), and the role of chance (κατὰ τύχην—3.49.4; cf. 3.45.6). See Connor (1984, 92 n31) on the themes of supplication, benefaction, and betrayal.

96. Spartan judges (dicastai) are so named at 3.52.2, 3.52.3; other legalistic

language includes *kategoria* (3.53.4) and the appeal to the impartiality of judges (μὴ οὐ κοινοὶ ἀποβῆτε—3.53.2; cf. 3.44.4, 3.46.4).

97. Hornblower (1991-96, I: 457) believes this boils the issue down to "free will versus force majeure."

98. Connor (1984, 93–94).

99. Macleod (1983, 105).

100. Connor (1984, 94) remarks that this calls to mind the Corcyrean alliance: the basis for that decision proved useful to the addressees of the speeches (compare the codas—1.44, 3.68—and see also 3.61.2 on the founding of the city). On neutrality as an option for Corcyra or Plataea, see discussion in chapter 5.

101. In episodes 2 and 3 no individual Plataean is mentioned; much of the activity in episode 1 is attributed to "the Plataeans." See also Hunter (1986, 1988). It should be noted that focalization occurs not only for the individuals involved, but also for various factions and cities as we saw in chapter 3.

102. Stahl (2003, 114) comments on the reminder at 3.36.1 and then compares the promise of help from the Spartan Salaithus to Mytilene and that of Athens to Plataea (2.71–78), noting that we look back to the opening of the tragic drama and the death of the Theban prisoners when the Plataeans are put to death.

103. Debnar (1996, 109) argues that the Plataean debate shows "the irrelevance of the past to Spartan policy," while "in book 5 the Athenians will exclude from their debate with the Melians all arguments concerning the future (5.87)." See Parry (1981), 190 on how the Plataean debate anticipates the Melian Dialogue.

104. For recurring phenomena in different guises, note Thucydides' remarks on the subject of civil war: such phenomena will continue to happen but "they are more or less severe and differ in form with every new combination of circumstances" (τοῖς εἴδεσι διηλλαγμένα, ὡς ἂν ἕκασται αἱ μεταβολαὶ τῶν ξυντυχιῶν ἐφ-ιστῶνται–3.82.2; English translation from Hornblower [1991–96], I: 481).

CHAPTER FIVE

1. Another unusual feature is that we encounter a rhetorical dispute in which the goal of each side is to convince not a third party, but the other speakers: in the first set of speeches, the Corinthians and Corcyreans attempt to persuade the Athenians; later the Thebans and Plataeans argue before the Spartans; individuals, such as Cleon and Diodotus, work to persuade the Athenian assembly.

2. As Meiggs (1972, 345) remarks: "Thucydides' treatment of the Melian episode cannot be satisfactorily judged in isolation."

3. De Romilly (1988, 290). Andrewes HCT, IV: 168 states: "Thucydides' presentation has the effect of weighting the sympathies of most readers in favour of Melos."

4. Bosworth (1993, 33). Andrewes HCT, IV: 185 remarks that in contrast with other massacres (Torone 5.3, Scione 5.32), here the Athenians are giving the Melians a choice of "peaceful surrender instead of useless resistance." The Athenians' decision to talk things over first with the Melians rather than simply

attack must be seen as humanitarian in a qualified sense, as Bosworth (1993, 43) acknowledges: "Humanitarian it certainly is in the limited sense that it is designed to force the Melians to accept the most advantageous terms from Athens and avoid bloodshed." Bruell (1974, 16) believes that the policy of Athens "is indeed compatible with, and to some extent conducive to, a remarkable gentleness." De Ste. Croix (1972, 14) argues: "the whole purpose of the Athenians is to persuade the Melians that they would be well advised to surrender, because resistance would be futile. It would be a bad mistake to say that Thucydides is "on the side of the Melians in any sense. The fact that they are being foolishly over-optimistic is made very clear by the Athenians." Connor (1984, 151) comments: "there is virtually no overt sympathy for the Melians." Cartwright (1997, 221) says that "the victims . . . were given the opportunity to save themselves from destruction. They rejected it, and the significance of this episode for Thucydides lies in part in the thinking behind this decision." Here Athenian action and rhetoric are consistent, as noted by Andrewes HCT, IV: 179–80: "There is almost a sincerity in this appeal to the Melians to 'behave sensibly,' to give up an opposition which can do them no good, and surrender." Stahl (2003, 165) describes the Athenians as "almost imploring" the Melians. For examples of miscalculating the likelihood of surrender in the twentieth century, see Chuter (1997). Even de Romilly (1988, 291) acknowledges that "from a rational and political point of view, one fact stands out immediately: the Melians were wrong to resist."

5. See Stahl (2003, 169–70). Thucydides refuses to tell the reader why Athens attacks Melos at this particular time or whether the Melians have done anything to provoke it. Amit (1968, 217) points out that Thucydides omits the "entirely Athenian debate in the Assembly" to determine the manner of punishment after the city is taken; we could add he also omits the debate in the assembly which originally sent the expedition. On Thucydides' omissions, see Herter (1954, 316–19); Andrewes (1960, 2); and nn44, 70, and 71 below.

6. Westlake (1968, 5).

7. Wasserman (1947, 27).

8. I find myself very much in agreement with Wasserman regarding Thucydides' balanced presentation, basing this interpretation partly on Thucydides' own remarks where he says that his work will lack "patriotic bias" (τὸ μυθῶδες–1.22.4)—this is discussed in chapter 2. Thucydides is claiming that he will avoid chauvinism; he will offer no biased or exaggerated stories of patriotism—Athenian or otherwise. In the case of Melos, Thucydides does not necessarily endorse the arguments of either side. I conclude that the reader is encouraged to look without prejudice at the dialogue from both the Athenian and Melian points of view. For the difficulty of deriving Thucydides' own opinions from speeches, see Hornblower (1987, 155–90) and his conclusion (185): "nothing can be straightforwardly extracted from the Melian Dialogue . . . about Thucydides's own position."

9. Another possibility other than Athenian success or defeat is simply giving up (cf. 3.91); see n67 below. Liebeschuetz (1968, 73) sees the outcome as inevitable: "In the first half of the dialogue the speakers discuss the expediency of forcing Melos into the Athenian Empire, in the second they discuss the likelihood of the Melians resisting successfully. But since the Melians are offered no alternative to becoming

subjects except complete destruction, and since they are clearly not ready to choose
the safe but dishonoring alternative, even though they have no chance of defend-
ing their city successfully, the inevitable destruction of Melos casts its shadow over
the whole of the negotiations." Macleod (1983, 57) remarks that "this cannot mask
that what is possible for Athens is conquest whereas what is possible for Melos is
surrender and that the Athenians are the real agents whereas the Melian must simply endure."

10.   Cleon and Diodotus have previously pointed out the value of intact cities
at 3.39.8, 3.46.3; cf. Sparta's motivations at 2.77.2 (discussed in chapter 4) and
Stahl (2003, 162). Amit (1968, 224) asserts that the business of the Athenian
troops "was to implement the decisions already taken by the Assembly, with the
minimum of casualties, expenses, and harm to Athens." On the Athenians' willingness to negotiate, cf. 3.3–5.

11   Cartwright (1997, 220) remarks: "The two sides are as far apart at the end
of the debate as they were at the beginning" (see 5.112.2). We may compare the
Plataean debate and how the Spartans ask the same question before and after the
Plataean and Theban speeches (3.68.1). See also Wasserman (1947, 22–24).

12.   "The Melians did not bring them before the common people but told
them to speak to the officials and a small group" (οἱ Μήλιοι πρὸς μὲν τὸ πλῆθος
οὐκ ἤγαγον, ἐν δὲ ταῖς ἀρχαῖς καὶ τοῖς ὀλίγοις λέγειν–5.84.3). Andrewes
HCT, IV: 159 comments that "ἀρχαί in Greek would include the council, often
the most powerful organ in an oligarchy, as well as magistrates in the more familiar sense; and ὀλίγοι will be the privileged voters."

13.   Cartwright (1997, 222) points out that those in power fear that the
Melian people may support Athens: see 5.84, 5.116.

14.   Yet see the brief exchanges at 1.53, 3.113, 4.97–99.

15.   This distinction between dialogue and set speech would have been familiar to Thucydides' fifth-century audience. While there were long speeches in the
law courts, assembly, and dramatic productions, dialogue (or *brachyologia*) occurred
in sophistic displays (prominently recreated in Plato's *Protagoras*) and the *sti-
chomythia* of tragedy. Cartwright (1997), 220 remarks upon Thucydides' experi-
mentation in featuring dialogue as part of the *History*. On the dialogue form, see
Hudson-Williams (1948). Macleod (1983, 67) notes that one of the reasons for the
dialogue is that it allows for "the peculiar privacy of the negotiations . . . [which]
gave the opportunity for a dialectical treatment of some major historical themes."

16.   In particular, the reader may be led back to the Mytilenian debate where
the value of debate is questioned by Cleon (3.37–38).

17.   Cf. 5.89 on the untrustworthiness of long speeches (λόγων μῆκος ἄπιστον) and Andrewes' comment (HCT, IV: 162): "the combination seems to imply
that a very long speech is, as such, less credible or persuasive than a short one."
Macleod (1983, 54) (with references) remarks on the "deceptiveness of the unin-
terrupted speech and the superior precision of dialogue." Beyond this, there is a
challenge to Athenian institutions as well. The basis of decision-making within the
assembly (and in the law courts) is voting based on speeches: this feature of
Athenian democracy is itself under attack. On Thucydides' criticism of Athenian
democracy, see Ober (1998, 78) where he concludes (for the Corinthian-
Corcyrean debate): "Thucydides' implicit lesson is that democratic knowledge

does not provide an adequate grounding for assessing the truth value of rhetorical discourse. And thus, badly—or at best indifferently—instructed by speech, the Athenian Assembly was likely eventually to fall into error and, as a result, to make bad policy."

18. Macleod (1983, 56–57) argues that "while the Athenians are claiming to give the Melians the chance of a free, rational and practical decision . . . the Melians know what is in store for them." Monoson and Loriaux (1998, 292) find that "language is not used for purposes of deliberation but as an instrument of siege." Regarding the Athenian restrictions on discourse, see Gomez-Lobo (1989, 12–23).

19. Wasserman (1947, 21) comments: "If Thucydides had had his Athenians refute their opponents by a speech in his usual way, we would not have had the dramatic intensity of a prizefight in which the Melians, though outmatched on the battle ground of expediency, rise again and again with new objections against the striking force of the apparently irrefutable Athenian arguments." Orwin (1994, 98) sees "in their choice of format the [Athenian] envoys reveal sovereign confidence in the power of their arguments." For an analysis of the Dialogue as exemplifying a "formal disputation" consisting of "move and countermove possibilities," see Alker (1988).

20. Macleod (1983, 54) asserts that the "stipulations" that there be no suppositions about the future and that the subject for discussion must be established are required by the methodology of practical deliberation and the principles of rhetoric.

21. σωτηρία: 5.87, 5.88, 5.91.2, 5.101, 5.105.4, 5.110, 5.111.2; cf. "not to be destroyed" (μὴ διαφθείραντες–5.93), and the idea of avoiding danger at 5.99.

22. ἀσφαλεία: 5.97, 5.98, 5.107, 5.111.4. By ruling more, the Athenians will be "safer" (5.97).

23. αἱ φανεραὶ ἐλπίδες, literally, "visible expectations," by which the Athenians evidently mean reasonable—or likely—expectations of the future, as opposed to "invisible hopes" (ἐπὶ τὰς ἀφανεῖς–5.103.2; cf. 5.102, 5.111.2, 5.113).

24. 5.89, 5.101, 5.111.4.

25. Allison (1997, 55) notes that "soteria has little to do with Athenians and Athens for the first half of the war even as a consideration of policy"; of the 37 uses of soteria, seven appear in the Melian Dialogue, yet here "soteria will only apply to Melos" (57); "as Book 6 gives way to Book 7 and the disaster in Sicily become palpable, soteria figures prominently in Athenian thought" (56).

26. 1.73–77, 2.62–64, 3.44–47. In building on what was implied at 1.73–77, Diodotus states quite bluntly that, when it comes to international issues, Athens is simply not interested in hearing about justice (3.44, 3.46.4, 3.47.4–5). Liebeschuetz (1968, 74) remarks that "the argument of Diodotus applied to the Athenian case at Melos suggests that the Athenian determination to press home their attack on the independence of Melos to the point of destroying that city completely is based on a misguided view of Athenian interest." The reason given for the rejection of justice's relevance is that Athens and Melos are not equal in power: "justice (δίκαια) is judged from equal [power of] compulsion (ἀπὸ τῆς

ἴσης ἀνάγκης κρίνεται) . . . the strong do what they are able, while the weak submit" (5.89). There may be a qualification on the prohibition against appealing to justice. The Athenians are not necessarily saying that justice is irrelevant to foreign policy or relations between cities (or at least to the discourse between cities); what they are maintaining is that when one power is much greater than another (as in this situation), discussion of justice is not applicable (see discussion in chapter 7).

27. This is, the Athenians assert, both a divine and a human law. Regarding divine aid, the Athenians believe they may count on the gods as much as the Melians (5.105.1).

28. Note that when the Athenians address the idea of shame (*aischune*), it boils down to the Spartans considering "what is pleasurable as fine and what is advantageous as just" (5.105.4; cf. 5.107), thus imputing moral reductivism to the Spartans. It is noteworthy that the Melian oligarchs' appeal to freedom and honor shows a sensitivity to popular morality and discourse, while the Athenians—a democracy—dismiss such concepts as mere words. Thucydides has already analyzed the collapse of such conventions in the plague at Athens and the civil war in Corcyra (2.52–3, 3.82–4). When Athens instructs the Melians to focus on expediency, they also play the role of a "violent teacher" (βίαιος διδάσκαλος–3.82.2); on such "schooling" metaphors, see Pouncey (1980, 3).

29. Andrewes HCT, IV: 161 comments: "In the privacy of this conference, the Athenians give up hollow pretense." Kagan (1981, 150–51) notes the "blunt" language of the Athenians. As Coby (1991, 76) puts it: "The Athenians are honest even about the deceptiveness of rhetorical speech. . . . The peace that is latent in the new morality depends on forthright communication between parties, not on deception of the weak by the strong." Liebeschuetz (1968, 76) goes so far as to call it "repulsive" and the Athenians as "bullying and arrogant to the weak, boundlessly self-confident, lacking humility even towards the gods." Pouncey (1980, 92) finds that "the tone of hardness is adopted prospectively to match the final outcome of the confrontation;" see also Bruell (1974, 14). Bosworth (1993, 31), however, believes that if the Melians capitulate, that would be "a decision which minimises suffering on all sides."

30. Diodotus' speech is an exception, but it is part of an internal discussion among Athenians, not diplomatic discourse between cities.

31. I reject the idea of de Ste. Croix (1972, 19) and Bruell (1974, 15) that appeals to justice always come from the losing side; cf. the Corcyreans at 1.32–36 and the Thebans at 3.61–67.

32. Andrewes (1960, 9).

33. Bosworth (1993, 37) believes that "by the time of the Melian dialogue Thucydides has given us a surfeit of propaganda. Now it is time for realities." Coby (1991, 73) argues that "relative and temporary peace is the promise of the new morality, which is judged to be more realistic than exhortations to virtue." As Forde (1992, 378) says, "The Athenians may wish to make the Melians better realists."

34. Williams (1998, 198) states that the Melians are "quite lacking in prudence, moderation, foresight, a willingness to negotiate or even to bend at all,

good planning, and the ability to consider reasonably both sides of an issue . . . in the unjust world of the fifth-century Greeks, the non-rational and unyielding posture of the Melians helped ensure their own destruction." For Realism in Thucydides, see Doyle (1991), which distinguishes between three types of Realism (minimalism, fundamentalism, and structuralism) and argues that Thucydides' own methods and lessons follow only the minimalist form of Realism, in which choices "depend upon a prior consideration of strategic security" (170). This the Melians fail to do. Forde (1992, 373) argues that while Thucydides is a Realist in international affairs, he "tried to defend the theoretically more difficult position that international realism need not entail universal moral skepticism." Garst (1989, 21–22) also finds that "Thucydides' history directs attention to the confusion underlying neorealist debates over power in international politics," for "in neorealism, this leadership [of hegemonic powers] lacks the moral dimension so heavily emphasized by Thucydides"; cf. Alker (1988).

35. At the very least, the Melians feel it is reasonable and understandable that they should have recourse to all kinds of arguments and points of view (εἰκὸς μὲν καὶ ξυγγνώμη ἐν τῷ τοιῷδε καθεστῶτας ἐπὶ πολλὰ καὶ λέγοντας καὶ δοκοῦντας τρέπεσθαι–5.88).

36. Pericles earlier argued against the "calculation of advantage" (οὐ τοῦ ξυμφέροντος . . . λογίσμῳ–2.40.5).

37. See Radt (1976, 35) on the reading τὰ εἰκότα καὶ δίκαια, although I do not agree with his conclusions.

38. Andrewes HCT, IV: 165 remarks: "the Melians seek to turn the Athenian position by claiming that the observance of conventional justice is in fact a general advantage, ξυμφέρον." Amit (1968, 230) feels that "the problem is to find what is χρήσιμον to both sides . . . it is the Melians who conduct the debate." Crane (1998, 239) observes that "the Melians . . . argue that justice, fairness, and interest are all interlinked." Coby (1991, 77) believes that "the Melians are attempting to make common cause with the Athenians, to connect their interest as a weaker state today with Athens' interest as a weaker state tomorrow"; cf. Alker (1988, 812).

39. In war, the situation and attitudes of people change, which leads to a new application of words (*dikaiosis*): see esp. 3.82.4–8.

40. Macleod (1983, 61) notes "a still more striking departure from the 'rules' . . . in chs. 100–11; for here the Melians are constantly appealing to those moral sanctions and those speculations about the future which the Athenians had ruled out." See also Andrewes (1960, 1) and Orwin (1994, 103).

41. Amit (1968, 234) argues that in the rhetorical contest, the Melians have "the upper hand." Crane (1998, 293) observes that by their actions the Melians prove that the Athenians are wrong in their contention that the weak always yield to the strong (5.89, 5.111.4).

42. Connor (1984, 153) points to the Melians' thesis that "restraint could be in the long term interest of the more powerful"; see also Crane (1998, 240). Liebeschuetz (1968, 75) comments: "The Athenians were also perfectly right that the Melians' own interest required that they should yield to the Athenians since they had not the strength to resist successfully. But ironically, as far as their own interest was concerned, the Athenians were wrong and deluded." Macleod (1983)

captures the conflicted essence of Athens with their "characteristic combination of forethought and folly" (65), concluding that "in attacking their puny neighbours, the Athenians are ruthless, realistic and yet also paradoxically blind" (67); cf. Forde (1992, 384). Pouncey (1980, xiii) sees Athenian action as proof of "Thucydides' essential pessimism," which he defines: "The conviction that human nature carries within itself drives that are destructive of its own achievements, that they are in fact the same drives as those that build historical achievements in the first place."

43. Debnar (1996, 109).

44. Andrewes HCT, IV: 168 speculates that past actions of Melos may have included making contributions to Alcidas in 427, resisting Nicias in 426, ignoring the assessment of 425, and perhaps some provocative action immediately before 416, but again Thucydides has told us nothing beyond the resistance in 426 (3.91). On possible contributions to the Spartan war fund, Loomis (1992, esp. 65–66, 74–75), argues that the Melians must have made a contribution in 427 (IG V 1.1); Seaman (1997, 401) argues that the contribution came from those who survived the Athenian expedition in 416; cf. Meiggs (1972, 314).

45. See de Ste. Croix (1972, 14) on the likelihood of divine aid or Spartan help.

46. The Melians at 5.102 state: Ἀλλ᾽ ἐπιστάμεθα τὰ τῶν πολέμων ἔστιν ὅτε κοινοτέρας τὰς τύχας λαμβάνοντα ἢ κατὰ τὸ διαφέρον ἑκατέρων πλῆθος. Andrewes translates (HCT, IV: 170) κοινοτέρας as "more impartial." Amit (1968, 231) translates more fully: "it happens that the odds are more even than could be expected from the difference in numbers." Reasons given for favoring the likelihood of Spartan aid include the proximity of Melos and Sparta's kinship ties with Melos (5.104, 106, 108).

47. Cf. Diodotus' words on the deceptive but irresistible power of hope (3.45).

48. Wasserman (1947, 29) remarks: "it is τύχη ἐκ τοῦ θείου, a sign of divine grace and justice, of help and protection beyond human planning and expectation. The sceptical and disillusioned mind of the Athenians sees only the blindness of chance." De Romilly (1988, 294) articulates a broader sequence: "On each occasion the Athenians admit that this danger [the fall of the empire] exists but are quite willing to accept it. On the first occasion, they only discuss how serious such a defeat might be; on the second, they mention only the people of whom they would be most afraid; and on the third and last occasion they simply reply by a threat."

49. Williams (1998, 199) criticizes Athenian efforts in subjugating the small island of Melos as "an action which suggests not only a fondness for brutality, but also a lack of moderation, self-control, and even of the foresight to consider the adverse impression such an action would cause."

50. Amit (1968, 229) observes that the Athenians "now indulge in fancy about the future and put instead of war, destruction of the city." Connor (1984, 150) sees this as prediction: "within the speech itself the outcome is foretold: the Melians will resist; the Athenians will conquer; the city will be destroyed." Lattimore (1998, 295) notes that—in spite of their prohibition at 5.87—"the entire situation is the result of Athenian 'suspicions about the future.'"

51. We should note that in the narrative frame—while the siege is still going

on—Thucydides tells us that the Spartans did not break their treaty with Athens, even though the Athenians had extensively plundered Spartan territory (5.115.2). That is, the Athenians' prediction in the dialogue about Spartan aid to Melos is correct: the Spartans do nothing, even when provoked by further Athenian aggression. Again the reader has a superior vantage point than do the Melians. On the accuracy of Athenian predictions, see Pouncey (1980, 93).

52. Regarding "this sort of misguided hopefulness," Ober (1998, 105) remarks that "as Thucydides' reader soon learns, the Melian oligarchs and the post-Periclean Athenian demos have much more in common than the Athenian generals supposed."

53. See Stahl (2003, 163). Garst (1989, 15) argues that "from beginning to end it is the Melians who put forward the ideas and proposals while it is the Athenians who reply. Because they have a response to everything, the Melians are constantly foiled and sent off to find another argument." Williams (1998, 201) notes that "The Dialogue stresses the need for compromise but neither side is willing to give in."

54. Macleod (1983, 58); he continues: "a concern for the future is also characteristic of statesmanlike forethought (cf. further 1.138.3; 2.65.6), and so to concentrate on the present may be simply shortsighted." See Edmunds (1975a, esp. 7–88).

55. For Themistocles' abilities, see 1.90–93, 1.136.1, 1.138.1; cf. Pericles (2.65.5, 2.65.13), and see discussion in de Ste. Croix (1972, 28–33). Monoson and Loriaux (1998) is more critical of Pericles' foresightedness.

56. Whether Thucydides considers the *History* to have a practical purpose is a vexed issue. De Ste. Croix (1972, 32) comments on the possibility of intelligent foreknowledge; see also Connor (1985, 11), Stahl (2003, 99), and Rood (2004, 123); cf. the more restrictive views of de Romilly (1956a) and Flory (1990, esp. 206–8). I discuss this further in chapter 10.

57. Bosworth (1993, 43) calls the Melian government "pig-headed" in refusing to acquiesce.

58. Melos advances the idea that Athens may be an example (*paradeigma*–5.90) to others in the future: if they abolish any notion of the common good and their empire falls, they would be left without any recourse. The Athenians use *paradeigma* in the present tense: "hatred of power is a clear proof to the ruled" (τὸ μίσος δυνάμεως παράδειγμα τοῖς ἀρχομένοις δηλούμενον–5.95). Williams (1998, 200–201) comments: "Idealism by itself, without the addition of foresight, intelligence, planning, and above all power, is incapable of survival. . . . As the Athenians discover in Sicily, if rational planning, action at the appropriate time, sufficient resources, unity, and military strength (all of which together can give confidence) are lacking, then military action based only on hope and fear is unable to succeed . . . Thucydides could not help but see some of the flaws in the Melian, as well as the Athenian, position."

59. Cartwright (1997, 220) comments that like Plataea, Melos was chosen "not because of its importance to the course of the war but for the issues raised in the accompanying negotiations." See Leibeschuetz (1968, 74); on page 74 n12, he argues that "The Melians are a perfect illustration of Diodotus' thesis." Orwin (1994), 112 believes that "indeed the very arguments of Diodotus would seem to

point to clemency in this case as well"; see Macleod (1983), 58, Connor (1984) 149–50, and discussion in chapter 7. Connor (1984), 154 argues that "for the reader . . . the Melian counterattack . . . changes the perspective from the narrow concentration on the events of 416 to the broader development of the war." This is the view of Kagan (1981), 149 n47. See Orwin (1994), 107–8 on the explicit mention of Brasidas (5.110), which looks back to book 4.

60. Williams (1998, 199) speculates: "if the Melians had possessed some sort of military advantage—if for example, the Spartans were already present on the island in a strong force, or if the Melians had developed a great fleet such as the Syracusans do later, or if the Melians had some sort of technological advantage that would give them the edge in warfare, or if they had united with many islanders who had fleets, unlike Sparta, then the Melians perhaps would have had good grounds for their confidence in their ability to withstand a siege."

61. Wasserman (1947, 30) asserts that "The most dynamic and most dangerous example of this indulgence in wishful thinking is the Sicilian Expedition with which the Melian Dialogue is so closely connected that it has to be regarded as its prelude." Kagan (1981, 167) believes both the Sicilian and Melian expeditions resulted from the same motive: to restore the balance of power after the Spartan victory at Mantinea and regain Athenian prestige; see also Cornford (1907, 182–85); Herter (1954, 330–32); and Amit (1968, 219–23). In linking Sicily with Melos, Gomme (1967, 187) comments: "The course of events may itself be dramatic, and the truthful historian will make this clear." On the links between Melos and the circumstances in 404, see de Romilly (1988, 275): "the characters made to speak by Thucydides show a strange foreknowledge of the events which marked the end of the war"; cf. Liebeschuetz (1968, 75–76). Connor (1984, 155–57) compares the Melian episode with the Persian war which forced Athens to become nautical (1.18.2, 1.93.3): the Athenians "confronted in that struggle precisely the preponderance of power and apparent hopelessness that Melos now faced"; cf. Crane (1998, 246–54). For the episode as a meditation on the nature of Athenian imperialism, see Andrewes (1960, 3–6) and de Romilly (1988, 274), who comments on Thucydides' "desire to give his own treatment of the question of imperialism as a whole."

62. Cartwright (1997, 221).

63. Connor (1984, 155). Allison (1997, 59) notes that "In this case greater force is given to the climax of Book 7 because the reader had not been accustomed to associating *soteria* with the Athenians. The absence from the Athenian program only becomes evident when the term recurs so often in the Melian Dialogue."

64. On the importance of *eikazein*, see chapter 2. Gribble (1998, 45) believes that "Thucydides imagines them [i.e., his readers] as motivated by the same intellectual and historical goals as the narrator-historian himself (1.22.4), like him possessed of highly developed intellects and sensibilities."

65. Garst (1989, 15) thinks that "the debate at Melos is about whether the Melians can maintain their neutrality. In rejecting the neutral status of Melos, the Athenians betray a new and urgent anxiety about their control over their allies and empire." Regarding evidence from the Athenian Tribute List (IG I³ 71) and whether Melos actually paid tribute, see Treu (1954), answered by Eberhardt (1959) and Keirdorf (1962). I am in agreement with Amit (1968, 221) regarding

the "'minimalist' view of Eberhardt, i.e., that the inclusion of Melos in the Cleon assessment of 425 (cf. ATL A9) does not prove that Melos was ever a member of the Athenian League or paid any tribute."

66. For a comparison of these two passages, see discussion in Eberhardt (1959, 303–7) and Keirdorf (1962, 255–56).

67. Williams (1998, 200) remarks that "it is possible that the Athenians' lack-luster earlier performance contributed to a Melian confidence that the Athenian threat was mere empty talk and may have caused them to have greater trust in the ability of their island's defenses to deter the Athenians."

68. They are called "ambassadors" (πρεσβεῖς) throughout (5.84.3, 5.85, 5.114.1). For the status of these envoys, see the brief discussion in Bosworth (1993, 32 n12).

69. This is Andrewes' conclusion (HCT, IV: 157). Seaman (1997, 388) argues against this interpretation: "First there is no supporting evidence which suggests that the Melians ever went to war with the Athenians (not to mention that doing so would have been quite foolish). Second, if the Melians had decided on war with the Athenians (and their allies) they would likely have concluded a treaty with the Spartans, an alliance for which there is again no evidence." Bauslaugh (1991, 116–17) argues that there was not necessarily any action of Melos which provoked the attack in 426; rather with Athens' desperate search for revenue the Melians' "refusal to contribute to the cost of the war hindered Athenian efforts to procure revenue from every possible source."

70. In endeavoring to "discern the reasons why the Athenians found it necessary to suppress the island in 416 B.C.," Seaman (1997, 386) maintains that "in spite of a clash of arms in 426, the Melians maintained their neutrality." For the Athenians' motivations, see Andrewes HCT, IV: 156–58 which concludes: "on balance, however, it seems likely that the attack in 416 was due solely to an Athenian whim, without any immediate antecedent quarrel . . . [still] if there were specific grounds for the attack in 416, we cannot now expect to discover what they were." Pouncey (1980, 88) comments: "the narrative is deliberately cleared of all contextual information, any record of grievance or politics attending the event, so that the Athenian action is made to appear a perfectly gratuitous act of aggression."

71. As Pouncey (1980, 88) points out, many facts pertinent to this specific situation are omitted by Thucydides: "we are not told how much tribute Melos would have to pay, whether they would have to give hostages, or whether an Athenian garrison would be posted there."

72. Seaman (1997, 388) concludes that ."in fact Melos emerges from the Melian Dialogue as a neutral state never having injured Athens"; Melos was "in fact both independent and neutral, just as Thucydides tells us" (409).

73. Seaman (1997, 390) thinks that "as Thucydides tells the story, Athens is guilty of unprovoked aggression against a harmless neutral"; "the motive for the expedition was in all probability Athenian imperialism, plain and simple" (414). Pouncey (1980, 97) suggests that "the notion that one must constantly expand to maintain national security seems patently false, yet Thucydides seems partly inclined to believe it."

74. In support of neutrality, the Melians assert that they have nothing to do with the Athenians, being colonists of the Spartans (τούς τε μὴ προσήκοντας . . . ἄποικοι ὄντες–5.96).

75. Regarding the Athenians' argument at 5.97, Seaman (1997, 390) believes

"the clear import is that successful resistance by a *weak* island would be *especially* dangerous." See Cleon's view on the hatred and fear of subjects at 3.40 and comments by de Romilly (1988, 287–88) on fear as motivation for the Athenians and Pouncey (1980, 98–101), who calls fear "the first impulse to imperialism" (99).

76. The prevalence of neutral states is preemptively dismissed by Thucydides, although see Bauslaugh (1991, 109): "Thucydides' self-promoting statement that the entire Greek world was involved in the war, some joining in immediately and other intending to do so (1.1.1), should not be taken as a pronouncement of definitive fact. The truth is that Thucydides knew full well that the situation was far more complicated, and he did not hesitate to acknowledge the existence of neutrals at the outset of the war."

77. Bauslaugh (1991, 132) notes that due to their rejection of neutrality, "the Plataeans gave their enemies a perfect legal pretext for annihilating them."

78. The islander status of Melos is emphasized at 5.84.2, 5.97, 5.99; cf. 5.109.

79. Bauslaugh (1991, 28) observes: "it seems that Thucydides considered this anomalous policy [i.e., neutrality] as a double-edged sword, simultaneously dangerous, even potentially fatal, for those who pursued it, and yet also useful, even necessary, for belligerents, whose interests, indeed whose very victory or defeat, were served by convincing uncommitted states, whose polarization might prove disastrous, that it would in fact be the best and securest policy (i.e., *sophrosyne*) to abstain from the conflict and remain at peace."

80. See Bauslaugh (1991, esp. 110–24, 146–60, 162–63).

81. See discussion of this passage in Bauslaugh (1991, 71–72).

82. Seaman (1997, 415) observes: "It is indeed ironic to consider that it was in fact her longstanding neutrality which left Melos as prey for Athens during the Peace of Nicias." Williams (1998, 306) finds a broader lesson: "The incident [of Mycalessus—7.29–30] also indicates that any state which has a powerful ally that can come to its aid has an important advantage. This is particularly true in the case of a small city-state that cannot defend itself well. Thucydides illustrates this point over and over in the *History*: States which act without allies, such as Plataea, Mytilene, and Melos frequently come to grief."

83. Bauslaugh (1991, 146).

84. For example, Thucydides explicitly links the Corcyrean conflict to the outbreak of the war (1.23.6, 1.55.2; cf. 1.146); this is discussed in chapter 3.

85. Connor (1984, 15–19, 233–40) discusses the development of the reader's reaction.

86. Bauslaugh (1991, 117) notes that all the previously neutral states "eventually became involved in the war," which "emphasizes how terribly difficult it was to remain uncommitted in a time of general conflict between powerful hegemonial alliances. Failure did not mean that no abstention was possible, only that it was difficult to maintain."

CHAPTER SIX

1. Hornblower (1991–96, I) considers this comparison in certain key passages noted below; in his earlier book (Hornblower 1987, 178), he emphasizes pas-

sage 3.82.2 because Thucydides introduces the comparison in his own voice (see discussion below). Farrar (1988, esp. 153–58) is extremely insightful.

    2. This translation owes much to Stahl (2003, 54).

    3. While more commonly *idiotes* contrasts with *polites* (a person in his private station as opposed to a citizen in his public capacity), here *idiotes* contrasts with polis. This is complicated by the immediately following expression ἕνεκα τῶν ἰδιῶν which refers to the separate interests of individual states as contrasted with the common interests of the Peloponnesian League. On the range of meaning for *idiotes*, see Gomme HCT, II: 192.

    4. 1.122.2–3, 1.124.2–3. Hornblower (1991–96, I: 200–201) remarks that the term *tyrannos* is applied to a city, yet "a tyrant is essentially an individual." The tyrant-city metaphor is explored in chapter 8.

    5. Gomme HCT, I: 417–18 translates with expansion: "if it is true [as of course it is] that identity of interests is the safest ground for action for states as for private individuals." He explores various readings and possible interpretations of this passage.

    6. Hunter (1988, 26) comments: "In Diodotus' view the city is very like a person, experiencing all the errors and feelings of the individual, including insolence, pride, hope, and greed."

    7. This translation is based on Connor (1984, 248–49).

    8. This is discussed in Strasburger (1954, 402–3).

    9. Cf. also the Corinthians' contrast between Spartans and Athenians at 1.70–71. While there are prominent individuals in books 1 and 2 (Pericles, Archidamus, et al.), it may be that too much focus on individual leaders' personalities early on would detract from Thucydides' establishment of cities as actors. Westlake (1968, 317–319) notes that the first half of the *History* focuses on communities—this far I am in agreement. He also argues (15) that Thucydides may have altered his judgment about historical causation and focused on individuals' personalities more extensively in the second half, yet here I am not convinced that introducing an evolution in Thucydides' ideas (and the whole composition question) is needed. It is interesting, though, how Alcibiades describes himself (an individual) as worthy of rule (6.16.1), possessed of glory (6.16.1), and outstanding in brilliance (*lamprotes*–6.16.5), for all these attributes have been assigned to the city of Athens (cf. 1.76.3, e.g.).

    10. Especially *Republic* 368–69, 434–35, 544; cf. Aristotle *Politics* 1253, 1261, 1323–24.

    11. See Knox (1964, 66). Both Protagoras and Democritus may have pursued the city-individual analogy. It is said that the whole of Plato's *Republic* was sketched out in Protagoras' *Antilogikoi* (see DK80 B5) though it is impossible to determine whether Protagoras pursued the analogy with respect to justice. Democritus was fascinated by the interplay between small and large: regarding political language and the individual, see DK68 B245, B250, B259.

    12. On the recycling of rhetorical topoi, see Hudson-Williams (1948). Regarding similar modes of expression in Thucydides and Isocrates, he says that they both "are following a well-established rhetorical tradition of taking old or conventional *dianoiai* and expressing them in their own words" (77).

    13. The comparison is not limited to democratic Athens: cf. Herodotus 1.5.4 on

power and influence that changes over time; this may well refer to both individuals and cities (or empires). It is interesting that Thucydides does not use the term for citizen (*polites*). While *idiotes* may connote a looser interaction with other citizens, it is also possible that Thucydides may be thinking of apolitical or pre-political individuals such as Homeric and tragic heroes and heroines, who seek their own preeminence and autonomy and fail to subject their desires and ambitions to the good of the community (note especially 1.144.3 on honor). On this reading, cities will pursue communal action only after giving up their heroic pretensions.

14. See discussion in chapter 2. Given the significance of the city-individual comparison both in Thucydides and Plato's *Republic*, we should note the sharp contrast in the status of "extrapolation and comparison" (*eikazein*—or at least the use of this term): in Thucydides this ability is highly honored, while in Plato's Divided Line *eikasia* is found on the lowest part of the divided line, farthest from apprehension of reality (*Rep.* 509d–511e).

15. Farrar (1988, 136) says that the "many echoes and recurrent patterns . . . [are meant to] . . . challenge him [the reader] to assess the genuine differences and similarities between two contexts, to think historically." She describes one of Protagoras' goals as "securing the audience's imaginative participation" (127); this could apply to Thucydides as well.

16. Farrar (1988, 155–57) says that Thucydides assumes "that the behavior of the political community is appropriately characterized both as the behavior of persons, of a collectivity, and as the behavior of a unit, an entity." Loraux (1986a, 270–74) analyzes the shift between depicting the city as a unity and as a plurality of individuals. While it is valuable to speak of communities as units, the key events leading up to the war, both at Epidamnus and Plataea, belie the notion of unanimity within a polis (see 1.24.4, 2.2.2, 2.3.2; cf. also 1.2.5–6, 1.12.2, 1.18.1, 1.23.2, e.g., and the generation gap at 6.18.6).

17. See esp. 1.70–71, 2.36–46, 6.16–18, 8.96.5. The possibility is also expressed that certain communities are hostile to one another by nature: see Hermocrates' remark that Sicilians are the natural enemies of Athens: τὸ φύσει πολέμιον (4.60.1). For a treatment of such "political" characteristics, see Crane (1992a).

18. 1.122.3, 1.124.3, 2.63.2, 3.37.2, 6.85.1 (discussed in chapter 8).

19. Hornblower (1991–96, I: 127; cf. 131). White (1984, 64) supports this notion: "it is apparent that the principal figures in this world are the individual cities, regarded as units, which can speak to each other through representatives in certain established places and modes. They are capable of making agreements and breaking them, hence of moral action."

20. The issue of cities unequal in power may be illuminated by examining individuals of unequal status in society, whether the disparity is brought on by slavery or poverty. While a comparable inequality among cities surely exists, see note 32 below.

21. Cf. 1.73–77, 2.62–64, 5.89, 5.107. See the interesting discussion in Heath (1990). When the Athenians say that the gathering of Peloponnesian allies has no authority to judge its actions (1.73.1), this raises the question: Does anybody have the power or legitimate authority to do so? If so, what would such a body be like? In any case, Diodotus' argument is not wholly consistent: see chapter 7.

22. It is also said that Athens is a teacher for the rest of Greece (2.41.2—discussed in chapter 8). On *paradeigmata*, see Hunter (1973a, 85–94); later she says: "For the reader earlier events exist as paradeigmata, model situations, the outcome and possibilities of which he knows. By bringing this knowledge of the past with him into the present, he is equipped to compare and judge, even to predict" (180). Regarding the feasibility of a Panhellenic forum, cf. the fourth century development of Panhellenism in Isocrates, for example, as discussed by Jaeger (1945, III: 74–82).

23. Farrar (1988, 145) maintains that while Thucydides shows how things happened and why, he suggests that it was not inevitable. On the question of contingency, see Flory (1988).

24. Arbitration is referred to a number of times in the *History* (1.82, 3.53, 3.56, e.g.; cf. the offer made by Sparta at 4.19–20 and the Peace of Nicias itself at 5.14–24). While in retrospect the Spartans rue their refusal of the Athenians' original offer in 432 BCE, they come to view the Athenians' rejection in 413 BCE as auspicious (7.18). See the discussion in HCT, IV: 394–95 and de Ste. Croix (1972, 290–92).

The suggestion has been made that Thucydides lived perhaps a full decade after the end of the Peloponnesian War; this reinforces the likelihood of his interest in the future of relations between Greeks cities. If Lichas, son of Arcesilas, is the *proxenos* of Argos and Thucydides knew of his death (in 397 BCE), then Thucydides himself of course lived past 397. See Pouilloux and Salviat (1983 and (1985); for a cautious reading of this evidence, see Cartledge (1984).

25. Jaeger (1945, I: 384) says that for Thucydides, "the central problem is the nature of the state." An extremely valuable account of the beginnings of political analysis is found in Strasburger (1954).

26. Of course, the terms of the comparison may work reciprocally. This is significant for the potential application of such models to the resolution of political conflict, both between citizens within a polis and between city-states. Among others, Connor (1991, 53) suggests that "war . . . is an analogue to *stasis*, the disintegration of community through internal tensions"; see also Price (2001).

27. On the utility of Thucydides' *History*, see chapter 5 n56.

28. White (1984, 63) endorses this idea (citing 1.34.2): the proper occasion for invoking the practice of arbitration is before resorting to arms. Pearson (1957) describes the degeneration of moral values as the war proceeds. Connor (1984, 250) says that while the *History* demonstrates the sufferings of mankind and that they are rooted in human nature, nevertheless he sees the "simultaneous insistence that they are mistakes to be avoided." It is up to later generations to find ways to avoid such mistakes, because "the work provides no resolution to this tension."

29. The fit is not always precise, for the differences have to be examined and reexamined, as Plato admits in his work exploring this same analogy (*Republic* 434e–435a).

30. The language of the judicial system (δικάστης, δίκας δοῦναι, ἐγκλήματα, ἀπολογέω , etc.) is applied to international conflict and attempted negotiation throughout the *History*. See the valuable discussion in Darbo-Peschanski (1987).

31. Farrar (1988, 161) discusses the importance of the collectivity. By extension,

we find all Greece suffering during war, when cities insist upon their own separate needs in opposition to those of other cities. Cf. also the case of Sicily where cities contemplate uniting for a common cause: for example, consider the situation described at 6.80, discussed in Connor (1984, 121): "At the center of his [Hermocrates'] speech is the idea of Sicily as a unit" (see 120–22). For the idea of Attic villagers viewing their villages as their own cities (2.16), see chapter 8.

32. 1.2–19, esp. 1.3.1, 1.10.5, 1.15.2, 1.17, 1.18.2. The Plataeans argues that the Greeks are joined in significant ways, including a shared set of laws (3.58–59; cf. 1.41.1, 3.67.6) and common religious beliefs (3.59). They emphasize the importance of Greek unity (3.54, 3.59); see Price (2001, 333–77). Creed (1973, 219–20) analyzes the various obligations a Greek might have to a friend, to his city, or to Greece itself (on loyalty, see 224). White (1984, 91) poses the following question: "But could equality be seen not as the factual precondition of the discourse of justice, but as its product, as something that it creates and makes real in the world? Could Athens, that is, have recognized that even cities unequal in power may have an equal interest in maintaining the discourse that gives them identity and community, that indeed makes their life and competition possible?"

33. Price (2001, 26); he also remarks that in some ways "*stasis* is basically different from a *polemos*" (5); cf. the caution in Kallet (2004).

CHAPTER SEVEN

1. Dover HCT, V: 396 (see also 436); Wassermann (1956, 30); cf. J. H. Finley (1967, 114–16). Gomme HCT, II: 167 remarks on the Athenian "passion for generalization in rhetoric such as we find it difficult to appreciate." Parry (1970, 14–15) locates the language of Thucydides at the third of five stages of abstraction where "abstract words are the staple of argument, yet they always have a human and dramatic reference"; cf. 12–13 on "proverbial abstractions."

2. Meister (1955, 13). For the range of meaning of *gnome*, see Rusten (1989, 148); cf. Edmunds (1975a, 7–14) and Huart (1973).

3. See Meister (1955, 23) on particles and conjunctions introducing maxims. Although maxims introduce general concepts, it is valuable to recall that Thucydides has no fixed terminology, describing each situation in a new way; for this point, see Stahl (2003), 120.

4. On adverbs such as *aiei, pollakis,* etc., see Meister (1955, 19–20); on general laws using a form of *pant-,* see 30–31.

5. In fact, the Corinthians argue that such an alliance would lead to war, not peace (1.40.1–2). The Corinthians cite the cases of Samos and Aegina when Corinth either acquiesced to Athenian dominion or helped the Athenians (1.40.5–1.41.3).

6. On Athenian mistakes, see Hornblower (1991–96, I: 129).

7. This proverbial quality is akin to sentiments such as "Early to bed and early to rise makes a man healthy, wealthy, and wise." The Corinthians also introduce a maxim at 1.42.4 (τὸ γὰρ μὴ ἀδικεῖν τοὺς ὁμοίους—"to avoid wronging equals"). Later they support their claim concerning the question of responsibility for the enslaving of Greece: surprisingly it is the Spartans who are "responsible" or

"guilty" (*aitioi*). οὐ γὰρ ὁ δουλωσάμενος, ἀλλ' ὁ δυνάμενος μὲν παῦσαι περιορῶν δὲ ἀληθέστερον αὐτὸ δρᾷ ("It is not the one who enslaves who more truly commits the act, but the one who was able to stop it but overlooked it"—1.69.1). Surprisingly the one who was able to stop such a deed is in fact the perpetrator. As Hornblower (1991–96, I: 113) remarks, the criticisms of Corinthians are "unreasonable."

8. Thucydides, of course, influences how his readers react to this argument, for he has already announced the coming of war several times in authorial statements, especially "the Athenians forced the Spartans to war" (ἀνακάσαι ἐς τὸ πολεμεῖν—1.23.6).

9. We may well find an echo in Pericles' warning: "I have come to fear our own mistakes (*hamartias*) more than the enemy's planning" (1.144.1); cf. also 2.65.7–13, esp. 2.65.11: ἡμαρτήθη . . . ἁμάρτημα.

10. Meister (1955, 50–90) outlines three levels of application for the maxim: within the passage, the maxim must be tested with respect to the specific argument that it supports; it may be gauged with respect to the speech as a whole; and the reader may apply the maxim to other situations found elsewhere in the *History*. See also Hammond (1973).

11. Gomme HCT, I: 251 translates 1.84.4 as "one educated in the necessary, and only in the necessary, virtues," or—what may amount to the same thing—"one brought up in the hardest school."

12. For a maxim on skill and courage, see 2.87.4. When the Spartans negotiate with Athens regarding the possibility of peace on more moderate terms than might be expected, they invoke a maxim on yielding and holding out (4.19.3).

13. Andrewes (1960, 5–6). Gomme HCT, I: 236 cites Democritus fr. 267: φύσει τὸ ἄρχειν οἰκήιον τῷ κρέσσονι ("Rule belongs by nature to the stronger").

14. See Rusten (1989, 112–13); he remarks that Archidamus' "generalisation accurately predicts the Athenian reaction to the divination in 2.21.2."

15. Hornblower (1991–96, I: 339) comments: "An organic view of the state is implied here." According to Meister (1955, 42), one-fifth of all maxims are found in Pericles' speeches. Other universal principles concern innovation (1.71.3) and the deluding effect of extraordinary good luck (4.17.4).

16. See Meister (1955, 17–49).

17. For comments on human nature in speech, see 1.76.2, 3.39.5, 3.45.3, 4.61.5, and 5.105.2; in narrative, see 1.22.4, 3.82.2, and discussion in Topitsch (1943–47) and Price (2001, 27–28). Further work on maxims in Thucydides might be carried out along the lines of Lardinois (1997), which applies modern "paroemiology" (emphasizing social and linguistic contexts) to Homeric *gnomai*.

18. The analogy, that is, may be thought of as reciprocal. To understand the cities of the classical Greek world, it would be valuable to look at the individuals of Thucydides' work. See chapter 6 n9.

19. See Meister (1955, 27) on the use of καὶ νῦν as a connective at 3.37.1 and 3.39.6.

20. Wassermann (1956, 29) finds confirmation for Cleon's description of subject allies in the characterizations voiced by Pericles and the Mytilenians themselves (2.63.2, 3.9–14).

21. See Meister (1955, 47–48) on the comparatives used in 3.37.3–4. As has been noted, Cleon speaks of "laws" (*nomoi*), when the issue at hand is a decree of the assembly to execute all adult male islanders. See Gomme HCT, II: 300 on decrees (*psephismata*) vs. laws (*nomoi*); cf. Macleod (1983, 93). Winnington-Ingram (1965, 71–72) translates *nomoi* as "tradition" and "principles."

22. See Macleod (1983, 94) on the "fact/word" contrast in this section. On Cleon's maxim at 3.38.1, Gomme HCT, II: 302 comments: "a direct, but not quite an open, claim that in such circumstances at least ὀργή and not λογισμός should guide our action"; and on 3.39.4, "another case of love of generalization making its way into a speech" (II: 307).

23. Meister (1955, 25) calls this maxim "parenthetical."

24. In their speech the Mytilenians also use the terms for revolt (*apostaseis*— 3.9.1–3 [4x], 3.13.1 [4x]); see Macleod (1983, 90). See Winnington-Ingram (1965, 74) on the distinction between revolt and insurrection. Gomme HCT, II: 307 thinks "the definition of ἀπόστασις is very forced, as though it were something which could not be helped."

25. Meister (1955) compares 4.98.6.

26. Once more Thucydides has anticipated Cleon's assertion—this time in the Mytilenians' speech in which they claim they were not truly "autonomous and free" (3.10.5–3.11.1). Again we might think of the proverbial "To err is human." Hornblower (1991–96, I: 425) finds much in common here with ideas of retaliatory justice.

27. On 3.39.5, Gomme HCT, II: 308 remarks: "another wide generalization, but more to the point than the last [3.39.4]." Hornblower (1991–96, I: 429) notes: "The admission, that what the Mytileneans have done is natural, sits uneasily with Kleon's claim earlier in the ch. that their behavior is exceptionally bad."

28. See Meister (1955, 40–41) on this "three-fold variation." Of course, this is an odd combination: the Athenians must resist enjoyment in argument *and* such "soft" feelings as pity; see Winnington-Ingram (1965, 75). Macleod (1983, 72) considers this a form of rhetorical amplification and offers parallels elsewhere in Thucydides. Winnington-Ingram (1965, 75) finds a range of meaning in *epieikeia*: "reasonableness," "fairness," and "decency." Gomme HCT, II: 309 links *epieikeia* to all persons, while *oiktos* or *eleos* refer only to particular individuals.

29. Hornblower (1991–96, I: 432) finds Cleon's suggestion about the Mytilenian attack "gratuitous" and notes that this argument is "hardly consistent with [Cleon's] view that Athens is a hated tyranny." Gomme HCT, II: 312 concurs: "it is another γνώμη not particularly apt to the context."

30. The term *transposition* is itself a metaphor deriving from mathematics and music, although both fields endorse its usage here. To transpose in mathematics is to transfer from one side of an equation to the other: this is precisely what happens with the city-individual analogy, for when something is said about individuals (one side of the equation) it is then transferred to the other side relating to cities. In music, to transpose means to rewrite a musical composition in a different key, and again this sheds some light on transposing ideas in a new political context.

31. See also 3.46.5 ("now we are doing the opposite [*tounantion*]") and cf. πρὸς τοὺς ἐναντίους (3.48.2); indeed, Diodotus calls his debate with Cleon a "competition" (*agon*—3.44.1). We might contrast this with Cleon's use of

homoios—especially at 3.40.3, on which Macleod (1983, 96) comments, "The last ironic twist of the knife is the repetition of τοὺς ὁμοίους; for these words refer in 40.3 first to notional friends and equals, who would be worthy of pity, but then to the unchanging hostility of Athens' actual subjects."

32. Hornblower (1991–96, I: 436) observes: "Note that in this ch. Diodotos moves without embarrassment between the behaviour and appropriate treatment of cities on the one hand and of individuals on the other." He then cites Knox's observation that while the gods are frequently mentioned by speakers in Thucydides, this is not true of Pericles, Cleon, Diodotus, or Alcibiades, and comments: "These four are perhaps represented as more interested in generalizing, as here [3.45.3], at a purely human level." Macleod (1983, 75) analyzes 3.45 in terms of Diodotus' contribution, namely, that human nature is what lies behind the behavior Cleon has condemned. Scanlon (1987, 294–95) thinks "the psychological schema . . . is conversely applicable as a description of motivation at the levels of both states and individuals and in the cases of both the rulers and the ruled"; see Lintott (1992, 29–30) and Hussey (1985, 120). Bodin (1940, 41–42) characterizes 3.45.3 and 3.45.7 as two aphoristic generalizations ("deux généralisations de caractère aphoristique"). Note that Diodotus at this point prefers *hamartanein* and its cognates to *adikia*, which he reserves almost wholly for Cleon's policy recommendation (this is noted by Gomme HCT, II: 318 who translates *hamartanein* as: "to make a mistake in judgment," not "to break a law"). Bodin (1940, 41) sees the idea of *adikia* being absorbed into *hamartema*. Conversely Cleon has used *adikia* and its cognates to characterize what Mytilene has done (3.38.1, 3.39.1, 3.39.3, 3.39.6, 3.40.5), but reserves *hamartia* to condemn the Athenians' mistaken act of reconsidering their decision (3.37.2). Wassermann (1956, 38) remarks: "A balanced view of man shows that he acts as he does under the necessity of a natural law whether as an individual or as a political group (Plato's later picture of the state as the individual writ large is already implied by Thucydides)." See also Hunter (1988).

33. Gomme HCT, II: 319 comments: "The external circumstances and internal passions, of individuals or states, are distinguished, and in the first two sentences particular circumstances and passions are mentioned, in the last both are generalized." It is of course extraordinary that Diodotus can claim that because sometimes crimes are committed in spite of the death penalty, either a harsher penalty must be discovered or the death penalty is no restraint at all (ἢ τοίνυν δεινότερόν τι τούτου δέος εὑρετέον ἐστὶν ἢ τόδε γε οὐδὲν ἐπίσχει). Surely, this does not follow. See Stahl (2003, 120–21) on this point and on Diodotus' argument in general.

34. It is difficult to determine whether the phrase ἐπὶ παντί is meant to be taken temporarily (at all times?) or for all situations (for both individuals and cities?); given its ambiguous formulation, it might be taken in both senses.

35. Winnington-Ingram (1965, 79) argues that these powers (hope, desire, chance) are "too strong to be resisted." Wassermann (1956, 30) finds "desire" and "hope" (*eros* and *elpis*) to be rooted in human nature, while "chance" (*tuche*) refers to external conditions and opportunities. Orwin (1994, 155) argues that "what earlier Athenians have offered as a defense of their empire [Diodotus] invokes as equally an excuse for rebellion against it. So, for instance, he adds freedom to

empire as one of the 'greatest things' that nature bids cities pursue. . . . The thesis thus proves, on reflection, to imply the sympathy of the strong for the very resolve of the weak to oppose them."

36. Regarding desire (*eros*), Diodotus' sketch might be applied to the Sicilian expedition (discussed briefly in chapter 8).

37. Again Diodotus' formulation applies both to the city and to the individual: a tyrant may hold power over citizens just as a city may hold power over other cities. Given the context, he is thinking of Athens' power over other cities, but one also speaks of the power (*arche*) over other individuals. Diodotus' remarks on unexpected luck may echo Cleon's words about unexpected success (*eupragia*) coming to a city and leading it to *hybris* (3.39.4). See Meister (1955, 41–42) on 3.45.4–6. Debnar (2000, 176 n57) notes "Diodotus' shift from the singular 'city' at 3.45.2 to 'cities' at 3.45.6."

38. Cf. Cleon's point at 3.39.7. Hornblower (1991–96, I: 429–30) distinguishes between Diodotus' argument that concerns individuals within a rebel state and Cleon's that argues "severity for crushed revolts"; indeed, the two situations are not precisely parallel.

39. Wassermann (1956, 37) comments on the discovery of Thucydides and the Sophists that "politics, like everything that has to do with man, is a natural as well as a moral science. Political attitudes and actions, such as the Mytilenean case under consideration, obey the unchangeable laws of human psychology, of ἀνθρωπεία φύσις. . . . Thus, the art of politics consists in observing the fact and conditions of human behavior and in both recognizing and applying the general law in the particular case (the integration of the general and the particular being one of Thucydides' most vital concepts)." Meister (1955) finds four broad categories for maxims: human psychology, the state, empire, and war; on maxims concerning human psychology, see 78–81. Orwin (1994, 156) oddly characterizes this as extending Diodotus' thesis *from* cities to individuals, rather than the other way around.

40. Hunter (1986) considers the collective psychology of armies, audiences of speeches, mobs, and cities. In a second article (1988), she remarks that "for a brief time [the crowd is] mentally homogeneous" (18); "the crowd has a personality and emotions of its own and is almost a single individual, thinking as one" (25); she goes on to argue that "in Diodotus' view, the city is very like a person, experiencing all the errors and feelings of the individual, including insolence, pride, hope and greed" (26). She concludes that Thucydides' "analysis remains at the level of the psychological" (30).

41. For fear as a motive for war, see Hornblower (1991–96, I: 32–33, 86, 120). Fear also keeps the Mytilenians in the Athenian alliance (3.11.2). On anger in a group, see Hunter (1988, 22); for courage (e.g., 6.63), see Hunter (1988, 23 and 23n28).

42. To this extent, Diodotus agrees with Cleon that the issue concerns expediency for the city of Athens (3.40.4, 3.44.2; see also περὶ πόλεως βουλευομένοις–3.38.7); they both also exclude emotion or mercy, yet Cleon considers both the Mytilenian oligarchs and the people guilty (3.39.6). Gomme HCT, II: 322 remarks that Diodotus' remark (3.47.2) "cannot be reconciled" with Thucydides' own view on pro-Spartan sentiment expressed at 2.8.4–5.

43. δεῖ δέ, καὶ εἰ ἠδίκησαν, μὴ προσποιεῖσθαι ("Even if they were guilty, we must pretend they were not"—3.47.4). On his earlier statement about not needing to be strict "judges" or "jurors" (ὥστε οὐ δικαστὰς ὄντας δεῖ ἡμᾶς μᾶλλον . . . ἀκριβεῖς—3.46.4), see Arnold (2000, 175): "The Greek word order . . . creates the initial impression that Diodotus advises the Athenians not to act as jurors. . . . But Diodotus does not ask the Athenians not to be jurors; rather he advises them as jurors not to be overly strict in their punishment."

44. See the ingenious solution by Debnar (2000, 170), who lays great emphasis on Diodotus' claim that all speakers must lie (3.43.2–3): "By alerting his audience to the possibility that here may be a distance between what he says and what he believes, Diodotus allows those Athenians inclined toward moderate punishment to detect in his words opinions that reconcile their sense of what is civilized with their notions of sound political counsel. The paradox allows these Athenians to assure themselves that although Diodotus appears to take into account only expedience, in reality he offers advice that he also believes is just."

45. Hornblower (1991–96, I: 438) notes: "here only does Diodotus explicitly invoke considerations of justice." Macleod (1983, 77) remarks that the argument here "leads to an appeal to considerations of justice, in spite of his declared preference for ones of expediency." Winnington-Ingram (1965, 77–79) explains that "Diodotus argues as Cleon's speech allows him to argue . . . [this is the] only place where [an appeal to justice] will help his cause." See Orwin (1994, 151).

46. Yet see Gomme HCT, II: 308 on 3.39.6: "there is no sign in Thucydides that the commons, at least in Mytilene . . . objected to what the ruling class was doing until defeat was certain"; cf. Orwin (1994, 142). The distinction between guilty and innocent has been anticipated in Thucydides' introduction to the speeches: πόλιν ὅλην διαφθεῖραι μᾶλλον ἢ οὐ τοὺς αἰτίους ("to destroy a whole city rather than the guilty ones"–3.36.4).

47. Ostwald (1979, 5).

48. On the topic of justice between cities, we find the concepts and terminology of judgment and punishment (which derive from within the polis itself) brought onto the international stage: cities accuse one another (katagoreuo, enklemata), defend (apologeo), judge (dicastes, dikazomai), are guilty (aitios), and pay the penalty (δίκας δοῦναι). Such an exploration is of the greatest importance not only for understanding the course of the war but also for contemplating the possibilities of peace (even if these opportunities are not taken advantage of). For this idea, see Darbo-Penschnski (1987), Sheets (1994), and Price (2001).

49. See especially Strasburger (1954).

50. See Hussey (1985).

51. On group psychology, Wassermann (1956, 39) remarks: "These emotions [desire, hope, daring], while already affecting the individual as part of human nature, play an even more vital part in the political sphere (Thucydides' foremost interest); here the controls and restraints of reason are even more endangered by the pressures of group psychology—a field which is one of the great discoveries of Thucydides"; in his discussion of Cleon and Diodotus' speeches, he continues: "on an even more general and higher level, where the historian turns into the political scientist and philosopher, politics presents itself as the supreme battleground

between the forces of reason and of emotion in human nature" (40; see also 40 n19). Meister (1955, 74) notes that the speeches in books 6 and 7 contain relatively few maxims.

52. Debnar (2000, 176) thinks it is Diodotus' paradox (all speakers must deceive) which has "stimulate[d] further analysis . . . [and] force[s] us to scrutinize more closely those concepts that underlie the debate."

53. Once again we are back to Thucydides' emphasis on the art of finding comparisons (or "extrapolating"–*eikazein*). This is precisely the skill needed of the reader, who is asked to consider in what situations such an analogical process is valid. When is it useful to speak of a city as being like an individual? When it is accurate to do so? Is it legitimate to speak of a city as having a character (e.g., 1.70–71, 8.96.5)?

54. Kagan (1975, 77–78) claims that the speeches are used for various purposes: "To express points of view with which Thucydides agrees, to expose the weaknesses in positions with which he disagrees, to set forth the character and ideas of major actors in the historical drama." Develin (1990, 58–60) puts it well: "Thought and speech, if not always logical, are logically prior to action. It is in the analysis of thought, intentions, attitudes, words that the real task of the historian lies . . . [Thucydides] saw the use of speeches in their context as his major concentration of interpretative focus" (60).

Chapter Eight

1. Bosworth (2000, 16) advances the idea that even the generalities of Pericles' Funeral Oration "are not timeless platitudes but sentiments totally appropriate to the contemporary political climate . . . there is much in the historical record of 431 that gives real bite to the rhetoric."

2. See below for a discussion of the historical Pericles' penchant for memorable language.

3. Tompkins (1972, 1993) and Debnar (2001).

4. Thucydides appears to be pulled in two directions. He does not wish to appear obsessed with the importance of Athens: this work will not be an Athenian history, but a history of the war, taking many perspectives into account; see Flory (1990). Yet Athens is important, not only for understanding the causes of the war and the course of the war, but also for understanding the development of human civilization: the significance of Athens derives in part from its standing at the height of power (1.1.1). For these reasons, the metaphors introduced early offer the reader a framework against which he or she may contemplate the complexity of democratic and imperial Athens.

5. Much of what Gribble (1998, 62) has to say about "narrative interventions" may be said of Thucydides' political metaphors: "Their purpose is not to tell the reader what to think . . . but to shape reader reaction in a wider sense. They highlight crucial analytical threads in the work, or preview issues which are to be explored more deeply by the future narrative as a whole."

6. Hornblower (1991–96, I: 223) comments that Themistocles' skill of improvisation (1.138.3) "is obviously and deliberately echoed by Pericles' claim to

be able to 'devise and explain a sound policy'" (2.60.5). On *eikazein* more general-ly, see discussion in chapter 2.

7. On metaphor, in addition to Lakoff and Johnson (1980), see also Black (1962, 25–47); Boys-Stones (2003); Danesi (1999); and Stanford (1972). Nogales (1999) offers a theory of metaphor in terms of "reconceptualization" and provides a valuable bibliography. While many metaphors apply to Athens, cf. 2.43.3 (and the comment of Parry [1972, 61]), 3.82, and 6.13.1 (and comment by Hornblower [1991–96, II: 294]). For other sorts of comparison, see, e.g., 5.11.1 and 7.75.5.

8. See my discussion of Thucydides withholding information in chapter 3 and misleading the reader (at 2.5.5–6) in chapter 4.

9. As Stahl (2003, 174) puts it, "we allow [Thucydides] to correct his speak-ers by his own presentation of the events"; this amounts to "elucidation of speech-es by the ensuing (or preceding) narrative of events."

10. On the tyrant-city, see Barcelo (1990, esp. 419–24); Connor (1977); Hunter (1973b); McGrew (1993); Raaflaub (1979, 2003); Scanlon (1987); Schuller (1978); Stahl (2003, 132–34, 141–43); and Tuplin (1985).

11. Here we find an allusion to Sparta's well-known hostility to tyranny: αἰεὶ ἀτυράννευτος, "forever free of tyranny" (1.18.1). This negative adjective first appears here in extant Greek literature—could Thucydides have coined the term?

12. Scanlon (1987, 288) comments: "Pericles rejects the 'slavery versus free-dom' slogan as facile, but accepts the Corinthians' tyrant analogy. The appearance of injustice and the danger of abandonment are typically a tyrant's burdens"; the tyrant-state is "a regrettable necessity whose consequences are to be endured."

13. Scanlon (1987, 289) notes in both Pericles' and Cleon's speeches a "recog-nition that there is an inherent danger for the tyrant-state in either relinquishing its rule or growing weak in its adminstration." On 3.37.2, Gomme HCT, II: 299 explains that Athens' empire is a tyranny "because it is a rule (*archen*) over unwill-ing subjects who are always conspiring against it." Winnington-Ingram (1965, 76) maintains that for Cleon to describe the empire as a tyranny is to imply that jus-tice has nothing to do with the case: "it cannot be unjust for subject [as enemy] to harm the tyrant." Tuplin (1985, 355) argues that Cleon "is deducing what he wants from a presupposition that empire equals tyranny which is not explicitly jus-tified." I do not think Thucydides supposed the Athenian empire to be *equal* to tyranny (as I will argue below), though Cleon may be pressing that point here.

14. On Euphemus' remarks (6.85.1), Scanlon (1987, 290) sees a "total inte-gration of tyranny with expediency."

15. For tyranny and its associations in the fifth-century historical context, see Raaflaub (2004, 89–102). Crowther (2003, 90) comments: "To be a metaphor is to posit an objectively significant connection, but in a way which provokes the con-nection to be made via avenues of imaginative, and thence, in part, personal asso-ciation, rather than immediate logical relations." On Athens the tyrant in Attic Comedy, see note 28 below.

16. Sicilian tyranny is associated with injustice, dislocation, and exile (6.4–5; cf. 1.14.2, 2.30); the Peisistratids were marked by virtue and intelligence (6.54.5) and their rule followed the constitution and was not burdensome—injustice only came later (6.53–59; cf. 1.20). We find tyranny elsewhere: Pausanias imitated tyranny rather than generalship (1.95.3); Alcibiades was

accused of aiming for tyranny (6.15.4; cf. 6.60.1, 6.89.1); see also 1.120.2–3, 1.126, 3.62.3, 3.104.

17. Beyond this, it is possible to juxtapose imperial and actual tyranny on the one hand with other descriptions of Athenian action as a way of testing the Athens-as-tyrant model.

18. δυνατωτέρας . . . χρημάτων . . . προσόδων μειζόνων . . . ναυτικά –(1.13).

19. By contrast, in the early fifth century, the united Greeks faced the Persians: τῶν ξυμπολεμησάντων Ἑλλήνων...κοινῇ τε ἀπωσάμενοι τὸν βάρβαρον ("The Greeks in common fought together and drove out the barbarian"—1.18.2; cf. 1.99.2).

20. Tuplin (1985, 366) notes that "direct characterizations of tyranny . . . mostly dwell on the illegitimacy, lawlessness, unrestrained power, dependence on force and arrogance of the tyrant, that other metaphorical uses of tyranny evidently derive from such characteristics, and that there is no good reason to require more of its application to empire." Scanlon (1987, 291) remarks that "as the narrative proceeds, we recognize that other typical characteristics of historical tyrants, especially violence and arrogance, do apply" to Athens. For references to tyrants in both Thucydides and other literature from the classical period, see Tuplin (1985): hubris, impiety, lawlessness, injustice at 361 n46; theft, greed, and wealth at 352 n17 (cf. 361 n46); tyrants are unable to trust anyone (354 n25); they rule over unwilling subjects (355 n27); they pursue their own self-interest (361 n46). Tuplin also notes (364) the correspondence between the tyrant as an anti-aristocratic benefactor of the demos and imperial Athens' favoring of democracies. See also Schuller (1978, 12–13). On the status of the cities of Athens' empire, see Type 8 of dependent *poleis* in Hansen (1997, 29): "a polis which is a member of a hegemonic league (*symmachia*) which has developed into an 'empire' (*arche*), e.g., the *hypekooi poleis* in the Delian League."

21. Barcelo (1990, 425) discusses the polarities within which the tyrant operates: power and obedience; serving state and self; oppression and tolerance; pleasure and risk; insolence and resistance; strength and weakness.

22. Fifth-century imperial Athens personified risk, sacrifice, and boldness: on risk, see the Athenians' description of themselves at 1.73.2, 1.74.2, 1.74.3 1.75.1; on sacrifice, see 1.74.2, 1.73.4 (cf. 1.70, 1.75.4–5, 1.76.1). De Romilly (1988, 266) notes that the boldness of Athens which had been criticized by the Corinthians (1.70.3) has been transformed into a compliment (1.73–4). In the Pentecontaetia, Stadter (1993, 59) finds a similar attitude toward danger: "Thucydides' staccato account forces the reader to note again and again Athens' resolve and acceptance of risk in mounting individual and multiple operations," and concludes: "In Thucydides' narrative, the Pentecontaetia is dominated by a strong, aggressive, and ceaselessly active Athens" (48). On *polypragmosyne*, contrast the picture of Athens at 2.41.4 with the tyrants' limited accomplishments (cf. also 1.10.2). On the tyrants' fear and desire for safety, see also 6.59.2.

23. Scanlon (1987, 301) concludes: "The dynamics are identical at the level of individual and state so that the tyrant-state is not a mere metaphor but the macrocosmic phenomenon corresponding to the microcosm of historical tyrants." Connor (1977, 106), however, finds "Thucydides is disassociating himself from this facile characterization of Athens as a new form of tyranny." Tuplin (1985,

366) notes the relative rarity of the tyrant-as-city metaphor and finds slavery to be a more "natural" metaphor for imperial authority.

24. Connor (1977, 105–106); only for the juxtaposition of the Peisistratid digression (6.53–59) with Athenian action concerning the profanation of the mysteries do we find that "Thucydides seems for once to be accepting the analogy between Athens and tyranny" (108).

25. See Macleod (1983, 69).

26. Lakoff and Johnson (1980, 5); specifically, "we tend to structure the less concrete and inherently vaguer concepts (like those for the emotions) in terms of more concrete concepts, which are more clearly delineated in our experience"; also "we typically conceptualize the nonphysical in terms of the physical" (59). Aristotle *Rhetoric* 1412a5 says that the use of metaphor involves the perception of similarity in apparently dissimilar things; see his discussion of metaphor at *Rhetoric* 1404ff. Black (1962) labels the non-metaphorical reference as the principal subject, while the metaphorical term is the secondary or subsidiary subject.

27. Parker (1998) traces the semantics of the term: for Solon, *tyrannos* designates "someone who . . . takes power which does not belong to him . . . a usurper, someone who grasps power, someone who wrongfully vaunts himself to the pinnacle of the state" (156). Parker then argues that "it is Attic speech which makes a sharp semantic distinction between *tyrannos* and *basileus*, a distinction which did not exist elsewhere and in other dialects," attributing this special difference in Attic to the fact that in Athens "tyrants never pretended to be kings" (170–71). In fact, Parker believes that "Thucydides distinguished first with absolute consistency between tyrants and kings . . . [and] is thus the first author who evinces a clear and consistent concept of 'tyranny' as opposed to kingship" (164).

28. Applying the label of tyrant to Athens is not original with Thucydides; see Aristophanes *Knights* 1111–14 (cf. 1330, 1333), *Wasps* 620, and discussion in de Romilly (1988, 126); Macleod (1983, 98–100); and Henderson (2003). On Athenian tyranny in tragedy, see Knox (1966, 59–66). Yet, as Scanlon (1987, 287 n4) comments: "the preexistence of the tyrant-state topos does not, however, preclude Thucydides' selective quotation of it . . . nor does it prevent an artistic, thematic use of the commonplace to characterize Athens and her subjects."

29. Lakoff and Johnson (1980, 112).

30. Ibid., 7–9, 22–24, 67; one of the modern examples they examine is "time is money."

31. Ibid., 13; on the "partial nature of metaphorical structuring," see 52–55. The metaphor does not "fit" the reality in all respects: if it did, it would be "identity," not "metaphor." They later stipulate that "our criteria for metaphor were (a) a difference in kind of activity and (b) partial structuring (use of selected parts)" (84).

32. Ibid. Connected to the notion of partial metaphorical structuring is the idea of highlighting and downplaying: Lakoff and Johnson observe that all metaphors, "by virtue of their entailments, pick out a range of experiences by highlighting, downplaying, and hiding" or suppressing certain aspects (152); "every true statement necessarily leaves out what is downplayed or hidden by the categories used in it" (163).

33. On the innate capacity to see likenesses, see Ar. *Poetics* 1459a7–8; cf.

Rhetoric 1405a9–10. Crowther (2003, 85) comments: "The basic predicative structure of language is simultaneously and manifestly affirmed by form and denied by content. Metaphor is, in ontological terms, inherently tensional."

34. Lakoff and Johnson (1980, 89).

35. Ibid., 44.

36. Lakoff and Johnson (1980, 94) remark: "The overlap of entailments between two metaphors . . . defines the coherence between them." On coherence, see 20–21. They note that metaphors are "more likely to involve coherence than consistency" (96).

37. Ibid., 97.

38. Ibid., 6.

39. See Orwin (1994, 59–60) on charges against the Athenians.

40. Cf. 1.69.6, 1.82, 1.84, 1.119; see also 1.72.1. In another context, Hornblower (1991–96, II: 274 [s.v. 4.83.5]) notes the "metaphorical use" of *dicastes* (cf. 6.87.3).

41. The Athenians acknowledge adjudication between cities, both within the empire between Athens and its subject allies (ἐν τοῖς ξυμβολίαις πρὸς τοὺς ξυμμάχους δίκαις, "in contract suits against our allies"–1.77.1; cf. 1.77.3–4) and between Athens and Sparta in accordance with the arbitration clause of the 446/45 treaty (τὰ δὲ διάφορα δίκη λύεσθαι κατὰ τὴν ξυνθήκην, "to resolve our differences justly in accordance with our agreement"–1.78.4). This raises the question of when it is appropriate for one city to judge another.

42. On Athens' rejection of such an international "court," see also 3.44, 5.89, 6.87.

43. See White (1984, 59–92).

44. See discussion in chapter 6. Cf. also 1.37.3, 3.46.4, 3.53, 3.68, 4.83.3–5, 6.87.3, and the Spartan *dicastai* at Plataea (3.52.2–3; cf. 3.56.3). For a full survey of "judicial" language, see Darbo-Peschanski (1987). On notions of international justice in Thucydides, see Cohen (1984), Nakategawa (1994), and Sheets (1994).

45. The sense of *eleutheros* as political freedom appears historically in the later sixth and fifth centuries; the "enslavement" of Greek cities by Persia has now been transferred to Athenian imperial behavior. For evolving senses of freedom, Raaflaub (2004) traces its meaning in interstate relations (118–165) and its use in propaganda (166–202); cf. Patterson (1991, 47–164). Scanlon (1987, 287) comments on Sparta as a "liberator"; see also Diller (1968). On polarities in Thucydides, see Connor (1991, 67): "Thucydides builds his work on a series of polarities—Greek and barbarian, justice and expediency, *logos* and *ergon*, reason and passion, land and sea, Athenian and Spartan. These are the foundation of his narrative, but the narrative reveals them to be constructs, not unchanging or inevitable realities."

46. Hornblower (1991–96, I: 150, 152). Cf. 2.8.4. Hornblower also remarks on the Corinthians' rhetorical attack (1.122.2), noting the "non-literal sense of 'slavery'" (I: 200). In his commentary on 1.98.1–2, Gomme HCT, I: 282 views ἐδουλώθη, as "a rhetorical word, here it means something very different from ἠνδραπόδισαν just above." Cartwright (1997, 59 [s.v. 1.98]) remarks: "the Greek . . . means 'was enslaved,' though this is not to be taken literally." Stadter (1993, 61 n93) also recognizes that Athens' actions lead to two types of slavery—sale of

captives (1.91.1f., 113.1) and subjection of allies (1.98.4)—but emphasizes the international plane (50): "The enslavement of Naxos was not unique, but as the first was a powerful paradigm, like the Corcyrean stasis." For enslaved individuals, see, e.g., 1.55.1, 1.98, 1.101.2, 1.103.1, 1.139.2, 2.78.4, 3.73. On one city "enslaving" another, see, e.g., 1.69.1, 1.121.5, 1.122.2, 1.124.3, 2.71.2–2.71.3, 3.10.3–3.10.4, 3.13.6, 3.58.5, 3.64.3 (in narrative, see 1.8.3, 1.98.4, 3.70.3, 3.71.1). Generally *andrapodizo* and its cognates designate slavery of individuals (2.68.7, 3.28.1, 3.36.2, 5.3.4, 5.32.1; but cf. 6.62.3) while *douleia/douleuein/douloo* refer to the enslaving of a polis (1.8.3, 1.121.5, 5.9.9, etc., but cf. 1.101.2, 5.23.3, 7.85.4). Thucydides does not maintain a distinction between metaphor in speech and literal use in narrative. See the valuable note in Rood (1998, 238–39 n50).

47. Flory (1993, 117) comments that Pericles is "known for his bold metaphors." Lakoff and Johnson (1980, 157) remark: "people in power get to impose their metaphors."

48. Parry (1972, 60). On the Athenians-as-islanders, see "The Old Oligarch" 2.14–16. Gomme HCT, I: 461 notes the differences between this and the passage in Thucydides: "the latter [Old Oligarch] adds the freedom from στάσις [civil war] that an island ruling the sea would enjoy." De Romilly (1988, 116) notes: "They must strive toward achieving the perfect condition that would be theirs, if Athens were an island." Spence (1990, 106) believes that 1.143.4–5 "represents an over-simplification of Perikles' ultimate strategy." The Athenians-as-islanders model differs from the previous models in this respect: it is not derived from a situation within a polis, such as slavery or tyranny, but is built on geography, as Wickersham (1994, 66) notes: "The power of Athens is so surpassingly wisely designed, that it can be said to spring from geography; it is limited not by politics but by nature." On the connection between the Athenians as "sea people" and democracy, see Amit (1965, 57–71).

49. See esp. 1.83, 2.62; cf. "The Old Oligarch" 2.2. Hornblower (1991–96, I: 8) calls the importance of sea power one of the two theses Thucydides attempts to establish in the Archaeology, remarking that the first expression of land and sea (1.2.2) "is surely programmatic," and anticipates the "great programmatic importance for the wartime narrative which is to come" (I: 55). See also Cawkwell (1997, 43–44). In Lakoff and Johnson's terms, the islander model would be a sub-category of the major category land and sea.

50. Connor (1984, 51). Syracuse, however, which is many ways is compared to Athens, is actually on an island. To what extent does this factor lead to Syracuse's victory in 413 over Athens, weakened by attacks from Decelea (a Spartan land base)?

51. A dig presumably at Sparta, which was said to have modeled its constitution on the Cretan constitution (see Herodotus 1.65.4). For a more detailed discussion of the contrast between Athens and Sparta, see E. M. Harris (1992, 162–63).

52. Connor (1984, 66) translates: "We enjoy a style of civic life that does not copy the *nomoi* of our neighbors and is more a model to some than an imitation of others."

53. Cartwright (1997, 110) notes this as "one of the many striking expressions in this speech." See discussion below.

54. Cartwright (1997, 110) argues: "The context suggests that Pericles has in mind the character of the Athenian citizen and the organization of the Athenian state." Hornblower (1991–96, I: 307 [s.v. 2.41.1]) comments on *xunelon* as an "odd formula because Pericles is not in fact summing up, but introducing a new idea: Athens as an education to Greece" and limits the reference to "a narrower front than culture generally." Wickersham (1994, 68) believes that "For Pericles, Athens 'sets the example' and demonstrates to the rest of Greece what a state ought to be (*paideusis tes Hellados*)." In noting that the image of Athens in the Funeral Oration neglects the architecture of the building program, Stambaugh (1974, 311) concludes: "what is important is the quality and conditions of life rather than the merits and effects of architecture. The image of Athens which emerges is based not on bricks and mortar . . . but on the principles of conduct, the administration of government, and the character of the people."

55. Rusten (1989, 158).

56. Pericles goes on to say that their city is worthy of admiration (ἀξίαν . . . θαυμάζεσθαι–2.39.4). Scanlon (1987, 300–301) remarks: "The proper balance of justice and force is the lesson of Pericles which is ignored by his successors." Williams (1998, 122) believes the recapitulation embraces the idea of "self-sufficiency, the opening theme of 2.36.3." Other paedagogical metaphors appear later in the *History* (e.g., 3.82.2; cf. 3.42.2, 5.30, 8.45.2). Within the Funeral Oration we learn that speech (*logoi*) is not an impediment to deeds; rather we must "learn ahead of time" (*prodidachthenai*–2.40.2; cf. *didaskalion*–2.42.1). Hornblower (1991–96, I: 432) notes that "Th. always uses διδάσκαλος metaphorically."

57. Havelock (1963).

58. Consider Thucydides' earlier dismissal of what poets have sung about (1.21.1; cf. 1.22.4).

59. See Loraux (1986a, 338) on Athens as a model; she distinguishes between the senses of *paradeigma* as example and as model (298).

60. Athenians in rural Attica lived with local "independence" (αὐτονόμῳ οἰκήσει–2.16.1). In fact, Bétant (1969, I: 168) lists this as the only instance of the word *autonomos* meaning *liber et solutus*; see also Hansen (1995). Bosworth (1992, 124 n7) discusses metaphorical uses of the term *autonomia*. Mackin (1991, 253) discusses rural citizens' sense of alienation. On the idea of a microcosmic polis and its relation to the philosophy of the atomist Democritus, see Hussey (1985).

61. Hornblower (1991–96, I: 346) translates: "something that was a democracy in name, but actually was a rule by the first man." Cf. Herodotus 3.82.4. Gribble (1998, 53) believes this paragraph "marks the culmination of the issues of the first two books."

62. In the *History*, arche refers to empire in 81 of 110 instances.

63. Pericles dominated, led, and brought to glory his fellow citizens much as Athens dominated, led, and perhaps brought to a kind of glory the cities of the Athenian empire. Williams (1998, 136) finds Pericles in some ways like a tyrant which raises the question: are all tyrants bad? Yet Pericles is legitimately elected each year.

64. See esp. 2.37–8, 2.42–4, 2.60–61.

65. Hornblower (1991–96, I: 311).

66. Monoson (1994, 257); she finds the suggestion that the beauty of "Athens

is capable of stirring the passions of individual citizens, moving them to choose to seek an intimate relationship with this particular city" (257).

67. Monoson (1994, 260–70). Lattimore (1998, 95) (note to 2.43) cites a paper by Kathryn Morgan which calls "attention to Thucydides' startling choice of words: 'lover' is overtly sexual and denotes the aggressor in relationships, so that Athens (whose power has just been mentioned) becomes a passive object." Again, the metaphor found in Thucydides does not appear to be original; see Aristophanes *Knights* 732, 1340–44, *Birds* 1279, and Connor (1992, 97 n14).

68. Monoson (1994, 261).

69. Ibid., 267.

70. See 6.24.3; cf. 6.54.2. For the association between tyrants and *eros*, see Connor (1984, 178–79 n53).

71. Monoson (1994, 276 n81). See Connor (1984, 176–80) on the conspiracy against the Peisistratids, calling it "an act of erotic boldness [which] link[s] the digression to the theme of *eros* so prominent in the work" (178); more specifically, "both the conspiracy against the Pisistratids and the invasion of Sicily, for example, are presented as acts of inappropriate or misdirected boldness, *tolma*" (179). See also Ober (1998, 113–15).

72. Hornblower (1991–96, I: 310) translates: "I have sung the city's praises." Gomme HCT, II: 130–31 remarks that the cluster of *eulogia, hymnesa,* and *katastrophe*—"all with a poetical colour . . . introduce one of the most elaborate, carefully phrased and difficult passages in Thucydides." See also Loraux (1986a, 271–72).

73. Gomme HCT, II: 128 observes: "It is interesting that just below, 42.2, Perikles says τὴν πόλιν ὕμνησα, a word normally used of poets, later of eulogists in prose (Plato *Rep.* 1.364A)." Kakridis (1961, 64) argues that the change in style to the language of a hymn of praise begins at 2.41.3. Loraux (1986a, 444 n39) emphasizes "the religious sense" of the term *hymnos*. Interestingly, if the city is the object of this religious song of praise, Pericles play the role of singer.

74. Hornblower (1991–96, I: 339) translates: "For everything living must eventually wither."

75. For the decline of cities, see Herodotus 1.5. Hussey (1985, 120) argues: "Body, soul and city are all taken to be analogous structures."

76. If Pericles has described Athens as a city in its healthy state in the Funeral Oration—citizen and city engaged in fulfilling mutual obligations and rendering benefits and respect to one another—with the plague, the city as a whole has become a victim of a disease, now sick and in need of treatment. On such "biological metaphors," see Hornblower (1991–96, I: 6) on *akmazontes* (1.1.1): "lit. 'in their prime'; a biological metaphor. Such metaphors are frequent in Th. and tell against attempts to argue that he distinguished between the behavior of states and the behavior of individuals" (cf. 134, 339). I agree with this assessment. Nicias introduces the medical model in the debate over the Sicilian expedition: "Become a doctor of the city: rule well, help your country, and do no harm" (τῆς πόλεως...ἰατρὸς ἂν γενέσθαι–6.14).

77. Wickersham (1994, 32) notes that Thucydides "practices reticence and saves the deepest material for the speeches." Parry (1970, 20) comments: "Thucydides distills the world into abstractions . . . [yet they] are never quite

commensurate. They resist the intellect which wants to put them into order"; all this makes Thucydides' style a "struggle." Regarding the possibility of recovering Thucydides' own opinions, Hornblower (1991–96, I: 114) cautions that "speeches cannot be used as a statement of Thucydides' views except when they correspond to an explicit authorial judgment"; see also Pope (1988, 286).

78. Much of Thucydides' historical analysis is metaphorical. Parry (1972, 51) describes his method: Thucydides "writes an exposition in which ideas and events are strongly marked by key terms. These key terms are semi-abstract nouns and verbs designed to distill the elements of experience into an articulate pattern." Scanlon (1987, 286) describes this as Thucydides' "method of explaining by recurrent paradigms," and claims that the metaphorical approach "provide[s] a key to the character of Athenian rule and to Thucydides' historical philosophy in general" (292 n16). On the didactic nature of paradigms, see Scanlon (1987, 300 n41) and Hunter (1973a).

79. Stanford (1972, 98) quotes Murry, *The Countries of the Mind* (1931): "Discussions of metaphor—there are not many of them—often strike us at first as superficial. Not until we have ourselves made the attempt to get farther do we begin to realize that the investigation of metaphor is curiously like the investigation of any of the primary data of consciousness: it cannot be pursued very far without our being led to the borderline of sanity. Metaphor is as ultimate as speech itself, and speech as ultimate as thought. If we try to penetrate them beyond a certain point, we find ourselves questioning the very faculty and instrument with which we are trying to penetrate them. The earth trembles and yawns beneath the explorer's feet."

80. E.g., Connor (1977, 95) seeks "to determine the extent to which this comparison reflects his [i.e., Thucydides'] own view of Athenian imperialism." While I am certainly not arguing that Thucydides does not have opinions, e.g., regarding tyranny, the fact is that we find that certain expressions—such as Athens the tyrant-city—appear in speech rather than narrative. Thucydides has chosen to explore this comparison in depth, returning to both actual tyranny and imperial tyranny in different settings, both in speech and narrative.

81. Gribble (1998, 56).

82. Ibid., 55.

83. As a definition of *paraplesion,* LSJ offers "about equal."

84. On occasion, Thucydides makes the juxtaposition explicit: see, e.g., 1.55.2, 1.146, 4.36, 7.77. For a valuable discussion of such echoes and anticipations, see Rengakos (1996). Thucydides openly tells his reader that the description of the plague is presented so that should the disease appear again—outside the period of the Peloponnesian War—it may be recognized and its course anticipated (2.48.4; cf. 2.51.6, 3.82).

85. Thucydides introduces the model of Athens as tyrant-city, asking the reader to explore the similarities between Athens' relations with other cities and a tyrant's with his fellow citizens. Gribble (1998, 45) describes this task: "Thucydides demands a sensitive and intelligent audience capable of responding to the complexities of a work of literature (rather than a compliant one, as in oratory)."

86. Two appear in the narrative alone: Attic villagers and the *arche* of Pericles.

87. Storey (2003, 133–34) discusses this fragment; his translation is found on page 14.

88. On Pericles' memorable expressions, see also Aristophanes, *Achamians* 530–534; Aristotle, *Rhetoric* 1365a34; and Plutarch, *Life of Pericles* 8, 28. As Connor (1977, 97 n14) remarks: "The extravagance of the language is fully appropriate to Pericles' love of the vivid phrase."

89. Macleod (1983, 97 n45).

90. Leidl (2003, 53).

91. See Rhodes (1998).

92. On the tyrant model, Macleod (1983, 69) comments: "Thucydides is seeking not merely to record that attempt [of e.g. 'Cleon and Pericles . . . seeking to persuade an audience'], but to show us how and why they succeeded or failed, to help us understand, and so also to judge, the speaker and his public. This purpose we can achieve in two main ways: by sifting the arguments and by examining their relation to the narrative."

93. On recognizing the similarities between events in Thucydides' *History* and those from the reader's own time, see de Ste. Croix (1972, 28–33).

CHAPTER NINE

1. It is interesting to compare this with Pericles' wave of superlatives in his description of Athens' greatness: μέγιστον . . . πλεῖστα . . . μεγίστην . . . πλείστων . . . μεγίστοις . . . εὐπορωτάτην . . . καὶ μεγίστην (2.64.3).

2. Thucydides expected the war to be great from the start (1.1.1, 5.26).

3. See Connor (1984, 23–26).

4. Elsewhere in the *History* Thucydides claims to "judge from evidence which I am able to trust after my most extensive inquiry" (ἐπὶ μακρότατον σκοποῦντί μοι πιστεῦσαι–1.1.3). Regarding accuracy (*akribeia*), see also 5.26.5; Hornblower (1991–96, I: 60) comments: "there is also present the idea of *precise* conformity with reality."

5. Cf. "what was truly said" (τῶν ἀληθῶς λεχθέντων –1.22.1; cf. 7.14.4). On the opposition between what is true and what is pleasant, see Edmunds (1993, 847–48).

6. For an explicit criticism of Hellanicus, see 1.97.2. To be sure, Thucydides acknowledges difficulties: his own lapses of memory (1.22.3); the difficulty of discovering events from the distant past (1.1.13, 1.9.2); even the difficulty of producing an accurate eye-witness account (7.44.1). One is left with no other choice than to conjecture based on the evidence (χρὴ εἰκάζειν –1.9.4), but success is not guaranteed (cf. 1.10.2).

7. In the Funeral Oration, Pericles very deliberately says that the remembrance of Athenian greatness that will last forever is not dependent on writing (2.43.2–3): this memory—set free from writing altogether (ἄγραφος μνήμη)— will guarantee eternal glory and praise which never ages (cf. Pericles' "unwritten laws" [ἄγραφοι νόμοι]–2.37.3). Loraux (1986a, 51) remarks: "the resemblance between the *kleos aphthiton* (imperishable glory) of the aristocrats . . . and the *athanatos mneme* (immortal memory) of the city is too evident to be gratuitous."

Yet Thucydides may be implicitly criticizing Pericles' assertion regarding what endures. Thucydides' audience is able to appreciate that the *preservation* of Pericles' words—and the idea of this unwritten memory—yet this is possible only by means of Thucydides' written history; see Morrison (2004, 115–16).

8. Again, this is common in the classical period: on Plato's competition with Homer, see Havelock (1963). The Sophists, such as Protagoras, tried to "one-up" Homer by pointing out mistakes (almost word by word) in the opening of Homer's *Iliad*. On Thucydides' relationship with Herodotus, see Hornblower (1992a), Hornblower (1991–96, II: 19–38, 122–45), and Scanlon (1994). On the influence of political debate on science and historiography, see Lloyd (1979, 226–67) where he concludes: "this very paradigm of the competitive debate may have provided the essential framework for the growth of natural science" (267).

9. Cf. the teachers in Aristophanes' *Clouds* who claim they are better teachers; these competitive assertions also appear in the Hippocratic corpus. On the competition among intellectuals, see Lloyd (1987, 87–102).

10. Both Themistocles and Pericles had the ability to foresee (*prognous, proegno*–1.138, 2.65.5, 2.65.13).

11. See Wallace (1998).

12. See Pericles' sentiments at 2.40.2.

13. On comparing the empires of Athens and Persia, see Rood (1999) and Price (2001, 363–71).

14. Regarding Thucydides' attendance at the Funeral Oration, see Bosworth (2000).

15. Hornblower (1991–96, I: 321) comments: "a rare autobiographical statement followed by an emphatic claim to autopsy (note the repeated use of 'myself')."

16. Thucydides says explicitly that he remembers (ἔγωγε μέμνημαι) that many said the war would last twenty-seven years (5.26). Memory is often connected to events of great magnitude: 1.23.3, 2.8.3, 2.47.3, 5.66.2, 8.41.2. Edmunds (1993), 850 argues that "when Thucydides speaks of memory, he is usually disparaging, never favorable," and concludes that ultimately the historian rejects "not only the poets' account but also their traditional authority, namely, memory" (851). Surely this goes too far, given the importance of recollection for Thucydides' informants' reports.

17. Cf. the speech of the Peloponnesian leaders, describing the effect of powerful emotion on memory: φόβος γὰρ μνήμην ἐκπλήσσει ("For panic strikes out memory"–2.87.4).

18. Thucydides notes that everyone thinks that the war in which he or she participates is the greatest war (1.21.2). Surely the historian attempts to transcend such tendencies, but is Thucydides wholly immune from such an inclination?

19. Westlake (1989b, 99) remarks that Thucydides may be anticipating objections that he was "too young to embark on historical research at the outbreak of the war"; similarly his remarks on having had the plague himself and observing others (2.48.3) might be seen as preempting any skepticism regarding his description there; see also Westlake (1962, 277 n1).

20. As Flory (1988, 53–54) remarks, "Thucydides . . . does seize this opportunity to make three significant hypotheses which touch intimately on his own participation [in the war against Brasidas]."

21. Flory (1988, 53) speaks of Thucydides' "sensitivity to the unpredictability of even trivial events."

22. Although Marincola (1997, 182–84) argues that "there is no overt justification or defense of his action" (183), see Westlake (1962); Ellis (1978); and Hornblower (1991–96, II: 338). On the possibility that Brasidas was Thucydides' source for this account, Hornblower (1991–96, II: 334) comments: "surely the two men talked between 424 and 422."

23. The term *dokimazo* certainly has a formal connotation familiar to Athenians from the various "vettings" of magistrates and other officials (*Ath. Pol.* 59.4, e.g.).

24. Hippias's name is listed (*gegraptai*) immediately after his father, Pisistratus (6.55.2). In interpreting this epigraphical material, Thucydides also reveals something of his method in making deductions and arguing from probability (εἰκός . . . οὐδὲ τοῦτο ἀπεοικότως —"it is likely . . . nor is it unlikely"–6.55.1–2). Thucydides also tells us that the text of the inscription (*epigramma*) on the Altar of the Twelve Gods "even still now is legible in faint letters" (ἔτι καὶ νῦν δῆλόν ἐστιν ἀμυδροῖς γράμμασι–6.54.7). Dover HCT, IV: 331 remarks, "Thucydides is not above pride in the trouble he has taken." Fortuitously, the inscription has survived: see Meiggs and Lewis (1989, 19–20) (#11). Thucydides also quotes another inscription, the monument (*sema*) in Lampsacus that commemorates the death of Archedike, Hippias' daughter (6.59.3).

25. Dover HCT, IV: 273–88 discusses the comparative evidence on these incidents from Andocides' *On the Mysteries* and Plutarch's *Life of Alcibiades*.

26. Connor (1984, 178 n52). For a discussion of Thucydides' sources, see Dover HCT, IV: 323–25.

27. The Athenians' lust for Sicily (6.24.3, cf. 6.13.1) is linked to the erotic triangle in the sixth century (6.54.1). Alcibiades' alleged aim at tyranny (6.61.7) may have triggered the Athenian people's nervous recollection of earlier Athenian tyrants. See Connor (1984, 178–80) and Stahl (2004, 121).

28. ἰστέον δὲ ὅτι στρατηγήσας ἐν Ἀμφιπόλει ὁ Θουκυδίδης καὶ δόξας ἐκεῖ βραδέως ἀφικέσθαι καὶ προλαβόντος αὐτὸν τοῦ Βρασίδου ἐφυγαδεύθη ὑπ᾽ Ἀθηναίων, διαβάλλοντος αὐτὸν τοῦ Κλέωνος ("It should be known that Thucydides was general in Amphipolis and was thought to have arrived there slowly—Brasidas took it in advance—so he was banished by the Athenians with Cleon attacking him"–Marcellinus *Life of Thucydides* 46). Cf. Nicias' fear of slanderous attacks in Athens if he were to withdraw from Syracuse (7.48.3).

29. Letters are also written by Pausanias, Themistocles, and Alcibiades. The verb *grapho* may also refer to inscriptions, *stelai,* and treaties.

30. W. V. Harris (1989, 78), and he goes on to say that Thucydides is merely "explaining it [i.e., this discovery] to the public." Edmunds (1993, 849) believes that "Nicias' view of the Athenians as presented by Thucydides, is exactly the same as the one that can be attributed to Thucydides himself on the basis of his methodological statements."

31. Connor (1985, 6–7) argues that Thucydides' authority derives in part from the demonstration of his historical method found in the Archaeology. See also Loraux (1986b, 147–53).

32. If we think of Thucydides' intended audience, certainly what many

Athenians would remember about Amphipolis was what Cleon said in the assembly against Thucydides. Hornblower (1987, 27) quotes Syme's remark: "exile may be the making of an historian."

CHAPTER TEN

1. For example, all the events and speeches in Athens from 424–404 must have been reported to Thucydides by others due to his exile. More generally, oral sources are referred to with phrases such as: ἀκοῇ ἴσμεν and ἀκοῇ λεγόμενα ("we know from oral report," "spoken in hearsay accounts"–1.4.1, 1.23.3, 7.87.5; cf. 1.20). M. I. Finley (1956, 296–99) examines Thucydides' confrontation with older oral tradition. W. V. Harris (1989, 80) remarks that Thucydides "still preferred oral testimony to written"; cf. Momigliano (1977, 192) on "the preference for oral tradition and visual observation."

2. See also 2.103.2, 3.25.2, 3.88.4, 3.116.3, 4.51, 4.104.4, 6.7.4, 6.93.4, 7.18.4, 8.6.5, 8.60.3; cf. 1.1.1, 2.1, 4.104, 1.22.2, 1.97.2. Dover HCT V: 390 notes the exceptions (2.47.1, 4.116.3, 5.24.2), but argues against the label of "signature." Related to this sort of self-reference, Ford (1985, 85) presents a fascinating interpretation of Theognis' "seal" (*sphragis*) as "an assertion of ownership rather than authorship," and goes on to explore the political dimension of the poet as "the Muses' spokesman and as a political envoy" (92–93).

3. Edmunds (1993, 837) uses grammatical tense to analyze Thucydides' use of the verb *grapho*. The primary tenses (present and perfect) allow Thucydides to speak "of his writing from the point of view of an ideal present time—his work is a possession ἐς αἰεί. If the adverb αἰεί is understood in its distributive sense, the work is a possession for each successive occasion." Marincola (1997, 185 n52) examines *grapho* by distinguishing between first- and third-person statements: "the first person is used for statements of opinion, reasoning, inference, autopsy, and methodology, that is, anything that affected the history *qua* history. The third person, on the other hand, is used by Thucydides for formal openings and closings." On the presence or effacement of the historian in his own work, see Loraux (1986b).

4. Crane (1996, 7); see now Yunis (2003).

5. Thomas (1992, 104).

6. As Rhodes (1998) notes, any sort of cross-referencing from one roll of papyrus to another would be extremely impractical. In addition, papyrus was an expensive import; the copying alone of such a long work would have encouraged such "sharing."

7. A tremendous problem for those studying the question of orality and literacy in the fifth century is that the terms for "speak" and "listen" (*legein, akouein*) may at times be used interchangeably with those for "write" and "read" (*graphein, anagignoskein*). Gomme HCT, I: 136 posits that "oral reports" (*akoas*–1.20.1) go beyond "hearsay" to include "all that has been said and written of the past," "all that we have heard or read of it." On the phrase "it is said" (*legetai*), Westlake (1977, 356) acknowledges that "the *legetai* phrase may point to the use of a written source." See further references in Thomas (1993, 234 n29

and 236 n31). In this case, however, "listening" (*akroasin*–1.22.4) does appear to mean *listening* and not *reading*, though Thucydides does contrast "a possession forever" (κτῆμά τε ἐς αἰεί) with "a competition piece *to be heard* for the moment" (ἀγώνισμα ἐς τὸ παραχρῆμα ἀκούειν–1.22.4); see discussion on this passage below.

8. Dover HCT, V:385 surmises that this official, the *grammateus*, may be the same one referred to in *Ath. Pol.* 54.5, yet he believes that composing a message in writing "was still a comparatively unusual procedure in 414." But Nicias refers to "many other letters" he has sent (7.11.1)—perhaps this practice was more common than Dover would allow, given the importance of reports and documents in the administration of the Athenian empire. See Rood (1998, 189–91) on 7.8.2.

9. It is hard for me to believe that Athenians would not have wanted to *hear* the speeches in the *History* (see Cleon's remarks at 3.38). Edmunds (1993, 840) remarks that "the illusion of the presence of the writer would have been strengthened by the practice of reading aloud." Flory (1980) argues that Herodotus probably read aloud only excerpts (14) and believes that both Herodotus and Thucydides had a "relatively exclusive audience" (26). Though focusing on Herodotus, Thomas (1993) argues for the "context of intense argument, and a careful assumption that there is an audience which listens" (234), and concludes "oral performances were not merely a survival of a primitive 'oral culture,' but continued, in different forms, as an important medium for the presentation and transmission of knowledge in the latter half of the fifth century" (244). For the limits on reading, see Woodbury (1976); on silent reading in the fifth century, see Knox (1968). In thinking of Thucydides' audience as readers, Arnold (1992) offers a provocative discussion, proposing that *even if* Thucydides could have remembered all the words of a speech (cf. 1.22.1), he would need to make significant changes in the nature of the language employed in order to "accommodat[e] rhetorical speech to his contemplative work" (47). The quality of the language—the style itself—must change. To achieve this, "Thucydides complicated the logic of the speeches and disguised the defects in their arguments even for an audience who can study, contemplate and reread his work at leisure" (46). A density of ideas and a greater difficulty of argument is required, on this view, if Thucydides is to reproduce something in a written medium for a contemplative reader equivalent to the aural experience of political oratory. Still I remain unconvinced that Thucydides would have envisioned his primary audience as those who read his work silently to themselves.

10. Edmunds (1993, 847).

11. Edmunds (1993, 847) comments that "democracy is given to the pleasures of the moment"; see also de Romilly (1966). Wallace (1996, 230–31) discusses the "political isolation of Athenian intellectuals." It is possible that as sections of the *History* were written by Thucydides in exile, these "chapters" might have been sent back to family and political friends in Athens. Even though Thucydides could no longer influence affairs directly in Athens, he might have provoked discussion among those friends and followers who themselves could still particpate in Athenian politics (see note 21 below).

12. This translation comes from Perseus 2006.

13. While Plato often seeks to recapture the golden days of fifth-century

Athens in his dialogues (the dramatic date of the *Parmenides* must be ca. 450), in this instance he may well be projecting into the mid-fifth century a fourth-century practice of reading aloud and consequent discussion.

14. Thomas (2003, 166). Hershbell (1995, 37) believes that one function of written works was to stimulate oral discussion: "Plato nowhere wrote down his most serious thoughts, and his negative views on the usefulness of writing may explain his choice of the dialogue form: written works need the 'help' from verbal discussion, oral debate, and a lively exchange of ideas." For a key difference between Plato and Thucydides, see Nightingale (1995, 52): "The politician, in short, is inside the system, whereas the philosopher is an outsider. Only a person who is completely disembedded from the social and political economy of the city can act in a disinterested manner." Thucydides' reader, I believe, was expected to be fully engaged with his polis—his social and political community—in a way which Plato's philosopher was not; cf. Rowe (1998).

15. This translation is based on Grube (1992).

16. The phrase "according to their perception of what was justified" comes from Price (2001, 39–45).

17. Rutherford (1995, 67); Yunis (1996, 136–71).

18. On the constitution of the 400, see *Ath. Pol.* 29–33; for a discussion of Pericles and Cleon, see sections 27–28.

19. Baltes (1993, 18); see also Hornblower (1987, 121–24).

20. That is, I would question the assertion in Loraux (1986a, 288) that "Thucydides rejects all forms of oral expression." On possible performances of Plato's dialogues, see Blondell (2002, 23–25); on Plato's intended audience, see Blondell (2002, 25–27); on stimulating the audience's engagement, see Blondell (2002, 47–48).

21. In addition to those in the philosophical schools, we might even go on to speculate that the homes of rich aristocrats, such as Callias' house described in Plato's *Protagoras,* would have provided a sympathetic audience for Thucydides' ideas. A further step would have been to voice those ideas in political institutions (the assembly or the council) and then transform them into political action.

22. Steiner (1994, 227); Ober (1998).

23. Thomas (2000, 267); see also Thomas (2003, 174): "Whether we call this oral style or epideictic style, or even simply early rhetoric, we seem to be dealing with an identical phenomenon—a style suitable for oral delivery to a live audience, lively, clear, argumentative, demonstrative, syntactically uncomplicated, possible even rhyming, with a strong first-person presence." For a valuable exploration of oral "style," see Gagarin (1999).

24. Thucydides' target may also have been a rhapsode such as Plato's Ion, who was so successful at provoking an emotional response from the audience. Thucydides—and Plato—may well have hoped to distinguish themselves by eliciting a more dispassionate reaction; see Robb (1994, 166–68).

25. Translation from Usher (1974).

26. Kahn (1996, 381).

27. Ibid., 382.

28. Dionysius remarks that "the author was not composing these writings of his for the man in the street, the workman at the bench, the artisan or any other

person who has not enjoyed a liberal education, but for those who have passed through the standard courses to the study of rhetoric and philosophy, to whom none of these usages will seem strange" (50).

29. See Yunis (2003, 189) on what he calls the problem of the "absent author" who must anticipate the reader's burden and guide the reader's pursuit of meaning.

30. Rood (2004, 123).

31. Frankel (2004, 19); see also Neustadt and May (1986, 1–16).

32. Price (2001, 282) interprets μεγίστη πρόφασις as the "most compelling occasion"—they have already resolved on war, but are seeking the best possible pretext. Gomme HCT, I: 425 translates πρόφασις here as "openly expressed reason or motive"; Hornblower (1991–96, I: 203) considers this to be "their grounds for going to war," yet earlier (s.v. 1.118.1) he translates this term as "reasons publicly alleged" (194).

33. A transcript of Bush's speech may be found at Bush (2002).

34. See UN (2002).

35. See Powell (2003a).

36. Powell then quotes selections from Blix's and ElBaradei's reports to the UN Security Council.
Blix: "Iraq appears not to have come to a genuine acceptance, not even today, of the disarmament which was demanded of it."
ElBaradei: "[Iraq's declaration of December 8] did not provide any new information relevant to certain questions that have been outstanding since 1998."
Blix (2004, 111) later comments that the large number of documents delivered by Iraq on 8 December 2002 were "rich in volume . . . but poor in information and practically devoid of new evidence."

37. See Powell (2003b). This same release notes that dozens of countries objected to war with Iraq and declared that they detected a willingness by Saddam to cooperate with weapons inspectors. For example, the South Africa UN ambassador, Dumisani Kumalo, said: "The inspection process in Iraq is working and Iraq is showing clear signs of cooperating more proactively with the inspectors." Several security council countries (Mexico and Chile) said privately they would abstain in a vote on the resolution to go to war.

38. See Largio (2004, 18). Blix (2004, 266) refers to the "now famous interview [in which] U.S. Deputy Secretary of Defense [Paul] Wolfowitz said that Iraq's weapons of mass destruction were chosen as the rationale for the war for 'bureaucratic' reasons, implying that while there were many other reasons, this was the only rationale that could rally broad support in U.S. public opinion and that stood a chance at having appeal outside the U.S. and inside the United Nations."

39. See Hussein (2003b).

40. In a statement to a delegation of Russian lawmakers on 20 February 2003, Saddam Hussein said that if the United States carried out its threat to attack, Iraq will "triumph over it, God willing . . . Iraq doesn't want war . . . [but peace] at any cost [was unacceptable]. . . . We will not relinquish our independence, our dignity and our right to live and act freely." See Hussein (2003b).

41. Chuter (1997, 381).

42. Ibid., 385.

43. Williams (1998, 201).

44. Blix (2004, 265). Much theoretical analysis has to do with rational choices, but irrational factors, such as the Melians' hope in divine aid or Saddam
Hussein's pride, should not be discounted. In this regard, we note that the
Athenians call into question frequently invoked motivations and speak scornfully
of men who are seduced by the name "shame": "In many cases, the men who see
what they're rushing into, let *the thing called shame* [τὸ αἰσχρὸν καλούμενον], by
the mere power of its seductive name, lead them on to a point at which they
become so enslaved by the phrase as in fact to fall willfully into hopeless disaster,
and incur shame more shameful as the companion of error, than when it comes as
the result of misfortune" (5.111.3).

45. The view that a lack of flexibility on both sides led to war is reinforced by
the report that in mid-February 2003—a month before the invasion—the Iraqis
broached (through Lebanese-American businessman Imad El Haje) the idea of
allowing U.S. experts and troops into Iraq to verify the absence of weapons of mass
destruction; see Landay and Strobel (2003).

46. Blix (2004, 263) finds the failures of intelligence to be a "deficit of critical thinking" on the part of the U.S. See Bulletin (2005).

47. Zizek (2004, 43–44).

48. Mearsheimer and Walt (2003, 51–52). See Clarke (2004, 263–64) on the
various factors influencing the U.S. government. Interestingly, Jervis (2003, 84)
points to "the combination of power, fear, and perceived opportunity [which] lead
it [the United States] to seek to reshape global politics and various societies around
the world." It is difficult not to see this as a version of the Athenian rationale for
empire: honor, fear, and advantage (1.76.2).

49. Theorists have found elements of realism, neo-realism, and constructivism
in Thucydides' work: on realism and neo-realism, see Crane (1998), Doyle (1991),
Forde (1992), and Garst (1989); on constructivism, see Lebow (2001); for valuable
discussions on theory, see Johnson Bagby (1994) and Snyder (2004). Others have
found useful lessons for U.S. foreign policy and commentary on the United States'
role in the world: for example, see Hanson (2001) and Lebow and Kelly (2001).

50. See Yunis (1991, 180) on the notion of "instructional rhetoric."

51. On bystanders and listeners (internal audiences) in Plato's works, see
Blondel (2002, 52).

BIBLIOGRAPHY

Alker, H. R., Jr. 1988. "The Dialectical Logic of Thucydides' Melian Dialogue." *American Political Science Review* 82: 805–20.

Allison, J. W. 1997. *Word and Concept in Thucydides*. Atlanta.

Amit, M. 1965. *Athens on Land and Sea. A Study in Athenian Sea-Power*. Brussels.

———. 1968. "The Melian Dialogue and History." *Athenaeum* 46: 216–35.

Andrewes, A. 1960. "The Melian Dialogue and Perikles' Last Speech (Thucydides V, 84–113; II, 60–4)." *PCPS* 186: 1–10.

Arnold, P. 1992 [=Debnar 1992]. "The Persuasive Style of Debates in Direct Speech in Thucydides." *Hermes* 120: 44–57.

Badian, E. 1993. *From Plataea to Potidaea: Studies in the History and Historiography of the Pentecontaetia*. Baltimore.

Bal, M. 1985. *Narratology. Introduction to the Theory of Narrative*. Tr. C. Van Boheemen. Toronto.

Baltes, M. 1993. "Plato's School, the Academy." *Hermathena* 155: 1–26.

Barcelo, P. A. 1990. "Thukydides und die Tyrannis." *Historia* 39: 401–25.

Bauslaugh, R. A. 1991. *The Concept of Neutrality in Classical Greece*. Berkeley.

Bernstein, M. A. 1995. *Foregone Conclusions: Against Apocalyptic History*. Berkeley.

Bétant, E.-A. 1969. *Thucydideum Lexicon* I-II. Geneva (first publ. 1843).

Black, M. 1962. *Models and Metaphors. Studies in Language and Philosophy*. Ithaca, NY.

Blix, H. 2004. *Disarming Iraq*. New York.

Bloedow, E. F. 1994. "Pericles and Athens' Alliance with Corcyra." *Classica et Mediaevalia* 45: 51–66.

Blondell, R. 2002. *The Play of Character in Plato's Dialogues*. Cambridge.

Bodin, L. 1940. "Diodote contre Cléon. Quelques aperçus sur la dialectique de Thucydide." *REA* 42: 36–52.

Bosworth, A. B. 1992. "*Autonomia*: The Use and Abuse of Political Terminology." *Studi italiani di filologia classica* 10: 122–52.

———. 1993. "The Humanitarian Aspect of the Melian Dialogue." *JHS* 113: 30–44.

———. 2000. "The Historical Context of Thucydides' Funeral Oration." *JHS* 120: 1–16.

Bruell, C. 1974. "Thucydides' View of Athenian Imperialism." *American Political Science Review* 68: 11–17.

Brunt, P. A. 1993. *Studies in Greek History and Thought*. Oxford.

"Bulletin: No W.M.D. Found." 2005. *New York Times* editorial. 13 January, A34.

Bury, J. B. 1964. "Cleopatra's Nose." In H. Temperley (ed.), *Selected Essays of J. B. Bury*, 60–69. Amsterdam.

Bush, G. W. 2002. Transcript at http://www.whitehouse.gov/news/releases/2002/09/mar/200212-1.html.

Calder, W. M., III. 1955. "The Corcyraean-Corinthian Speeches in Thucydides I." *CJ* 50: 179–80.

Cartledge, P. A. 1984. "A New Lease of Life for Lichas, Son of Arkesilas?" *LCM* 9: 98–102.

Cartledge, P. A., and F. D. Harvey (eds.). 1985. *CRUX. Essays in Greek History presented to G. E. M. de Ste. Croix on his 75th birthday*. London.

Cartwright, D. 1997. *A Historical Commentary on Thucydides. A Companion to Rex Warner's Penguin Translation*. Ann Arbor.

Cawkwell, G. 1997. *Thucydides and the Peloponnesian War*. London and New York.

Chuter, D. 1997. "Triumph of the Will? Or, Why Surrender Is Not Always Inevitable." *Review of International Studies* 23: 381–400.

Clarke, R. C. 2004. *Against All Enemies. Inside America's War on Terror*. New York.

Coby, P. 1991. "Enlightened Self-Interest in the Peloponnesian War: Thucydidean Speakers on the Right of the Stronger and Inter-State Peace." *Canadian Journal of Political Science* 24: 67–90.

Cogan, M. 1981. "Mytilene, Plataea, and Corcyra: Ideology and Politics in Thucydides, Book Three." *Phoenix* 35: 1–21.

Cohen, D. 1984. "Justice, Interest, and Political Deliberation in Thucydides." *QUCC* 45: 35–60.

Connor, W. R. 1977. "Tyrannis Polis." In J. H. D'Arms, J. W. Eadie (eds.), *Ancient and Modern: Essays in Honor of Gerald F. Else*, 95–109. Ann Arbor.

———. 1984. *Thucydides*. Princeton.

———. 1985. "Narrative Discourse in Thucydides." In *The Greek Historians. Literature and History: Papers Presented to A. E. Raubitschek*, 1–17. Saratoga, CA:

———. 1991. "Polarization in Thucydides." In R. N. Lebow and B. S. Strauss (eds.), *Hegemonic Rivalry. From Thucydides to the Nuclear Age*, 53–69. Boulder.

———. 1992. *The New Politicians of Fifth-Century Athens*. Indianapolis (first publ. 1971).

Cornford, F. M. 1907. *Thucydides Mythistoricus*. London.

Cowley, R. 2001. *What If? Two Eminent Historians Imagine What Might Have Been*. New York.

Cowley, R., et al. 1998. "The Road Not Taken." *Quarterly Journal of Military History* 10.3: 65–80.

Crane, G. 1992a. "The Fear and Pursuit of Risk: Corinth on Athens, Sparta and the Peloponnesians (Thuc. 1.68–71, 120–21)." *TAPA* 122: 227–56.

———. 1992b. "Power, Prestige, and the Corcyrean Affair in Thucydides 1." *CA* 11: 1–27.

———. 1996. *The Blinded Eye. Thucydides and the New Written Word*. Lanham, MD.

———. 1998. *Thucydides and the Ancient Simplicity. The Limits of Political Realism*. Berkeley.

Creed, J. L. 1973. "Moral Values in the Age of Thucydides." *CQ* 23: 213–31.

Crowther, P. 2003. "Literary Metaphor and Philosophical Insight: The Significance of Archilochus." In G. R. Boys-Stones (ed.), *Metaphor, Allegory, and the Classical Tradition. Ancient Thought and Modern Revisions*, 83–100. Oxford.

Danesi, M. 1999. "Kisses Sweeter Than Wine: Metaphor and the Making of Meaning." In M. Danesi (ed.), *Of Cigarettes, High Heels, and Other Interesting Things*, 91–112. New York.

Darbo-Peschanski, C. 1987. "Thucydide: historien, juge." *Metis* 11: 109–40.

Davidson, J. 1991. "The Gaze in Polybius' *Histories*." *JRS* 81: 10–24.

Debnar, P. 1992 [= Arnold, P. 1992]. "The Persuasive Style of Debates in Direct Speech in Thucydides." *Hermes* 120: 44–57.

———. 1996. "The Unpersuasive Thebans (Thucydides 3.61–67)." *Phoenix* 50: 95–110.

———. 2000. "Diodotus' Paradox and the Mytilene Debate (Thucydides 3.37–48)." *RM* 143: 161–78.

———. 2001. *Speaking the Same Language. Speech and Audience in Thucydides' Spartan Debates*. Ann Arbor.

Develin, R. 1990. "Thucydides on Speeches." *AHB* 4.3: 58–60.

Diller, H. 1968. "Freiheit bei Thukydides als Schlagwort und als Wirklichkeit." In H. Herter (ed.), *Thukydides. Wege der Forschung.* 98: 639–60.

Doyle, M. W. 1991. "Thucydides: A Realist?" In R. N. Lebow and B. S. Strauss (eds.), *Hegemonic Rivalry. From Thucydides to the Nuclear Age*, 169–88. Boulder. Rpt. In W. Blanco and J. Roberts (eds.), *The Peloponnesian War*, tr. W. Blanco, 489–501. New York, 1998.

Eberhardt, W. 1959. "Die Melierdialog under die Inschriften ATL A9 und IG I² 97+." *Historia* 8: 284–314.

Edmunds, L. 1975a. *Chance and Intelligence in Thucydides*. Cambridge, MA.

———. 1975b. "Thucydides' Ethics as Reflected in the Description of Stasis (3.82–83)." *HSCP* 79: 73–92.

———. 1993. "Thucydides in the Act of Writing." In *Tradizione e Innovazione nella Cultura Greca da Omero all'Età Ellenistica. Scritti in Onore di Bruno Gentili*, 831–52. Rome.

Ellis, J. R. 1978. "Thucydides at Amphipolis." *Antichthon* 12: 28–35.

Farrar, C. 1988. *The Origins of Democratic Thinking. The Invention of Politics in Classical Athens*. Cambridge.

Ferguson, N. (ed.). 1997. *Virtual History. Alternatives and Counterfactuals*. London.

Finley, J. H. 1967. *Three Essays on Thucydides*. Cambridge, MA:

Finley, M. I. 1956. "Myth, Memory, and History." *History and Theory* 4: 281–302.

Flory, S. F. 1980. "Who Read Herodotus' *Histories*?" *AJP* 101 (1980): 12–28.

———. 1988. "Thucydides' Hypotheses about the Peloponnesian War." *TAPA* 118: 43–56.

———. 1990. "The Meaning of τὸ μὴ μυθῶδες (1.22.4) and the Usefulness of Thucydides' History." *CJ* 85.3: 193–208.

———. 1993. "The Death of Thucydides and the Motif of 'Land and Sea.'" In R. M. Rosen and J. Farrell (eds.), *Nomodeiktes: Greek Studies in Honor of Martin Ostwald*, 113–23. Ann Arbor.

Ford, A. L. 1985. "The Politics of Authorship in Archaic Greece." In T. J. Figueira,

G. Nagy (eds.), *Theognis of Megara*, 82–95. Baltimore.

Forde, S. 1992. "Varieties of Realism: Thucydides and Machiavelli." *Journal of Politics* 54: 372–93.

Fowler, R. L. 2001. "Early *Historie* and Literacy." In N. Luraghi (ed.), *The Historian's Craft in the Age of Herodotus*, 95–115. Oxford.

Frankel, M. 2004. *High Noon in the Cold War: Kennedy, Krushchev, and the Cuban Missile Crisis*. New York.

Gagarin, M. 1999. "The Orality of Greek Oratory." In E. A. MacKay (ed.), *Signs of Orality. The Oral Tradition and Its Influence on the Greek and Roman World*, 163–81. Leiden.

Garst, D. 1989. "Thucydides and Neorealism." *International Studies Quarterly* 33: 3–27.

Gomez-Lobo, A. 1989. "El diálogo de Melos y la Visión histórica de Tucídides." *Nova Tellus* 7: 9–31.

Gomme, A. W. 1967. *Essays in Greek History and Literature*. Freeport, NY.

Gould, S. J. 1989. *Wonderful Life: The Burgess Shale and the Nature of History*. New York.

Gribble, D. 1998. "Narrator Interventions in Thucydides." *JHS* 118: 41–67.

Griffith, G. T. 1961. "Some Habits of Thucydides When Introducing Persons." *PCPS* n.s. 7: 21–33.

Grube, G. M. A. (tr.). 1992. *Plato: The Republic*. Rev. by C. D. C. Reeve. Indianapolis.

Halliwell, S. (tr.). 1987. *The Poetics of Aristotle*. Chapel Hill.

Hammond, N. G. L. 1973. "The Particular and the Universal in the Speeches of Thucydides, with Special Reference to that of Hermocrates at Gela." In P. A. Stadter (ed.), *The Speeches in Thucydides*, 49–59. Chapel Hill.

Hansen, M. H. (1993). "The Battle Exhortation in Ancient Historiography." *Historia* 42: 161–80.

———. 1995. "The 'Autonomous City-State.' Ancient Fact or Modern Fiction?" In M. H. Hansen and K. Raaflaub (eds.), *Studies in the Ancient Greek Polis*, 21–43. Stuttgart.

———. 1997. "A Typology of Dependent *Poleis*." In T. H. Nielsen (ed.), *Yet More Studies in the Ancient Greek Polis*, 21–43. Stuttgart.

———. 1998. "The Little Grey Horse—Henry V's Speech at Agincourt and the Battle Exhortation in Ancient Historiography." *Histos* 2: n. pag.

Hanson, V. D. 2001. "A Voice from the Past. General Thucydides Speaks about the War." *National Review Online* Nov. 27.

Harris, E. M. 1992. "Pericles' Praise of Athenian Democracy: Thucydides 2.37.1." *HSCP* 94: 157–67.

Harris, W. V. 1989. *Ancient Literacy*. Cambridge, MA.

Harrison, E. L. 1959. "The Escape from Plataea: Thucydides 3.23." *CQ* 9: 30–33.

Harvey, F. D. 1966. "Literacy in the Athenian Democracy." *REG* 79: 585–635.

Havelock, E. A. 1963. *Preface to Plato*. Cambridge, MA.

———. 1982. *The Literate Revolution in Greece and Its Cultural Consequences*. Princeton.

———. 1986. *The Muse Learns to Write*. New Haven.

HCT= Gomme, A. W., A. Andrewes, K. J. Dover. 1945–81. *A Historical Commentary on Thucydides*. 5 vols. Oxford.

Heath, M. 1990. "Justice in Thucydides' Athenian Speeches." *Historia* 39: 385–400.

Hedrick, C.W. 1993. "The Meaning of Material Culture: Herodotus, Thucydides, and Their Sources." In R. M. Rosen and J. Farrell (eds.), *Nomodeiktes: Greek Studies in Honor of Martin Ostwald*, 39–54. Ann Arbor.

Hedrick, C. W., J. Marincola, E. O'Gorman, and J. Moles.1999. "Exchange and Reply." *Histos* 3: n. pag.

Henderson, J. 2003. "Demos, Demagogue, Tyrant in Attic Old Comedy." In K. A. Morgan (ed.), *Popular Tyranny: Sovereignty and Its Discontents in Classical Athens*, 155–79. Austin.

Hershbell, J. P. 1995. "Reflections on the Orality and Literacy of Plato's Dialogues." In F. J. Gonzalez (ed.), *The Third Way. New Directions in Platonic Studies*, 26–39. Lanham, MD.

Herter, H. 1954. "Pylos und Melos." *RM* 97: 316–43.

Hinds, S. 1998. *Allusion and Intertext. Dynamics of Appropriation in Roman Poetry.* Cambridge.

Hogan, J. C. 1972. "Thucydides 3.52–68 and Euripides' *Hecuba*." *Phoenix* 26: 241–57.

Hornblower, S. 1987. *Thucydides*. Baltimore.

———. 1991–96. *A Commentary on Thucydides*. 2 vols. Oxford.

———. 1992a. "Thucydides' Use of Herodotus." In J. M. Sanders (ed.), *ΦΙΛΟΚΑΛΩΝ. Lakonian Studies in Honour of Hector Catling*, 141–154. London.

———. 1992b. "The Religious Dimension to the Peloponnesian War, Or, What Thucydides Does Not Tell Us." *HSCP* 94: 169–97.

———. 1994. "Narratology and Narrative Techniques in Thucydides." In S. Hornblower (ed.), *Greek Historiography*, 131–66. Oxford.

———. 1995. "The Fourth Century and Hellenistic Reception of Thucydides." *JHS* 105: 47–68.

Huart, P. 1968. *Le vocabulaire de l'analyse psychologique dans l'oeuvre de Thucydide.* Paris.

———. 1973. *ΓΝΩΜΗ chez Thucydides et ses contemporains (Sophocle—Euripide—Antiphon—Andocide—Aristophane)*. Paris.

Hudson-Williams, H. LL. 1948. "Thucydides, Isocrates, and the Rhetorical Method of Composition." *CQ* 42: 76–81.

———. 1950. "Forms of Debate and the Melian Dialogue." *AJP* 71: 156–69.

Hunter, V. 1973a. *Thucydides. The Artful Reporter*. Toronto.

———. 1973b. "Athens *Tyrannis*: A New Approach to Thucydides." *CJ* 69: 120–26.

———. 1986. "Thucydides, Gorgias, and Mass Psychology." *Hermes* 114: 412–29.

———. 1988. "Thucydides and the Sociology of the Crowd." *CJ* 84: 17–30.

Hussein, S. 2003a. Transcript at http://www.cbsnews.com/stories/2003/02/20/iraq/main541277.sthml.

Hussein, S. 2003b. The transcript for this interview may be found at http://www.cbsnews.com/stories/2003/02/26/6011/main542151.sthml, and http://www.cbsnews.com/stories/2003/02/26/6011/main542152.shtml, and http://www.cbsnews.com/stories/2003/02/26/6011/main542155.shtml.

Hussey, E. 1985. "Thucydidean History and Democritean Theory." In P. A.

Cartledge and F. D. Harvey (eds.), CRUX. *Essays in Greek History presented G.E.M. de Ste. Croix on His 75th Birthday*, 118–38. London.

Iser, W. I. 1974. *The Implied Reader*. Baltimore.

Jaeger, W. 1945. *Paideia: The Ideals of Greek Culture*. 3 vols. tr. G. Highet. Oxford.

Jervis, R. 2003. "The Compulsive Empire." *Foreign Policy* July–Aug.: 83–87.

Johnson Bagby, L. M. 1994. "The Use and Abuse of Thucydides in International Relations." *International Organization* 48: 131–53.

de Jong, I. J. F. 1987. *Narrators and Focalizers. The Presentation of the Story in the Iliad*. Amsterdam.

———. 1997. "Homer and Narratology." In I. Morris and B. Powell (eds.), *A New Companion to Homer*, 305–25. Leiden.

———. 2001. *A Narratological Commentary on the Odyssey*. Cambridge.

———. 2002. "Narrative Unity and Units." In E. J. Bakker, I. J. F. de Jong, and H. Van Wees (eds.), *Brill's Companion to Herodotus*, 245–66. Leiden.

de Jong, I. J. F., and J. P. Sullivan (eds.). 1994. *Modern Critical Theory and the Classics*. Leiden.

Kagan, D. 1969. *The Outbreak of the Peloponnesian War*. Ithaca.

———. 1975. "The Speeches in Thucydides and the Mytilenian Debate." YCS 24: 71–94.

———. 1981. *The Peace of Nicias and the Sicilian Expedition*. Ithaca.

———. 1995. *On the Origins of War and the Preservation of Peace*. New York.

Kahn, C. H. 1996. *Plato and the Socratic Dialogue. The Philosophical Use of a Literary Form*. Cambridge.

Kakridis, J. Th. 1961. *Der thukydideishe Epitaphios: Ein stilistischer Kommentar*. Munich.

Kallet, L. 1993. *Money, Expense, and Naval Power in Thucydides' History 1–5.24*. Berkeley.

———. 2001. *Money and the Corrosion of Power in Thucydides. The Sicilian Expedition and Its Aftermath*. Berkeley.

———. 2004. Review of Price (2001). CW 97: 208–9.

Kierdorf, W. 1962. "Zum Melier-Dialog des Thukydides." *RM* 105: 253–56.

Kitto, H. D. F. 1966. *Poiesis. Structure and Thought*. Berkeley.

Knox, B. M. W. 1964. *The Heroic Temper. Studies in Sophoclean Tragedy*. Berkeley.

———. 1968. "Silent Reading in Antiquity." *GRBS* 9: 421–35.

Lakoff, G., and M. Johnson. 1980. *Metaphors We Live By*. Chicago and London.

Landey, J. S., and W. P. Strobel. 2003. "Saddam wanted secret negotiations with U.S., officials say." Knight Ridder Newspapers: 5 Nov.

Lang, M. 1995. "Participial Motivation in Thucydides." *Mnemosyne* 48: 48–65.

Lardinois, A. 1997. "Modern Paroemiology and the Use of Gnomai in Homer's *Iliad*." CP 92: 213–234.

Largio, D. 2004. "21 Rationales for War." *Foreign Policy* Sept.–Oct.: 18.

Lateiner, D. 1975. "The Speech of Teutiaplus." *GRBS* 16: 175–84.

———. 1977. "Heralds and Corpses in Thucydides." CW 71: 97–106.

———. 1989. *The Historical Method of Herodotus*. Toronto.

Lattimore, S. (tr., intro.). 1998. *Thucydides. The Peloponnesian War*. Indianapolis.

Lebow, R. N. 2001. "Thucydides the Constructivist." *American Political Science Review* 95.3: 547–60.

————. 2003. *The Tragic Vision of Politics: Ethics, Interests and Orders*. Cambridge.

————. 2004. "Constructive Realism." *International Studies Review* 6.2: 346–52.

Lebow, R. N., and R. Kelly. 2001. "Thucydides and Hegemony: Athens and the United States." *Review of International Studies* 27: 593–609.

Lebow, R. N., and B. S. Strauss. 1991. "Thucydides and International Relations: Introduction." In R. N. Lebow and B. S. Strauss (eds.), *Hegemonic Rivalry. From Thucydides to the Nuclear Age*, 1–19. Boulder.

Leidl, C. G. 2003. "The Harlot's Art: Metaphor and Literary Criticism." In G. R. Boys-Stones (ed.), *Metaphor, Allegory, and the Classical Tradition. Ancient Thought and Modern Revisions*, 31–54. Oxford.

Liebeschuetz, W. 1968. "The Structure and Function of the Melian Dialogue." *JHS* 88: 73–77.

Lintott, A. 1992. "Civil Strife and Human Nature in Thucydides." in J. H. Molyneux (ed.), *Literary Responses to Civil Discord*, 25–35. Nottingham.

Lloyd, G. E. R. 1979. *Magic, Reason, and Experience. Studies in the Origins and Development of Greek Science*. Cambridge.

————. 1987. *The Revolutions of Wisdom. Studies in the Claims and Practice of Ancient Greek Science*. Berkeley.

Lloyd-Jones, H. 1971. *The Justice of Zeus*. Berkeley.

Loomis, W. T. 1992. *The Spartan War Fund. IG VI, 1 and a New Fragment*. Stuttgart.

Loraux, N. 1986a. *The Invention of Athens. The Funeral Oration in the Classical City*. Tr. A. Sheridan. Cambridge, MA.

————. 1986b. "Thucydide a écrit la Guerre du Peloponnese." *Metis* 20: 139–61.

Lord, A. 2000. *The Singer of Tales*. S. Mitchell, G. Nagy (eds.). 2nd ed. Cambridge, MA.

MacDowell, D. M. (ed., intro., and trans.). 1993. *Gorgias. Encomium of Helen*. Bristol.

Mackay, E. A. (ed.). 1999. *Signs of Orality. The Oral Tradition and its Influence on the Greek and Roman World*. Leiden.

Mackie, C. J. (ed.). 2004. *Oral Performance and its Contexts*. Leiden.

Mackin, J. A., Jr. 1991. "Schismogenesis and Community: Pericles' Funeral Oration." *Quarterly Journal of Speech* 77: 251–62.

McGrew, J. F. 1993. *Tyranny and Political Culture in Ancient Greece*. Ithaca, NY.

Macleod, C. 1983. *Collected Essays*. Oxford.

McNamara, R., with B. VanDeMark. 1995. *In Retrospect. The Tragedy and Lessons of Vietnam*. New York.

Marincola, J. M. 1989. "Thucydides 1.22.2." *CP* 84: 216–21.

————. 1997. *Authority and Tradition in Ancient Historiography*. Cambridge.

————. 1999. "Genre, Convention, and Innovation in Greco-Roman Historiography." In C. S. Kraus (ed.), *The Limits of Historiography. Genre and Narrative in Ancient Historical Texts*, 281–324. Leiden.

Mearsheimer, J. J., and S. M. Walt. 2003. "An Unnecessary War." *Foreign Policy* (Jan.–Feb.): 50–59.

Meiggs, R. 1972. *The Athenian Empire*. Oxford.

Meiggs, R., and D. Lewis (eds). 1989. *A Selection of Greek Historical Inscriptions to the End of the Fifth Century B.C.* Oxford.

Meister, C. 1955. *Die Gnomik im Geschichtswerk des Thukydides*. Winterthur.

Missiou, A. 1998. "Reciprocal Generosity in the Foreign Affairs of Fifth-Century Athens and Sparta." In C. Gill, N. Postlethwaite, and R. Seaford (eds.), *Reciprocity in Ancient Greece*, 181–97. Oxford.

Moles, J. 1999. "*Anathema kai Ktema:* the Inscriptional Inheritance of Ancient Historiography." *Histos* 3: n. pag.

———. 2001. "A False Dilemma: Thucydides' *History* and Historicism." in S. J. Harrison (ed.), *Texts, Ideas, and the Classics. Scholarship, Theory, and Classical Literature*, 195–219. Oxford.

Momigliano, A. 1942. "Terra Marique." *JRS* 32: 53–64.

———. 1977. "Time in Ancient Historiography." In *Essays in Ancient and Modern Historiography*, 179–204. Middletown, CT.

———. 1978. "The Historians of the Classical World and Their Audiences. Some Suggestions." *Annali della scuola normale superiore di Pisa, Classe di lettere e filosofia* 8: 59–75.

Monoson, S. S. 1994. "Citizen as *Erastes:* Erotic Imagery and the Idea of Reciprocity in the Periclean Funeral Oration." *Political Theory* 22: 253–76.

Monoson, S. S., and M. Loriaux. 1998. "The Illusion of Power and the Disruption of Moral Norms: Thucydides' Critique of Pericles' Policy." *American Political Science Review* 92: 285–97.

Morrison, J. V. 1992. *Homeric Misdirection: False Predictions in the Iliad*. Ann Arbor.

———. 1994. "A Key Topos in Thucydides: The Comparison of Cities and Individuals." *AJP* 115: 525–41.

———. 1997. "*Kerostasia*, the Dictates of Fate, and the Will of Zeus in the *Iliad*." *Arethusa* 30: 273–96.

———. 1999. "Preface to Thucydides: Rereading the Corcyrean Conflict (1.24–55)." *CA* 18: 94–131.

———. 2000. "Historical Lessons in the Melian Episode." *TAPA* 130: 119–48.

———. 2004. "Memory, Time, and Writing: Oral and Literary Aspects of Thucydides' *History*." In C. J. Mackie (ed.), *Oral Performance and its Contexts*, 95–116. Leiden.

———. 2006. "Speech-Narrative Interaction in Thucydides." In A. Rengakos and A. Tsakmakis (eds.), *Brill's Companion to Thucydides*. Leiden.

Murari Pires, F. 1998. "The Rhetoric of Method (Thucydides 1.22 and 2.35)." *AHB* 12.3: 106–112.

Murry, J. M. *The Countries of the Mind*. Oxford.

Nakategawa, Y. 1994. "Forms of Interstate Justice in the Late Fifth Century." *Klio* 76: 135–54.

Neustadt, R. E., and E. R. May. 1986. *Thinking in Time. The Uses of History for Decision Makers*. New York.

Newman, J. K. 1988. "Protagoras, Gorgias, and the Dialogic Principle." *ICS* 11: 43–61.

Nightingale, A. 1995. *Genres in Dialogue. Plato and the Construct of Philosophy*. Cambridge.

Nogales, P. D. 1999. *Metaphorically Speaking*. Stanford, CA.

Ober, J. 1993. "Thucydides' Criticism of Democratic Knowledge." In R. M. Rosen and J. Farrell (eds.), *Nomodeiktes: Greek Studies in Honor of Martin Ostwald*, 81–98. Ann Arbor.

———. 1994. "How to Criticize Democracy in Late Fifth- and Fourth-Century Athens." in J. P. Euben, J. R. Wallach, and J. Ober (eds.), *Athenian Political Thought and the Reconstruction of American Democracy*, 149–71. Ithaca.

———. 1998. *Political Dissent in Democratic Athens. Intellectual Critics of Popular Rule.* Princeton.

Ong, W. J. 1982. *Orality and Literacy. The Technologizing of the Word.* London.

Orwin, C. 1994. *The Humanity of Thucydides.* Princeton.

Ostwald M. 1979. "Diodotus, Son of Eucrates." *GRBS* 20: 5–13

———. 1988. *ΑΝΑΓΚΗ in Thucydides.* Atlanta.

Parker, V. 1998. "Τύραννος: The Semantics of a Political Concept from Archilochus to Aristotle." *Hermes* 126: 145–72.

Parry, A. 1970. "Thucydides' Use of Abstract Language." *Yale French Studies* 45 (1970): 3–20.

———. 1972. "Thucydides' Historical Perspective." *YCS* 22: 47–61.

———. 1981. *Logos and Ergon in Thucydides.* Salem, NH.

Parry, M. 1971. *The Making of Homeric Verse. The Collected Papers of Milman Parry.* A. Parry (ed.). Oxford.

Patterson, O. 1991. *Freedom. Volume I: Freedom in the Making of Western Culture.* New York.

Pearson, L. 1957. "Popular Ethics in the World of Thucydides." *CP* 52.4: 228–44.

Pelling, C. 2000. *Literary Texts and the Greek Historian.* London and New York.

Perseus. 2006. English translation of Plato's *Parmenides* on-line at http://www.perseus.tufts.edu/cgi-bin/ptext?doc=Perseus:text: 1999.01.0174:text=Parm.:section=126a.

Plant, I. M. 1999. "Thucydides and Forensic Oratory." *CQ* 49: 62–73.

Pope, M. 1988. "Thucydides and Democracy." *Historia* 37: 276–96.

Pouilloux, J., and F. Salviat. 1983. "Lichas, Lacédémonien, Archonte à Thasos et le Livre VIII de Thucydide." *CRAI* 20: 376–403.

———. 1985. "Thucydides après l'exil et la composition de son Histoire." *RP* 59: 13–20.

Pouncey, P. R. 1980. *The Necessities of War. A Study of Thucydides' Pessimism.* New York.

Powell, C. 2003a. Transcript at http:/www.whitehouse.gov/news/releases/2003/02/ 20030205-1.html.

———. 2003b. Transcript at http://www.cbsnews.com/stories/2003/02/20/iraq/ main541277.sthml.

Price, J. J. 2001. *Thucydides and Internal War.* Cambridge.

Pritchett, W. K. 1994. "The General's Exhortation in Greek Warfare." In W. K. Pritchett, *Essays in Greek History*, 27–109. Amsterdam.

Raaflaub, K. 1979. "Polis Tyrannos: Zur Entstehung einer politischen Metapher." In G. W. Bowersock, W. Burkert, and M. C. J. Putnam (eds.), *Arktouros. Hellenic Studies Presented to Bernard M. W. Knox on the Occasion of His 65th Birthday*, 237–52. Berlin and New York.

———. 1985. *Die Entdeckung der Freiheit: Zur historischen Semantik und Gesellschaftsgeschichte eines politischen Grundbegriffs der Griechen.* Munich.

———. 2003. "Stick and Glue: The Function of Tyranny in Fifth-Century Athenian Democracy." In K. A. Morgan (ed.), *Popular Tyranny: Sovereignty and Its Discontents in Classical Athens*, 59–93. Austin.

————. 2004. *The Discovery of Freedom in Ancient Greece*. Tr. R. Franciscono. Chicago.

Rabinowitz, P. J. 1987. *Before Reading. Narrative Conventions and the Politics of Interpretation*. Ithaca, NY.

Radt, S. K. 1976. "Philologische Kleinigkeiten zum Melierdialog." *Mnemosyne* 29: 33–41.

Raubitschek, A. E. 1973. "The Speech of the Athenians at Sparta." In P. A. Stadter (ed.), *The Speeches in Thucydides*, 32–48. Chapel Hill.

Rengakos, A. 1996. "Fernbeziehungen zwischen den Thukydideischen Reden." *Hermes* 124: 396–417.

Rhodes, P. 1998. "'Epidamnus is a City': On Not Overinterpreting Thucydides." *Histos* 2: n. pag.

Ridley, R. T. 1981. "Exegesis and Audience in Thucydides." *Hermes* 109: 25–46.

Robb, K. 1994. *Literacy and Paideia in Ancient Greece*. New York.

————. 1997. "Orality, Literacy, and the Dialogue-Form." In R. Hart, V. Tejera (eds.), *Plato's Dialogues. The Dialogical Approach*, 29–64. Lewiston, NY.

de Romilly, J. 1956a. "L'Utilité de l'histoire selon Thucydide." *Fondation Hardt* 4: 39–66.

————. 1956b. "La crainte dans l'oeuvre de Thucydide." *Classica et Mediaevalia* 17: 119–27.

————. 1966. "La condamnation du plaisir dans l'oeuvre de Thucydide." *WS* 46: 142–48.

————. 1988. *Thucydides and Athenian Imperialism*. Tr. P. Thody. 2nd. ed. Oxford.

Rood, T. 1998a. *Thucydides. Narrative and Explanation*. Oxford.

————. 1998b. "Thucydides and his Predecessors." *Histos* 2: n. pag.

————. 1999. "Thucydides' Persian Wars," in C. S. Kraus (ed.), *The Limits of Historiography. Genre and Narrative in Ancient Historical Texts*, 141–68. Leiden.

————. 2004. ".Thucydides." In I. de Jong, R. Nünlist, and A. Bowle (eds.), *Narrators, Narratees, and Narratives in Ancient Greek Literature. Studies in Ancient Greek Narrative*. Vol. I: 115–28. Leiden.

Rosenbloom, D. 1995. Review of Hornblower (1994). *BMCR* 95.12:11.

Rowe, C. 1998. "Democracy and Sokratic-Platonic Philosophy." In D. Boedeker and K. A. Raaflaub (eds.), *Democracy, Empire, and the Arts in Fifth-Century Athens*, 241–53. Cambridge, MA.

Rusten, J. S. (ed.). 1989. *Thucydides. The Peloponnesian War. Book II*. Cambridge.

Rutherford, R. B. 1995. *The Art of Plato. Ten Essays in Platonic Interpretation*. Cambridge, MA.

Ryle, G. 1966. *Plato's Progress*. Cambridge.

de Ste. Croix, G. 1972. *The Origins of the Peloponnesian War*. Ithaca, NY.

Scanlon, T. S. F. 1987. "Thucydides and Tyranny." *CA* 6: 286–301.

————. 1994. "Echoes of Herodotus in Thucydides: Self-Sufficiency, Admiration, and Law." *Historia* 43: 143–176.

Schneider, C. 1974. *Information und Absicht bei Thukydides. Untersuchung zur Motivation des Handelns*. Hypomnemata 41: Göttingen.

Shrimpton, G. S. 1998. "Accuracy in Thucydides." *AHB* 12: 71–82.

Schuller, W. 1978. *Die Stadt als Tyrann–Athens Herrschaft über seine Bundesgenossen*. Konstanz.

Scodel, R. 1997. "Pseudo-Intimacy and the Prior Knowledge of the Homeric Audience." *Arethusa* 30: 201–19.

Seaford, R. A. S. 1994. *Reciprocity and Ritual: Homer and Tragedy in the Developing City-State*. Oxford.

Seaman, M. 1997. "The Athenian Expedition to Melos in 416 B.C." *Historia* 46: 385–418.

Shapiro, S. O. 1996. "Herodotus and Solon." CA 15.2: 348–64.

Sheets, G. A. 1994. "Conceptualizing International Law in Thucydides." *AJP* 115: 51–73.

Small, J. P. 1995. "Artificial Memory and the Writing Habits of the Literate." *Helios* 22: 159–66.

———. 1997. *Wax Tablets of the Mind: Cognitive Studies of Memory and Literacy in Classical Antiquity*. London.

Smith, P. C. 1997. "Tensions in the *Phaedrus:* Dialogue and Dialectic, Speech and Writing." In R. Hart and V. Tejera (eds.), *Plato's Dialogues. The Dialogical Approach*, 169–99. Lewiston, NY.

Snyder, J. 2004. "One World, Rival Theories." *Foreign Policy* (Nov.–Dec.): 53–62.

Spence, I. 1990. "Perikles and the Defence of Attika during the Peloponnesian War." *JHS* 110: 91–109.

Stadter, P. A. 1983. "The Motives for Athens' Alliance with Corcyra (Thuc. 1.44)." *GRBS* 24: 131–36.

———. 1993. "The Form and Content of Thucydides' Pentecontaetia (1.89–117)." *GRBS* 34: 35–72.

Stahl, H.-P. 1966. *Thukydides: Die Stellung des Menschen im geschichtlichen Prozess*. Munich.

———. 1973. "Speeches and the Course of Events in Books Six and Seven of Thucydides." In P. A. Stadter (ed.), *The Speeches in Thucydides*, 60–77. Chapel Hill.

———. 2003. *Thucydides. Man's Place in History*. Swansea, Wales.

Stambaugh, J. E. 1974. "The Idea of the City: Three Views of Athens." *CJ* 69: 309–21.

Stanford, W. B. 1972. *Greek Metaphor. Studies in Theory and Practice*. 2nd ed. Oxford.

Steiner, D. 1994. *The Tyrant's Writ. Myths and Images of Writing in Ancient Greece*. Princeton.

Storey, I. C. 2003. *Eupolis. Poet of Old Comedy*. Oxford.

Strasburger, H. 1954. "Die Entdeckung der politischen Geschichte durch Thukydides." *Saeculum* 5: 395–428. Rpt. in *Thukydides, Wege der Forschung* 98, H. Herter (ed.), 412–76. Darmstadt 1968.

Thomas, R. 1989. *Oral Tradition and Written Record in Classical Athens*. Cambridge.

———. 1992. *Literacy and Orality in Ancient Greece*. Cambridge.

———. 1993. "Performance and Written Publication in Herodotus and the Sophistic Generation." In W. Kullmann and J. Althoff (eds.), *Vermittlung und Tradierung von Wissen in der griechischen Kultur*, 225–44. Tübingen.

———. 2000. *Herodotus in Context. Ethnography, Science and the Art of Persuasion*. Cambridge.

———. 2003. "Prose Performance Texts: *Epideixis* and Written Publication in the

Late Fifth and Early Fourth Centuries." In H. Yunis (ed.), *Written Texts and the Rise of Literate Culture in Ancient Greece*, 162–88. Cambridge.

Tompkins, D. P. 1972. "Stylistic Characterization in Thucydides' Nicias and Alcibiades." YCS 22: 181–214.

———. 1993. "Archidamus and the Question of Characterization in Thucydides." In R. M. Rosen and J. Farrell (eds.), *Nomodeiktes: Greek Studies in Honor of Martin Ostwald*, 99–111. Ann Arbor.

Topitsch, E. 1943–47. "ἀνθρωπεία φύσις und Ethik bei Thukydides." WS 61–62: 50–67.

Treu, M. 1954. "Athens und Melos und der Melierdialog des Thukydides." *Historia* 2: 253–73.

Tuplin, C. 1985. "Imperial Tyranny: Some Reflections on a Classical Greek Political Metaphor." In P. A. Cartledge and F. D. Harvey (eds.), *CRUX. Essays in Greek History Presented G. E. M. de Ste. Croix on His 75th Birthday*, 348–75. London.

Turasiewicz, R. 1990. "Le problème du style de Thucydide." *Eos* 58: 79–89.

UN. 2002. A transcript of UN Resolution 1441 may be found at http://www.state.gov/p/nea/rls/15016.html.

Usher, S. (tr.). 1974. "On Thucydides." In *Dionysius of Halicarnassus. The Critical Essays*. Vol. 1, Loeb. Classical Library. Cambridge. MA.

Varnedoe, K. 1990. *A Fine Disregard: What Makes Modern Art Modern*. New York.

Walbank, F. W. 1975. "*Symploke*: its Role in Polybius' Histories." YCS 24: 197–212.

Walker, A. D. 1993. "*Enargeia* and the Spectator in Greek Historiography." *TAPA* 123: 353–77.

Wallace, R. W. 1996. "Book Burning in Ancient Athens." In R. W. Wallace and E. M. Harris (eds.), *Transitions to Empire*, 226–40. Norman, OK.

———. 1998. "Sophists in Athens." In D. Boedeker and K. A. Raaflaub (eds.), *Democracy, Empire, and the Arts in Fifth-Century Athens*, 203–222. Cambridge, MA.

Wasserman, F. M. 1947. "The Melian Dialogue." *TAPA* 78: 18–36.

———. 1956. "Post-Periclean Democracy in Action: The Mytilenean Debate (Thuc. III 37–48)." *TAPA* 87: 27–41.

Weil, R. 1975. "Lire dans Thucydides." In J. Bingen, C. Cambier, and G. Nachtergael (eds.). *Le monde grec*, 162–68. Brussels.

West, W. C., III. 1973. "The Speeches in Thucydides: A Description and Listing." In P. A. Stadter (ed.), *The Speeches in Thucydides*, 3–15. Chapel Hill.

Westlake, H. D. 1962. "Thucydides and the Fall of Amphipolis." *Hermes* 90: 276–87.

———. 1968. *Individuals in Thucydides*. Cambridge.

———. 1973. "The Settings of Thucydidean Speeches." in P. A. Stadter (ed.), *The Speeches in Thucydides*, 90–108. Chapel Hill.

———. 1977. "ΛΕΓΕΤΑΙ in Thucydides." *Mnemosyne* 30: 345–62.

———. 1989a. "Personal Motives, Aims and Feelings in Thucydides." In *Studies in Thucydides and Greek History*, 201–23. Bristol.

———. 1989b. "The Two Second Prefaces of Thucydides." In *Studies in Thucydides and Greek History*, 97–102. Bristol.

White, J. B. 1984. *When Words Lose Their Meaning. Constitutions and Reconstitutions of Language, Character, and Community*. Chicago.

Whitlock Blundell, M. 1989. *Helping Friends and Harming Enemies: A Study in Sophocles and Greek Ethics*. Cambridge.

Wickersham, J. 1994. *Hegemony and Greek Historians*. Lanham, MD.

Williams, M. F. 1998. *Ethics in Thucydides. The Ancient Simplicity*. Lanham, MD.

Wilson, J. 1987. *Athens and Corcyra. Strategy and Tactics in the Peloponnesian War*. Chippenham, England.

Winnington-Ingram, R. P. 1965. "τὰ δέοντα εἰπεῖν. Cleon and Diodotus." *BICS* 12: 70–82.

Woodbury, L. 1976. "Aristophanes' *Frogs* and Athenian Literacy: *Ran.* 52–53, 1114." *TAPA* 106: 349–57.

Yunis, H. 1991. "How Do the People Decide? Thucydides on Periclean Rhetoric and Civic Instruction." *AJP* 102: 179–200.

———. 1996. *Taming Democracy. Models of Political Rhetoric in Classical Athens*. Ithaca.

———. 1998. "Constraints of Democracy and the Rise of the Art of Rhetoric." In D. Boedeker and K. A. Raaflaub (eds.), *Democracy, Empire, and the Arts in Fifth-Century Athens*, 223–40. Cambridge, MA.

———. 2003. "Writing for Reading: Thucydides, Plato, and the Emergence of the Critical Reader." In H. Yunis (ed.), *Written Texts and the Rise of Literate Culture in Ancient Greece*, 189–212. Cambridge.

Zizek, S. 2004. "Iraq's False Promises." *Foreign Policy* (Jan.–Feb.): 43–49.

Index Locorum

Aristophanes
Acharnians 530–34, **251n88**
Birds 1279, **249n67**
Knights 732, **249n67**; 1111–14,
    245n28; 1330, **245n28**; 1333,
    245n28; 1340–44, **249n67**;
Wasps 620, **245n28**

Aristotle
Ath. Pol. 27–28, **256n18**; 29–33,
    256n18; 54.5, **255n8**; 59.4,
    253n23
Poetics 1451, **20**; 1452, **214n4**;
    1455, **20**; 1459, **246n33**; 1460,
    18
Politics 1253, **233n10**; 1261,
    233n10; 1323–24, **233n10**
Rhetoric 1365, **155**, **251n88**; 1405,
    246n33; 1407, **155**; 1412,
    245n26

Demosthenes
59.103, **216n33**

Diogenes Laertius
3.35, **176**; 3.37, **176**

Dionysius of Halicarnassus
On Thucydides 9, **206n29**; 13,
    206n29; 49, **181**; 50, **257n28**;
    51, **181**

Eupolis
Demoi fr. 102, **154**

Gorgias
Helen 9, **203–4n11**

Herodotus
1.65, **247n51**; 1.86–87, **214n4**;
    3.82, **248n61**; 9.27, **220n73**

Homer
Iliad 9.613–14, **218n54**

"Old Oligarch"
2.2, **247n49**; 2.14–16, **247n48**

Plato
Parmenides 127, **176**
Phaedo 97, **176**
Phaedrus 230, **199n4**
Republic 332–36, **218n54**; 364,
    249n73; 368–69, **120**, **233n10**;
    434–35, **233n10**, **235n29**;
    509–11, **234n14**; 544, **233n10**;
    560–61, **177**; 606, **8–9**

Plutarch
Life of Pericles 8, **251n88**; 28,
    251n88
Moralia 346, **203–4n11**

Polybius
1.4, **218n51**; 3.32, **218n51**

Sophocles
Antigone 821, **6**

Thucydides
Book 1: 1.1, **3, 9, 16, 37, 160, 179,**

273

Book 5: 5.3, 223n4, 246–47n46;
5.9, 246–47n46; 5.11, 243n7;
5.14–24, 235n4; 5.17, 215n16,
217n47; 5.20, 206n29; 5.23,
246–47n46; 5.24, 254n2; 5.26,
9, 166–67, 199n3, 205n21,
251n2, n4, 252n16; 5.28.2, 98;
5.30, 248n56; 5.32, 223n4,
246–47n46; 5.66, 252n16;
5.84, 84, 90, 95–96,
224n12–13, 231n68, 232n78;
5.84–116, 81, 112, 184; 5.85,
84; 5.86, 83, 85–86; 5.87,
85–86, 91, 222n113, 228n50;
5.88, 225n21, 227n35; 5.89,
72, 84, 86, 91, 131, 184, 194,
205n24, 224n17, 224n21,
n24, 225–26n26, 227n41,
235n21, 246n42; 5.90, 86, 89,
92, 229n58; 5.91, 84, 89, 184,
225n21; 5.92, 89; 5.93, 89, 93,
185, 225nn21–22; 5.94, 96;
5.95, 97, 194, 229n58; 5.96,
231n74; 5.97), 90, 184–85,
225n22, 231n75, n78; 5.98,
90, 92, 97, 225n22; 5.99, 90,
225n21, 232n78; 5.100, 82,
86, 91; 5.100ff., 90; 5.100–111,
227n40; 5.101, 86–87,
225n21, n24; 5.102, 92,
225n23, 228n46; 5.103, 92,
225n23; 5.104, 82, 86, 91–92,
185, 228n46; 5.105, 86,
91–93, 194, 225n21,
226n27–28, 237n17; 5.106,
92, 228n46; 5.107, 91, 93,
131, 205n24, 225n22, n28,
234n21; 5.108, 92, 228n46;
5.109, 90–91, 232n78; 5.110,
92, 225n21; 5.111, 87, 91,
225n21–24, 227n4, 258n44;
5.112, 91–92, 97, 185,
224n11; 5.113, 82, 93,

225n23; 5.114, 231n68; 5.115,
229n51; 5.116, 224n13

Book 6: 6.1, 95; 6.1–5, 138; 6.4,
243n16; 6.7, 254n2; 6.8, 174;
6.13, 243n7, 253n27; 6.14,
249–50n76; 6.15, 243n16;
6.16–18, 234n17; 6.18, 234n16;
6.24, 249n70, 253n27; 6.27–28,
168; 6.53, 168; 6.53–59, 138,
243n16, 245n24; 6.53–61, 168;
6.54, 138, 169, 243n16,
249n70, 253n24, n27; 6.54–55,
169; 6.54–59, 168; 6.55,
169–70, 253n24; 6.59, 224n22,
253n24; 6.60, 168–69, 224n16;
6.61, 168–69, 253n27; 6.62,
246–47n46; 6.63, 240n41; 6.85,
108, 138, 234n18, 243n14;
6.87, 246n40, 246n42, n44;
6.89, 243n16; 6.93, 254n2

Book 7: 7.8, 170, 255n8; 7.8–15,
168, 200n11; 7.10, 173; 7.11,
255n8; 7.14, 170, 251n5; 7.16,
173; 7.18, 215n16, 235n24,
254n2; 7.28, 216n31; 7.29–30,
232n82; 7.31, 213n75; 7.44,
213n75; 7.48, 253n28; 7.57,
213n75; 7.63, 212–13n65; 7.71,
203n7; 7.75, 243n7; 7.77, 95,
250n84; 7.85, 246–47n46; 7.87,
254n1

Book 8: 8.6, 254n2; 8.41, 252n16;
8.45, 248n56; 8.48, 210n40;
8.60, 254n2; 8.96, 234n17,
242n53; 8.98, 67

Xenophon
Hellenica Graeca 2.2.3, 95
Memorabilia 1.6.14, 176

General Index

243n15, 243n16, 244n20, n22,
245n26–28, 253n27
tyrant-city, 12, 111, 133–41, 152,
155–56, 185, 233n14, 243n10,
n12–13, 244n17, 244n23,
250–51n85, 251n92

United States, 186–95, 258n46, n48

writing, 7–9, 160, 162, 165, 172–88,
200n8, 253n24, 254n2–3

universal principles, 116–20, 124,
126–27